Akan Pioneers
African Histories, Diasporic Experiences

Akan Pioneers
African Histories, Diasporic Experiences

Second Edition

Kwasi Konadu

Diasporic Africa Press

Diasporic Africa Press, Inc. | New York
www.dafricapress.com

Copyright © 2018 Kwasi Konadu

Originally published as *The Akan Diaspora in the Americas* by Oxford University Press, 2010.

All rights reserved. No part of this publication may be reproduced,
stored in a retrieval system, or transmitted, in any form or by any means,
electronic, mechanical, photocopying, recording, or otherwise,
without the prior permission of Diasporic Africa Press.

LCCN 2018907390
ISBN 978-1-937306-66-3

I dedicate this book to the African lives and histories submerged under water and under foreign soil, toiling and fighting for the right to be. I hope my attempt to recover something of their lives in Africa and in the Americas allow them to go home.

I also dedicate this book to our daughters, Yaa, Afia, and Abena. May they walk that path to the river and find balance in all they say and do.

Mpaeɛ (Libation) and Acknowledgments

Onyankopɔn, Asase Yaa, abosompem, meda mo ase bebree. Na monim sɛ meresua; momma menhu. To my family in Ghana, Jamaica, and North America, I thank you for your continued support and understanding. I am expressly grateful to Amma, Abena, Yaa, and Afia for everything. To Nana Kwaku Sakyi, Nana Kwabena Brown, Scot Brown, Kofi Sapɔn, Kwasi Bempong, Obadele (Kwame) Kambon, Clifford Campbell, Kwame Essien, Harry N. K. Odamtten, and Kwasi Odaaku, thanks for all those exchanges and support. Both Dr. James Turner and Dr. Kweku Agyeman have been and continue to be important elders in my intellectual life, and here I want to record my deepest thanks.

This research would not have been possible without the pioneering work done by so many writers, whose interpretations I attempt to engage, and by "local" historians in Ghana who collected and wrote histories—from the late nineteenth century to the 1970s—of persons and communities we would otherwise never have encountered. In this regard, the effort to collect oral histories across a nascent Ghanaian landscape by the late Kwame Daaku has been a key contribution and a source of inspiration. Though those oral histories should be read critically, they have provided the archaeologist a path to sites of cultural and historical value, provided the historian a window through which to envision how Akan societies and culture moved through their histories, and have confirmed some of the findings of both modes of inquiry.

I began this project in 2001. Since then, several scholars have kindly answered questions about sources, made suggestions, and even provided copies of source materials. To them all, I say thank you once more. I am also greatly indebted to friends and colleagues who assisted with translations and to the staff of repositories in Europe, Ghana, the Caribbean, and North America. Your contributions have helped to increase the book's value. The usual disclaimers apply.

Contents

	Maps, Figures and Tables	x
	Preface to the Second Edition	xi
1	On Diaspora and the Akan in the Americas	3
2	Quest for the River, Creation of the Path: Akan Cultural Development to the Sixteenth Century	27
3	History and Meaning in Akan Societies, 1500–1800	55
4	"The Most Unruly": The Akan in Danish and Dutch America	93
5	The Antelope (*Adowa*) and the Elephant (*Esono*): The Akan in the British Caribbean	122
6	"All of the Coromantee Country": The Akan Diaspora in North America	162
7	Diaspora Discourses: Akan Spiritual Praxis and the Claims of Cultural Identity	202
	Select Bibliography	237
	Notes	241
	Index	283

Maps

[Map 1]	Key Archaeological Sites in Contemporary Ghana	35
[Map 2]	The Gold Coast	56
[Map 3]	Eight Principal Slaving Regions	94
[Map 4]	Eighteenth-century Caribbean	128
[Map 5]	South Carolina Lowcountry	186

Figures

[Fig 3.1]	"Heads of Gold Coast men and women"	63
[Fig 3.2]	Engraving of Asante Prince Adom and his son	79
[Fig 4.1]	A Saramaka maroon garden camp	118
[Fig 4.2]	Spiritual healer woman in Paramaribo, Suriname	120
[Fig 5.1]	Prisoners serving sentences for Obeah in Antigua	141
[Fig 5.2]	Retreat of British colonists during the Demerara uprising	145
[Fig 5.3]	Accompong maroons singing and making music	152
[Fig 5.4]	Illustration of encounter between Cudjoe and a British officer	158
[Fig 6.1]	A South Carolina rice field	182
[Fig 7.1]	Axim Wesleyan Methodist church congregation	210
[Fig 7.2]	Group portrait of church girls with dolls in Kumase	211
[Fig 7.3]	Oba Ofuntola Oseijeman Adelabu Adefunmi at Oyatunji Village	214
[Fig 7.4]	Cape Coast Castle, 2005	227
[Fig 7.5]	"Black is beauty" billboard, Accra, Ghana, 2006	234

Tables

[Table 4.1]	Select Danish voyages from the Gold Coast	97-98
[Table 4.2]	Select Akan lexical items among maroons	115-116
[Table 5.1]	Gold Coast African imports to the British Caribbean, 1785-1795	125-126
[Table 6.1]	Estimated African and white population in Georgia, 1751-1870	168
[Table 6.2]	Estimated African and white population in Maryland, 1710-1850	173
[Table 6.3]	Estimated African and white population in Virginia, 1624-1850	178
[Table 6.4]	Estimated African and white population in South Carolina, 1715-1850	184
[Table 6.5]	Estimated African and white population in New York, 1698-1850	194

Preface to Second Edition

While searching online at the start of the new year, I came upon a blog maintained by a PhD student of history at one of the University of California schools. Interested in Atlantic history and "slave ethnicity," this future historian had posted an historiographical essay, probably written for a class, which asserted, "Even more dogmatic are such scholars as Kwasi Konadu, who has argued that Coromantees were essentially the early modern precursors to modern Ghanaians, joined together by a 'shared genetic culture.'" Curious, I emailed the student, who responded, "I meant to quote your phrase 'shared (genetic) language.' I have changed the quote, and I also rewrote the sentence to reflect that my opinions are coming from Rucker's reading of your work."[1] The student accepted Rucker's verdict without reading my book, and yet I am dogmatic. Nonetheless, I contemplated this student's essay and response—less an apology and more a confession—and wondered if this is the kind of scholarship Atlantic studies and its stepchild, black Atlantic history, inspires, and to which it aspires.

Rather than accept the received wisdom of the academic grapevine, I set aside gossip and book reviews and carefully read Walter C. Rucker's *Gold Coast Diasporas* over the course of the spring semester, giving it the seriousness it deserved and making marginal notes from the acknowledgements to the bibliography.[2] This book sets out to examine "the formation of the Gold Coast diaspora from the 1680s to the 1760s," identifying "the early decades of the eighteenth century [as] a period when Coromantee and (A)mina ethnic groups formed in the Americas" from Akan, Ga, Adangme, and Ewe speakers originating in Africa's Gold Coast (p. 23). Using sociologist Orlando Patterson's well-worn notion of "social death" and historian Michael Gomez's "ethnicity to race" paradigm, Rucker argues that "Gold Coast Africans reinvented, redefined, and transformed Gold Coast cultural materials and deployed them in unprecedented ways in the Americas," informed by a "commoner consciousness" and new notions of masculinity and womanhood (p. 9). My aim in this preface is threefold. First, I assess the validity of Rucker's case study through an examination of the sources used and the reading practices or interpretive techniques employed. Second, taking Rucker's work as representative of a recent trend in Atlantic and black Atlantic studies, I suggest some implications for the fields of African and diasporic African history. Finally, I hope to reintroduce readers to the case *The Akan Diaspora in the Americas* (henceforth, *TADA*) made for doing African and diasporic history as partners rather than odd couples, and against academic conformity and what's trending.

Though there are readers of this book who are very familiar with the rich historiography of the Gold Coast and Ghana, it is worth emphasizing the depth and somewhat unique range of sources which make serious historical research a daunting task. Besides a dense and growing archaeological record, most of the linguistic communities and polities now sliced up among Ghana's regions have recorded—and living—oral traditions with important historical content, transcribed and mostly translated in published and unpublished forms. Key manuscript collections in Arabic and Ajami (modified Arabic script used to write African languages) remain untranslated and thus underutilized. Documentary records supplied principally by Europeans constitute thousands of primary materials scattered in European repositories in Portuguese, Spanish, Dutch, Swedish, Danish, German, and French. Further, in those documents and on their own exist archived indigenous and foreign language sources deposited in the Public Records and Archives Administration Department of Ghana in Accra and its regional branches in Cape Coast, Koforidua, Kumase, Sunyani, and Tamale. In Kumase, we have the Manhyia Archives for Asanteman, and in Ghana we have languages (e.g., Akan/Twi, Gã, Hausa) that constitute their own archives through which scholars might fruitfully source and interpret proverbs, lore, bodily gestures, drum and flute texts, as well as a range of material culture. It is against these sources, especially so for historical research, that we might measure scholarship claiming competency in them. How does Walter Rucker's work measure up? First, some background, and then the appraisal.

Rucker is a US historian fluent in American English, and who, along one of his academic stops at Ohio State University, began to work on what he then called "the Akan Project." Previews of this project appeared in his first monograph, *The River Flows On*, published in 2006. In 2010, when *TADA* was released, Rucker published an article in *Afro-Americans in New York Life and History* subtitled, "Akan Culture and Community in Colonial New York City." In it, he claimed "Coromantee" was "an appellation associated with Gold Coast Akan speakers ... [in] the wider Akan Diaspora," and concluded Akan "day names," loyalty oaths, Ananse folktales, and a "belief in spiritual transmigration represent core elements in the cultural geography of the Akan Diaspora," where "emerged one 'Akan' identity in the Americas" (pp. 80, 110). In *Gold Coast Diasporas*, there's a sudden reversal. Rucker's "Akan Diaspora" and "one 'Akan' identity" argument is now a problem because an "Akan Diaspora" represents "a monolinguistic or 'ethnic' diaspora" devoid of "cultural plasticity" (p. 7). *Gold Coast Diasporas*, then, is a disavowal of Rucker's "Akan Diaspora" project and, in his view, a necessary caricature of *TADA* as "Konadu's essentialist views of the persistence and continuity of Akan culture in the Black Atlantic" (p. 13). The black Atlantic idea was transformative for Rucker, enabling his dramatic U-turn—conversion?—and providing the framing tools for his case study. Indeed, the study begins with a religious deliverance, where that idea was crucial in his "scholarly rebirth," "reinvention," and his "reincarnation as an early modern Black Atlantic historian" (pp. ix, xi). Having no methods or theories unique to it, the black Atlantic view is an ideological, even theological, position where adherents frequently invoke prophets such as literary and cultural critics Paul Gilroy and Stuart Hall, with a penchant for theorizations set against secondary literature and the fetishes of hybridity, plasticity, (re) invention, fluidity, "liminal space," and "cultural scripts" (pp. 6–9). Armed with this view and having read books that "facilitated [his] fluency in Black Atlantic studies," allow me to assess the product of that reading and two tourist trips to Ghana (p. x).

Besides the deficits in Rucker's scholarly repertoire, his book argues Africans from the Gold Coast accepted European trademarks assigned to them, much like hot iron brandings on the enslaved body, or better yet the terms *negro* and *nigger* which African descended peoples used long after Europeans who became "white" created these categories for them. For Rucker the "Coromantee and (A)mina" brandings were "ethnic groups" better suited for his black Atlantic ideology than an "ethnic" Akan diaspora. His choice of terminology, however, is an overreach because it ignores the power European or white slavers had to name Africans in print and as property and that Akan is a non-ethnic, non-monolingual concept. I presented this concept in *TADA*, and apparently it problematized his in-process project on the Akan diaspora.

Gold Coast Diasporas is divided into two parts and bookended by two tales—one of an individual named Don Juan and the other of a well-known folktale character, Ananse. Don Juan's tale is shorthand for the study and its ethnogenesis argument for a "Coromantee" identity, but also representative of the way evidence is used throughout the book. A standard four-page form with fill-in blanks constitute Don Juan's discharge record and the basis of Rucker's snapshot, but he reads out of this clerical document "Don Juan's claim to a Coromantee natal origin" when it was British colonial officials, not Don Juan, who, not knowing his place of birth, crossed out 'the county of' and ascribed an identifier by writing in its place "Coromantee in Africa." Though probable Don Juan could have uttered those words, the fact is he did not. Another discharged serviceman and contemporary also named Don Juan, in fact one of fourteen servicemen named so by colonists, had his birth place recorded as "Accoo" (i.e., Aku, a referent to Yorùbá speakers in Freetown), having served "at Sierra Leone in the county of Africa," but more importantly his discharge came at "his own request."[3] Even the physical description and attributes Rucker extrapolates from his Don Juan to stand in for Coromantee's "well-earned reputations" in the Americas is at odds with his own evidence. Don Juan's record places him in "Africa, Bahamas, Honduras [and] Jamaica," not specifically the Gold Coast or Sierra Leone (pp. 2–3); he is discharged for "being unfit for further service" and "seldom in hospital," not "never visited the hospital for treatment nor complained about injury" and for "physical fortitude" (p. 2); the "country marks" ascribed to him ("three scars on each corner of the mouth [and] cheeks [and] forehead") do not match Rucker's illustration of a "Coromantee youth" (on page 3) nor Akan scarifications, but they do conform to Yorùbá and perhaps Ewe ones—the Ewe migrated to the Gold Coast around 1650 from Yorùbá-speaking regions. In the end, the declaration to be made and signed by discharged soldiers "at his own request" was left blank by Rucker's Don Juan, and an "x" mark on the second page of his record is perhaps the only place where this individual made a self-induced claim.

Rucker promises "a historical optic" through which "the Gold Coast past mattered," and by focusing on "Gold Coast history through the mid-eighteenth century" he intends to examine "the early modern Gold Coast with a particular focus on speakers of the Akan, Ga, Adanme, and Ewe languages" (p. 22). Besides lacking competency in any of these languages and never having consulted the national or regional archives in Ghana, he also brought serious problems of his own to this undertaking. Principal sources for the late-fifteenth to early-seventeenth centuries are in Portuguese, in various European archives, or in published transcriptions such as António Brásio's twenty-two-volume *Monumenta Missionaria Africana*. From that period to the nineteenth century, Dutch, German, Danish, French, and English language sources dominate. Though there are no original, non-English language sources or archives consulted for his study, this does not deter Rucker from claiming, in two of many instances, "Beginning in 1482, Atlantic creole culture was given birth in the Gold Coast," and, "By the late-sixteenth century, the Gold Coast ... was thoroughly balkanized" (pp. 74, 107). Even if we suspend our disbelief, ignore such claims, and assess Rucker's evidentiary base from within this 1680s-to-1760s period, we find that his "primary sources" boil down to a handful of translated and deftly annotated travel accounts, his cartographical evidence is a translated and trite 1629 Dutch map (eschewing maps from 1471 onward), and oral evidence is reduced to a heavy dose of Carl Reindolf's highly redacted English version butchered by Basel Mission (BM) editors as compared to his fuller, handwritten Gã version in the BM archives. A 1764 text on the Fante and Gã languages by polyglot and African-Danish clergyman Christian Protten would have helped, but this too is inexplicably absent for someone so concerned with ethnogenesis and "polyglottal" communities.

The European accounts used are few and very familiar: Pieter de Marees, Dutch merchant with observations on Cape Coast and Accra (c. 1600–01); Wilhelm Müller, German-speaking pastor at a Danish fort in Fetu near Cape Coast (c. 1662–9); Jean Barbot, French merchant with observations mainly on Elmina, Cape Coast, and Accra, though he probably remained mostly on a ship (c. 1682); Willem Bosman, Dutch merchant with observations on Elmina and Axim (c. 1688–1704); Johannes Rask, Danish pastor at Fort Christiansborg in Osu, Accra (c. 1709–12); and Ludewig Rømer, Danish merchant with observations mainly on Accra (c. 1739–49). Not only are these accounts restricted to the specific locales of Elmina, Cape Coast, and Accra, there are chronological gaps compounded by spatial limitations in addition to their colored optics and the plague of plagiarism. Rather than engage his sources or check them against the originals or the archives in Europe or on Ghana's coast, these accounts—a mixture of hearsay, observation, printed sources, and plagiarism—are taken at face value. For instance, Rucker concluded, "Both Barbot and Bosman, reflecting on the decades leading up to the 1690s, concur on the ability of Akyem to serve as a balance to Akwamu's regional influence," or other statements with the prompts, "As Bosman and Barbot note," without interrogating Barbot's known plagiarism of Bosman or consulting Albert van Dantzig's multi-articled corrections to Bosman's flawed English translation published in *History in Africa* (pp. 51, 55, 77).[4] And so, we end up with concurrence or "matches" between such accounts that are as contrived as a single-minded commitment to one line of argument.

Some might see the disregard for the rules of evidence, archival research, issues of authorship, or critical distinctions between original and published (and translated) sources as quibbles, but we must treat these matters with the deference they deserve because central to Rucker's argument is "that Atlantic Africans carried their histories—both distant and present with them to the new worlds ... [where] the distant and immediate pasts of Gold Coast Africans helped frame a collective liminal experience in the Americas" (pp. 64–

65). If the early chapters on Gold Coast history were the prologue, Rucker next sets his sights on the Americas and offers more of the same well-known, published, and secondary English-language references that readers are told will distil "a sharper and more defined picture of" polyglottal diasporas "as opposed to a monolinguistic" one (p. 7). Instead of a masterful portrait, we get, ultimately, a low-grade collage of a literature review. This convenient overview of a specific literature, which features his wife and friends, is then grafted onto a repurposed version of his first book, *The River Flows On*, itself a revised dissertation and half of whose chapters were previously published. In that book, Rucker's argument bears a striking resemblance to his *Gold Coast Diasporas*: "enslaved Africans adopted these seemingly false ethnonyms and actively referred to themselves as 'Coromantee'" (2006, p. 8). His "Atlantic world approach" (p. 12) and sources (scant US archival materials, some published travel accounts, hefty secondary literature) are roughly the same. Shocking as this may seem, while conceding literature reviews do have a place in scholarly production, the act of repurposing and the slight handling of evidence is a normative practice among black Atlantic specialists, which might explain his targeted references to a specific black Atlantic literature.[5]

For the uninitiated reader, a few names from Rucker's bibliography—which also appear among the endorsements—should suffice. For as much as scholars like John Thornton have argued for the existence of "Atlantic creoles" in Africa, he and others neither have the data nor can they show *how* most West-Central Africans became seduced by Portuguese and Catholic ideas and how "creolized" their daily lives became.[6] Instead, the records show that expressions of faith (chiefly among the ruling elites) were linked to political expediency, while the region disintegrated amid fraudulent "mass" baptisms, persistent warfare, acute slaving, and exile. Staying in that region, Jason Young's *Rituals of Resistance* attempts to examine religious traditions of "precolonial Kongo" and coastal Georgia and South Carolina around the ideas of "change, innovation, and creativity [that] were crucial to the development of black cultures around the Atlantic," but he has no fluency in Kikongo or related languages, no consultation of original archival sources in Portugal, Rome, or the Congo-Angola region, and resigns himself to well-known travel accounts, missionary documents, and to some published Portuguese sources, strangely, in French translation (2007, p. 3). Likewise, in the Gold Coast context, Rebecca Shumway draws on an "Atlantic world paradigm" to argue for a "distinctive [Fante] language and culture" beginning in the fifteenth century and the formation of a new "coastal coalition" in the eighteenth century, but she, like Rucker, references no Portuguese- or Dutch-language sources, relying instead on secondary literature and, ironically, on her "conversational" Asante/Twi, not Fante.[7] Is it, then, surprising that Shumway, like Rucker, often confuses the names of language groups, peoples, and polities? Or that her major claim for the change or newness of the Fante language is voided by her confession, "Further linguistic research is needed to more precisely explain how and when the language began to be used along the coast" (p. 152)? Scholars are adept at invoking the omnipresence of "change" related to culture contact—as if Europeans were magic wands that upon contact remained impervious yet able to transform Africans into a new species called "creoles"—but are less skillful at demonstrating its precise mechanisms and layered contexts with deep empirical accuracy. What do we call Europeans who, on African soil, consumed African crops and cuisine, bodies through intercourse, ideas through "fetish oaths" and indigenous therapeutics, and who spoke African languages?

The evidence Rucker summons for his case study might be suitable for a literature review or even a constrained survey, but the historical arguments he makes by way of thin, taken-at-face-value evidence exposes serious flaws in his reading practice. A few of the more crucial ones will do. First, Rucker's allegation that *TADA* proffered "essentialist views of the persistence and continuity of Akan culture" based on "some ethereal sense of a shared or 'genetic' Gold Coast or Akan cultural 'heritage' existing ... since time immemorial" is a gross misreading of *his own* evidence (pp. 13, 33). The PhD history student—the one mentioned in the opening anecdote of this preface—had not read *TADA*, but accepted at face value Rucker's facile interpretation because both shared similar beliefs and reading practices. Rucker had plucked the phrase "shared (genetic) language" from *TADA* and confused "genetic" with biological determinism—hence, his caricature that *TADA* viewed "Akan culture as genetic"—when, in linguistics, a genetic relationship exists once languages or dialects belong to the same linguistic grouping and where influence does not constitute a genetic relationship. In fact, Rucker cites an article by linguist Florence Dolphyne entitled, "The languages of the Akan peoples," in which Dolphyne concluded, "all these dialects are closely related genetically."[8] It is tricky to believe someone ignorant of the languages and sources when they critique another, who is fluent in both, for being "essentialist." The truth is, essentialism is not a boogeyman but rather an ideological commentary poorly disguised as an argument based on scholarship. Secondly, on the note of scholarship, *TADA* was the first book on the Akan peoples in the Americas, covering much of the substantial ground over which Rucker has traveled. Rather than build upon that groundwork, Rucker instead appropriated my concepts, analyses, cast members, sources used, and even reproduces two of *TADA*'s illustrations (see pp. 171, 223), while seeking to undermine the book by lifting specific words out of context and splicing them together to create a distorted meaning.⁹ In fact, what is actually being undermined here is the ethics of the historical profession through Rucker's lack of integrity.

Rucker claims *TADA*'s view of Akan culture is timeless, essentialized, and impervious to change because the project was about "persistence and continuity," but the word "persistence" occurs nowhere in *TADA*. Rather, *TADA* stressed "transformation and continuity" by demonstrating "how Akan culture formed in the West African forest and its continuity and transformation in dialogue with Islamic forces to the north and northwest of the forest and European forces on the coast after the fifteenth century" (*TADA*, p. 23). Not only does Rucker's reading practice commandeer the "commoner consciousness" idea from Ray Kea's seminal work (produced when Marxist analysis was in vogue) and the "Akanization" and "(A)mina" constructs from *TADA* without attribution, his interpretive use of both show (a) his hypothesis of such a group consciousness fails to accord with his evidence, as conjecture often passes for data (e.g., over 50 "may have been" instances), and (b) in his argument against an "Akan diaspora" but for "Gold Coast diasporas," he consistently writes about "the dominance of Akan cultures in the Gold Coast" and "the influence of Akan-speaking peoples and polities" (pp. 69–70). Rucker, thus, contradicts his argument in *The River Flows On*, in that "'Kormantee' does refer to most Akan-speakers from the Gold Coast who were transported to the Americas," and vindicates, even accentuates, *TADA*.¹⁰ Finally, a very common interpretative technique that weakens Rucker's book is, first, the suggestion of extensive research, then followed by a definitive claim. He says, "From the cartographical evidence alone, a few interrelated historical factors become crystal clear," but this is based on the 1629 Dutch map, not all the available maps from the 1471 Portuguese map to those of later centuries. Then, Rucker claims, "All historical references to 'queen-mothers' in the Gold Coast originate in, or refer to, the nineteenth and twentieth centuries," suggesting figures like "Queen" Nanny of Jamaica were a "new" feature of exile, when English records from the Royal African Company at Cape Coast prominently featured not only "Queen" Tituba of Agona in the 1680s but also the "Queen of Fetoo [Fetu]" in the early eighteenth century.¹¹

Turning from an assessment of Rucker's sources and his interpretations, what implications might his work, and more broadly, (black) Atlantic perspectives hold for the fields of African and diasporic African history? I think there are three takeaways. The first concerns language—both the mechanics and documented history of African languages as well as the way we talk about each other to show disagreement. I was born in Jamaica, and although I have Maroon and Akan ancestry—my great-great-grandmother was named Adwoa Konadu—no one in my family, even those with more ability, took their African-based histories and languages as seriously as I did. And so, I had to learn; I learned by audio tapes, books, and most important, spending time in Ghana and surrounding countries. This aided me in learning Akan/Twi, and later, European languages when it came to the archives. Cutting corners in the archives or the "field" is as dangerous as using conjecture and accusation in place of scholarship—it says more about the accuser than the target of such allegation. If that PhD history student in California is any indication, there may be equal—if not greater—danger in the combination of graduate programs requiring only French or another European language in lieu of African *and* diasporic language training (e.g., Haitian Kreyol, Jamaican Patwa), and the fashion of (black) Atlantic world perspectives where Africans remain largely invisible yet legible only as "Europeanized" or "Americanized" souls.

The tragic irony is that Robert F. Thompson of Yale University coined the term "Black Atlantic" in his 1983 book that took African and diasporic languages and perspectives seriously, only to be appropriated by Paul Gilroy and then remixed, so much so this version eschews Africa and diasporic connections to it and scandalously incriminates Thompson as an essentialist. The revised black Atlantic idea therefore represents a ratification of a default "white" Atlantic and academia, and for Rucker and company, the apparent goal is "to take over black academe," that subservient niche in partnership with the fashionable views and values of white academia (p. x). Here, á la James Baldwin, "white" is a metaphor for power, and as that power was exercised routinely over the lives of the enslaved and their descendants, especially in naming property, one of the most remarkable aspects of the African presence in the Americas is the ubiquity of Akan "day names" and specimens of their language in the records of repression. *TADA* makes this clear and its push for a fuller accounting shows that African and African-based or -derived languages are both archives of knowledge and a perceptive lens through which we can better grasp social and intellectual histories on multiple shores of the Atlantic.

The second takeaway is about belief, evidence, and what some scholars do either to make one fit the other or make belief (ideology) come before or surpass a dense body of evidence. Rucker's belief in "social death" transforms this abused metaphor into a lived experience in which Africans "suffered a series of social deaths," only to contradictorily conclude they did not suffer "social death" because that death was only a "temporal waypoint" (whatever this is supposed to mean) (pp. 7, 229). Like Orlando Patterson before him,

Rucker offers no evidence from the enslaved that they subscribed to this "social death" view. Likewise, as Rucker believed the trial records for Gabriel's 1800 plot to revolt in Virginia contained too much African content for whites to invent and so the plot must have been true, he also believed the veracity of a 1736 Antigua plot and its trial records, supposedly through a Gã leader named "Court" who built an alliance with "Coromantee" and "creole" participants (pp. 108–11). The facts paint or at least points to a different story: Antiguan authorities recovered no weapons or gunpowder (supposedly, to blow up a ballroom, signaling the start of the revolt), hundreds were arrested and tortured on suspicion, spies were placed by authorities in the jails where inmates hatched stories to save their own skin, the owner of "Court" denied the charge, and the judges claimed the two leaders—"Court" and "Tomboy"— confessed, but there is no record of their trials nor confessions.

The records do, however, reveal something about Akan cultural forms and language, and yet a second look at those records also indicate a misidentification on my part, which I will correct here to make a broader point about the cruciality of linguistic and archival competency. In the first version of this book, I had rendered a reference to "Court," that is, "Coquo Tackey," as Kwaku Takyi, when in fact the correct transliteration is "Kokuroo Takyi" (Great Takyi). "Kokuroo" is an Akan/Twi adjective for "great, large, big," modifying the noun or proper name "Takyi," which is Akan, not Gã, placing in doubt the belief "Court" was crowned king. Antiguan officials claimed, and Rucker believed, "Coquo Tackey" meant "Great King," but the closet approximation of "king" in Gã is Lumɔ and Maŋtsɛ, the Gã rendering of the proper name is "Taki" (phonetically different from Takyi), and the earliest references to Taki in the archived Gã records is Nii Taki Kome (1825–56) and Nii Taki Tawiah I (1862–1902). Finally, as the Antiguan judges' report noted, "The language and ceremonies used at it being all Coramantine," shorthand for the Akan language. That language *is* a composite or combination of three to four mutually intelligible variants—Bono, Fante, Asante, Akuapem. That language was also the predominant one recorded on the Gold Coast by the Flemish Eustache de la Fosse in 1479–80, Englishman William Towerson in 1555, Dutchmen Pieter de Marees in 1600–01 and Wilhelm Müller in the 1660s, and Frenchman Jean Barbot in 1682. For Gã-Adangme and Ewe speakers in the Accra region "the city and entire Accra plains," according to Gã linguist Mary Kabuku, "were dominated by Akan speakers from 1660 until the end of the nineteenth century."[12] This historically informed yet tightly-braided linguistic, cultural, and political reality is at sharp odds with the single-minded case for "Coromantee" or "(A)mina" ethnogenesis. As far as "ethnic" categories and ethnogenesis are concerned, there is evidence for African categories of self-identification, as indicated in eighteenth-century newspapers ads for "Fantee, and Ashanti [Asante] Negroes," that contest if not undermine the inflated importance of "Coromantee" and question why academics continue to take their cues—and script—for African and diasporic histories from European trademarks and theologies.[13]

The third and final takeaway is about the question of African history and diasporic African history. Are they odd couples? If they are, they need not be. My concern in TADA was to explicate "collective self-understanding as Akan persons or culture bearers and the pattern of individual lives shaped by diasporic experiences," using the notion of "a composite Akan culture ... calibrated among those of Akan origin and a 'diaspora' of 'Akanized' communities on the Gold Coast littoral and forest periphery (e.g., the Ewe, Gã-Adangme, Guan, Dagomba), that found its way to the Americas." That argument called "attention to an important rethinking of the historical formation of Akan culture in West Africa and its reach into the Americas" (TADA, pp. 4, 6). "Composite" meant and still means "complex, amalgamated, fusion" between various clans, many of whom formed polities, fought wars yet engaged in extensive diplomacy, traded with yet competed against one another, and ultimately their members became a force in the Americas, despite their relatively small numbers. They did the same on the Gold Coast through Greater Asante, which was larger in size than present-day Ghana, itself a "composite" nation that grew out of the British colonial division of Greater Asante into a tripartite colonial state (Northern Territories, Crown Colony of Ashanti, Gold Coast Colony). This is a simplified version of more intricate historical processes, but the storyline is clear as to how the complex Akan cultural forms and norms became so influential in the Americas and into the twentieth-century Gold Coast/Ghana, especially its southern half. If ethnogenesis is about the formation and development of an "ethnic" group through either a process of self-identification or assimilating an outside identification, the Akan case enriches and transcends this process.

The Akan peoples were more than an "ethnic" or "monolinguistic" group, and so scholarship that focuses on Europeans cataloged or taxonomized African peoples, ascribed indiscriminately "ethnic" labels onto them, or incredulously argues "out of many, they became one [race]" impoverishes our understanding and our need to fully account for their lives and their histories (p. 6). By "their histories," I mean that all historians study and write about lived experiences that do *not* belong to them, because those experiences—human actions, if you will—are the sole intellectual property of those who lived them. Some of us think such experiences are the historian's possession because they "discovered" them in the archives, and therefore they can contort the documented parts of those lives in ways that suit an argument. Viewed from this perspective, *TADA* embraced this view and imperfectly pushed for a fuller accounting upstream—when we do have the sources of self-understanding to excavate *their* histories—precisely because the scholarship on diasporic African histories was shallow. In the sixteenth- and seventeenth-century records supplied by Europeans, we find repeated references to Africans on the Mina/Gold Coast categorizing a European as a "lagoon person" (ɔburɔni) from lands across the sea (*aburɔkyire*), but more importantly references (spelled variously) to Akani, Equafoɔ, and Twifoɔ. They tell a story. The suffix *-foɔ* is a plural marker for "people," while *-ni* is the singular, declarative marker for a "person." Thus, Equa*foɔ* meant "trading people" (as in de Marees's *aguaede*, "trade goods") and Twi*foɔ* was "Twi people" (as in de Marees's *batafou*, "long-distance commerce people"), whereas Akani or Aka*nni* meant "this is an Akan person." While the former were self-identification statements of peoplehood, or what kind of people they were and what business they did, the latter was a declarative statement, most likely in response to the question, "Who are you?" This "Akani" term runs its course through the sixteenth to eighteenth centuries, and is picked up in the nineteenth century by Basel Mission evangelists who, in their conversations with indigenes in *their* own language, decided to reduce to writing one variant of the Akan language called "Twi," or, more recently, Akan/Twi. The root word in "Akan" is *kan*, meaning "first, foremost, pioneer" in that most Akan/Twi peoples claim to be autochthons—the "first" to settle in their respective homelands. We have, then, in the terms "Akan" and "Twi" mutually intelligible languages and cultural forms—constituted by sharing a common linguistic root or ancestor—and shared (not identical) histories and self-understandings from which white Europeans took their cues. I only wish scholars would do the same.

So why this new preface, this need to reintroduce readers to a book originally published in 2010 (paperback in 2012)? Is it to teach graduate students a lesson or two, scold self-proclaimed black Atlantic specialists, or exact some sort of vague revenge against academics who have decided that my originality and competence threatens their ideological position, even sociopolitical goals? Perhaps all three could be implicated, though they stand as tertiary targets. Besides influencing recent scholarship on Igbo and Gã diasporas in the Americas, the primary reason for a reintroduction to *TADA* is threefold.[14]

All productions, including book publishing, have a backstory. Whereas moviegoers might get some behind-the-scenes snippets, consumers of books are rarely so privy. This book was slated to be my first "big book" with an elite academic publisher. Initial optimism was warranted, for I was working with a VP and executive editor, having made my case through a successful proposal and a subsequent contract. Based on two reviews of the proposal—one by John Thornton, the other by the late James Miller, who died of cancer in 2015—I made substantial changes by scrapping the sample chapters and starting anew, since I was still writing when I submitted the proposal. I delivered the final manuscript, but that wasn't the end of it. I had exceeded the 300-page limit in the contract and had to grudgingly remove a chapter and substantial parts of the first three chapters, including a discussion of the very notion and genealogy of the term "Akan." I complied because I was a new scholar, only some years removed from graduate school, and because I wasn't as versed in the politics and criminality of book publishing as I am now. I was also a new father with another child born the year the book was released, which meant publishing took a backseat to parenting. Only years later did I finally put the pieces together—Thornton's puzzling absence at my Boston University talk in fall 2010, Rucker's swift attempts to undermine the book at the 2011 ASWAD conference in Pittsburgh while I was absent, and book reviews that triggered several head scratches. I then realized the manuscript was not peer-reviewed, a standard academic publishing practice. The promotional blurbs on the back cover came from my proposal review, which is to say Thornton and Miller never saw the full manuscript and I didn't get the benefit of feedback, so as to address shortcomings or anticipate criticisms. The editor had led me to believe otherwise, but that belief ended when I confronted her about reports the book, well into its third or fourth year, was not selling. The "best seller" label above the book in the publisher's catalog was a marketing ploy, I was informed, which only added to my frustration. A year or two later, I requested my rights to the book, which were granted. The publisher defended his editor and doubled down on any claim of wrongdoing. Since this publisher rarely reverted publishing rights to authors, especially not long after publication, readers can judge for themselves, as I offer the book, once more, with this crucial caveat.

Peer review came by way of several book reviews, published around the release of the paperback edition. A most important takeaway from these reviews is the diametrical ways historians of Africa and those of US history viewed the book, revealing a crucial divide between the two, though the book sought to bring both into closer partnership. In other words, rather than accept the challenge, the intersectional path, prompted by this book on African histories and diasporic experiences, most reviewers took sides. The US historians assumed I was a Ghanaian personally "familiar with Akan language and culture." Apparently, I was so skilled I had fooled these scholars to believe I had "a native's perception"; but I was born in Jamaica and they had read too much into my name rather than into the book's contents. I now see where these graduate students inherit their ideology and reading practice from. Indeed, both Vincent Brown and Rucker remained on the introductory chapter; the former apparently didn't read past it, citing only pages 5, 6, and 16 and "the work of Walter C. Rucker," his companion. (Parenthetically, is it odd Brown celebrated Rucker's *The River Flows On* when seven or more scholars in Rucker's field of US history disparaged the book). If Brown had actually read the book carefully, or at least in its entirety, he might have noticed I do more than highlight "perseverance" of cultural practices; I *demonstrate* how specific practices and ideas took shape or the lines along which they did in West Africa and in the Americas. Not surprisingly, Brown's review was mute on the Africa chapters, where the story begins. And yet the competency required for African history is the most acute weakness of these scholars and of the "diaspora" histories they claim from their North American platforms. We simply can't do African diaspora histories without African history, with the converse holding relatively true from at least the eighteenth century onward. Viewed from this perspective, it is little wonder the likes of Brown and Rucker fixated on the book's introduction, evading the African histories that would factor into diasporic experiences. It is as if they tasted an appetizer, stopped, fabricated faults, then wrote about the main course and dessert. Fortunately for us, Africa historian Ray Kea, who is African American like Rucker and the reviewers, but also a specialist on the Gold Coast and (Danish) Caribbean, stepped into the kitchen, and like a chef masterful on both sides of the Atlantic, offered the most accurate appraisal to date.

Published in the *New West India Guide / Nieuwe West-Indische Gids* in 2012, Kea's review is thorough, critical in the questions it raises, and balanced in its coverage, showing that a book review requires reading the book and that competent book reviews should be performed by those who know the sources, geographies, and peoples covered. Rather than reproduce Kea's full review, which is worth it, I advise readers to consult it, along with another perspective on *Gold Coast Diasporas* by Gérard Chouin, who, like Kea, knows the multilingual primary sources for the Gold Coast region.[15] But if readers need another inducement to read further, here are the final six sentences of Kea's review:

> While Konadu seems to postulate a cultural continuity through time, he attempts to avoid reifying this idea by viewing continuity in terms of a cultural biography, over the long duration, of a range of practices, ideas, rituals, institutions, and attitudes among Akan speakers. In this conceptual setting ideational culture stands as a relatively auton-

omous formation which created its own context(s). Konadu demonstrates that this culture was historical, mobile, and mutable and that it was embedded in different networks and strategies. Furthermore, his work shows that diasporic studies can be profitably examined at different spatial levels. At one level he localizes the material and historical conditions of Akan ideational culture; at another he places the conception, production, circulation, and consumption of this culture within an Atlantic basin context. This is an important and intellectually refreshing study and I recommend it with much enthusiasm.[16]

To new and returning readers, this book's principal argument and methodology remain true: African diasporic cultures in the Americas took shape through processes of transformation *and* continuity, and the extent of each has been shaped decisively by, on one hand, the Africans who lived in colonial and Maroon societies, and on the other, the sheer barbarity and racial violence of neo-European colonies-turned-states in the region. We have to remind ourselves that as much as we celebrate modernity and the "Atlantic world," both subsidized by transoceanic slaving, the "Atlantic world" killed the creativity and cultures of non-Europeans more than it promoted them. This was no clearer than in the so-called 1736 plot to revolt in Antigua, where historian Jason Sharples has not only confined my findings (see Chapter 5), but has shown how colonial slaving regimes, through white fantasy and fear, destroyed community building among Africans and their progeny. Antiguan judges established kangaroo courts to investigate a dead-end plot, recruited enslaved Africans as spies in jails in exchange for a pardon—witnesses named the dead, the jailed, and the convicted. Together, judges, informants (who became suspects) and suspects produced knowledge of a conspiracy that did not exist before incarceration through the use of physical and psychological coercion.[17] Community and culture cohesion suffered.

In Antigua and in other colonial territories throughout the Americas, this book focuses on the African and diasporic experiences of a cluster of peoples—*akan*, or "pioneer peoples" in fact—who coalesced around a set of cultural ideas and practices, and despite their relatively small numbers, ultimately became a force in the Americas. My goal in this book, therefore, is simple: tell the story of their experiences as fully as the sources (as I knew then) allow and to build that story around their disproportional influence, struggles, contradictions, and contributions. Where else in the last few centuries have a people become the cultural nucleus in their homeland among competing factions as well as national heroes in diasporic places (e.g., Jamaica in the Caribbean basin and Guyana in South America)? We have to explain—not just theorize about—this stream of related and historicized processes, their formation, transformation, and continuity.

My concern, which I announce in the first chapter, was never about cultural "survivals" or "retention" or even perseverance. Nor is my concern to follow trends that elide lived historical experience. In the Americas, the majority of Africans and their descendants experienced marginal differences in terms of freedom in the period the book covers, and so I see no need to use "free people of color," though I do distinguish layers of lived experiences among Maroons, the manumitted, the enslaved, and the like. Besides, all people have "color" and so "people of color," modified or not by "free," remains an empty category of little analytical value. This book focuses on the multiplicity of experiences, at various scales, at different times and places. Because it reflects a point in my experience as a scholar, I have decided to republish it with only necessary revisions and updates. To have completely revised the book with what I know now would require a new book and would betray the charting of my growth. I judge each book project's success not by sales or awards or even kind remarks, but by this question: Am I getting better, sharper in my thinking and writing, clearer in the case I make? I hope you, the reader, make your way through this book fully, then judge it accordingly.

Notes

1. Devin Leigh, email message to author, January 16, 2017. Leigh is a PhD candidate in Atlantic history at UC Davis.

2. Walter C. Rucker, *Gold Coast Diasporas: Identity, Culture, and Power* (Bloomington: Indiana University Press, 2015).

3. The National Archives, Kew (TNA): War Office (WO) 97, 1715/141, 16 August 1839.

4. See Albert van Dantzig, "Willem Bosman's New and Accurate Description of the Coast of Guinea: How Accurate Is It?," *History in Africa* 1 (1974), 101–108; idem, "English Bosman and Dutch Bosman: a Comparison of Texts," *History in Africa* 2 (1975), 185–216; idem, "English Bosman and Dutch Bosman: a Comparison of Texts," *History in Africa* 3 (1976), 91–126; idem, "English Bosman and Dutch Bosman: a Comparison of Texts," *History in Africa* 4 (1977), 247–276; idem, "English Bosman and Dutch Bosman: a Comparison of Texts," *History in Africa* 5 (1978), 225–258; idem, "English Bosman and Dutch Bosman: a Comparison of Texts," *History in Africa* 6 (1979), 265–285; idem, "English Bosman and Dutch Bosman: a Comparison of Texts," *History in Africa* 7 (1980), 281–291; idem, "English Bosman and Dutch Bosman: a Comparison of Texts," *History in Africa* 9 (1982), 285–302; idem, "English Bosman and Dutch Bosman: a Comparison of Texts," *History in Africa* 11 (1984), 307–329.

5. Refurbishing is a black Atlantic contagion. Rucker's close friend and a series editor for *Gold Coast Diasporas*, Herman Bennet, repurposed his revised dissertation-cum-first book, *Africans in Colonial Mexico*, for his second book, *Colonial Blackness: A History of Afro-Mexico*, by using essentially the same source materials and black Atlantic paradigm. His most recent project, *Soiled Gods*, takes its inspiration from the first chapter of the first book. I have only seen two chapters of the "new" book project, and so any further judgment must wait.

6. See Linda M. Heywood and John K. Thornton, *Central Africans, Atlantic Creoles, and the Foundation of the Americas, 1585–1660* (New York: Cambridge University Press, 2007). This work builds upon an earlier volume: Linda Heywood, ed., *Central Africans and Cultural Transformations in the American Diaspora* (New York: Cambridge University Press, 2002). For doubts about the "creolized" nature of those from the region, see Roquinaldo Ferreira, *Cross-Cultural Exchange in the Atlantic World: Angola and Brazil during the Era of the Slave Trade* (New York: Cambridge University Press, 2012), 247–48. For non-creolized views of the culture and identities of West Central Africans, see Christina F. Mobley, "The Kongolese Atlantic: Central African

Slavery & Culture from Mayombe to Haiti" (PhD diss., Duke University, 2015); Barbaro Martinez-Ruiz, *Kongo Graphic Writing and Other Narratives of the Sign* (Philadelphia: Temple University Press, 2013); Maureen Warner Lewis, *Central Africa in the Caribbean: Transcending Time, Transforming Cultures* (Mona: University of West Indies Press, 2003).

7. Rebecca Shumway, *The Fante and the Transatlantic Slave Trade* (Rochester: University of Rochester Press, 2011), 12.

8. Florence Dolphyne, "The languages of the Akan peoples," *Research Review* 2, no. 1 (1986): 11.

9. Dereliction and distorted messaging is also rife in Rebecca Shumway's *The Fante and the Transatlantic Slave Trade* and her historiographical essay, "From Atlantic Creoles to African Nationalists: Reflections on the Historiography of Nineteenth-Century Fanteland" (*History in Africa* 42 (2014): 139–164), where her argument for a historiographical neglect or slighting of "Fanteland" is muted by her omission of Thomas McCaskie's seminal essay "Nananom Mpow of Mankessim: An essay in Fante history" and my own "Euro-African Commerce and Social Chaos: Akan Societies in the Nineteenth and Twentieth Centuries" (*History in Africa* 36 (2009): 265–292) published in the same journal! The Fante receive their fair share of attention in *Akan Pioneers*.

10. Walter C. Rucker, *The River Flows On: Black Resistance, Culture, and Identity Formation in Early America* (Baton Rouge: Louisiana State University Press, 2006), 30.

11. TNA: Treasury (T) 70, 1463, Memorandum Book, Cape Coast Castle, 7 June 1704.

12. M. E. Kropp Kabuku, *Korle meets the Sea: A Sociolinguistic History of Accra* (New York: Oxford University Press, 1997), 113.

13. *Daily Advertiser* (Kingston), vol. 1, issue 5, 22 December 1789 and 6 January 1790.

14. On the Igbo diaspora, see Toyin Falola and Raphael Chijioke Njoku, eds., *Igbo in the Atlantic World: African Origins and Diasporic Destinations* (Bloomington: Indiana University Press, 2016); Douglas B. Chambers, *The Igbo Diaspora in the Era of the Slave Trade: An Introductory History* (Enugu, Nigeria: Jemezie Associates, 2013). On the Gã diaspora, see Harry N. K. Odamtten's *Edward W. Blyden's Intellectual Transformations: Afropublicanism, Pan-Africanism, Islam, and the Indigenous West African Church* (Michigan State University Press, forthcoming).

15. Gérard Chouin, review of *Gold Coast Diasporas: Identity, Culture, and Power*, by Walter C. Rucker, *The William and Mary Quarterly* 73, no. 4 (2016): 767–771.

16. Ray Kea, review of *The Akan Diaspora in the Americas*, by Kwasi Konadu, *New West Indian Guide / Nieuwe West-Indische Gids* 86, no. 1 & 2 (2012): 130.

17. Jason Sharples, "Hearing Whispers, Casting Shadows: Jailhouse Conversation and the Production of Knowledge during the Antigua Slave Conspiracy Investigation of 1736," in *Buried Lives: Incarcerated in Early America*, eds., Michele Lise Tarter and Richard J. Bell (Athens: University of Georgia Press, 2012), 37–38, 53.

Akan Pioneers
African Histories, Diasporic Experiences

1

On Diaspora and the Akan in the Americas

Se wokɔ a, twa w'ani hwɛ no nkyi na taa bra fie—When you go, turn your eyes to look back, and come home frequently.
—Akan proverb

Close to 10 percent of the total number—a little more than 1.2 million—of the Africans shipped to the Americas between 1520 and 1865 came from the Gold Coast (contemporary Ghana), but the vast majority, who were carrying a composite Akan culture, could not temporally realize the opening proverb. Any Akan who travels in the temporal and does not return home or visit frequently is considered a *kwaseapanin* ("eldest of the fools")—an insult of the highest caliber. However, this would have been an inappropriate charge for those who were transported to the Americas: Their journey was characteristically one way and not of their own volition, and they were certainly not immigrants on a "middle passage" but rather uprooted captives-turned-commodities-turned enslaved captives. Nonetheless, the pull to look back and go home was so strong that a small group in early nineteenth-century Jamaica "told some of their shipmates, whom they solicited to go with them, they would proceed to the sea-side by night, and remain in the bush through the night, and the first canoe they found by the seaside they would set sail for their country, which they conceived was no great distance."[1] Justifiably, their eyes had turned back in the hope of going home despite the nautical miscalculation (if the ideas in the source matched the aspirations of those for whom it was written). Others probably did the same but in their hearts and minds while resigned to the processes of social death and rebirth on the immobile slave vessel (i.e., the plantation complex), on which they revolted or jumped overboard or were forcibly transshipped between the Caribbean and mainland colonies possessed by the British, Dutch, Spanish, and French. Efforts to reverse the one-way voyage were rare, but the further instability and trauma of transshipment remained quite frequent, particularly between the Caribbean and North America.

On 14 September 1786, Coffee (Kofi), after being shipped from Jamaica, arrived at a Louisiana port during its period of Spanish occupation (ca. 1770–1803) and was sold within two days to a Luis Boisdore. The seller,

Daniel Clark, also sold a shipmate named Cudjoe (Kwadwo) to Joseph Cultia and another Coffee to Pedro Surget.[2] Cudjoe and the two persons named Coffee were categorized as *bozal* or "newly arrived from Africa," and they likely knew each other prior to and during their brief stay in Jamaica. Shipmates on board the *Nueva Orleans*, these adult male "blacks" from the Gold Coast (also known as the "Mina" coast) via Jamaica were part of the influx of Africans from the Gold Coast to Jamaica between 1781 and 1785, an import of nearly twenty-five thousand people, or 42 percent of all Africans transported to Jamaica during that short period.[3] Two other Mina males named Cofi (Kofi) in late eighteenth-century Louisiana were among a bevy of black males bearing the Akan name Kofi (and its variants), and though these two men were likely shipmates, they were definitely cellmates. Both were among a number of agricultural workers in the semitropical and humid Louisiana climate, which closely mirrored many other parts of the Americas and West Africa. Incarcerated, the elder Cofi died in jail, and the other—a nineteen-year-old born in 1771 (probably on the Gold Coast, like his shipmates)—was released from jail in 1793.

What became of young Cofi once released from jail? We do not know. Nor do we know the interior lives of the group in Jamaica that sought to reverse the one-way voyage. The same applies to 25-year-old Ama, Anne or Pablo from the Gold Coast, 25-year-old Coffy (Kofi) the Maroon, persons named Coffi and Coffy who were involved in the 1795 Pointe Coupee conspiracy, or Quaco (Kwaku), a 63-year-old individual that married the 53-year-old Abba (Aba, Yaa, "Thursday-born female").[4] Both Quaco and Abba were sold to Eulogio de Casas at the start of the nineteenth century, when John Joseph, an Asante prisoner of war, was transported directly to New Orleans. Joseph traveled the same routes as other Akan individuals in North America, working in Louisiana, South Carolina, Virginia, then emigrating to England around 1843, where he related his story. These sketches situated between the Caribbean and North America reflect the kinds of Akan persons relocated to the Americas; they also constitute an appropriate setting for explicating their collective self-understandings as Akan culture bearers and patterned lives shaped by diasporic experiences. By turning our eyes to give the Akan diasporic strand its well-deserved attention, we deepen our understanding of African and transatlantic lived experiences, for they condition the present and are thus histories without closure. In unearthing those lives, we provide proper "burial" so the 1.2 million who embarked from the former Gold Coast can at last go home.

In the Americas, the Akan peoples became identified through an uneven series of characteristics which made them—in the eyes of planters and other Africans—valued as agriculturalists and (un)skilled laborers endowed with great physical strength, as practitioners of indigenous African therapeutics and spirituality, and as Maroons and freedom seekers. These characteristics do not mean the Akan had a monopoly on resistance or maroonage, for the Sereer and the Wolof of Senegambia, for example, had an equally strong tradition of resistance to enslavement in the seventeenth and eighteenth centuries and carried that perspective to the Americas. What is clear is that Akan men, women, children, and their further progeny did fulfill those roles in some places and in some historical moments more than others and that many were inconsistently assigned the pervasive identities of "Mina" or "Coromanti" (and its variants) across distinct linguistic and temporal landscapes. In some historical moments, the Akan bring into sharp relief the diasporic themes of maroonage, resistance, betrayal, and freedom, but they also complicate these themes, for all were delimited by an assumption of coexisting *within* the same deculturizing and neo-European social order. Maroons lived on the periphery of the social order and depended upon it for concessions or provisions, while other freedom seekers carved out contested social and political spaces within the laws and limits of that order. Some Akan went further: They envisioned, as was the case in the Danish and Dutch colonies, a complete overthrow of that draconian social order of European import with one of their own making and based on foundational cultural understandings, thus contributing a significant lens by which to study a layered African diasporic culture, experience, and identity.

The Akan case shows that emancipation, for instance, did not end but rather reorganized the unequal power and labor relations of enslavement and that resistance and revolts did not necessarily end enslavement but exposed its bankruptcy and inability to control uncontrollable property. Undoubtedly, the Akan consistently and in far-reaching ways contributed well beyond their numbers to the themes of maroonage, resistance, and the forging of polities in the Americas, and it is this kind of sustained force that extended the cumulative costs of the slave trade, its termination, and the prevention from exportation of at least another million Africans.[5] These considerations and the experiences of those who did not fit so neatly into any of the aforementioned stereotypic identities and themes constitute the focal point of this book. Precisely, it interweaves the contexts of West Africa and the Americas in terms of the development of a specific Akan culture shaped by continental and diasporic exigencies, and it maps this trajectory, its input toward a composite diasporic cultural identity and ideology, and its engagement with contemporary realities on both sides of the Atlantic. This process ultimately aims at locating the Akan variable in the African diasporic equation and intends not to unravel the quilt but to clarify one of its neglected constituents so as to better understand how the quilt came to be and is still becoming.

The Akan never constituted a majority among other African cultural groups shipped to various parts of the Americas, including Jamaica, throughout much of the "slave trade" (henceforth, "international enslavement enterprise"). However, their leadership skills in war and political organization, expertise in medicinal plant use and spiritual practice, and their very presence as archived in the musical traditions, language, and patterns of African diasporic life far outweighed their actual numbers (whatever the ultimate total might be). The argument herein is that we should look no further than a composite Akan culture for an explanation since it was that culture, calibrated among those of Akan origin and a "diaspora" of "Akanized" communities on the Gold Coast littoral and forest periphery (e.g., the Ewe, Gã-Adangme, Guan, Dagomba), that found its way to the Americas. This argument calls attention to an important rethinking of the historical formation of Akan culture in West Africa and its reach into the Americas, particularly in view of the fact that African diaspora studies, which have marginalized the Akan, have merely engaged in a numerical debate based on a limited number of Gold Coast ports and via the entangled and ultimately European slaving trademarks of "Mina" or "Coromantee." None of the studies has moved beyond those debates or European taxonomies to examine Akan culture in terms of how it has moved through its African and African diasporic histories through persons who may or may not have been Akan. Certainly, this sort of engagement presupposes a working definition of "Akan." Before we define "Akan," however, it is first necessary to clarify the trademarks of "Mina" and "Coromantee" in relation to the Akan in West Africa and the Americas and to explain my approach to Akan culture at the intersections of historical and cultural studies. In doing so, the rationale and limits of my argument, as well as the historical treatment of the Akan experience to follow, will be more intelligible.

MINAS, COROMANTEES, AND AKAN PEOPLES

The purpose of this section is to unpack the historically and geopolitically situated terms (the trademarks) "(A)mina" and "Coromantee." Though their usage overlapped somewhat in the European colonies in the Americas, Coromantee was more a British and to a lesser extent Dutch possession, whereas the Danish, Spanish, French, and Portuguese employed Amina or Mina. Mina and Coromantee both have their origins in the Gold Coast—itself part of a taxonomy representing European interests in West Africa—but Mina preceded Coromantee by more than a century. The idea of "Mina" had its origin in the Portuguese West Africa base at the Castelo de São Jorge da Mina (ca. 1482–1637) or "Elmina" fort, which was built on a rocky peninsula formed by the Benya Lagoon and the Atlantic Ocean, and as part of a region that became known as "Costa da Mina" and later Gold Coast.[6] Though the Dutch seized the Elmina fort in 1637 and helped to terminate all hopes of a recapture with the help of Eguafo and Asebu, Portuguese activity continued on the Gold Coast until the late seventeenth century. For these European interlopers, the Tanɔ and Volta rivers, respectively, demarcated the western and eastern limits of the Mina coast, but the term "Mina" included areas east of the Volta on the former "Slave Coast." On the Gold Coast, "Mina" referred to the peoples of the Elmina settlement and fort, at once distinct from other Akan peoples but inclusive of the former as members of the settlement and on the Gold Coast; beyond this coast, "Mina," in a generic way, denoted Africans from the Gold Coast itself.[7] In fact, the provenance of "Mina" or *Mina de oro* ("mine of gold"; Gold Coast) formed part of the 1503 entries of the Spanish Crown records of Valencia for enslaved Africans from "Minne d'or" (i.e., Gold Coast), and the 1629 map of Dutch cartographer Hans Propheet lists several "Mijna" (Mina) fishing settlements west of Elmina toward Komenda and to the east in coastal settlements adjacent to Accra.[8]

The term "Mina" in a broader sense linked Europe, São Tomé, the Gold Coast, Bénin, Kôngo, and the Americas for several centuries and has been the source of much discussion and confusion, especially in terms of its meaning and application on the West African coast and in the Americas. Off the coast of West Central Africa, São Tomé developed into a nexus of the international enslavement enterprise with the Gold Coast and the Americas in the sixteenth and seventeenth centuries. The island of São Tomé supplied food, acted as a conduit for enslaved persons, and used cowries for the São Jorge da Mina fort and the enterprise itself. In São Tomé, enslaved persons for export were known as *escravos minas* (mina slaves), *negros minas* (mina blacks) or *minas* (Africans from the Mina coast). Many of these Minas were in transit in São Tomé and destined for export (usually to and through São Jorge da Mina) during the sixteenth and seventeenth centuries, particularly as São Tomé became not only a key entrepôt in the slaving and spice enterprise that linked the Kôngo, Bénin, the Gold Coast, and Europe but also an important sugar producer.[9] The Portuguese imported captive Africans from Bénin and the Kôngo to Elmina and Axim from the late fifteenth through the early seventeenth centuries, linking a flow of captives and commodities between the Ivory Coast, Gold Coast, and Slave Coast. But the number of captives from the Gold Coast were relatively small, and so only between 600 and 2,000 captives were exported to São Jorge da Mina from São Tomé before 1550, and the majority of the *escravos de resgate* (enslaved persons destined for export rather than settlement) were thereafter sent to the Americas, principally Brazil and the Caribbean.[10]

Given the extensive coverage on the term "Mina," there should be little by way of new interpretation to offer, particularly with the recent publication of Gwendolyn Hall's *Slavery and African Ethnicities in the Americas*. Hall argues that Africans in the Americas often self-identified the very "ethnicities" found in documentary sources and that the "ethnic" designation of "Mina" referred to "different ethnicities over time and place, but it certainly sometimes meant people from Little Popo, originally Akan speakers who had migrated from west of the Volta River."[11] On the former "Slave Coast" (contemporary southeastern Ghana, Togo, and Bénin), the people of "Little Popo" (Aného) were originally Akan immigrants who formed a "diaspora" west and east of the Volta River, which demarcated the former Gold Coast and Slave Coast in the late sixteenth or early seventeenth century and who were either bi- or multilingual. Although the Gã-Adangme and Ewe languages were spoken on the eastern end of the Gold Coast and across the Volta River farther east, Akan remained the lingua franca of the entire Gold Coast, stretching across its western and eastern frontiers as areas immediately west and east of the Volta became multilingual and thus multicultural in the latter half of the seventeenth century. According to Jesuit missionary Alonso de Sandoval, "Popo," which was probably "Little Popo," as distinct from "Popo" (Hula), bordered the Volta River to the west and Allada to the east, and Allada was situated between (Little) Popo and Bénin. Relying heavily upon Sandoval's work, published originally in 1627, Hall further argues that the Mina "nation" comprised Gbe language speakers (i.e., Aja or Adja, Fon, Ewe) of the "Slave Coast" and that, at the time of Sandoval's observations, there was "an ethnicity named Mina whose members identified themselves with or were identified as part of the Aja/Fon peoples of the Slave Coast and were Gbe sublanguage group speakers, although they most likely spoke Akan as well."[12]

It is questionable whether a Mina "ethnicity" already existed or was the product of historical displacement or the imagination. Sandoval, as well as Portuguese and Dutch observers, geographically situated the Minas on the Gold Coast and viewed "Mina" as a wider area beyond Elmina and the Minas as Akan.[13] We know that Akan and other persons from the Gold Coast had established independent communities, or what the "Negroes call crooms" (*kurom*, "town") on the Slave Coast as refugees, canoemen, traders, and the like as early as the seventeenth century. Moreover, Thomas Philips, a British slaver, noted the presence of Mina canoemen from Elmina, who had settled at Ouidah to help the Dutch with their business in the late seventeenth century.[14] Displaced peoples and cultural strangers forming "new" communities or peoples were not new to the region in the period under discussion.

Further, the Akan polity of Akwamu had extended its hegemony as far east as Ouidah at the start of the eighteenth century and thus reinforced an Akan presence and influence to the extent that the kind of Akan (descended) communities Philips encountered are still referred to as "Minas," as distinct from the appellations used by Gã-Adangme descendants.[15] If the Mina "nation" consisted of Akan migrants who moved into parts of the Slave Coast and were multilingual speakers eventually shipped to the Americas, why would its members unproblematically "identify themselves," or would Hall render them as primarily Gbe speakers? The Baule and other Akan peoples in the Ivory Coast, for example, were early Akan migrants in the region, and although they became fluent in the non-Akan linguistic and cultural worlds of the area, they still identified with and have maintained an Akan-related language, ethos, and cultural praxis. Indeed, simply because designations of "Mina" encountered in the documentary sources suggest that peoples of this grouping arrived from the Slave Coast does not necessarily mean that they were predominantly Gbe speakers—a historically recent nomenclature. They could have also been multilingual Akan persons who were recorded as other than Akan speakers, granted that multilingualism in West Africa and in captivity was an invaluable asset.

Scholars such as Hall have examined the cases of Cuba, Saint Domingue (Haiti), Brazil, and Louisiana and have used these places as sites where the Mina presence, which was thought to be of Akan derivation, was rather of largely Gbe constitution. As a result of this approach, scholars have placed too much weight on a literal reading of the sources and have at times misconstrued the sources. In support of her argument for Cuba and perhaps other Spanish-speaking locales, Hall relies on the work of Cuban historian Moreno Fraginals, who uncovered several African "ethnic" designations through an examination of Cuban sugar and coffee estates from the second half of the eighteenth to the late nineteenth century. Fraginals has tabulated 976 (or 5.2 percent of a total of 18,731) "Minas" between 1760 and 1870. However, these "Minas," like Sandoval's, were distinct from other ethnic categories such as "Lucumi" (Yorùbá, Nagô), "Arara" (Ajá, Fon, Mahi, Ewé), and "Bibi" (Ibibio).[16] In other Spanish colonies, such as Costa Rica and what became Panama, many of the Minas from the Gold Coast came to the region by the mid-seventeenth century, and, despite Spanish Crown prohibition, a number of them—under names such as Antonio, Andrés, and Miguel—entered places like Costa Rica (sometimes via Panama) in the first decade of the eighteenth century and thereafter.[17] In 1680 the likes of Antonio and Andrés were described as "habitual runaways" and were listed under the trademark of "Mina." Those who arrived after 1713, such as Francisco and Nicholás Mina, likely came via South Sea Company vessels since the British company was granted an *asiento* or exclusive license to supply Spanish colonies with African captives under the 1713 Treaty of Utrecht.[18] The South Sea Company landed at least 35,000 African captives in the Americas between 1714 and 1737, and thirty-two of its voyages from the Gold Coast accounted for the embarkment of more than 9,000 captives to mostly Spanish Central America, Rio de la Plata (between Uruguay and Argentina), and Cuba.[19]

Though the Akan were less represented in Cuba and Saint Domingue, the "Minas" and "Caramanty" were also distinct from the Gbe speakers in both eighteenth-century colonies. This would have differed little in the previous century, for Gold Coast captives were in demand in Guadeloupe and Martinique among planters and merchants such as Jean Barbot, who found "Gold Coast Blacks... much more acceptable in the French Islands."[20] Thus, French and Cuban estate owners or the agents who recorded the "ethnicities" under discussion did not see the Minas as a part of the constellation of Gbe speakers or "Araras." In fact, "Minas" referred to peoples from the Gold Coast, for Gbe speakers were placed into a distinct category in Cuba, and even in the local *cabildos* (brotherhoods) we find the Cabildo de Ashanti and, in the larger society, the "Minas Popo Coast da Oro" (Mina-Popo from the Gold Coast), who were Akan and Gã-Adangme migrants who had settled at Aného. In the first three decades of the nineteenth century, those from the "country" of "Mina Janti" (Mina-Asante) and "Mina" continued to enter the ports of Cuba, and the names of those Mina captives brought before the Court of Mixed Commission at Havana were stubbornly Akan. On condemned vessels like the *Voladora*, the vast majority had Akan names such as Cuame (Kwame), Quocu (Kwaku), Cofi (Kofi), Ata, Sechi (Sakyi), Ofori, Sare (Asare), Adu, Quameapea (Kwame Appia), Amangua (Amankwa), Cuasicum (Kwasi Kuma), Ochere (Okyere), and Achampol (Akyeampɔn). Those designated as Mina-Popo and Mina-Ashanti (Mina-Asante) also appeared in documents in colonial Mexico and Brazil.[21]

We find the vast majority of Mina in Brazil during the late seventeenth and eighteenth century, and baptismal documents from Rio de Janeiro list "Mina" but as only one of several very broad ethnic designations. Captives from broad regions such as the Costa da Mina were often funneled through a limited number of ports, such as Ouidah in the eighteenth century, and Africans from the Slave Coast (Bight of Bénin) were listed under "Mina" in Brazilian documents, but "Mina" was a general term used to include a number of different peoples other than Gbe speakers. In nineteenth-century Rio de Janeiro, the term "Mina" came to include Yorùbá-speaking peoples, and we can be sure of the inclusive yet restrictive meanings of "Mina" for at least one mid-nineteenth-century observer in Rio de Janeiro noted the presence of "Ashantee" and "Mina" persons.[22] That Africans from the Volta delta and east of the Volta were still being shipped to Brazil after the British abolition of the slave trade suggests both a continued yet numerically small Akan presence and the choice of broader categories of identification by multilingual Akan persons if the umbrella of "Mina" strategically provided for security and identification through ethnic and later religious mutual-aid organizations. In spiritual organizations, Gwendolyn Hall and Robin Law note the presence of the Casa das Minas, a so-called Dahomian cult house in São Luis, Maranhão, Brazil; however, in São Luis, there were and still are other important *terreiros* (spiritual centers) such as the Casa das Minas-Jeje (Fon-Ewe), Casa de Nagô (Yorùbá), and Casa Fanti-Ashanti (Akan), all embodiments of distinct spiritual-cultural practices (with overlap) under the umbrella of Candomblé.[23] Although the Akan in Brazil were not numerically significant, their presence and spirit remain part of the popular consciousness among African Brazilian organizations such as Ilê Aiyê (House of Life), which not only made "Ghana Ashanti" its 1983 carnival theme in Salvador (Bahia) but also composed and performed a song dedicated to Akan-Asante history. That history and its people hold significant meaning for cultural consciousness and identity formation among those in Brazil who self-consciously and institutionally define themselves as African and see the Akan, in this instance, as a source of inspiration and remembrance. Composed by César Maravilha, the words to the song "Negrice Cristal" are as follows:[24]

Viva o rei Osei Tutu	Long live to king Osei Tutu
Ashanti a cantar	The Ashanti [Asante] sing
Para o nosso rei Obá	To our king, Obá
Salve o rei Osei Tutu	Greetings to the king Osei Tutu
Negrice Cristal	Negrice Cristal
Liberdade, Curuzu	Liberdade, Curuzu[25]
Tema Gana Ashanti	The theme Ashanti [Asante] Ghana
Ilê vem apresentar	Ilê comes to present
Ashanti, povo negro	Ashanti [Asante], black people
Dessa rica região	From this rich region
Gana império Gana	Ghana empire Ghana
Do ouro e do cacau	Of gold and cocoa
Sudaneza, Alto Volta	Sudanese, Upper Volta [Burkina Faso]
E África Ocidental	and West Africa
A influencia Ashanti	The Ashanti [Asante] influence
Se fazia sentir	It was made to spread
O Togo, Daome	Togo, Dahomey [Bénin]
E a Costa do Marfim	and the Ivory Coast
Viva o rei	Long live the king

The last stanza of "Negrice Cristal" affirms a historical development that has both much relevance for our discussion of "Mina" and two implications for clarifying the Akan experience in the Americas. First, the idea of Asante and, broadly, Akan influence to the west and east of what is now Ghana is rooted in the historical record. A reading of that record brings into question the proposition that we can unproblematically disaggregate multilingual and mobile speakers who occupied contiguous areas and thus claim that one group was more numerous than another in the Americas. Second, regardless of the ethnic categories that were ascribed to those same peoples, they did not necessarily share similar thinking about "Mina" as a marker of self-identification, as might be the case in the minds of scholars. Of the 8,442 identified ethnicities from Gwendolyn Hall's Louisiana Slave Database (ca. 1719–1820), "Mina" was listed as a distinct category from other ethnicities, including the Aradas (Allada)—and this was the case for Cuba, Saint Domingue (Haiti), and Brazil—but these Minas constituted only 628 persons or 7.4 percent of the total number.[26] Among those ethnicities Hall identified quite a number of Africans from the Gold Coast under the category of "Mina" with Akan and non-African names, but it remains unclear how they were distinct from "Minas" listed as Gbe, Fante, and other African language speakers, particularly among Africans who unambiguously had Akan names yet were listed as "Bamana" or from the "Congo."[27]

Joseph Mina, for instance, is said to have taken "the ethnic name of the Mina slaves who reared him," according to Hall, but since the term "Mina" was a distinct category of identification and assumed a meaning inclusive of different peoples in Louisiana and elsewhere, what did it mean with regard to Joseph or those who reared him? It is not immediately clear whether Joseph or the Minas in Hall's calculations were largely and unambiguously Gbe language speakers. Was Antonio Cofi Mina, a leader of the enslaved Mina community that was involved in the 1795 Pointe Coupee conspiracy and accused of conspiring to overthrow the institution of slavery, a Gbe language speaker with an Akan name or a multilingual Akan bearing a Spanish first name followed by a name of Akan origination?[28] The latter seems more plausible until further evidence becomes available. Nevertheless, after the conspiracy Antonio was shipped to Cuba, where he in all likelihood joined that distinct group of Minas of Gold Coast provenience and of Akan cultural origin. It would appear, then, that, rather than diminishing the Akan presence in the Americas, we must significantly reduce the number and presence of Gbe language speakers clustered under the "Mina" experience there. Robin Law rightfully argues that the name "Mina" was specific to the Gold Coast and its inhabitants—even if they settled elsewhere as Akan and Gã-Adangme speakers—in West Africa, and although the elasticity of the term came to sometimes include Gbe speakers in the Americas, particularly Brazil, "it is questionable whether ["Mina"] ever denoted Gbe-speakers as distinct from speakers of Akan or Gã-Adangme."[29]

The Mina experience thus raises some critical questions about African social formation and cultural transformation in the Americas. Did Africans use language, "religious" affiliation (e.g., as adherents to African and African-based spiritualities in the Americas, Islam, or Christianity), or the structures of African polities as remembered from Africa, or did they use all three in varying degrees and as principles by which to organize themselves? If the mechanism of organization was primarily language, did cultural groups identify themselves and others by the principal and perhaps mutually intelligible languages they spoke? What might have been the decision-making process of bi- or multilingual speakers from contiguous areas and those accessible by land and water? Africans may have identified with localized or broader polities in West Africa as a source of security and thus would have given their loyalty to those bases of social unity, and this would have been true for centralized Akan polities. However, religious affiliations via Islam or Christianity would have been meaningless for most Akan, who were non-Christian and non-Islamic and had been that way for centuries. Significant numbers of Akan persons began to yield to Christianization—albeit with resistance—only in the late nineteenth and early twentieth century and largely on the coast decades after they were shipped to the Americas. Indigenous spiritualities, unlike those proselytizing religions of the "book," were rooted in the cultural order of their birth, and the wider net they cast upon the spiritual, sociopolitical, and linguistic lives of members were far reaching and permeable in that "divinities" and their meanings could be adopted, shared, used, and discarded across larger political and cultural landscapes without conflict of allegiance. Yet, these spiritualities, like those of the Gold Coast, were in and of themselves not unifying forces and thus principles around which Akan or other Africans would have coalesced in Africa or the Americas since they were so integral and almost indistinguishable from one's culture and were not externalizing and hegemonic "faiths" built upon ultimate, exclusive, and Universalism-like claims.

The topography and commercial networks of West Africa, as well as the roads and waterways that facilitated those networks, also assisted the convergences of cultural traditions through either the volition of the groups involved or political domination. As a result of either process, a kind of multilingualism and multiculturalism emerged in a region where a high degree of diversity or ethnicity has been greatly exaggerated. It has been easy to imagine African diasporic groups as "ethnies" or "nations" as broadened expressions of "ethnicity," but these approaches have not fully grappled with the issues of African language competency among scholars who do diasporic and "Atlantic" history and the locating of "Africa" and African lives in European scribal sources.[30] These sources still confound the process of locating African identities, and they continue to shape the perspective of scholars who remain true to their perceptions of "nations." The "nation" (*nación, nação*; Spanish and Portuguese, respectively) and "country" (*terre*, French) of Africans inventoried in neo-European documents were based less on Europeans' perceptions of African polities and more on language (or at least what they believed were a plethora of indiscriminate languages). Thus, these "nations" and "countries" were early inventions that anticipated the concept of "ethnicity," a colonial creation based largely upon the European idea of a nation and built upon the early process of determining African language or "ethnolinguistic" groups as found in the ethnographies and vocabulary lists compiled by seventeenth-to-nineteenth-century European missionaries. Though commerce was the common denominator between Africa and Europe of the late fifteenth and nineteenth centuries, very few European merchants were and even fewer scholars of "diaspora" are fluent in African history and languages. Scholars have grounded their works in assumed linguistic knowledge gleaned from European missionary ethnographies and lexicons. If 537 million (or 82.6 percent) of 650 million Africans of non-Arab and non-European origin used no more than ten to twelve root African languages—as bi- and multilingual speakers, based upon a mutual intelligibility of at least 85 percent—as of 2004, we cannot start with Joseph Greenburg's flawed classification scheme nor a missionary's catalog of phrases in order to clarify the linguistic or "ethnic" map of the African past.[31] Rather than debate the extent of African ethnicities in the Americas—a discourse that privileges the "nation" and "ethnic" notions such as "Mina" and "Coromantee"— perhaps we should start with the Africans' self-understandings and identities in Africa and then use both as a compass to chart their shapes in the Americas.

As was the case with Joseph Mina and Antonio Cofi Mina, the terms "Mina" and "Coromantee" used by European slavers also raise a fundamental question: How can one be sure that the Akan names used in this study were the cultural property of Akan persons? Were Akan names employed (only) by Africans of Akan cultural origin, or did other Africans not of Gold Coast provenance also adopt and use these names (as Akan names or in translation, such as "Monday" or "Thursday")? It is certainly possible and even probable that some Africans or their progeny born in the Americas might have carried an Akan name in the Americas through their parents, relatives, or another person or fictive kin. Yet, it is more likely that those who bore transparent Akan names were actually Akan or Akan descendants since these names were distinct in cultural origin and spelling, were restricted to those on the contiguous Gold Coast and Slave Coast, and were usually found where the British, Dutch, and Danish had colonies and commercial ties with other European nations. The Akan were also very aware of who they were on the Gold Coast littoral and on the forest fringe, and they engaged the Americas through these foundational self-understandings. Though cultural authentication as an Akan did not always follow the matrilineal principle in the Americas (in that a key criterion of Akan personhood presupposed birth by an Akan mother), it was more the case that Akan (descended) fathers who married or who fathered children with non-Akan women gave their children Akan names.

One example of such a scenario, in which an Akan fathered a child with a non-Akan woman and gave his child an Akan name, involves Paul Cuffee, the well-known, African-descended maritime entrepreneur. Though Cuffee's mother Ruth was a Wampanoag, his father Kofi was apparently an Asante person seized on the Gold Coast and then enslaved and remembered as Kofi—the source of "Cuffee." Beyond the certainty that Akan names might or might not have been granted to or adopted by persons of Akan cultural origin, the point in either case is this feature of Akan culture—its distinctly patterned naming system and the character of each name—took root and flourished as a resource for carving out a cultural identity (out of several African and non-African options) in the Americas. The Africans referred to as Akan in this book were selected as such based upon transparent Akan names, augmented by evidence of Akan culture and language use, historical demography, most frequent places of disembarkation in the Americas from primarily the Gold Coast (and areas east of the Volta River), scarification or "country marks" (consistency recorded by Europeans as marks of discrete identification since Renaissance Europe), and thematic characterizations and categories of identification (e.g., "Coromantee" or "Mina") in the primary and secondary literature. As the mushrooming slave trade literature attests, the overwhelming presence of males and of Akan male names owes much to the structure and demographics of the international enslavement enterprise: Almost two-thirds of those exported to the Americas via ports on the African littoral were male, and since men were primarily the merchants and fought the wars, it is clear that the vast numbers of Africans thus exploited were victims of an insidious commerce and war.[32] When and where the evidence exists and I have been able to find it, Akan (descended) women form part of the larger experience since, without question, they played integral roles from facilitating revolts on board the slave vessels to shaping the cultural and spiritual realities of their captivity.

CULTURE, HISTORY, AND SPIRITUALITY

The nature of this study requires a prefatory note on my approach to a "cultural history" and some important delimitation of my use of culture and spirituality in general and Akan culture and spirituality in particular. Many historians have an undying loyalty to their field and its boundaries, but there are those who moonlight in other areas of knowledge production such as archaeology or anthropology. Nevertheless, historians of either persuasion are often unable to escape the gravity of disciplinary conflicts between anthropology and history; they may also remain confined to theories and methods identified as their own. These conflicts facilitate much of the confusion in the interpretive use of "culture" and "religion" to the extent that neither is tenable as an analytic concept since in those disciplines there are no unambiguous parameters as to what constitutes or distinguishes "culture" and "religion" and the historical development of either (in relation to one another) among those studied. All cultures and therefore all human beings have a fundamental framework that they use to interpret and respond to historical, sociopolitical, cosmic, and temporal environments, and, in turn, those interpretations and responses become codified as foundational understandings in terms of the composite "way of life" that people choose to live over time and in specific locales.

Culture, as defined here, is a composite of the spiritual, ideational, and temporal dimensions of life as experienced by people across historical time and place; it is also a process that provides a procedural framework for living, interpreting, and responding to human, ecological, and climatic realities. As such, *temporal culture* refers to the physical, technological, or tangible part of life that people use, make, and share, which includes all of the physical manifestations of a culture. *Ideational culture* includes ideas, symbols, values, principles, and ways of feeling, thinking, and acting, as well as a stock of knowledge and ways of making sense of reality as constructed or filtered by a group. An ideational culture not only embraces the temporal dimension of the world but also accepts the notion that a nonphysical, immaterial reality is real and apprehensible. *Spiritual culture* constitutes what we may call cosmological understandings and, in a sense, is very much interconnected with the temporal and yet part of a temporal, ideational, and spiritual continuum. In other words, if this continuum were a tree, the temporal would be the trunk and its branches, the ideational would be the roots, and the spiritual would be both what nourishes the roots and the unseen activities of sustainability well beneath the soil and beyond the eye of the microscope. This all implies a theory of culture.

Each of these dimensions forms a composite called "culture" (in lieu of a more encompassing term), and this concept, in spite of its embattled nature, remains a widely accepted way to refer to a people, their universe, and their place in and vision of that universe. In other words, people, ultimately, boil down to their core culture, and their historical evolution—in terms of the pragmatics of day-to-day living, collective ideas, or spiritual strivings—are cultural histories. For our purposes, culture is both multilayered and mobile; that is to say, if movement, whether coerced or consensual, defines human life in a myriad of ways, then culture is portable and geographically unfixed so as long as the composite integrity of a distinct (spiritual and ideational) culture is maintained. To the idea of cultural durability, the Akan proverbially claim, *ɛkyɛm tete a, ɛka ne mmeramu* (when the shield wears out, its framework remains [intact]), and here human material culture, like the shield, may give way, but its core ideational and spiritual understandings remain. For the Akan, the term *amammerɛ*, which is the confluence of *ɔman* (cultural group) and *merɛ* (manner, way), is often used for "culture." *Amammerɛ* is premised on people rather than polity, and, in the same way that members give birth to and sustain the life of an organization worth having, it is the people or the "cultural group" and their "ways and manners" that are ultimately at stake when it comes to both humans and the ideational and material practices they create. Therefore, "Akan" is used in this study to mean the composite culture designed by West African forest settlers (the "first, foremost, and pioneer" peoples) between the Komóe and Volta rivers from the coast to the edge of the forest and defined by a distinctiveness in culture and spirituality in terms of a shared common language, ethos, calendrical system, traditions of origin, sociopolitical order, and a high degree of ideological conformity. These shared features organized an indigenous culture that although shaped in some ways by other African societies, it became "Akan" not out of sameness, as the Fante are not replicas of the Asante, but they offer connective points of culture for study. In sum, Akan cultural identity is a broad, non-ethnic identifier, and Akan spiritual culture—a constant presence noted in the accounts of European merchants, sailors, clergymen, soldiers, and missionaries from the late fifteenth century onward—has been the most enduring marker of that identity on its own terms and in interactions with the variables of Islam, Christianity, colonialism, and all the exigencies of globalization.

Akan culture and spirituality were and still are symbiotic, and to understand the dynamic of the former, one must have a simultaneous grasp of the latter. A pervasive misreading of this fundamental understanding might explain why the Akan are one of most written-about peoples in West Africa, but their spirituality and, by extension, their indigenous culture remain scandalized as "fetishism" (or whatever contemporary phrase is used in its place), are left to those in religious studies or anthropology, and continue to be poorly investigated beyond those who are interested in political and economic history. Spirituality, as defined herein, is distinct from religion. Religion as an institution or a belief system does not presuppose a culture in which it is rooted in the sense that any Akan can also be a Muslim, Buddhist, or Christian, but not any Muslim, Buddhist, or Christian can become an Akan, as one would adopt a religious orientation. In the normal course of Akan living, one must be born of an Akan mother, at a minimum, to be considered an ɔkani ba (child of the Akan), in addition to speaking *Twi kasa kronkron* (sacred Twi language) and being well grounded in the core understandings that formed Akan culturally structured thought and behavior. These are indigenous criteria of identity making, some of which were altered or muted in the Americas due to the abnormality of living and dying under racialized captivity. Both religion and spirituality, therefore, must be operationally distinguished so that when we talk of spirituality we are engaging in a cultural rather than a religious discourse that can be examined in the context of Akan sources of knowledge and interpretation and also distanced from the anthropological notion of "belief."

Often in academic discourse there exists a subtle yet important disjuncture between knowledge and belief. The idea of "belief" has undergone significant semantic change in several European languages over the past few centuries, and "belief as it is employed in anthropology does indeed connote error or falsehood," for "cultural others" possess "belief systems" with attendant "folk scientists," while Europeans and their ideological progeny have "knowledge systems" of a distinctly scientific, reasoned, and assured quality.[33] Thomas McCaskie's engaging and, at times, profound account of Asante (Akan) history and society is grounded in a study of "belief" in Asante history, but that very anchoring raises some questions. McCaskie argues the historical Asante polity structured and controlled the beliefs of its citizens through the lens of civil or public expressions of Asante "belief" wherein the polity's "ideologies of control—its structuration of belief and knowledge in society—depended upon the blurring of epistemological distinctions rather than their sedulous reinforcement."[34] According to that argument, coercive leaders of the historical Asante polity seemingly exploited and subordinated its people through the control of a belief system characterized by passivity, resignation, and "weak thought," and it suggests that the Asante were defeated, at least ideologically, by the "theologically highly developed" Christianity of the British.[35] For McCaskie, the battle between Christianity and indigenous "beliefs" was "immediately and directly about lived ideologies," and the former seized upon the latter's rootedness in ambiguous prognostications via the *abosom* ("properties of and in nature") and the lack of rigorous search for "alternative epistemological possibilities" as found in "the Cartesian and Kantian tradition."[36] In the end, what we have is not Asante history contextualized in Asante society and "belief" but rather a Gramscian version of Asante (state) history reduced to state politics deduced from state-centered action of a religious or ceremonial sort without much attention to the private, nonstate manifestations of "belief" in the broader Asante society. Though McCaskie charges Ivor Wilks with imposing Weberian models of the state on nineteenth-century Asante, he himself imposes a Gramscian model also of Western import. In doing so, McCaskie, as he advises, did not assess Asante "belief" on its own terms and "in relation to the specifics of its social and individual meanings" but focused on state actors and (ceremonial) actions and synchronically reduced too much of Asante "belief" and knowledge to a deceptive exterior and an endeavor without personal, sacred meanings.

Akan spirituality in the Asante context was more than an exercise in postmodern historiography given that the profundity of Asante or Akan ideas, material culture reflective of cosmological concerns, and spirituality cannot be interpreted solely in terms of mnemonic devices and hermeneutical master texts. We simply do not have the sources that could capture the full range of meanings and interpretations of cultural practices and reflections in historical Asante or the courage to cease telescoping Asante or Akan ideas and actions through the lens of Marx, Weber, or Gramsci and claim to present the former on their own terms and in their own right. Here, the larger issue is not the postmodernist readings of McCaskie or the focus on political narrative by Wilks—though one could argue for an intermediary position between culture and political context—but the very sources employed in the interpretation of Akan history. For the Asante in particular, McCaskie relied on the accounts of two Wesleyan Methodist missionaries, Thomas B. Freeman and Thomas R. Picot, for key utterances of Asantehene Kwaku Dua Panin and Asantehene Mensa Bonsu in support of arguments related to state coercion or control of beliefs. As direct quotes from missionary journals, the utterances of both Asantehene were used in such a way that those sources were presented as unproblematic in relation to their author's missionary depositions, sensibilities, and what each actually heard, no doubt in translation, especially with regard to Asante "beliefs." Thus, as the case of local leader and Gold Coast merchant John Kabes (1650s?—1722) illustrates, "our knowledge and understanding of Kabes [or any key indigenous person] is dictated to us by his relationship with the Europeans with whom he came in contact. That confused and distorted image [that] emerges is not surprising [and thus, for instance, we lack...] his own attitudes toward the Europeans with whom he dealt so closely during so many years."[37]

As we move beyond the almost exclusive dialogue with European sources in order to locate indigenous persons and practices, a critical reading of Akan culture requires a simultaneous reading of its authored spirituality in order to arrive at meanings that make sense in the intellectual and cultural histories of Akan peoples in Africa and in the Americas. In the Americas, the claim that displacement ruptured the Akan spiritual or ancestral connection to both the land and their personality is a misreading, for Akan persons who left a record of some sort envisioned a spiritual return to their homeland. This homeland was not necessarily the Gold Coast, and thus they seemed to have developed the idea that *asamando* (where the ancestors dwell) was more a space where one could gain entry, in spite of immediate geographical places of birth and death. Under normal circumstances in Akan life, all efforts were made to secure the body of a deceased cultural member within reasonable distance; beyond this boundary of reason, of which the Americas marked a great temporal distance from home, the Akan conceded to its logic, and perhaps it was this idea that compelled a spiritual homegoing unbounded by time, space, or distance. What was critical here was not necessarily a connection to land but to ancestors and spiritual agencies that would facilitate entry to *asamando* through the appropriate rituals since Akan cultural ties to their Creator were linked to principal, water-based *abosom* (spiritual agents) rather than land- or forest-based manifestations of that Creator. In *asamando* and through the *abosom*, cultural knowledge of historical and spiritual value was archived, retrieved, shaped, and reused to gain entry to and communicate with those in *asamando*, as well as secure cultural knowledge of pragmatic value. After thirty-five years of research among the Saramaka Maroons of Suriname, Richard Price admittedly came to realize the fuller value that we have placed on spiritual culture: "Indeed, the importance of spirit possession as a means for the transmission of historical as well as spiritual knowledge was something I only dimly understood before I met Tooy."[38] Tooy was a Saramaka healer whom Price had recently encountered, and Price's realization is more than instructive. In sum, my approach to culture and spirituality has much to offer African diaspora studies and the study of the Akan "diaspora" as a variable in that equation.

ON DIASPORA AND THE AKAN LENS

The term "diaspora," as applied to the worldwide dispersal of African peoples, has been in use only for the past few decades, though its implied "transnational" focus has been an intellectual concern of African descended thinkers and activists for much longer. In fact, several of those thinkers recognized that human history began with African history and that the first (voluntary) "diaspora" was an African one. Current thinking about African descended communities and identities as imagined or invented have become popular and even fashionable in diasporic studies in spite of the very conceptual difficulties embedded in notion of "diaspora" in general and the "African diaspora" in particular.[39] The conceptual and even methodological problem is that "diaspora" subsumes historical processes of voluntary and involuntary movement, dispersal, and exile with little distinction between them and to the exclusion of the ways in which each process singularly and symbiotically has shaped the histories of African peoples across time, geography, gender, and place in respective social orders. An additional challenge is the expanding yet consolidating and interlinked character of African global communities and the difficulty of comprehending the dynamism of human movement, which, unlike tectonic plates, disperse and retract by way of multiple peripheral and proximate factors. For instance, reducing the international enslavement enterprise and the coerced displacement of Africans in the Americas to notions of "middle passage" or "migrations" puts Africa on the periphery of that history, fails to account for the human subjectivity of Africans in their one-way crossing of the Atlantic, and apologizes for the unsanitized realities of enslavement.[40] The psychic terror and social violence of enslavement is further reduced to a joint corporate venture over labor demands and African "migrant" laborers, one in which the invisible yet legally real corporation of slavery is held liable for its debts rather than the shareholders who created and profited from that corporation and the reduction of Africans to chattel. Chattel enslavement then bookmarks the start of an African diasporic narrative that makes the "American experience" of Africans and their descendants seem like "progress" (juxtaposed to slavery as a beginning), an advancement marked by an ambiguous partnership with the dominant views and values of neo-European societies in the Americas.

Since the days of the often-referenced Herskovits-Frazier debate, studies of the African diaspora in the Americas has been marked by an intense focus on West Africa to the exclusion of West Central Africa and certainly southern East Africa in places such as Mozambique and Madagascar. In the past two decades, however, we have seen two significant conceptual shifts in African diasporic studies: one from West to West Central Africa and the other from the "saltwater" Africans, who came to dominate the American landscape since the seventeenth century, to the "Atlantic creoles." In the shift to West Central Africa, the works of John Thornton, Linda Heywood, Maureen Warner-Lewis, Monica Schuler, and others have opened up new vistas of scholarship. The most recent text by Thornton and Heywood argues that West Central Africans rather than West Africans were the founders and creators of African American culture, wherein the acculturation in European values, religion, dress, and language began in Africa for these "Atlantic Creoles," making them well suited for their subjugated colonial and enslaved roles in America.[41] Ira Berlin makes the same argument, though his North American narrative focuses on a limited number of European port towns in West Africa.[42] In Berlin's and Heywood and Thornton's work, we see a continued tension between West Africa and West Central Africa in terms not only of which created "African American culture" but also of the ways in which both are popular representatives of an "Atlantic world" chorus that lacks attention to the logic of its melody and the evidence used to author the musical composition. Works on "Atlantic Creoles," like "Atlantic world" historiography, have become their own worst enemies: In appealing to a universal expectation of evitable Americanization, Africa remains neglected in Atlantic histories because many scholars lack competency in the African histories and languages of the people they study; national historical narratives of European or North American origin are privileged, and Africans are denied *their own* agency in the patronizing ways they are "founders and creators" of a culture that ultimately flowed from Europe.

When and where the sources make it possible, the challenge is to focus our studies more on the nexus between specific African cultural groups and individuals in terms of how their culture moved through their history in Africa and the Americas. Here, the idea is not the pursuit of "African survivals" belonging to a distinct cultural group or the embattled notions of syncretism and creolization but rather an African culture and society that was composite in origination and reconstituted—at the level of foundational self-understandings—in its dialogue with other Africans and their externalizing world across historical time. The historical and cultural specificity of the Akan provides one such case because it articulates the identity of a composite Akan culture as informed by their African history and diasporic experiences, as well as the ways in which their culture shaped the African experience in the latter context. This study contributes to a necessary shift from the tradition of privileging an Atlantic or North American ownership of the African diaspora and makes that diaspora a shared property by properly examining it through African history in terms of continuity and transformation rather than by seeing the Atlantic as a threshold that, upon crossing it, produced "new" human beings and histories once African.[43] The Akan diaspora in the Americas is one of the most important African cultural groups to settle the region since at least the seventeenth century, yet it has received no scholarly treatment, whereas a number of studies have noted the importance of the Yorùbá, Igbo, or Kôngo-Angola diasporas in the making of the Americas.[44] The published literature on those diasporas have focused on enslavement, "middle passage," and the "American experience" of a single cultural group or region and attempted to move beyond descriptions of generalized African experiences. The Akan, a cultural group of the West African forest, contributed in specific and integral ways to the diasporic themes of maroonage, conspiracies and rebellions, self-help organizations and communities, and an African spiritual-ideational-material culture in the Americas.[45]

The book thus seeks to contribute to the discourse on the history of African transnational cultures in the Americas since the African diaspora is unique in its formation and constitution, and, as such, the most enduring and explicit marker of that composite diaspora in the Americas is found in the domain of culture and its influences. Yet, that culture subsisted through the accumulative experiences of raids, captures, escapes, uprisings, incarcerations at West African coastal ports, languishing in the holds of ships, disease and suffering, death and the one-way Atlantic crossing, commodification, and life in the slave societies of the Americas. In this respect, Stephanie Smallwood's *Saltwater Slavery* is somewhat comparable to this book, though they fundamentally differ. I focus exclusively on the Akan to examine the Akan, whereas Smallwood's text uses the Gold Coast case and primarily Royal African Company records, though relying too heavily on the secondary literature for Akan culture, to examine important concerns of commodification and the "saltwater" terror experienced by Africans who did not encounter a geographically stable "Atlantic world" so popular in contemporary scholarship. An interpretive history with a thematic approach, *Akan Pioneers: African Histories, Diasporic Experiences* uses Guyana, Jamaica, Antigua, Barbados, former Danish and Dutch colonies, and North America (i.e., Georgia, South Carolina, Virginia, Maryland, and New York) and Canada from the mid-seventeenth century as cases to explicate the Akan experience in the region. These cases are, however, preceded by an examination of how Akan culture formed in the West African forest and its continuity and transformation in dialogue with Islamic forces to the north and northwest of the forest and European forces on the coast after the fifteenth century. In so doing, I focus on the historically situated processes of cultural transformation and continuity in West Africa and the Americas and use those early experiences to examine the contemporary engagement and movement of diasporic Africans and Akan persons between Ghana and the Americas, particularly North America.

The Akan provide a unique case of African cultural continuity and transformation in the Americas, for, although they engaged in commercial interactions with Arab Islamic and European Christian forces for centuries in West Africa, they rarely became Islamic or Christian (until the twentieth century, and even then with resistance) and many did so in the Americas, though more so in Maroon communities. In the area of spiritual culture and political leadership, the Akan contributed to the composite identity and culture of Africans in the Americas through an "internal dialogue" with other Africans and the exigencies of their own historical moments. That conversation is recurring as the "slave castles" of Ghana become both contested sites of meeting and reinterpretation and a crossroads where diasporic Africans are adopting Akan cultural institutions and spiritual practices, while Akan persons in Ghana are becoming increasingly Christianized and are leaving for North America and parts of Europe. The latter process has led many in diasporic communities to travel to and study in the Akan homeland. These phenomena associated with the Akan diaspora strongly suggest that the study of a composite African diaspora must be one of ongoing movements and transformations in specific and shared dialogue among African-based and African-descended communities.

The Akan experience also provides an important perspective on the neo-European societies used as case studies and in which Akan peoples found themselves under captivity. Therein we gain insight into the Akan and an additional perspective on other Africans and their descendants in those (colonial) societies. This project enlarges our understanding of some of the lived experiences and their meaning for Akan persons in the Americas and the continued (dis)engagement with Akan culture among diasporic Africans and Akan persons from Ghana, who, ironically, meet frequently at the site where many ancestors of both groups departed—the "slave castles" that line the coast of what is now the republic of Ghana. In sum, the aim herein is to capture the processes associated with the formation of an African society and diasporal communities that were and are Akan in origination, as well as the forces and factors that have shaped these communities, identities, representations of Africa and Africans, and African self-understandings. This way, we engage in a conversation about real rather than invented peoples and, in exploring the Africanness of their humanity, shift one of the methodological foci of African diasporic studies from the quantification of aggregate numbers and the Eurocentric documentary evidence employed in slave trade studies to an interdisciplinary setting that foregrounds the African or Akan experience in the Americas.

Overall, the chapters that follow are organized to proceed, geographically, from the early West Africa forest and its fringes and the later Gold Coast to the Dutch and Danish colonies, the British Caribbean, and North America. Thematically, the chapters take on specific shapes to underscore the composite nature of Akan cultural history and identity on both sides of the Atlantic. The next chapter, therefore, provides a largely original perspective on how and why Akan culture and society developed the way they did through some of the early and key formative processes. Those processes facilitated early population growth, communal labor and reproductive strategies necessary for forest clearance and settlement during periods of malaria adaptation, and an agrarian sociopolitical order. Akan societies and culture were largely an indigenous development in the forest and on its fringes, and the necessary levels of commercial development placed the Akan in local and regional networks in food, trade goods, and locally exploited gold that predated the trans-Saharan trade. By the late fifteenth century, the Portuguese encountered Akan societies characterized by sophisticated cultural and commercial knowledge and skills after centuries of experience. The Akan societies approached these and other Europeans with tact, though consequences such as transatlantic slaving, through which 1.2 million Africans left the Gold Coast between 1520 and 1865, were rarely anticipated.

Chapter three examines in detail the state of Akan coastal settlements and those of the interior between the sixteenth and eighteenth centuries. By the end of the sixteenth century, the Portuguese dominance in the trade in gold and enslaved persons on the Gold Coast began to feels the influence of European rivals, and local African knowledge of that competition allowed them to skillfully adapt to the increased demand for gold and enslavable peoples on the coast. Gold Coast societies were less organized to specifically exploit the slave trade compared to the Europeans and the varied industries and port cities (e.g., Liverpool, Bristol) borne of that trade. The traffic in captives was not as integral to indigenous societies in that confluence of competition and commerce. During the seventeenth and eighteenth centuries, Akan settlements consolidated themselves into polities and confederations in their interactions with each other and with commercial forces on the northern limits of the forest, those on the northwestern frontier in Begho and the Bono areas, and the European merchants on the coast. The expansion of Asante was facilitated rather than caused by Asante's participation in the international slave trade, which was managed by European commercial interests. Those exported between the seventeenth and the early nineteenth centuries came from Akan and non-Akan societies, but all found themselves sharing a collective lot as enslaved captives in the Americas.

Chapter four explicates the lives of Akan people and their roles in the evolution of broader African cultural forms shaped by diasporic experiences in the Americas, beginning in the Dutch and Danish colonies, where Akan persons were known as "(A)mina." It examines Akan politics and culture in the Danish colonies and the theme of maroonage and Akan culture in the Dutch colonies of the Americas. The fifth chapter examines Akan political, spiritual, and expressive culture in the British Caribbean, particularly Barbados, Antigua, Guyana, and Jamaica. The Gold Coast figured prominently in the minds of planters and merchants in the British colonies of the Americas, and British control of key Gold Coast ports and an institutional and industrial framework built, in large part, upon the international enslavement enterprise and its protocolonial extension facilitated the passage and settlement of Akan persons outside of their homeland. Though one could argue that Akan culture lent itself to and its peoples were active participants in revolts and conspiracies throughout the Americas, our understanding of a composite Akan culture in the region is best served by using those moments of insurrection not as ends but rather as means to examine the cultural dimensions of those sovereignty-driven acts as a way to approach Akan peoples and their experiences.

Chapter six focuses on some of the lived experiences of Akan persons in the states of Georgia, Maryland, Virginia, South Carolina, New York, and, to a limited extent, Massachusetts and Rhode Island. The final chapter continues where chapter six leaves off and focuses thematically on issues of culture and diaspora in the Akan experience in North America and Canada. This chapter takes a contemporary look at the phenomenon of African-descended persons and their engagement with Akan culture and spirituality by telescoping this concern through the efforts of the late Nana Yao Dinizulu of New York and of Nana Kwabena Brown of the District of Columbia, as well as the issues of diaspora and internal dialogue on both sides of the Atlantic Ocean. Unfortunately, even those scholars of Akan cultural origin that attempt to examine the "new African diaspora" in North America fail to grasp the significance of the parallel practice of indigenous Akan culture and spirituality by relatively few Akan from Ghana and a growing number of diasporic Africans. That failure amplifies the very need for examination in light of a large body of literature on Santería in Cuba, Candomblé in Brazil, and Vodun in Haiti and New Orleans, as well as the implications of the frequent crossing of paths via the Atlantic Ocean.

2

Quest for the River, Creation of the Path

Akan Cultural Development to the Sixteenth Century

> Mo nyinaa mma yɛnkɔ kwan no
> (you all should allow us to go on the path)
> Mo nyinaa mma yɛnkɔ kwan no
> (you all should allow us to go on the path)
> Nnipa dodo a yɛkɔeɛ, yɛmmae
> (the multitude of people that went, they did not come)
> Mo nyinaa mma yɛnkɔ kwan no
> (you all should allow us to go on the path)
>
> —Akan drum text

Beyond the academic quest to explicate how West African societies emerged in one temporal form or another, the question of Akan origins owes much to the structure of their histories and the cultural claims made with regard to settlement, custodianship of land, and the prerogative of establishing and maintaining social order. However, most peoples' origins in (West) Africa are obscure beyond the chronological time-depth of several centuries, and the further one probes, the more fragmented and conflated the reconstituted historical narrative tends to become depending upon whose interests the narrative serves. Renewed interest in the origins of Akan social orders and institutionalized cultural practices on one hand, and the more fervent use of methods and data sources outside the domain of history in the reconstruction of African societies on the other has yielded new insights and prompted critical questions about old data and established interpretations. Such a convergence between questions, methods, and sources has also provided a path for what many have called for but for one reason or another have been less than vigorous in actualizing—that "a convincing historical scenario can only be constructed by a combination of disciplines."[1]

In *Forest of Gold*, Ivor Wilks explains that various events and processes that occurred between the fifteenth and the seventeenth century came to define the Akan as, essentially, sedentary agriculturalists, socially distributed between matriclan and matrilineage, politically organized into "states," and culturally bonded by language, religion, and a common sense of shared history.² The processes from which those characteristics originate were the cumulative outcome of the transformation from forging to an agrarian economy involving large-scale forest clearance. Therein the *abusua* ("matriclan structure") evolved in the context of a political authority based upon manipulation of the demands for gold and supplies of enslaved labor, and the ɔman ("state") political structure in the forestlands emerged as the Akan peripherally participated in both the old Mediterranean economy and the expanding "Atlantic economy."³ Wilks's uncertainty about whether there was an era of massive land clearance or a piecemeal process extending into antiquity and his argument for "slave labor" clearance of the Akan forest have prompted at least one historian to question Wilks's model.⁴ Others may also question his certainty that the Akan were driven out of the savanna and into the forest by a northern incursion.⁵ The general strategies of defense or responses to hegemony, particularly with the advent of western Sudanic polities and then Islam in the West African savanna, varied from fighting, finding refuge, withdrawal to remote and defensible areas, creating structural defenses, and conversion to Islam with the hope that this would offer some measure of protection. There is no evidence that one or a combination of these responses either contributed to Akan movement into the high forest or was a causal or facilitating factor in Akan settlement and cultural development. Precisely when, how, or who subdued and expelled the Akan from the savanna, if this was their "homeland," are left unattended by Wilks, though his model for the emergence of Akan polities still continues to enjoy wide, uncritical acceptance.

In his review essay of *Forests of Gold*, A. Norman Klein argues that slavery was the "unifying idea" that informed Wilks's thinking on Akan origins and the Asante polity, the most notable Akan society in eighteenth- and nineteenth-century documentary sources. According to Klein's reading of Wilks's "unifying idea," enslaved persons were imported (in exchange for gold) to clear the forest, and this led to a population boom, a "new class formation" led by "slave-owning entrepreneurs," and an agricultural revolution that initiated the formation of southerly Akan states.⁶ For Klein, this is an "academic myth" that has uncritically received wide acceptance. The backbone of Wilks's myth, according to Klein, is anachronism in that Wilks used nineteenth-century data to make fifteenth- and sixteenth-century interpretations; that is, Wilks "project[ed] well-known historical conditions into an unknown past," particularly by using oral histories.⁷ In response to Klein and in the end, Wilks remained unconvinced by Klein's argument and by archaeological research that casts doubt on his chronology for the emergence of southerly Akan polities in the forest and suggests a much earlier presence. The issue here is the lack of specific historical data, since the number of enslaved persons imported by Portuguese and Mande (Juula) traders to clear the forest and engage in farming and goldmining is unknown, and details about the formation of the matriclan structure in which they were incorporated is lacking. No data exists for the size or productivity of seventeenth century (or earlier) peasant or "slave-worked" farms to support a population boom, and the forest fallow system believed to have been part of an "agricultural revolution" only appeared in the historical record in the early nineteenth century.[8]

In an effort to offer a counternarrative to Wilks's, Klein has argued instead (based upon archaeological and biomedical data) that for millennia the Akan forest was inhabited by agriculturalists, who responded to later Eurasian diseases and slave raiding by clustering into denser populations, which placed a greater emphasis on fertility (especially of imported women) as a weapon against social dislocation, slavery, and disease in the late fifteenth to early eighteenth centuries.[9] Klein dates the early Akan in the southern forest of contemporary Ghana to approximately two millennia ago.[10] Indeed, Klein's approximate dates for forest occupation are consistent with the archaeological record for Ghana. They also suggest that those early Akan settlers were embedded in the economies of a forest-savanna mosaic prior to Islam, that commerce and mobility were cornerstones of society, and that an early Akan agrarian order existed, one based upon egalitarian and "classless" principles, as was found among Akan societies such the Eotile on the Ivory Coast around 1000 CE.[11]

In this chapter I use a number of relevant archaeological, historical, linguistic, biomedical, and oral sources to extend Klein's contribution and to interrogate some of the resilient propositions articulated by Wilks over the course of his career. I argue that the development of proto-Akan society and culture began much earlier in the forest and on its fringes, and that it was this extended period of formation that shaped the composite culture Europeans first encountered in the late fifteenth century rather than the events Wilks and others attribute to later centuries. I also argue that, contrary to the idea that key Akan cultural practices derived from Mande cultural diffusion (the "northern factor"), a process of Akanization has been the result of social assimilative processes, the forging of a sociopolitical order with an attendant spirituality, and adaptive strategies for survival in the forest and its disease-ridden environs. The idea of cultural practices originating in the north is not new, and such thinking goes beyond the Akan orbit to include so-called sub-Saharan Africa as a recipient of "northern" and Islamic or Islamicized African culture.[12]

There is a need to explore how and why Akan culture and societies formed the way they did in order to understand larger issues of cultural and social formation in the forested West African region and Akan culture in the Americas, in addition to challenging accepted propositions that assign Akan cultural practices and ideas to others. There is no den-ying, to be sure, that some Akan practices may have been informed or shaped in some way by cultures external to it. However, the issue here is the wholesale manner in which these relatively "empty-headed" peoples appropriated ideas and cultural structures not of their own agency or the that the culture identified as "Akan" was engendered by the confluence of northern Islamicized and southern Christianized forces from the fifteenth to the seventeenth century. These historical scenarios demand reassessment and an alternative narrative if the Akan are to be understood, first, in the context of their own cultural development and historical trajectory and, second, in relation to those exogenous to an Akan cultural orbit. What follows is an examination of some of the formative processes in the development of Akan culture and society between 1500 BCE and 1500 CE with a focus on cultural development in the forest and on its fringe, the factors of disease and language in that process, and a reconsideration of Islamization through supposedly Islamized Mande language speakers and the process Akanization to the sixteenth century.

IN THE FOREST AND ON ITS FRINGES

Ghanaian archaeologist Kwaku Effah-Gyamfi regards the period 1500 BCE–1000 CE as crucial to the study of the origins of any Akan social order and suggests that archaeology had a key role to play in that endeavor.[13] Archaeology, however construed, can provide only a partial perspective on those that temporally preceded us, and archaeology in the African context continues to be dominated by significant issues of settlement, urbanism, and the origins of metalworking, but it does so to the neglect of other integral factors such as trees and their relation to the processes of cultural development.[14] For instance, oil palm (*Elaeis guineensis*) is among the most widespread species to appear in West African archaeological sites. Not only are these trees associated with levels of pottery and polished tools that are indicative of technoeconomic traditions and connected to sacred sites of early settlements, but the very name of specific trees informed the names of significant Akan settlements (e.g., Kumase [under the kum tree]; Odumase [under the odum tree]). Oil palm also remains one of the most important indigenous food crops in the economies and cultural practices of the West African forest.[15] In the vegecultural and tropical forest zone, oil palm and root crops such as yams have been integral to the history of food production and the culture of those who consumed and used them, though both oil palm and yams were principally found near the forest edge before finding a home in cleared forestland. However significant and longstanding these food crops may be, the moisture of the tropical forest severely constrains the preservation of archaeological evidence, and thus we have to read the equatorial forest as a peculiar kind of archive.

As an archive, the forest and its fringes have much to tell us in its silences and disclosures. In fact, the very expansion of the tropical forest between approximately 9000 and 2000 BCE is significant since our starting point is precisely the period that covers half a century following this expansion. The expansion of the forest reveals much about the processes of agricultural and cultural development germane to early Akan settlements between the Komóe and Volta rivers and from the coastal mangrove swamps to the edge of the forest at approximately 8° N.[16] The high forest occupied by the proto-Akan was inclusive of the principal indigenous food crops of yam and oil palm, and oil palm pollen was prominent after the expansion of the forest from 1550 BCE onward.[17] Yams, a key source of carbohydrates, were harvested between the key periods of *kitawonsa* and *ɛbɔ* (July and September) in the forest and on its fringes. By 800 BCE there was a "sudden and remarkable increase in oil palm trees concurrently with a decrease in forest trees and the appearance of weed pollen strongly indicates that the oil palm expansion [near stream valleys in the forest and on its fringes] was due to the artificial opening up of the forest for farming purposes."[18] Oil palm, a source of fat and vitamin A, was initially restricted to the forest fringe especially along rivers, but dense strands of oil palm found in the rainforest indicate its domestication, human occupation, and clearance, feasibly with Neolithic axes, of which many are found in the forest of contemporary Ghana. One such clearing occurred around a Kintampo industry archaeological site close to what is now Kumase—located in the heart of the moist, semi-deciduous forest and later capital of the Asante polity—between 1655 and 1255 BCE. By then, the forest had reached its greatest expanse, and the prominence of oil palm pollen points to human occupation and forest clearance by way of stone tools, in addition to a nascent agrarian and sociopolitical order.[19]

The clearance of the forest proximate to Kumase falls relatively within a series of key processes and within a zone thought unsuitable for a sizable, sedentary population with a food producing economy to organize political and economic life. Those processes include the prominence of oil palm pollen after the expansion of the forest and a dramatic regression in the levels of Lake Bosomtwe, south of Kumase, around 1800 BCE because of the drier climatic conditions as vegetation resembled more cultivated forests. One of the foremost examples of a food-producing economy in West Africa, as well as one of the earliest Kintampo industry sites, dated between 1750±90 and 1545±100 BCE, was extant in central Ghana, in addition to other Kintampo industry sites at Boyase Hill and Nkukua Buoho in the forest zone proximate to Kumase.[20] Boyase Hill is a ceramic Late Stone Age site located northeast of Kumase on a granite inselberg (an island of savanna vegetation) distinct from the surrounding forest, while Nkukua Buoho is a granite hill found near Kumase. Findings at Nkukua Buoho suggest both a mixed economy based on farming and gathering and a sedentary population between 1800 and 500 BCE.[21] Drier conditions deduced from the dramatic but brief fall in the levels of Lake Bosomtwe are also indicative of adaptations that included the use of hills such as Nkukua Buoho and rock shelters for settlement, as was the case in southern Libya between 3050 and 850 BCE, given its ecological similarities to the fringes of the forest.[22]

Akan oral narratives of movement and settlement are replete with references of founding settlers emerging from "holes in the earth," which were caves and rock shelters used as either transitory or initial sites of residence, and, consequently, such places become sacred and environmentally protected as ancestral sites.[23] In fact, the Bosompra cave, a metal and Stone Age site occupied between 3500 and 500 BCE, is one prime example, and, in similar cases, caves or rock shelters have been very suitable sites for both transitory or longer settlement and the development of societies.[24] Akan narratives of movement and settlement, in which the vast majority—like the preponderance of Kintampo industry sites—are restricted to areas in contemporary Ghana, primarily talk about descending from the sky on golden chains or in brass vessels or emerging from "holes in the ground." The Akan use the term *ɛsoro* to mean "sky," as well as "north" and "convulsions" (during a convulsion, a person tends to look up toward the sky). The term *ɛsoro* is thus a cosmologic reference to the sky and a reference to places or people "above" one's relative position, whereas "holes" in the earth provide a temporal reference to caves, rock shelters, and, in some cases, sources of water and ancestry. Combined, the sky and "holes" provide a "vertical" framework for the entry and departure points of the early ancestors.

The occupants of large, aboveground rock shelters and subterranean caverns, such as the Bosompra cave, experienced less humidity and a drier climate—as West Africa was quite arid between 2500 and 300 BCE—and thus less rainfall, which would have contributed to their movement into a dense, shady forest that received heavy rainfall most of the year.[25] The amount of rainfall is largely responsible for the type of vegetation found in a particular area. Thus, the very dense vegetation formed principally by shrubs and oil palm, silk cotton (*kapok*), and similar trees in secondary forests was also home to both common and vital root crops that provided much of the starch and calories for population growth and the equally vital oil palm used for food, brooms, and soap making. A diet that included fruits and berries, seeds and nuts, fish, giant snails, grasscuttters, and small animals supplemented those root crops and the use of oil palm. Oil palm grows with an annual rainfall of 50 inches or more, and the Akan forest, in the early part of the first millennium CE, received approximately 40 to 80 inches of annual rainfall from the coast to its forest fringes.[26] These were periods of moderate rainfall. The arid period, combined with the cultivation and use of oil palm and root crops, suggests an early period of entry and settlement into the forest by proto-Akan peoples who developed a food-producing economy based on shifting cultivation and an agrarian social order. They also reached a level of cultural development in which their spirituality was linked to the agricultural cycle and the ancestral sites and groves were held sacred. The material culture excavated at Kintampo archaeological sites in contemporary Ghana support this scenario, and although archaeologists do not know the identity of the people of "Kintampo culture" sites, they are, nonetheless, hesitant to entertain continuity between Kintampo and proto-Akan culture or even to link the two based upon the available evidence to date.

The evidence archaeologists consider circumstantial and derived from Kintampo deposits—stone axes; beads; buildings of stone, mud, and wood; domestic pots; miniature ceramic sculptures depicting humans, cattle, sheep, goats, and dogs—is consistent with the evidence originating from related deposits for indigenous proto-Akan development.[27] The evidence from associated deposits, which argue for an indigenous proto-Akan cultural development, include similar material culture found at Kintampo archaeological sites in the form of oil palms, cowpeas, guinea fowl, pottery and rasps, and wattle and daub (i.e., wood and clay) building technology. Akan architecture and building construction traditions employed coursed clay and wood technologies in the creation of rectangular or square structures that, like those of the Batwa-occupied Congo forest, predominate in a landscape with very few round or conical houses, which remain on the outskirts of villages and are usually reserved as "shrines" of northern (i.e., foreign) origin or areas north of the forest. These building traditions began somewhere between 2000 and 1500 BCE, a period that corresponds to the end of an expanding forest, drier climatic conditions, and human settlement in the forest interior, during which local and regional trade intensified. Square or rectangular structures existed at some Kintampo sites, and continuity in material culture among the thirty or so pre-Kintampo and Kintampo sites found in contemporary Ghana strongly suggests indigenous development.[28] Chronologically, as Ann Stahl notes, that the oldest dates for Kintampo sites—usually exhibiting low density in landscape and settlements of small hamlets—cluster near the Kintampo village on the forest fringe, while sites to the north of the forest yield consistently younger dates.[29]

The archaeological record on Akan settlements and Kintampo sites in the forest, at the forest-savanna nexus, on the coast, and in neighboring regions to the east and west of contemporary Ghana, in addition to biomedical and ecological factors, tells a story that casts serious doubt on much of the received knowledge about early Akan society and settlement. The coastal and eastern parts of Ghana have received less treatment, and, as a result, archaeological findings for the coastal sites must be considered tentative until further investigation.[30] Of the twenty-seven known Kintampo archaeological sites in Ghana, most are located in the forest or on its fringes, and approximately six exist in the true savanna (see map 1). The major archaeological sites of the forest interior—most of which are positioned east, south, and north of Kumase as an axis—show overlap in occupation and evidence of settled life and of advanced social and cultural development. A number of these archaeological sites were substantial in size and had permanent structures that suggest large populations and long-term occupation. The age of the majority of those sites ranges from 3500 BCE to the nineteenth century in terms of occupation and include the Bosompra cave on the eastern forest fringe, Bono-Manso and Bew (Begho) on the northern forest fringe, Nkukua Buoho, Boyase Hill, Asantemanso, Adansemanso, Dawu-Akwapem, Akwamu, and the Krobo mountains of inhabited caves.[31]

Oral and archaeological evidence from two of the oldest Akan towns in the forest interior, Asantemanso and Adansemanso, indicates continuous occupation from 700 BCE to the present and 393 to 1650 CE, respectively, although Adansemanso was occupied mainly in the first half of the second millennium CE, a long dry period in West Africa and the second major regression in the levels of Lake Bosomtwe.[32] The excavated material culture of Asantemanso and Adansemanso supports the oral historical sources, which are consistent with Akan spiritual, ideational, and material culture through a constellation of evidence of iron smelting, ritual and festival practices, indigenous medicine, functional and artistic wares and figurines, social organization, and trading activities.[33] At both sites we find sacred groves and forests with shrines in close proximity to streams, ancient roadways, and fields indicative of agriculture. Although Peter Shinnie, who carried out excavations at Adansemanso and Asantemanso, seems certain "there was permanent settlement [with a population of several thousand] at Asantemanso as early as the last few centuries B.C.," he, however, would rather speculate on the presence of Guan speakers in the central Ghana forest than where the evidence points—to a proto-Akan presence.[34]

In the northern and northwest parts of the forest, areas associated with Akan origins are generally dated from the fifth century CE onward, and, in addition to continuity in pottery styles, rock shelter sites show the use of microlithic industries and ground-stone artifacts into the first millennium.[35] Like Asantemanso and Adansemanso of the forest interior, the two best-known sites of the northern and northwest forest are the Akan settlements of Bono-Manso, capital of the polity, and the township of Bew (commonly referred to as Begho). All of the sacred sites associated with

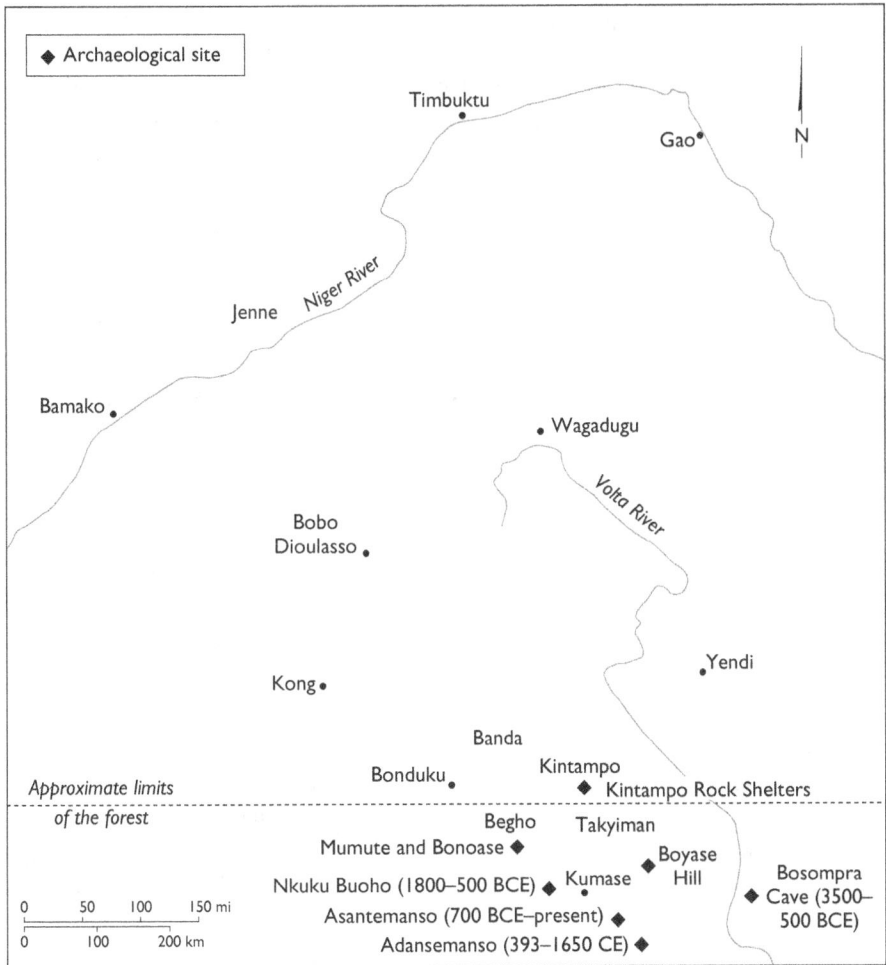

Map 1. Key archaeological sites in contemporary Ghana. Most of these important sites are found within the tropical forest and tend to yield higher calibrated dates than those above the forest. This suggests longer human occupation and settlement in the Akan region.

Bono settlement in the northern forest and on its fringes are located either next to inselbergs—as was the case with early sites in and around Kumase—or in caves and rock shelters, of which the Amowi rock shelter of the Bono was inhabited no later than 400 CE.[36] Some archaeologists date Bono-Manso to 1000 CE despite the early occupation of Amowi, iron smelting at Abam in Bono-Manso (ca. 300 CE) and in the eastern limits of Begho (ca. 100 CE), and the rock shelter of Atwetwebooso and the Nseserekeseso ancestral site in southeastern Begho.[37] The archaeology of these ancient sites confirms the frequent references in Akan oral narratives of founding settlers emerging from "holes in the earth." The archaeological record also provides no evidence of an intrusive northern people moving into the region, but it does support the claim that several Akan societies were autochthonous to areas where Kintampo cultural sites on the fringe and in the forest interior are found.

One of the key features of the commercial and cultural life of Kintampo rock shelters is evidence of the exploitation of domestic goats (*Capra hircus*), sheep (*Ovis aries*), giant snails (*Achatina achatina*), and grasscutters (*Thryonomys swinderianus*). The significance and prevalence of these animals may lie in the fact that trypanosomiasis-carrying tsetse flies made cattle, more suited for the savanna, unfit for the forest. Where trypanosomiasis is endemic in West Africa, goats and sheep are as common as Kintampo sites and Akan settlements, which shows evidence of the socioeconomic and cultural meaning of these animals. In the Akan forest, goats, sheep, and the grasscutter (*akrantee*) have had a longstanding history in the inhabitant's diet and culture. Even today, the Akan continue to exploit the grasscutter and use sheep (*ɔdwan*) in rites for the purification of society, resolution of dispute and debts, and the exchange of goods and services as evidenced by the term *peredwan*, which was the largest "weight" and monetary unit in the Akan payment or "gold weight" system. In the Akan language, *pere* means to "struggle, strive, or bargain," while *ɔdwan* indicates a "sheep." *Peredwan*, therefore, suggests bargaining with a sheep or struggling to set oneself free from debt or calamity. In cases that involve large-scale fines, debts, or calamities or perhaps a transgression related to a serious taboo, a sheep would be used. It is therefore likely that sheep played a critical role in the commercial and cultural life of those who settled Kintampo industry sites and lived in Akan communities of the past.

During the late phases of Kintampo culture, in particular the occupation at the K-6 rock shelter near the village of Kintampo, Ann Stahl suggests that an intensification of trade occurred around 1545 BCE and that most of the historical dates for Kintampo sites in and around the village of Kintampo range between 1800 and 1150 BCE.[38] If there was such a period of intensified trade, then proto-Akan people were embedded in key commercial networks through a food-producing economy that exploited oil palm and root-crop cultivation and supported a growing population, moved or settled in greater numbers into the dense forest in an arid period, established an agrarian social order, and reached a necessary level of cultural development so as to maintain a social order linked to a spiritual one. Indeed, and consonant with the archaeological record, Akan architecture and building traditions embedded in historical places of settlement provide an appropriate parallel for the broader proto-Akan culture as "an essentially indigenous phenomenon" that integrated some foreign components.[39] The continuity of that architectural and building tradition was evident in two historically recent, yet overlapping Akan societies—sixteenth-to-eighteenth-century Bono society on the forest fringe and nineteenth-century Asante society in the forest interior. In all likelihood, this architectural tradition reflects the very adaptive strategies employed during both the forging of culture in the forest and on its fringes and the societies' response to a climatic and disease-ridden environment that placed some pressure on reproduction and clan formation.

MALARIA AND THE MOLDING OF CULTURE

Refined over centuries, early African cultural practices, including technologies employed in efficient hunting and fishing methods that supported larger populations, allowed for an early entry into and intensive exploitation of the tropical forest and adaptive strategies to combat a malarial environment. It is likely that physical resistance to *vivax* and *falciparum* malaria—the two principal malarial parasites—developed more widely during the processes of exploitation and agricultural development in oil palm and yams several millennia before the adoption of seed agriculture and Neolithic tools, which occurred around 3000 BCE.[40] By then, the wet period in West Africa was reaching its end and about to give way to an arid period, the expansion of the forest was reaching its limit, and the metal and Stone Age site of the Bosompra cave was occupied—perhaps by proto-Akan peoples—as in similar rock shelters in southern Libya. In tropical Africa, mosquitoes, which are the principal carriers of malaria, developed a distinct affinity for human rather than animal blood, and, unlike *vivax*, the transmission of *falciparum* malaria (the most dangerous malarial parasite) depends more on continuous rather than seasonal, high-population density.[41] Descendents of *falciparum* sufferers developed the sickle cell gene that offered protection, and both parents with this gene gave birth to offspring who developed sickle cell anemia, victims of which usually died before the age of reproduction.[42] It was probably in this context but during an unknown period that childbearing emerged as one of the strongest pressures exerted on individuals in early Akan societies, and, as such, children were held in high demand and esteem, and annual rituals performed for mothers of ten (*owoduo*) and mothers of twins (*ɔwonta*) would rightly have corresponded with that development.[43]

In biochemistry, a homozygote is an organism with identical ("pure") forms of a gene or genes, while a heterozygote has two different forms of a gene or genes, and thus the three genotypes that an offspring can receive from both parents are either AA, AS, or SS. The normal hemoglobin (i.e., oxygen- and iron-transporting red protein in the blood) is A, whereas hemoglobin S is a mutant. At low oxygen levels, hemoglobin S hardens, and the red cells become sickle shaped, which prevents them from carrying sufficient oxygen. Although these cells die, they reproduce quickly, and the "sickling" in S homozygotes (SS or hemoglobin S from both parents) is sickle-cell anemia. Persons who are SS are not protected against malaria. Moreover, AS carriers with the sickle-cell trait have partial protection against *falciparum* since they inherit either hemoglobin A or S but not both, which was advantageous in malaria-prone regions. In the West African forest, Africans whose languages fall under the cluster of Kwa languages, such as the Akan, have the greatest presence of hemoglobin S in their blood. As noted earlier, those with the hemoglobin S mutation have a high probability of dying before maturity or the reproductive age; thus, the normal A form of the gene cannot replace the S form. Though the "hemoglobin S mutant can spread rapidly in the presence of malaria but tends to stabilize around the gene frequency" of 10 percent, a balanced polymorphism will occur: If we started "from one mutation in a population of 50,000 individuals, the process for reaching the equilibrium value takes about 2000 years."[44]

The 2000 years needed to reach that equilibrium—corresponding to greater genetic protection against malaria, as well as individuals living longer and producing offspring with that protection in greater numbers and in a settled environment—would take 80 generations at a rate of 25 years per generation or 66.7 generations at a rate of 30 years. The archaeological evidence of human occupation and settled, agrarian communities overlaps with the time it would take to reach the foregoing equilibrium among tropical forest and forest-edge dwellers. Distributed in restricted areas where the malaria parasite is diffused and against which the heterozygote is protected, hemoglobin mutants "usually confer a strong selective advantage on heterozygotes and a strong disadvantage on homozygotes," though this may not be the case for the common hemoglobin C in West Africa.[45] In the case of the glucose-6-phosphate dehydrogenase (G6PD) gene, which gives rise to the red blood cell enzyme of the same name, female heterozygotes, who usually have lower parasite counts, are protected against *falciparum* because of a G6PD deficiency or a mutant that confers protection against malaria by inhibiting the growth of the malaria parasite. Heterozygotes exist only in females since the G6PD deficiency links to the X chromosome, and women have two X chromosomes, though one is inactive, and thus female carriers produce both a deficient and a normal population of red cells for each chromosome, whereas men have only one X chromosome and are either deficient or normal since the trait is transmitted from mother to son. Some studies suggest that G6PD deficiency developed in places like tropical Africa as a response to malaria. If so, the "maternal advantage" it conferred against the most fatal malarial parasite may have been a key factor in the matrilineal order of the proto-Akan settlers.

Most scientists agree that *falciparum* malaria parasites developed within tropical woodland and rainforest environments, though the irony is that survivors of the initial *falciparum* malaria developed greater immunity in settled environments, where infections were stable, but such immunity decreased as the hosts left those environments for more than a year.[46] Thus, it appears that this situation provided a reason to stay in the forest, and permanent settlements were established as population expanded throughout the forest environment. However, hunters and gathers suffered high levels of mortality and morbidity upon successive contact with these permanent settlers and settlements, where *falciparum* infection was stable. This has implications for West African population settlement and interaction over time in that *falciparum* malaria is responsible for the highest frequency of hemoglobin S—one of three abnormal and widely distributed variants in West Africa—and if this variant emerged between 3000 and 2000 BCE, that emergence would be in line with root- and vegetable-crop cultivation in the forest and on the woodland borders. Moreover, hemoglobin B is highest in Liberia, and hemoglobin S is highest in Nigeria; perhaps hemoglobin C, the third variant, lies somewhere in between and thus provides a gradient that may tell us about early West African settlement and interaction, especially between settled forest communities and hunter-gathers of the savanna.[47] George Brooks speculates that proto-Mande peoples' movement south between 2500 and 300 BCE was restricted to the savanna or savanna-woodland zone and certainly not the forest (because of its unfamiliar environmental conditions). Perhaps it was this unfamiliarity and the risk of malarial contact that allowed southeastern Mande groups to develop commercial ties with Kwa-speaking groups, such as the Akan, during the 700–1100 CE wet period but not sooner.[48] Survival of early, family-based Akan communities led to cooperation in labor and leadership and to the creation of cultural strategies to combat diseases such as malaria; in addition, the architectural traditions of coursed clay and wood supported the spatial design of matrilineal-based family dwellings. In such sedentary communities, which clustered together in response to a particular disease environment, language underwent little differentiation, and this was probably the Akan language and orthography (with marginal dialectical differences) that Portuguese and Dutch observers recorded in their fifteenth- and sixteenth-century accounts.

THE LANGUAGE OF AKAN CULTURE DEVELOPMENT

The morphology of key Akan concepts provides further insight into the early processes of social and cultural development and reveals much about the psychology of early Akan ancestors in terms of the social and political orders that sustained their agrarian settlements. The clearing and occupation of the dense forest by proto-Akan settlers and agriculturalists, who cultivated oil palm and high-calorie root crops through communal labor and used efficient reproductive strategies, helped to sustain population growth during an era of aridity and adaptation to malaria. These processes shaped a proto-Akan culture that achieved levels of development concomitant with an agricultural cycle and a calendrical matrix that regulated daily life and rituals associated with the identification of an Akan Creator as manifest in a myriad of ways—expressed as *abosom*, "children" of that Creator—in the natural order. In this context, the ritual consumption of yams—harvested in *kitawonsa* and *ɛbɔ* (July and September)—and palm oil likely developed during harvests and periodic ceremonies where both indigenous crops were prominent and became staple offerings to ancestors. These cycles informed the calendrical matrix (*adaduanan*, calendrical cycle of forty-two days) that ordered patterns of cultural activity and ideas in short cycles, yet placing greater emphasis on peace, cleansing, sacredness, contentment, settlement, balancing strength and compassion, and the drive to temper human feelings and actions based upon arrogance and warlike aggressiveness. Temporally, the *adaduanan* might have been a calculated response to the potential of conflict, sabotage, tyranny, and self-interest over group interests, and thus it ordered society in terms of travel and (social) transactions, cleansing when chaos or transgressions occurred, peace rather than long-term war, avoidance of the overuse of the earth and its resources, and compassion and courage in the face of the inescapable human realities of death, pain, and suffering.

In the natural order, the forest and the farm were afforded respect as homes to spiritual and human occupations (the latter as tenants who used rather than owned these life-sustaining areas), and the restrictions placed upon farming on specific days (via the *adaduanan*) illustrate the translation of that respect into cultural practice. Thus, out of a respect for such restrictions and to meditate on the meaning of temporal life within the natural order through offerings and the pouring of *mpaeɛ* (libation), one would receive the appropriate *nhyira* (blessings) and be empowered by the spiritual presence of the ancestors, or *abosom*, invoked. Many trailblazing hunters explored new territory beyond the recognizable *asasetepa* (barren land), established frontier zones in cooperation with other hunters, and became custodians of such land and the various types of *abosom* they encountered in the forests and rivers and on the mountains. Those spiritual entities were then "domesticated," imbued with spiritual meaning, and deemed to be facilitators of life and its human dimension. *Ohyeɛ* denoted "boundary land," and the *ɔ-de-hyeɛ* (*ɔdehyeɛ*), usually rendered as "royal," were actually those who knew the boundaries as descendants of the principal hunter (*abɔfoɔ*, master hunter) who became the ruler of the new settlement. These hunters not only paved the way for new settlements and provided leadership to them, but the very pathways they created connected towns and villages and would be crossed and recrossed by other hunters, merchants, farmers, and travelers. In doing so, hunters helped address common problems encountered in the moist forest—inadequate transportation, communication, and food supply— and, rightfully, became integral actors in shaping society.

Though they were forest dwellers, most of the integral and oldest *abosom* of the Akan were and still are water and not forest derived, and the highest *ɔbosom*, Tanɔ or Taa Kora, came to be embodied by the sacred Tanɔ river, which originated inland near the edge of the forest in Takyiman and merged into the southerly *ɔbosompo* (ocean) near Assinie. In a "standard text" played on the *atumpan* drums, the creation of Tanɔ and the world of the Akan is symbiotically revealed: *Ɔkwan atware asuo, asuo atware kwan, ɔpanin ne hwan* (The path crosses the river, the river crosses the path, which is older [or came first]?) The response is *yebɔɔ kwan no kɔtoo asuo no* (we created the path to meet the river). And thus the river was created not only before the pathways in the forest, but before the humans who created the paths! How could this be? The drum text continues: *asuo no firi tete, asuo no firi ɔdomankoma ɔbɔadeɛ, konkon Tanɔ*... (this river is from ancient times, this river is from the beneficent Creator, sacred Tanɔ...). A hunter found Tanɔ, or Ta Kora, in a cave; a town, Tanoboase ("Tano under the rock"), was founded and the hunter became the ruler and the custodian of Ta Kora. This scenario re-occurred as often as the paths in the forest were crossed, and as the Tanɔ river and Akan societies stretched from the edge of the forest to the coast, Tanɔ provided life facilitators in the form of the *abosom*, and many gold-producing settlements emerged on or near the river. Rivers and streams also marked the internal divisions of settlements and demarcated frontiers, and, in their crossing, hunters and other trailblazers often encountered and later revered those water-derived *abosom*. Rivers and streams held added significance, for they were sites for retrieving life-sustaining water, washing clothes, bathing, and periodic purification and meditation rituals—rituals that were more or less regulated by the *adaduanan*. The pioneering hunters (*abɔmmɔfoɔ*, "one who creates something new") who established new settlements were referred to as *ɔhene*, a term indicative of the hunter's itchy body in terms of his ability to create pathways and settlements in the forest; hence, *ne ho yɛ hene* ("his or her body is itchy"). The phrase "ne ho yɛ hene" connotes a person well versed in the lie of the land and is usually the first person on that unoccupied land, who thus has rights to be custodian of the land and the spiritual agencies embedded in its environs. The Akan matrilineal clan and political system likely evolved through these processes of scouting, settlement, and custodianship.

The case of early Dɛnkyira, an Akan polity of the western forest, and Assin offer two of several instances that serve to underscore these processes. Led by Nana Ayɛkra Adebɔ, it is said that those who became known as the Dɛnkyira people reached Takyiman and settled at Nkyira for a century or so before establishing their capital of Abankɛseese (or Abankeseeso), by the Ofin river. The capital became a large urban center with seventy-seven streets watered by seven streams, home to a number of *abosom*. The likely mother or maternal kin of a hunter, Nana Adebɔ (ca. 1500–1518) was regarded as a powerful woman in the Agona *abusua* (clan, family) and the founder of the *Abankan* stool of Dɛnkyira—the stool represented the leadership of the polity. She is credited with the founding of Sasatia (special war [*ɔbosom*] for executioners and warriors), the creation of Wieme (a special stick that formed the physical abode of an *ɔbosom*), and the founding of the Agona settlement, which became known as Dɛnkyira.[49] Much like the Asante Sika Dwa Kofi (golden stool) of a later date, the Dɛnkyira people argue that all these items of reverence descended from the sky during the reign of Nana Adebɔ. As the founder and first occupant of the Dɛnkyira stool, Nana Adebɔ and her clan, Agona, came to occupy the stool and thus acquired the leadership of Dɛnkyira.[50] Though the people of Dɛnkyira migrated again during the eighteenth century to Jukwa, and some returned to their ancestral homeland a century thereafter, it is noteworthy that Jukwa remained the site of the Dɛnkyira stool, a place that was founded by an elephant hunter and where important rituals were performed. Indeed, *abɔfoɔ nni hɔ a anka kuro amma* (without the hunters there would be no town) and *ɔman safoa hyɛ abɔfoɔ nsam* (the keys of the nation are in the hunter's possession).

The hunter's duty, like that of other trailblazers who preceded him and became the custodians of lands and the spiritual agencies thereof, "was to study the land, and to report whether it would be suitable for farming and yield enough food to feed the population."[51] Like early Dɛnkyira, a number of Assin settlements make a similar case in that women, too, established their society, while hunters and their early ancestors first emerged from "holes in the ground."[52] For example, the people of Assin Akenkasu recall that they were initially governed by women, the first of whom was Nana Kɔkɔɔ Gyaanewa and then Nana Ofaa, whose son, Nana Afum Afram, a renowned hunter, founded a settlement but had to move to Assin Akenkasu due to attacks by those who lived in Dɛnkyira. The streams and rivers often noted in the traditions of origin, such the aforementioned, also lent themselves to key *abosom* that guided the polity and provided a means for its people to actualize their spiritual concepts and practices. Bosomfoɔ, a river-derived *ɔbosom* of the Assin polity in general and of the Attandansu settlement in particular, lay within the Konkom sacred forest in Assin. Bosomfoɔ was joined by a host of others, not the least of whom was a set of differentiated Tanɔ *abosom*, Bona, Kobiri, Afram (River), Bosompra (River), (Lake) Bosomtwe, and Bosomkeseɛ (the last three are associated with the *ntorɔ* paternal groups, to which many *ahene* of Asante belong).

The concept of *ɔhene*, an indicator of the hunter's itchy body in the dense forest and connoting pioneering abilities, was not gendered as in the term "king" (of a polity or division thereof), to which it is often reduced. The corresponding term, *ɔhemmaa*, which derives from *ɔhene* and is often translated as "queen mother," comes from *a-hem-foɔ* (*ahemfoɔ*; sg. *ɔhene*), wherein the plural affixes of a- and -*foɔ* are dropped, and the singular prefixes ɔ- and -*baa* (*ɔbaa*, woman) are added. Plurals are formed in Akan by using the nasals "n" and "m." For instance, whenever the nasal "m" converges with an initial consonant "b" (as in -*baa*), the combination becomes "mm" due to linguistic assimilation, hence, ɔ-hem*m*aa. An earlier meaning of *ɔhemmaa* or *ɔhene baa* (female *ɔhene*), as reflected in the account of Nana Ayɛkra Adebɔ of Dɛnkyira, suggested one who embodied the trailblazing and custodial role of an *ɔhene* who (and whose clan) assumed sociopolitical leadership. The *ɔhemmaa*, the sister or mother of the hunter, became the temporal basis of the settlement's matrilineal order, sustained by her cosmological parallel, *aberewa* (the ancient ancestress of the Akan), and wielded appropriate authority accordingly as the female *ɔhene*. The *ɔhemmaa* or *ɔmanhemmaa*, the ɛna (mother) or *onua-baa* (female sibling) of the present male *ɔhene*, has been reduced to mean a female leader of the indigenous sociopolitical structure, as well as the head of organizations and office holders in recent times. In early agrarian settlements, hunter-trailblazers and their descendants played integral roles in finding unsettled land, assuming custodianship of that land, and developing a sociopolitical order. Indeed, there might be a greater correlation between food production in early and present-day Akan societies, trade activities, the growth of towns, and the women who have not only traditionally dominated local food-trading activities but were also key in the founding of new settlements. Further, the linguistic dimension of Akan history has much to offer in terms of rethinking the foundational concepts of *ɔhene, ɔhemmaa, abɔfoɔ, ɔdehyeɛ,* and *abosom* in dynamic social and agrarian orders. Language, like the forest, is another archive that not only prompts us to reconsider the ways in which those foundational concepts were formed and the historical processes they have captured but also helps us to interpret claims of culture contact and diffusion among the Akan and Islamized Mande speakers.

Recently, linguists have examined Akan and Mande languages in an effort to map the history of contact and cultural diffusion between the two, in addition to the origins and structure of Akan settlements as result of that encounter. One of the key articles published in the 1960s by Ivor Wilks and

John Stewart discussed Mande linguistic diffusion among the Akan, and, more than forty years later, linguists such as Mary Dakubu have reexamined Mande loanwords in the Akan language. Dakubu argues that Mandekan (that is, mutually intelligible variants of the Mande linguistic family) "has had an important effect on Akan [language]," and, apparently convinced by recycled historical interpretations of Mande cultural diffusion, as well as Akan "state" formation in the fifteenth century, she states that the "main linguistic impact" of Mande was felt during "the formative years of the Akan state system."[53] The locus of this supposed impact unfolded in the northwest vicinity of the Brong-Ahafo region in Ghana—an area proximate to the site of ancient Begho and where much of the archaeological work related to the Kintampo village and Bono-Manso has been undertaken. In this vicinity of important linguistic diffusion, only two "linguistically Mande" towns were uncovered: Namasa and Bosuaba. If these towns were Mande in character, it is difficult to tell, for both were encircled by a preponderance of Akan towns, and even towns situated to the west, across the contemporary Ghana–Ivory Coast border, possess the Akan town-marking suffix, -*krom* or -*kro* (e.g., Kouakissikro, Jabunakrom), the remnants of early Akan migration and settlement.

If Namasa or Bosuaba were sites of cultural diffusion, the oral historical sources of Nasama regarded the Mande as invaders who were defeated by the "cave people" (Bono), along with the support of other local inhabitants, and there is no mention of the Mande as either autochthonous or having the town under their control.[54] In settlements with linguistically extant Mande language users, the lingua franca remains the Asante variant of the Akan language, and speakers of Mande languages such as Ligbi and Juula were bilingual in their own language and Akan, but this was not the case for Akan speakers.[55] Where might we find the evidence for the significant linguistic effect on Akan in areas supposedly dominated by Mande Juula traders from the fifteenth century or earlier? Dakubu provides little more than conjecture and a list of suggested additions to Wilks's original twenty Mande loanwords in Akan, of which most were related to trade and transportation and some were ultimately of Arabic and other non-African derivation. Yet, the presence of Arabic rather than "Mandeized" terms in this limited lexicon adds to the archaeological records, which indicate that Akan societies were engaged in local and regional commerce in West Africa well before and after the Arab-Muslim conquest of North Africa in the seventh and eighth centuries CE.[56] Apparently, the source of Wilks's list of loanwords was Delafosse's *Essai de manuel pratique de la langue mandé ou mandinque*; a review of that text and Delafosse's *La langue mandingue et ses dialectes* reveals little to no real Mande lexical items employed in Akan and found in either the Asante or the Bono variant of Akan.[57] Since the Bono employ the greatest number of proto-Akan linguistic elements had sustained contact with Mande traders for a longer time than any other Akan society, Mande linguistic elements in the proportion of "linguistic impact" should have been archived in the Bono variant of Akan speech. However, this is not the case. What is even more doubtful is the "stimulating or catalyzing sociolinguistic" impact Mande languages have had on Akan according to the speculative use of historical sources fraught with bias and error and on the grounds of recovering twenty or so words, some of which were disclaimed as "probable" and "possible."[58] What emerges, then, is quite the opposite of the Mande diffusion myth in the northwest and coastal regions of Akan occupation. On the contrary, the Akan were the ones who linguistically and, by extension, culturally transformed those Mande residents and their descendants in the forest, on its fringes, and even in contemporary northern Ghana.

A most explicit instance of "Akanization" occurred among non-Akan groups in northern Ghana, who adopted a myriad of Akan institutions rather than retain their Mande cultural forms in those areas of importation.[59] This process, however, was not solely the result of Asante expansionism in the eighteenth and nineteenth centuries, a period that corresponded to the height of the international enslavement enterprise and its gradual decline. The process of Akanization began much earlier—possibly in the eighth or ninth century CE, according to Brooks's suggestion of Mande commercial contact with Kwa-speaking peoples such as the Akan—as did, in that context, an exertion of continued Akan influence through an Asante hegemony that built upon historical processes. Be that as it may, other linguistic factors also translate into further evidence that dissolve the Mande myth and support an Akanization process based upon distinctive linguistic features in and early transformations of the Akan language. Akan is situated in the Niger-Congo linguistic family: Niger-Congo, Atlantic-Congo, Volta-Congo, New Kwa, Nyo, Proto-Tano, Central Tano, Akan.[60] In relation to members of its immediate linguistic family, "Akan is the only language which has substantial remains of the old noun prefixal system...which must have existed in Proto-Tano," and enshrined in Bono speech are the most Proto-Akan elements of all of the present mutually intelligible variants of Akan, which are the least affected by linguistic change in the typical history of a language.[61] To a much lesser extent, the coastal Fante variant of Akan shares some Proto-Akan elements as well. For instance, Bono and Fante speech includes the use of full noun prefixes and optional markers on the verb to indicate subject agreement, and other Proto-Akan features shared by both are consistent with oral (historical) sources that establish a chain of historical and cultural links between the Bono of the northern forest and the Fante on the southern coast.[62] It would appear that these distinctions in the structure and pattern of Akan speech occurred during the early historical movements and settlements of Akan people in the forest interior and on its northern and southern extremes, and this contention finds some support in the direct relationship between environmental adaptation, geographic dispersion, and linguistic differentiation evident in other West African societies.[63]

Kweku Osam argues that since noun classification systems are rooted in the culture of a people, Proto-Akan "must have been based on Akan ontology," in which its hierarchical foundation is reflected in the organization of society and underpinned by the power realized in spiritual, sociopolitical, and economic terms.[64] Though Osam's linguistic observation is noteworthy, there are issues with his conceptualization of Akan ontology. For instance, he makes "Onyame," one of several gender-neutral terms used for the Akan Creator, equivalent to "God," even though the Judeo-Christian idea of "God" and the Akan idea of Onyame emerged from two distinct conceptual and historical points of origin. Nonetheless, Osam observes that the "human class" of nouns, which is inclusive of all living entities such as ɔ-nyame (Creator; lit. "the shining one"), ɔ-bosom (offspring of the Creator), ɔ-saman (ancestor), ɔ-nipa (person), is reflective of Akan ideational and spiritual culture; he also maintains that it has been the least affected by noun class decay and is the only class affected by the new process of a plural marking system (i.e., human nouns marked by both old prefixes and certain suffixes).[65] This movement from "prefixal plural formation to both prefixal and suffixal plural formation" is a fascinating one, and Akan variants that show evidence of the "old" noun system might very well reflect Akan societies that were proximate in spatial distribution either in earlier times or before dispersal and linguistic differentiation.[66] The latter prospect can yield much in terms of the nature of Akan settlement patterns and the spatial extent of movement and settlement relative to the dense forest. In Akan settlements, the names of villages, towns, and polities were (and still are) usually demarcated by the suffixes -kurom or -kuro (town or permanent settlement of large households) and -ɔman (cultural group, nation), while a village (akuraa; pl. nkuraa) or semipermanent agricultural settlement appeared to follow less of a linguistic rule and more of a cultural one. Many villages and some towns, however, also had (and still have) the suffix -so, such as settlements named Boinso, Krabonso, Tanoso, and Manso in the Bono-Takyiman area. Manso, a generic and composite term referring to a "cultural group" located "in a certain place" became a suffix itself in the construction of the names of several old Akan towns, including Bono-Manso, Asante-Manso, and Adanse-Manso. There are at least four distinct "manso" towns or villages in the forestland, in addition to Manso Amenfi and Manso Nkwanta, southwest of Kumase. Akan towns that have the suffix -man (e.g., ɔ-man) suggest a reassessment of the use of and interpretations embedded in the idea of "state" in the (West) African context.

In the Ivory Coast (Côte d'Ivoire), the Akan occupy large and significant urban centers and settlements between the Bandama River to the west and the Tanɔ River to the east. Those urban centers with the suffix -*kuro* or -*kro* (town) occur largely in the central part of the country, and this clustering translate into areas where the Akan first entered or primarily settled. Beyond the center of the Ivory Coast, emanating from Bouaké in all four directions, there are more than seventy-seven towns, which all have the Akan suffix -*kuro*, as evidenced in towns such as Kokobokro, Koffikro, Koffi Yaokro, Tano Broukro, and even the country's capital, Yamoussoukro. Evidence of the Akan spatial distribution and settlement in the Ivory Coast also exists in the form of Akan terracotta traditions in southeastern Ivory Coast. These traditions date back to Akan migrations from at least 1000 CE to the present and include "mma" (produced by the Agni and Aboure), "ba" (by the Akye), and "assongou" (by the Eotile, Aboure, Agni, and Nzema). *Assongou* (a so-called fetish tradition) developed in the Aby lagoon region to provide protection against external material and spiritual forces and, unlike *mma* and *ba*, is still practiced today. The culture of the Aboure, one of the producers of *assongou*, represents a convergence of lagoon and Akan forest culture, with the latter dominating until recently. According to Robert Soppelsa, the matrilineal Eotile of the southeastern Ivory Coast are "the sole remnant of 'old lagoon' culture surviving today. Speaking the oldest form of the Akan language, they represent the last vestige of what was probably the original Akan culture...Their society has no centralized organization, nor class structure."[67]

The Eotile and other Akan in the Ivory Coast have archived antecedent forms of Akan culture and society and provide a convincing case for the study of Akan development in spatial and cultural perspectives in places other than Ghana. In Togo, there is less convincing evidence from the names of towns, though several tentative settlements have the Akan suffix -*man*, such as Toman, Koudyoman, and Tafdeman in northern and central Togo, in addition to the town of Adoukrom in central Togo. What is most interesting is a town named Asanté or Assanté, which occurs in both central Togo and Bénin. This observation reflects what might have been either early Akan settlements in what is now Togo and Bénin—with seventeenth- and eighteenth-century settlements that the "Negroes call crooms" [*krom*]—or the result of Asante expansionism, which at its height in the eighteenth and early nineteenth centuries extended northward into what is now Burkina Faso, westward into Ivory Coast, and eastward covering a good portion of Togo.[68] In sum, the linguistic evidence does not support the Mande myth of cultural or linguistic diffusion. On the contrary, a process of Akanization occurred in settlements that came into contact with Islamized Mande cultures, and the Akan remained, in large part, linguistically and culturally unaffected by those cultures. Over time, the Akan have adopted and adapted some foreign elements, while those same non-Akan cultures have imported much. The Guan hills (now Akuapem) in the eastern region of Ghana were transformed by Akanization via the Akan polities of first Akwamu and then Akyem, and the Gã-Adangme and Ewe of the coastal regions of Ghana have been shaped by Akan language and institutions, so much so that, for instance, not only do Ewe weavers produce Akan textile designs (e.g., *kente* cloth), but many "have [also] been apprenticed to Akan weavers."[69]

AKANIZATION AND ISLAMIZATION IN CONTEXT

A well-known *adrinka* symbol says, *kramo bɔne amma yɛanhu kramo pa* ("The bad Muslim does not allow us to see [or know] a good Muslim"). Although this symbol is used as a warning against hypocrisy and deception, it might have had its origins in the relations between Akan peoples and adherents to Islam. It is important to examine Islam or purveyors of Islam in Akan history, for much has been assumed in terms of the acculturating factor of the former in the latter's movement throughout their history and as part of the Mande myth, which makes similar claims. Though the Akan made commercial exchanges with Muslims, their societies never became Islamized, and the Akan rarely if ever settled in towns controlled by others in the forest, including areas where Muslims took up residency. The operative questions are, why were the Akan not Islamized, and if they were culturally and commercially affected by Islamic forces, particularly after the expansion of Islam and the limiting of Akan movement on West African trade networks in the second half of the second millennium? In Levtzion's scheme of Islamic expansion, an unspecified number of Berbers gradually accepted Islam after the Arab conquest of North Africa, and these Berbers transmitted Islam across the Sahara to the Soninke in the *sāhel*, who in turn transmitted it to the Malinké to the south, and Malinké-speaking traders or Juula spread Islam as far as the forest fringes.[70] In the Soninke polity of Wagadu (ancient Ghana), eleventh-century Muslims lived in separate quarters (like the *zongos* of contemporary Ghana) under a non-Muslim leader. The reoccurrence of Muslim communities, whose inhabitants lived in distinct quarters or on the periphery of towns governed by non-Muslims, is a key pattern in Islamic African encounters of West Africa from the incursion of Islam to the present. Indeed, "as long as Islam was confined to trading communities, it operated in the fringes of the West African societies."[71]

Islam penetrated West Africa after 1000 CE, and even then, Islamization was largely gradual and indirect until the later centuries since Arab and Berber converts were preoccupied with controlling the Iberian Peninsula and engaged in the process of Islamizing Berber and other indigenous cities in North Africa. Those African rulers who introduced Islam and supported Muslims and perhaps came under the influence of Islam could not relinquish the "traditional basis of their authority" and, therefore, did not become "unqualified Muslims" since the adoption of Islam was nominal for some and not total for even the most devout. Such rulers sought to control trade routes and exploit the trade in gold and other commodities. The mainstay was the gold trade involving Wagadu, "land of gold" to Arab writers of the ninth century; Mali, with its major trading and learning centers; and Songhay (or Songhai), centered on the trading and political capital of Gao, while its empire was established at Timbuktu and Jenné. Around Lake Chad, those societies in places like Kanem and Bornu relied mainly on slaving as a commercial link with Islamizing North Africa. In the wake of Songhay's collapse in the late sixteenth century, the trans-Saharan trade shifted to the east, migrations followed largely southwestern and southeastern paths (including those absorbed through Akan assimilation processes that prohibited disclosure of origins), and several polities emerged between the late sixteenth and the nineteenth century. The latter included, for instance, the polities of Kong, Gonja, Mamprusi, Dagomba, Nanumba, and others. Except for Kong, the rest were situated in northern Ghana.

Gold and enslaved persons (ʿabd, "slave" and "black African" in common Arabic parlance) were the most important commodities of the trans-Saharan trade with North Africa and beyond, and Juula traders played an integral part in the exchange of both commodities.[72] The trading network north of the forest and the routes that extended to the gold fields of the Akan forest were largely in the hands of Islamic merchants and intellectuals by the middle of the fourteenth century, though most Muslim intellectuals who wrote about West Africans between the ninth and sixteenth centuries had never seen those Africans on their own soil and in their own culture.[73] Nonetheless, Islam affected little of the gold trade and internal politics of Akan societies, including the few scribes in nineteenth-century Kumase, and the contact between Malinké-Juula traders of the savanna and Akan peoples of the forest beginning in the fifteenth century was no different.[74]

The Juula (or Dyula) were found in Wangara trading communities in the Malian heartlands and were first referenced in 1068 by al-Bakri of Cordoba. Juula-Wangara refers to a group of Malian Muslim traders dispersed from the Gambia region to Hausaland, which specialized in the management of long-distance commerce such as the gold trade. The Juula established networks of gold and kola trade between the Middle Niger and the forest, where, Ivor Wilks speculates, "probably in the early fifteenth century, the Juula established a highly lucrative trade with the Akan of the forest country."[75] Wilks's account does not consider either an Akan gold trade before the fifteenth century or the trans-Saharan gold trade, which was inclusive of the Akan region before that period. During the early fourteenth century, it was reported that a *mansa* (ruler) of Mali attempted to extend his power and Islam over the gold-mining communities under Mali's hegemony, and production fell off drastically. Though the Akan gold fields were never under the control of Mali, the idea that non-Muslim producers could halt the production of gold once they felt their indigenous spiritual and political sovereignty was threatened demonstrates one of several responses to Islamic hegemony or the potential thereof, as well as the way in which Islamized West Africans had to engage those communities of "unbelievers" (Arabic: *kuffār*) living on the periphery of their trading towns largely with tact.

One of the most notable trading towns and subject of much of the discussion about the Mande myth of cultural diffusion was Begho (ca. 1100–1800), for it became a key commercial link between the Akan of the forest and the Mande of the Middle Niger. There was a Begho founded in the second half of the sixteenth century, but this "enigmatic region" was not the same as the "gold town" of Bitu mentioned in the *Ta'rikh al-Fattash* and the *Ta'rikh al-Sudan*. Both of these works also speak of Bitugu, Bindugu, and Bindoko, which might have been additional references to Begho.[76] However, Bitu was the Hausa name for Begho, Bitugu was the Hausa-Mande variant, and Bindoko and Bindugu referred to Bonduku since, in Mande languages, the suffix for a country, land, or people is *-dugu*. Thus, the references in the *Ta'rikh al-Fattash* and the *Ta'rikh al-Sudan* to Bindoko-Bindugu are to the location of Bonduku-Gyaman, and Bindoko-Bindugu were also collective terms for non-Muslims such as the Abron (Bono).[77] On the other hand, Bitu-Bitugu in the *Ta'rikh al-Fattash* and the *Ta'rikh al-Sudan* refers to the Mande-Juula and Muslim Hausa peoples of older Begho and the more recent Bonduku. These settlements had non-Islamic and Muslim quarters—a demographic pattern in communities of Islamic and non-Islamic peoples in West Africa—and such quarters in Begho and Bonduku represented attempts to structure life and living according to Islamic ideological prescriptions. Those prescriptions differentiated a social order by way of *dar-al-Islam* ("community of believers" in Islam) and *dar-al-kufr* ("community of unbelievers"), and, in this context, the term *zongo* (*zango* in Hausa) became a generic one applied to Muslim immigrant quarters in or on the periphery of Akan societies.

In western and central Sudan, Akan speakers were known as "Tonawa" in Hausa, "Tõ" or "Tõ-na" in Malinké and as "Toom," as in Pacheco Pereira's "country of Toom," an early sixteenth-century reference to the region north of contemporary Asante in what was then Bono-Manso and Begho.[78] At its height, the ancient commercial town of Jenné-Jeno was inhabited as early as 200 BCE and extended to the eastern bank of the Black Volta's northern bend, and its territory bordered Begho, suggesting that the gold-bearing regions of the Akan gold fields were involved in early commercial exchanges between the forest and savanna zones.[79] Begho, called Bew and Nsokɔ by the Akan, was the northern frontier town of Akanland and the southern frontier of the Malian world, as well as a trading town for the distribution of gold from the Lobi and Akan gold fields. It was Begho's proximity to these gold-rich sites that led to its rise as a commercial center. Begho's peak between the fifteenth and the eighteenth century corresponds to a period of supposed Juula commercial influence and radiocarbon dates for the central areas of the town. The history of Juula settlement and commercial control of Begho is, however, questionable in light of settlements like Namasa, which was contemporaneous with Begho and located five miles north of Begho's ruins. Namasa was inhabited and controlled by autochthones such as the Bono and its traditions do speak of Mande invaders, likely the Juula, who were not among the autochthones.[80]

The Juula were not the first to settle Begho, and the Mande cosettlers in Begho designated the indigenous inhabitants in the area as Brong or Bono. The traditions of Hani (the reconstituted Begho) and Nsokɔ (Nsawkaw) recall that the population of Begho included Bono, *nkramofoɔ* (Mande Muslims), and Nafana or Tomfo-Numu.[81] Tomfoɔ is an Akan term for "blacksmith," while *numu* is a Mande counterpart. The traditions of Namasa, the urban capital of Nsokɔ, mention the "cave people" (Bono) and the "horsemen" (Mande Muslims) as separate groups, and that the Bono quarter with its "royal residence" controlled the market town. There is little doubt that Begho, where the "foreigners" lived in distinct quarters, was an indigenous Akan terminus of trade where foreign traders initially settled on the periphery and after centuries formed more permanent, yet segmented settlements in quarters or on the edge of the larger perimeter of the Begho township. The antiquity and structure of Begho and Bono-Manso strongly suggest that both became principal links between the Akan forest and the Mande of the Middle Niger, and their respective formations were stimulated by trade, as is evidenced by improved agriculture, expanding indigenous technology and commerce, pottery and occupation mounds, and separate Akan capitals and peripheral Muslim sections.[82] For the Bono polity, a Muslim quarter (*kramokurom*, Muslim town) was situated approximately 2.5 miles west of Bono-Manso, but Islam had little to no effect on the capital or the polity itself.[83] The archaeology of Bono-Manso reveals a capital virtually surrounded by streams, baobab trees, deceased persons buried with food offerings and cup in hand—practices supported by oral historical sources—and iron smelting dated at 300 CE.[84] Many of what are now old settlements still contain fragments of funeral effigies (*asodee*), broken pottery (*nkyenfere*), and graves (*adakamana*). Recent archaeological investigations also provide insights into the cultural landscape occupied by the old habitants of Begho and the Bono (Akan) in particular.[85]

Largely consistent with accounts of Bono-Manso, the township of Begho was a composite of Akan, Guan, Senufo, Mande, Kulango, and Grusi-Mo communities, and oral historical sources refer to it both as a settlement governed by horseback-riding and palanquin-borne Akan "chieftains" and as a multicultural borough with suburbs ordered along "ethnic" and functional lines.[86] The Bono occupied the capital and seat of governance and were the main population. They pursued farming, hunting, and trapping and maintained an old and complex "ethnomedical" and nutritional system, in addition to blacksmithing and architecture that utilized the wattle and daub method.[87] The compounds occurred in rectangular courtyards with dates ranging from 1000 to 1700 CE, and evidence abounds for the creation and use of copper and copper alloy objects, pottery, wares, and the domestication of cattle, sheep, and pigs. If pottery and its attendant ceramic tradition served as an indicator of an Akan settled and controlled Begho, the "ceramic evidence of Begho indicates no appreciable influences by the Mande on local ceramic traditions. It is doubtful whether the alien element dominated the local population in large numbers."[88] In sum, the evidence points to a Bono-controlled Begho, as well as significant commercial activity between the market towns of Jenné-Jeno on the Niger and Begho and Bono-Manso on the forest fringe, while the role of Akan settlers and cultural developers in shaping the early gold trade has key implications.

Through Jenné-Jeno, early Akan trade and items of that trade, such as its gold weights, might have reached Roman North Africa, for the geometric Akan gold weights have all of the graphic signs (and more) found in North African scripts but among no other West African peoples.[89] We are told that the gold weight system and currency used by the Akan was adopted from one introduced by Juula traders stationed at Begho, which would date the Akan gold weight and currency system to the fifteenth century CE. There is no evidence, however, that the system employed by the Akan existed (or exists) among the Mande or, for that matter, the Juula. Brian Vivian's excavated items from Adansemanso (dated 393–1650 CE) include "two brass cast geometric gold weights [as well as "two formed cubes" referred to as "strike stones," possibly associated with the gold trade, which] suggest gold weighing and trading activities were taking place."[90] Crossland's excavation of the ancient site of Begho found similar stone objects: "Some of these small stones could have been simple gold weights as examples of these were found by the present writer mixed with an old collection of geometric weights of Bondakile [north of ancient Begho]."[91] Highly dubious, therefore, is the arbitrary date of the fourteenth century CE proposed by Timothy Garrard for the earliest gold weights, which were introduced by Mande-speaking traders from the north and based on the units of the Islamic *mithqal* and ounce, the Portuguese and troy ounce standard.[92] In his reconsideration of thirty-eight hundred geometric and figurative "gold weights," Hartmut Mollat concludes that the "geometric forms [rather than the figurative ones] were the genuine weights for weighing gold dust," based on the indigenous Akan *taku* seed and that the "European standards and the Arabian trade standards were not incorporated in [the Akan] system," as postulated by Garrard.[93] Both the elaborative nature and the exorbitant quantity of the gold weights, as well as the writing and philosophical system encoded in those weights, are found only among the Akan and in no other West African society. Certainly, it is plausible that through trade or cultural contact the Akan incorporated—as all societies have done—some modicum of African and non-African cultural motifs into their gold weight production, but most of the gold weights derive from indigenous Akan conceptualizations as evidenced, for instance, by the predominance of gold weight names that remain obstinately Akan.

TOWARD THE NEXT CENTURIES AND ENCOUNTERS ON THE COAST

On the evidence for early society and culture in the forest and on its borders, a likely scenario is that the clearing of the dense forest began by at least 1500 BCE, using stone tools just after the forest reached its farthest expanse and during a suitable period of aridity between 2500 and 300 BCE. The concomitant prominence of oil palm pollen, which is indicative of human occupation, suggest the dense forest was being settled by proto-Akan peoples with a food-producing economy erected around oil palm cultivation and the exploitation of high-calorie root crops, which facilitated population growth. This society also made use of communal labor and reproductive strategies needed for forest clearance and settlement during a period of malaria adaptation. In addition, it utilized an agrarian sociopolitical order where hunters and their descendants played key roles in finding unsettled land and assuming custodianship. These processes must have shaped the proto-Akan culture of settlements both within and on the periphery of forests. Indeed, there is a direct correlation between food production, trade activities, the growth of towns, and the women, who have traditionally dominated local food-trading activities and allowed for both population growth through procreation and matrilineal processes for assimilating others into the cultural order. These forest and forest-fringe dwellers achieved levels of cultural development, and their spirituality became linked to an agricultural cycle, sacred ancestral sites, and so-called totemic association and the identification of an Akan Creator as manifest in a myriad of ways in the natural order.

Proto-Akan societies and culture were largely an indigenous development, and this interpretation of early culture and society is well supported by the archaeological, historical, and linguistic evidence. The combined evidence does not support the Mande myth or the idea that integral Akan cultural practices were the product of Mande cultural or linguistic diffusion. On the contrary, a process of Akanization has occurred in settlements that had contact with non-Akan cultures. Akan peoples, on the whole, shaped those cultures in significant ways, when the opposite should have occurred. Akan peoples have adopted some foreign elements, and yet many said non-Akan cultures have imported and adopted much from the Akan. The Akan had many commercial and cultural contacts with Muslims, yet they were never Islamized as a group and were little influenced in cultural and commercial terms. Akan peoples seldom lived in settlements headed by others in the forestland and on its edges, including areas where Muslims took up residency, such as the town of Begho. Those towns, which were established principally for trade, were on the northwestern edge of the forest, and Mande traders made it clear that they rarely entered the high forest; in fact, in Begho and Bono-Manso, these traders remained in distinct quarters or on the periphery of each capital. Even when Islamicized Africans took up residence in the Akan forest in later periods and in places like nineteenth-century Kumase, they resided in separate living areas.

Akan peoples were marginally affected by Islam, and one of the key reasons for this is that Akan societies were built on spiritual agencies (e.g., *abosom*), foundational ideas, and emblematic and objects (e.g., sacred swords, stools). Those agencies functioned as facilitators of the social and natural order and shaped the cultural self-understandings, settlements, and the polities as sources of identification and belonging on the later Gold Coast. In the late fifteenth century and early sixteenth century, the Portuguese came upon Akan societies who exhibited sophisticated cultural knowledge, spiritual understandings of divine and social order, and commercial skills after centuries of experience in local and regional trade and were able to approach these Europeans with tact. The Portuguese, like other Europeans to follow, were invariably limited to the Gold Coast littoral, but the nature of the Portuguese encounter with Akan societies set the pace for other Akan European interactions, particularly Akan response to Christianization. As with Islam, Akan peoples thwarted most attempts at Christian conversion for their social worlds were crafted around a spiritual culture attentive to the *abosom* and structured toward agriculture and regional commerce. Where commerce and (spiritual) culture were at odds, the apparent contradictions were perhaps accurate reflections of those same encounters and their immediate and distant consequences.

3

History and Meaning in Akan Societies, 1500–1800

Sensan yi firi tete
(This Sensan [tree] comes from ancient times.)
Ogyedua bɛsen no tenten
(The Ogyedua [tree] will surpass it in height.)

—Akan drum text

The *sensan* is a small, bamboolike tree or grass, while *ogyedua* (lit., the receiving tree) is a large shade tree that represents chieftaincy and is thus a place where rulers and councils of elders have convened their meetings in the recent past. Though *ogyedua* is also a place where anyone may go and rest, it is largely a synonym for an *ɔhene* (ruler), that is, the one who provides shade for the cultural group or polity. Both trees provide appropriate symbolism, for the *sensan*, or Akan spiritual culture—of some antiquity and deeply rooted—endured and frustrated the ideational forces of Christian merchants and clergy alike, whereas the *ogyedua*, or Akan polities and persons that were seduced by European trade and human trafficking, grew in illusionary heights and by the nineteenth century had been surpassed by the rulers of Britain. This chapter examines the commercial interactions between Akan polities and persons and the European nationals that established trading posts and fortified bases on the Gold Coast (map 2). Between 1500 and 1800, many of the early sources pertaining to the Gold Coast were written down or published with a bias toward commerce, owing to the relative extent of the international enslavement enterprise, which included the Americas and the first European "scramble for Africa" on the Gold Coast. But commerce is used herein as a window to examine issues relevant to Akan culture and society.[1] In other words, commercial interactions allow us to examine not only cultural institutions and identity in the period under discussion but also internal politics and conflicts borne of Europeans in the equation; the rise, fall, or consolidation of key polities; the Asante factor in Akan history and regional matters, and attendant issues of warfare, firearms, and the international enslavement enterprise on the Gold Coast.

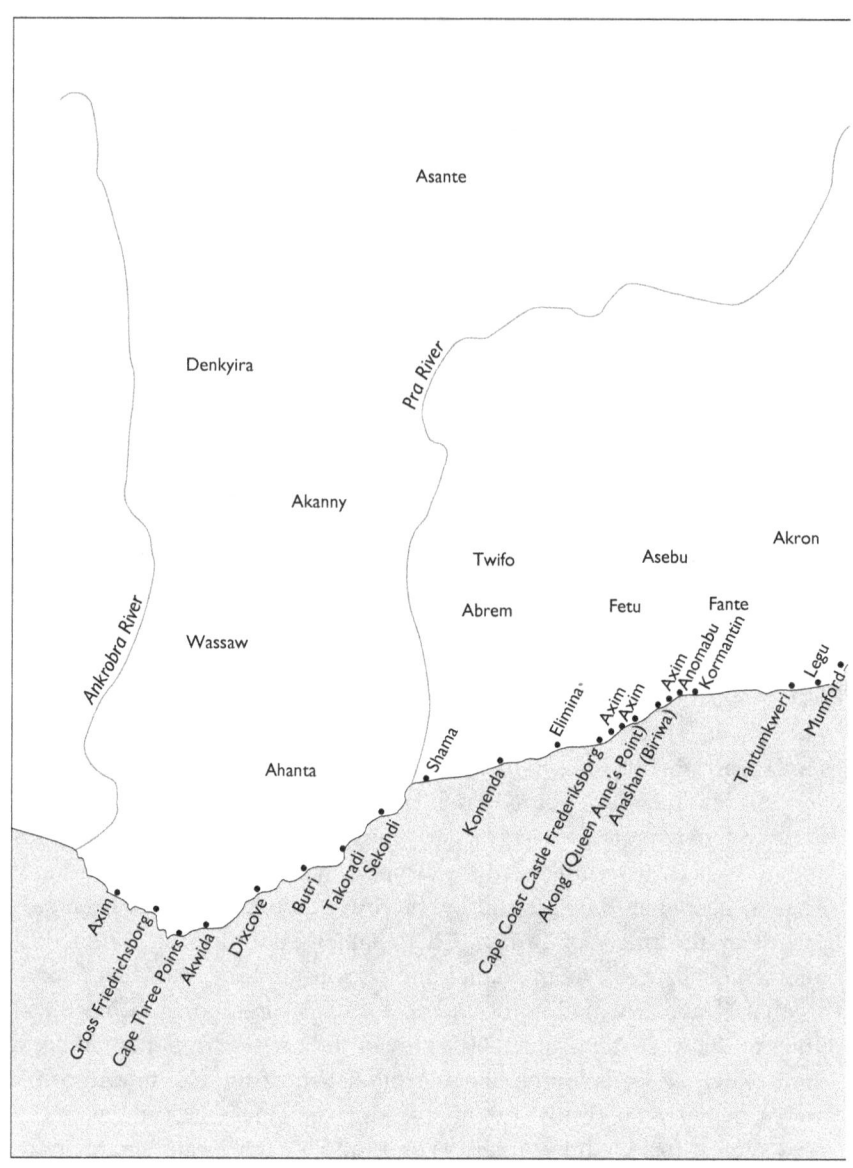

Map 2. The Gold Coast. Most of these settlements were inhabited between the late sixteenth and the early nineteenth century. The coastal ports of embarkation were significant contact points between European nationals and Akan societies. Reprinted by permission of the Royal Danish Academy of Sciences and Letters from *Danish Sources for the History of Ghana*, ed. Ole Justesen.

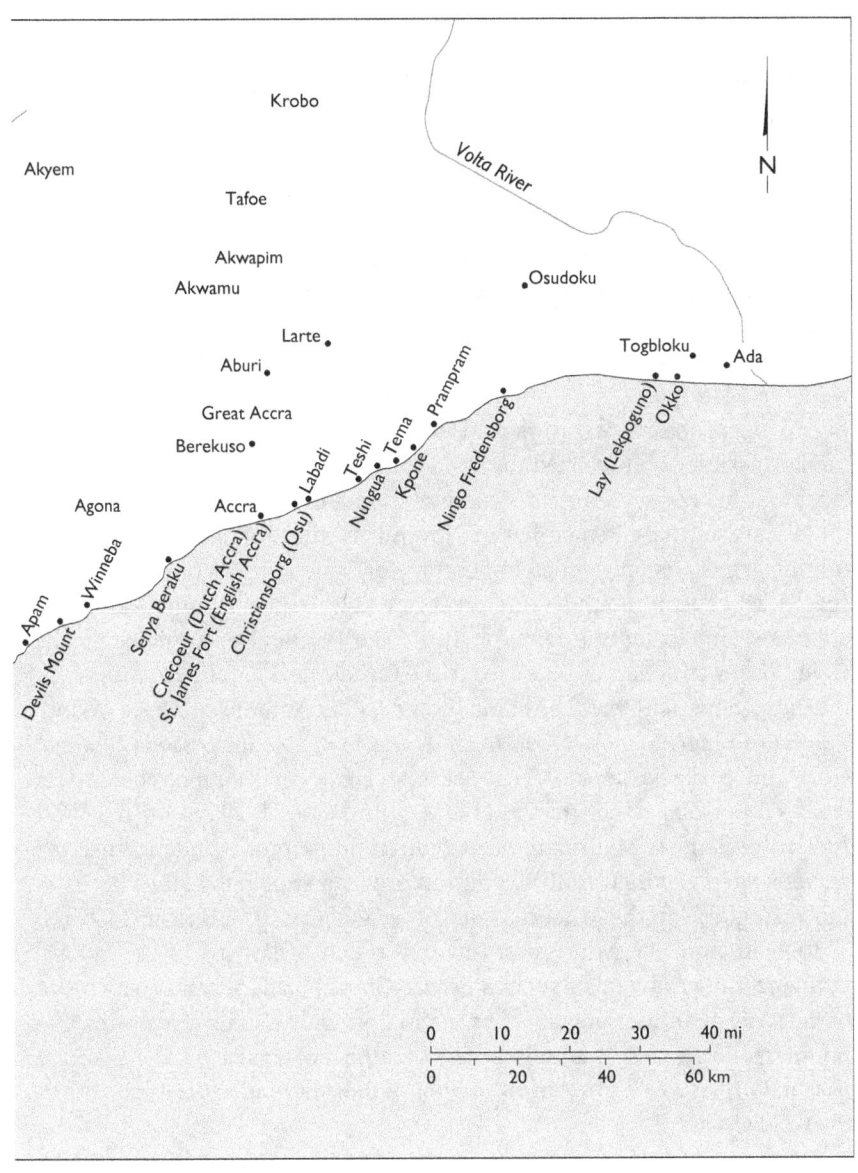

AKAN SOCIETIES AND CULTURE IN COMMERCIAL ENCOUNTERS

The Akan concept of *oburoni* (colloquially, white person) referred to a "lagoon person," and its complement, *aburokyire* (the place behind the lagoon), represented a foreign world and the southern limits of Akanland; the former was applied to Europeans encountering Akan peoples at "the mouth of the ocean" (*mpoano*) in the late fifteenth century. The first Europeans to encounter the Akan and engage in commerce on the coast were the Portuguese, who found a vast territory of forests and lagoons connected by the politics of commercial and social networks. Upon their arrival, the Portuguese soon realized that gold could be obtained in Gold Coast villages and fishing settlements. Gold was mined in shallow shafts mostly in the dry season (late September or November) after the harvests, and this mining activity usually ended in February or March, just before the sowing season, when yam mounds were made, crops were planted, and Akan agriculturists anticipated the rains of April. The Portuguese presence on the Gold Coast was generally restricted to the Castelo de São Jorge da Mina near the indigenous settlement of Edina (Elmina), São Antonio de Axem (Axim), Fort São Francis Xavier at Osu (Accra), and Fort São Sebastião at Shama.[2] Gold and enslaved persons were early and key commodities, but it was enslaved persons rather than gold at Arguim, a small island off the West African coast near Mauritania, that brought huge profits.[3] Some enslaved persons were exported from Arguim in order to supply the labor needs of the Portuguese on the Mina coast (i.e., the Gold Coast).[4] Between 1480 and 1530, gold from the Mina coast financed much of Portugal's brief global eminence, and individuals such as Fernão Gomes made a fortune as a result of the large quantities of gold that went to Portugal.[5] São Jorge da Mina, the premiere Portuguese trading center, became Portugal's most important base in Guinea (Western Africa) in light of the gold trade at Elmina and on the Gold Coast.

On the whole, the Portuguese remained in their forts, which were distanced from the indigenous peoples of the Gold Coast and certainly its hinterlands, used the sea as lines of communication rather than land, and employed force and terror, all of which marked a sharp contrast between Portuguese policy on the Gold Coast and other parts of West Africa. Portuguese policy on the Gold Coast derived in large part from the fraudulent and conflictual nature of the encounter between Caramansa (Kwamena Ansa?) and Diogo de Azambuja, and de Azambuja's tactics of engagement became part of the strategies employed by Portuguese officials after the São Jorge da Mina fort was built in the late fifteenth century.[6] The rulers of Eguafo and Fetu laid claim to both Edina and the territory on which the fort was constructed, though Eguafo controlled the land west of the Benya Lagoon, including the peninsula on which the fort and the adjacent settlement lay. The Portuguese sought immediately to cultivate friendships with the two rulers and their senior officials, but even such overtures did little to prevent a combined attack on the fort by Eguafo and Fetu in 1570. By then, Elmina—with Portuguese support—had achieved its independence from Eguafo and Fetu. Portuguese officials became acquainted with local politics by persuading some Akan to allow (distant) merchants to come to the Mina fort unmolested and without heavy tolls and by compelling a few villages to become the new township of Elmina through a severance of ties with Eguafo, a large polity, and Fetu (Afutu), described as a hamlet and fishing village ruled by Sasaxy in 1503.[7]

The Fante settlements of Edina (Elmina), Eguafo, and Komenda all trace their origin to Takyiman (the successor of Bono-Manso). Upon their pre-sixteenth-century arrival on the coast, the Fante settled occupied lands and established themselves at Mankessim and created new villages, though the Etsi claimed to have left Takyiman well before the Fante migrants (known as Borbor Fante), who encountered them at Mankessim.[8] The Edina people came to the coast under the leadership of Kwaa Amankwaa, a great hunter, and established the village of Anomansa or Anomee near the Benya Lagoon—this village later became Edina. Edina and Komenda formed part of Eguafo until Edina (or Elmina) cut its ties in the late sixteenth century, whereas Komenda remained under Eguafo up to the early eighteenth century, and this explains why Komenda and Eguafo were often conflated or confused until that period. During the early eighteenth century, the small fishing and salt-making village of Akatakyi (Little Komenda)—which Pacheco Pereira referred to as Acomane (village of Torto) and its ruler as Xeryfe in 1503—developed into the port town of a Komenda polity that came to rival and eventually surpass Eguafo. Eguafo was once the primary trading and political ally of the Portuguese, and it established a town, Amankwakurom, with a quarter for foreign traders. Komenda, like other Akan settlements on the coast and to the edge of the forest, regarded the "ɔbosom [as] created by [an Akan Creator]," and in "every house or family house we [had] an ɔbosom in this state," including a village of "priests" in the seventeenth century.[9] The rise, expansion, and notoriety of the port town of Komenda (Akatakyi) and Edina grew out of the ways in which European rivalry and active intrusion into local politics subverted indigenous political structures—as evidenced by frequent destoolment and enstoolment cases. It was that subversion that led to an Elmina township (under Portuguese and then Dutch protection) and a Komenda polity in the midst of a weakened Eguafo and Fetu. Indeed, Elmina grew under European protection, received the support of other settlements that had once aligned themselves with Eguafo and Fetu, and became a settlement governed by local elders ("braffoes") and the Portuguese governor of the Mina fort. In port towns representing large polities on the Gold Coast, the ɔbrafoɔ (braffoo) or divisional ɔhene was subordinate to the ɔmanhene of those polities, and thus Caramansa or Kwamena Ansa of Edina would have been under the authority of Eguafo (or the Eguafohene) during his late fifteenth-century encounter with the Portuguese via Diogo de Azambuja.[10]

The cultural and sociopolitical structure of Elmina was relatively the same as that of other Fante or Akan groups, but since Elmina remained independent of its coastal neighbors (under European protection) from the early sixteenth century on and maintained good relationships with the forest-based Asante of almost two centuries later, it came to view its history and institutions as distinct from those of other Akan peoples.[11] The ɔmanhene of coastal polities such as Komenda and Elmina was the political, military, judicial, and spiritual head of the "state," who was advised by less than a dozen divisional ahene (sg. ɔhene), who commanded the divisional armies and dealt with the day-to-day administration of the polity in collaboration with five asafo (paramilitary) group heads. A male child automatically joined his father's asafo company in lieu of a standing army, and, in Komenda and Elmina, the asafo leadership came to wield considerable power. The asafo companies of Komenda, which were led by the Tufuhen, were the most powerful in the polity, for they fought and held custodianship over its lands and had the prerogative of enstooling or destooling the ɔmanhene. For Elmina, the head of the asafo companies was called the Ekuwesuonhin, and its divisional ahene and ɔmanhene (called ɔhen) structure, unlike in Komenda, developed perhaps in the early eighteenth century, when the term ɔhen appeared in the documentary sources. By then, Akan migrants seeking refuge in Elmina and the ɔhen selected by Elmina officials had to be authenticated by the Dutch director general through an oath to the second Dutch West India Company.

The early Fante polities and many of its settlements were already established by the fifteenth century, and in the early sixteenth century Pacheco Pereira spoke of "great Fante" at Mankessim and "little Fante" at Anomabu in the vicinity of Cape Coast (Cabo Corço in European records; Oguaa among the Akan).[12] The coastal Fante and Labadi towns were positioned east of the Pra River, and the constellation of Fantin (Fante) settlements included Cormantin (Kormantin, Kormantse), Anamabo (Anomabu), Weamba (Winneba), and several fishing and salt-making villages. Kormantin (Cormanti[n] and its variants) referred to a coastal town positioned just east of Mori and west of Accra, but the name of this town would become a trope for many Akan or Gold Coast Africans who were captured and exported to the Americas. Perhaps "kormantin" derives from "korɔmante," a contracted form of mekorɔɔ no nanso mante ("I went, but I did not hear [about the ruler's death]), that is, an oath (*ntam*)—sacred statement that should not be uttered because it conjures up negative memories and invokes the very event that prompted the oath to reoccur upon articulation. Be that as it may, most coastal towns of the fifteenth century were divided in wards (*abron*), an apparent import from Takyiman, and the town of Elmina, for instance, was divided into two wards that evolved into three and then seven in the seventeenth and eighteenth centuries. The *asafo* companies corresponded to these wards, and membership in a company or ward followed a patrilineal principle, as did stool succession, though most of the inhabitants adhered to a matrilineal principle. In the sixteenth and early seventeenth centuries, each ward had a governor, known as a "brasso" (perhaps from "braffoo"), assisted by various minor officials, and the Portuguese armed and defended the inhabitants. In return, those inhabitants, reportedly Christianized by the early sixteenth century, according to Pacheco Pereira, defended the fort against common enemies or enemies of the Portuguese.[13]

Portuguese and African Christianization and miscegenation occurred primarily in and around the town of Elmina—where chapels were built on and across the peninsula at Edina and St. Jago—with very limited success at Shama, Axim, Fetu, and Komenda.[14] However, no private Portuguese subjects settled on the Gold Coast, as opposed to other parts of West Africa, where Portuguese *lançados* (runaway adventurers) and Portuguese African offspring and descendants, especially at Cape Verde and on the Upper Guinea coast, rivaled the French, Dutch, and English for trade between the sixteenth and eighteenth centuries.[15] Though intense European rivalry and commerce unfolded on the populated Akan coast, the miscegenation and Christianization that occurred elsewhere in West Africa did not take place on much of the Gold Coast on account of Portuguese policies shaped by the encounter with Caramansa or Kwamena Ansa and the spiritual culture of Akan societies. The process of Christianization on the early Gold Coast was confined to areas of proximate African European contact, and indigenous spirituality contested and even thwarted Christian evangelization, foregrounded by early commercial encounters and the strength of the Akan spiritual culture. Akan social orders seem to have been built on spiritual agencies (*abosom*) that functioned both as facilitators of the social and natural order and as important sacred objects that consolidated those understandings. To fully disregard these agents would be to destroy the cultural self and the polity as sources of identification and belonging. The preponderance of the *abosom* and of Akan spirituality remained a fact of life not only on the coast but also to the edge of the forest—and here the European sources are vague, but the oral historical sources provide some insights—in places like Wenchi (Wankyi), Nsokɔ, Inta (Tafo), and the Bono area, home of the sacred Tanɔ River and source of all Tanɔ River–derived *abosom*.

In fact, there has been continuity in Akan spirituality amid significant technological and socio-political change, in part, initiated by the Portuguese five centuries ago.[16]

Portuguese sources report that the São Jorge da Mina fort was built where the first reported Catholic mass on the Gold Coast occurred in 1482. The surviving records suggest that the Portuguese stationed at the Mina fort had a greater interest in gold, liquor, and so-called mulatto women than in their faith or the propagation thereof. Indeed, the zeal of the Christian crusade was surpassed by the greed of merchants, and the Portuguese were largely unsuccessful in converting most African rulers and their subjects on the Gold Coast, with the early exceptions of Sasaxy and Xeryfe.[17] In 1503 the Portuguese baptized Sasaxy of Fetu (renamed Dom João) and built a chapel, apparently at his request, while Xeryfe of Komenda entertained the idea of baptism.[18] Such sparse conversions were part of a mutually attractive commercial package generally formed between Portuguese and African ruling factions.[19] The price of Portuguese support included an acceptance of Christianity and its God, "especially where Portuguese troops or shipments of arms were requested."[20] With an overwhelming priority on commerce, Christianity was no more than a situational exterior assumed in most Portuguese-African interactions, and the strongest evidence remains the lack of a large body of Gold Coast converts. Even when local Portuguese governors were given cash rewards for each convert, most converts did not remain so.[21] The religious state of the affairs on the coast was described in a Portuguese report of 1632 that complained how few Africans practiced the Christian faith and instead secretly consulted indigenous healers who provided advice through divination and protective medicines, and took part in festivals at a sacred rock on the coast. Converts such as Grace of Elmina were accused of "fetish worship" and "when she was questioned about Jesus Christ, the Holy Virgin, and her own salvation, Grace replied that she had little interest in any of those matters."[22] Portuguese accounts also note the difficulty of and lack of progress in Christianization due to the place of spiritual culture in Akan societies and the trade concerns of the Portuguese. Trade and its profits became a sustained endeavor even among Portuguese chaplains at Elmina.[23] The nature of Portuguese encounters with and policy toward Akan societies structured by an indigenous spiritual culture set the pace for and underscored much of the layered interactions between Akan societies and the merchants and clergy of subsequent European nations.

During the seventeenth and eighteenth centuries, Akan polities consolidated their resources and structures in their interactions with each other, with commercial forces on the northern limits of the forest and on the northwestern frontier in Begho and the Bono areas, and with the European

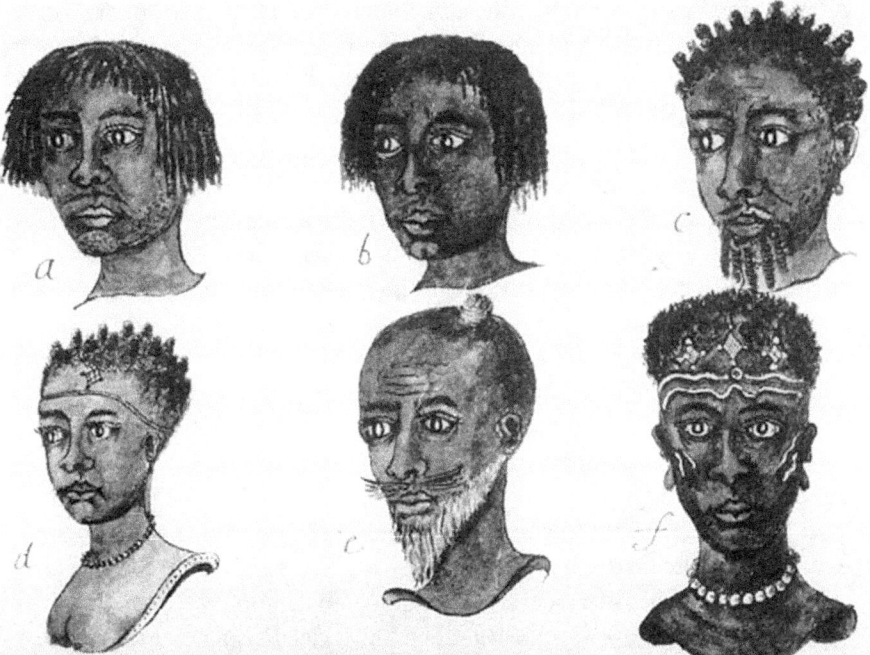

Figure 3.1. "Heads of Gold Coast men and women," as illustrated by Jean Barbot, ca. 1680s. Some scholars presume that these men and women in the illustration were Akan persons, but two of them were labeled "Quaqua men" (of the contemporary Ivory Coast and western Ghana), whereas person (c) was perhaps typical in Accra and on the Cape Coast, and person (e) was an "old man." Reproduced by permission of the Hakluyt Society.

merchants on the Atlantic seaboard. On the one hand, these centuries were characterized by raids, warfare, and political instability with the British, Dutch, and Danish trading companies that were in solid command of the European commerce on the Gold Coast. On the other hand, the Akani merchants represented a powerful commercial and political force that facilitated trade in gold—above all and at a time when gold was central to trade—between peoples of inland and coastal communities between Axim and Accra on the Gold Coast (see figure 3.1).

The Akani, an indiscriminate term often applied to inland Akan traders, were part of a trading organization that stretched from the coast to the edge of the forest, but the origins of this organization remains unclear. In the sixteenth and seventeenth centuries, the Accany or "Great Acany" represented on European maps included the three divisions of Akyem—Akyem Abuakwa, Akyem Kotoku, and Akyem Bosome—which originated from

Adanse and assumed these divisional identities after their migration. However, seventeenth- and eighteenth-century European accounts do not distinguish the three, which are often subsumed under "Akim" (Akyem) and its variants. What those accounts referred to by the name Akyem (Akim) was apparently Akyem Abuakwa, the largest division, established east of the Pra River in the seventeenth century.[24] Pieter de Marees referred to the Akani as "batafou" (batafoɔ, long-distance traders), and the rise in Akani power in the seventeenth century—with its apogee around 1650—suggests an increase in gold mining activities in the forest during that period.[26] The latter half of the century witnessed an increased focus on warfare and thus firearms acquisition as the Akani came more and more into conflict with inland and coastal polities. By the end of the seventeenth century, in consideration of the fall of Dɛnkyira and the rise of Asante, the Akani presence and strategic position was greatly reduced. European competition on the coast increased, new and more powerful inland polities emerged, and the centrality of gold began giving way to traffic in enslaved persons. Thereafter, the Akani disappeared from the historical records and were no longer considered a power on the Gold Coast in the eighteenth century.[25]

In largely coastal Akan societies, the main social disagreement from the fifteenth to the late seventeenth century was the conflict between social groups of an upper ranking and those with less power, wealth, and authority over the control of agricultural surplus in the context of a mosaic of independent polities, little military conquest of territory, and regional unity through key trading centers and lower-level yet strategic commercial sites. In the seventeenth century, Pieter de Marees and Johann Wilhelm Müller observed efficient levels of agricultural productivity with relatively little labor or effort (in their minds) that nonetheless produced high yields of maize (corn) and millet.[27] Some accounts indicate that the yam was used when *millie* (Turkish corn or wheat) was unavailable, though yam *fufu* (a dish made of pounded yams) appears to have been popular in coastal towns.[28] Game was a key item in the diet of inland town dwellers during the seventeenth century as evidenced by the rise in livestock prices (while the prices of food crops, particularly staple foods, remained constant) during the second half of the century. Commoners, at least in the coastal communities, generally consumed meats on festive or feasting days throughout the year; otherwise, they ate fish and chicken, and where these were unavailable, they ate largely vegetarian diets that included yams, fruits, vegetables, *millie*, palm oil, salt and pepper, maize, millet, rice, plantains, legumes, eggs, sugar cane, honey, and palm wine. Other seventeenth-century European observers noted that the coast was indeed "rich in palm wine" and remarked on the good quality of the bread produced from *millie* and the consumption and medicinal use of plantain (*borɔdeɛ*, brody), for instance, as a cure for diarrhea.[29] Those who controlled and derived tax from the land ensured not only their income but also that the towns—in a period of increasing urbanization and population growth—would receive a regular supply of the diverse foodstuff noted above. Under government authority, officeholders in the seventeenth century imposed heavier taxes on commoners in various (coastal) polities, and, according to Ray Kea, rural banditry emerged on a significant scale along with riots, revolts, and insurrections over the source of the main disagreement: appropriation and distribution of agricultural surplus.[30] This dispute was arguably born of the interactions between commerce and culture in terms of the intensification of African and European trade and rivalry, the shift from gold as the primary commodity to enslavable peoples, rampant kidnappings and pawning, the greater consumption of European trade goods by ordinary members of coastal and some inland societies, and the introduction and increased use of firearms.[31]

In the interactions between commerce and culture, the domain of "religion" remained an enduring spectacle to outward-looking European officials, clergymen, merchants, and general observers, who, more often than not and in varying degrees, filtered that outlook through their Christian lenses and reached conclusions about the internal workings of Akan culture and spirituality that were actually at variance with the reality. Pieter de Marees, an early seventeenth-century Dutch trader, wrote much about internal Akan trade at markets between the coastal and the interior peoples, and observed that the linen traded for gold became the standard clothing on the coast at beginning of the seventeenth century, trade items such as large basins were placed on the graves of the deceased and were used both as abodes of the *abosom* and as divining vessels.[32] Johann Wilhelm Müller, a seventeenth-century Lutheran pastor, also noted the use of linen to wrap corpses and to serve as an offering to the *abosom*.[33] Pieter van den Broeke, a contemporary of de Marees and a fellow Dutch merchant, became convinced that Accra provided "the most and best gold of this whole coast, but the people here are very bad and evil people," echoing Willem van Focquenbroch's sentiment that "...be the country ever so bad, the Gold is good."[34] These were common readings of culture and commerce.

At coastal markets, both Müller and de Marees observed sacred trees in the middle of these centers of extensive commerce in Cape Coast and Fetu, and though one was a pastor and the other a merchant, they and van Focquenbroch focused on the individual "who also acts as a Seer, or Prophet, and they call him *Fetizero* ["priest"]."[35] De Marees wrote that a "fetissero," on Tuesdays, "sits on a Stool in the middle of the Market, opposite the little Alter or scaffold where they make sacrifices to their *Fetisso*."[36] The "priest" was an *ɔkɔmfoɔ* (spiritualist), and most of these spiritualists served their community after a three- to seven-year period of training.

During training, the ɔkɔmfowa (lit., small ɔkɔmfoɔ, or initiate) was admonished to salute his or her elders appropriately and not to drink, gossip, quarrel, fight, or socialize with peers at night. Initiates were solemnly commanded or enjoined by their ɔbosom not to kill anyone and were required to fast all day on ceremonial days, for if they were full, they would not hear (i.e., understand) the voice of their ɔbosom.[37] Indeed, de Marees depicted one ɔkɔmfoɔ "performing another prayer, praying to their God" with two of three persons kneeling on the right knee as adherents to Akan spirituality do in various contexts. He also described the use of "straw-wisps" (i.e., raffia) or abamkyere, "which they also tie to their legs and arms."[38] On sacred Tuesdays (benada), fishermen "are not to go to sea to fish. The Women or Peasant women are not to come to Market with their fruits either, but stay at home with their merchandize... People abstain from doing any manual work on that day or engaging in any trade with each other."[39] On that "(sacred) day of rest," fishermen dared not catch fish at sea, and farmers did likewise on Thursday or Friday. De Marees's encounter with Akan spiritual practitioners and practices, such as his observation of sacred days and labor restrictions, left him with the impression that "If the Dutch see them observing such customs and laugh and mock them because they look so foolish, they are much ashamed and no longer dare to make their Fetisso in our presence."[40] Perhaps. An entrenched Akan spiritual culture, however, persisted well beyond what de Marees and others would have liked and complicated the commercial and ideological interests of men like him from various parts of Europe.

The Portuguese were not unique in their unsuccessful pursuit of Gold Coast converts or Christianization through commerce; in fact, the experience of other Europeans, such as the Danish, was no different. The Lutheran pastor Johann Wilhelm Müller, then stationed at the Danish fort in Fetu, unsuccessfully attempted to train African preachers and create an Efutu (Fetu) version of the King James Version of the Bible. Equally, the Capuchins—an independent order of Franciscan friars founded in 1525 in Italy—came to Assinie in the first half of the seventeenth century, only to suffer from unsuccessful religious proselytization; they retired shortly thereafter to Axim. Diseases such as fever and guinea worm contributed to their physical suffering as well. In April of 1701 Godefroy Loyer, Dominican friar and author of *Relation du Voyage du Royaume d'Issyny* (1714), left for Assinie accompanied by one Aniaba, who was at once presented as both the son of the Assinie ruler and an enslaved person captured in war. Loyer most likely thought that Aniaba would soon ascend to the leadership of Assinie and that his own ties to Aniaba would facilitate his "civilizing" and proselytizing mission. However, due to Aniaba's difficulty in assuming the leadership position of his "father," his fight with the then regent, Akasini, and the Akan matrilineal principle of leadership succession (where the ruler's nephew—and not the son—inherits his position), Aniaba was probably not the son of the ruler of Assinie. Loyer, like many of his predecessors, could not relate to the African coastal peoples, had no ally in Aniaba and no antidote for the strong attachment to indigenous spirituality (which he called "fetishism"), and returned to France in 1706.

That attachment and the extreme difficulty of conversion was echoed by Jean Barbot toward the end of the seventeenth century; Barbot and Dutch officials feared that the "mulattoes" would revert to "paganism."[41] Even the Gold Coast merchants, who, it would seem, were preoccupied with commerce, managed to fulfill obligations or cultural mandates related to Akan spirituality. On 6 April 1667, Jantie Snees, a wealthy Cape Coast merchant and chief revenue collector, hosted large festivals at Cape Coast and Amanfro, and two years later he sacrificed more than twenty goats to his ɔbosom.[42] Müller reported that the people of Fetu honored the abosom by spreading imported linen along the main roads of the polity ("linen, which one finds strewn on the roads"). Willem Bosman described an Apoɔ festival, which originated in the Bono area of Takyiman, at Axim in the late seventeenth century. The festival was held every year "at an appointed time" and was an eight-day ceremony of "lampooning," where commoners "freely [sang] of all the Faults, Villanies and Frauds of their Superiours as well as Inferiours without Punishment."[43] This ceremony, which opened and ended with rituals involving the abosom, took place in "one hundred Towns at the same time."[44] The widespread nature of Akan (spiritual) culture, even in a deeply commercialized and intensely militarizing historical context, is telling. Indeed, it would appear that the process of Christianization was limited on the greater Gold Coast and even in areas of proximate European-African contact and that indigenous spiritual practices rooted in Akan culture contested and even thwarted Christian evangelization.

The heightened nature of the seventeenth- and eighteenth-century international enslavement enterprise was paralleled by Protestant evangelization, yet the Africans who were born of African and European parentage and trained as missionaries—such as Christian Protten and Frederick P. Svane (both of Danish and African parentage), Anton W. Amo, and Philip Quaque—were less than successful, and the European missions, which had expected greater proselytization, were disappointed. Protten had no interaction with Africans beyond the Danish fort in Accra, Amo had little to no influence in his "native country," Svane found it nearly impossible to express Christian doctrine in the Gã language and found little support for his efforts, and Quaque used an interpreter when he preached due to the distance he created between himself and his Fante language and culture. At Cape Coast, Philip Quaque met and corresponded with Reverend Thomas Thompson of the Church of England

and chaplain at Cape Coast Castle in the 1750s. Though Thompson's relentless Christianization efforts failed miserably, Philip went to England as a youth from Fetu for twelve years and returned to the Gold Coast in 1766 as an ordained priest. Philip labored in the spirit of Thomas Thompson for fifty or so years and died with not much more success than Thompson. Ironically, a female ɔkɔmfoɔ performed the appropriate indigenous rituals at Philip's funeral.

In the mid-eighteenth century, Thompson, while stationed in Cape Coast, recorded what he called a "country prayer" to "Jan Compon" or "Yancumpong" (Onyankopɔn), the Akan Creator. The "country prayer," "Yancumpong m'iphih meh, mah men yeh bribbe ummouh," was translated as "may God preserve me and grant I may do no evil."[45] A transliteration and translation of Thompson's or his informant's Akan is striking: *Onyankopɔn nhwɛ me, mma mennyɛ biribi mumuo* ("Onyankopɔn should look after me, do not allow me to do something wicked"). Thompson probably recorded what he heard, and the proximity between what he recorded and the revised Akan language text suggests that Thompson had an ear for the language and a level of sensitivity to its speakers and spirituality. However, this was not the case for Thompson or his predecessor clergyman, Johann Wilhelm Müller. Müller, like many of those who came before and after him, did not respect Akan spiritual practices, and those he encountered and questioned on the coast felt his disdain as a Lutheran pastor and a biased observer. For instance, Müller asked to see an *ɔbosom* during consultation and was denied in each instance. Müller noted the changing fashion and tastes of Africans on the coast as if such capricious behavior were exceptional when compared to other parts of the world, including Europe, from which he came. He also noted Africans cheating in trade and the consequences thereof but was silent on European cheating and its consequences in terms of Euro-African trade and rivalry on the Gold Coast.

INTERNAL POLITICS AND CONFLICTS: THE EUROPEAN FACTOR AND AKAN RESPONSES

The Dutch, like other Europeans, were particularly prone to be involved in the politics and wars between polities or settlements on the coast. Such meddling occurred in the context of European rivalry and attempts to gain trust and trade leverage with Akan societies, such as Asebu, with whom the Dutch entered an informal trade agreement in 1598, which was replaced by a definite agreement in 1624.[46] The Dutch attacked the Portuguese-controlled Axim and Elmina between 1607 and 1625, established another fort west of Elmina in 1617, which placed greater Dutch control over the gold trade, and soon captured Elmina in 1637, Shama in 1640, and Axim in 1642. The Dutch followed the Portuguese in terms of cultivating trade alliances with coastal polities during their entry into the gold, commercial goods, and international enslavement enterprises. Two representatives of the Asebuhene won Dutch support against the Portuguese as part of a mission to Holland in 1612 as a result of the informal Dutch-Asebu agreement more than a decade earlier. Six years later, Samuel Brun, a surgeon stationed at the Dutch Fort Nassau between March 1614 and May 1616 and later from September 1617 to August 1620, reportedly observed an Akan-Abrem battle in which forty thousand men were killed (the counting was reckoned through a display of the heads of the slain).[47] This number is probably exaggerated, and it is unlikely that Brun counted all forty thousand heads, if there were that many. Such a sharp observer would have also reported whether that battle was solely between the Akan and the Abrem or whether the Dutch or other Europeans played some role in what appears to have been a very gruesome battle. Brun noted, "We [Dutch] too were to some extent obliged to take sides and give assistance to those well disposed towards us, especially the King of Sabou [Asebu], who was often defeated. Had we not supported him, he would almost certainly have been driven out; for the majority of these people had taken a great hatred to our King of Sabou, Henna Jany Jafarr Jafarry [ɔhene Gyan Gyafari Gyamfi?], because he had given the Dutch the aforementioned site, where I stayed three years."[48]

However, the Dutch were "well disposed" toward not only the Asebu but also many of the coastal polities in the seventeenth century. The year the Dutch entered into a formal trade agreement with the Asebu and built Fort Nassau at Mori, they also made a military agreement with the Fante. Through one such early seventeenth-century treaty the Dutch provided arms to the Fante to help them against the Portuguese on land, in addition to the use of Fante canoes at sea.[49] The Dutch made trading agreements with Axim, Accra, Jabi, and Komenda after they captured Elmina and established posts at Cape Coast and "Little Komenda" (Akatakyi); the seizure of Elmina was strategic, for the Dutch inventoried more than 90 different trade goods at Elmina in 1645, 150 in 1699, and 218 in 1728.[50] However, trade agreements were transitory and within a year or so, allies became enemies and vice versa. The Dutch fought a war against Axim in 1649, Adom in 1659, and Komenda in 1694; Axim and Komenda were trading partners before the mid-seventeenth century. Indeed, the nature of European rivalry and attempts to gain trade leverage with Akan societies shaped (and were shaped by) alliances and conflicts among coastal and inland polities themselves, and some sought direct trade relations through European sovereigns. The latter phenomenon was no more evident than when Komenda sent an ambassador to France to ask Louis XIV to direct traders toward their polity in the 1660s. French interest in Komenda in the 1660s, perhaps to attack nearby Dutch Elmina, was likely to establish a French commercial and military base on the Gold Coast, but this vision was largely unrealized even with repeated attempts from Komenda.

On 14 April 1672, two ambassadors from Komenda reached France but did not meet the king and were sent back to their home with presents, though the French were able to establish a short-lived post at Komenda in 1687.[51] The Dutch and the British fared no better, for the Dutch trading post at Akatakyi (port town of Komenda) in the 1670s and early 1680s was destroyed by Komenda in 1681 (but reestablished the next year), and the British post was burned in 1682 and subsequently abandoned in 1683 and 1687. These events forestalled the well-known Komenda wars in the last decade of the seventeenth century, a series of wars that reflects the multiple ways in which the British, Dutch, and (to a much lesser extent the) French shaped internal politics and in which Akan polities yielded to or refused such external hands, fought among themselves, and formed alliances with and without European encouragement.[52] On the one hand, we have cases such as the coastal Agona entering an alliance with the inland Akwamu and assisting them in their victory over Accra—a rival of Agona.[53] On the other hand, we have Fetu, wherein a victory over Abrem did not resolve its internal conflicts. When the Danes handed over the Frederiksborg castle to the English on account of increased debt, Fetu was divided into pro-Dutch and pro-Danish factions, and at least six different rulers held power between 1694 and 1715, notwithstanding a Dutch reciprocal military agreement with Fetu.[54]

As was the case with the Portuguese, the Dutch monopolized a rapidly expanding enterprise in enslaved persons to the Americas via a range of commercial goods produced in northwest Europe and acquired elsewhere. From the late fifteenth century to the mid-nineteenth century, the goods that Europeans traded from India, Europe, and the Americas penetrated African markets because the Guinea coast of West Africa apparently did not produce those items, the most important of which were cloth and metal goods.[55] The range of goods included practical, ostentatious, and poor-quality items in the form of cloth and clothing products, metal wares and non-metal containers, firearms, beads, tobacco, glassware, ceramics, foodstuffs, alcohol, and symbolic items meant to facilitate commerce.[56] Cloth was the primary and most consistent commodity traded by Europeans, and even cloth from West and West Central Africa was traded on the Gold Coast, including Manding cloth, which was exchanged for salt, foodstuff and other commodities from north of the forest. There was also a demand on the Gold Coast for Bénin cloth and *akori* beads from what is now southern Nigeria, linking the Gold Coast to the so-called Slave Coast and the Niger delta.[57] In terms of metals, manilas (copper bracelets) were an enduring commodity and functioned as ornament, currency, and a source metal for smiths. On the Gold Coast, however, manilas were never used as currency.[58] Those on the Gold Coast tended to use gold and gold dust as currency, but by the seventeenth century gold was being used as a European trade good with Akan societies, who tended to keep their gold.

By the early seventeenth century, English commercial agents were beginning to reexplore the Gold Coast, and although Samuel Purchas's publications of the period offer no English account of this region, it is clear that the British had interrupted a Dutch monopoly on the Gold Coast between securing a base at Kormantin in 1631 and then Cape Coast Castle in 1663.[59] In this context and with the entry of the British as rivals to other Europeans on the Gold Coast, Paul Hair asserts that sixteenth-century Anglo-African contact consisted largely of nonslave trading and argues that, although the English were aware of slave trading and John Hawkins's voyages, "their trade in Africa" did not involve "dealing in slaves before the 1640s."[60] In the mid-sixteenth century, four to five Africans from the Gold Coast were brought to England, where they were taught English and then returned to act as interpreters, but it is unclear whether they were captured, went to England on their own violation, or were the male offspring of local leaders sent to that country. However, the British did bring back "certeyne blacke slaves" from the coast in the 1550s, and these "slaves" were probably the four to five Africans since some of them eventually acted as intermediaries between the British and the Africans.

Generally, British contact with a local ruler was made before trade began, and the latter was often described as willing to negotiate on terms of trade, such as the meeting with *ɔhene* Kwabena Abaan on the Gold Coast. But this did not mean trading was neither contentious nor filled with perils borne of the kind of tactics employed by Diogo de Azambuja and his encounter with Caramansa (Kwamena Ansa?) of Edina. In 1558, "the English set fire to two Gold Coast villages which under Portuguese pressure had rejected trading and had used force against the traders."[61] The British attempted slave raids of villages but failed early due to local resistance, which killed several English men. The British then sided with African Portuguese merchants as a means to satisfy commercial interests and also acted as mercenaries for African rulers during a local civil war to procure enslavable peoples. Further insight into the nature of interactions between the British and the Africans on the Gold Coast is embedded in Robert Baker's narrative and reflective poem.[62] The poem describes two British voyages to two unstated points on the coast of Guinea, including the Gold Coast, made in the early 1560s, while Baker was a commercial agent driven—like many of his contemporaries—by economic motivations.[63] The events described by Baker show the Africans as contemptuous and "slaves"; though he was hostile and disrespectful, they were supportive and compassionate. Baker and others traded with the Africans ("blacke burnt men") "with weights to poise their golde so fine, yea speaking euery word in Portuguesse right well" on the Gold Coast.[64] Shipwrecked, Baker contemplated whether to surrender to the Portuguese at "Myne" (Mina) or to seek refuge among the Africans. According to Baker, he and his crew were greeted on shore with hospitality by "fiue hundred Negros," including the king and the "Kings chiefe sonne," who saved him and his men from drowning after a "waue ouerwhelms us and there in sea we lie." The Gold Coast Africans brought them onto land and fed them. Baker or his men convinced them that a British ship would soon come and trade would take place, but after the Africans realized no ships were coming, the English men were abandoned.[65] The compassion and humanity shown to Baker and his men and the fact that these Africans also wept with joy when a relative returned from a journey and in sorrow when someone passed are pieces of information that are often lost in accounts that largely focus on exoticism and commerce.

In the late sixteenth and early seventeenth century British trade with Guinea was regulated by royal letter patents, such as the one received by the Guinea Company, headquartered at Fort Kormantin, in 1631 and renewed in 1651. But the remainder of that 1651 lease was purchased by an East India Company (EIC) eager to profit from the Guinea trade.[66] The EIC exported ivory, gold, and enslaved peoples, and though EIC directors instructed company agents not to participate in the slave trade, these directors did order the shipment of such peoples and Africans at Fort Kormantin to EIC factories in India, St. Helena (an island in the South Atlantic), and Bantam (now western Java and southern Sumatra). The Africans at Fort Kormantin were reluctant to leave.[67] Textiles formed the bulk of exports from India and St. Helena to Guinea in quantity and value, and Indian calico was the most important textile sold by England to Africa in the seventeenth and eighteenth centuries. Local market preferences on the coast and in Europe, however, changed from year to year considering the nature of merchandise being sold by Dutch, Swedish, and Danish rivals to the British.[68] The EIC servants in Guinea promoted their own interests through illicit private trade as evidenced by reports of such activities to the company, and, in addition to these internal issues, conflicts such as the one around the occupation of Cape Coast Castle for its strategic trade and gold-acquiring position caused the company additional troubles.[69] In this conflict, Jan Claessen (John Cloice), a key African merchant and de facto ruler of Fetu, manipulated the European rivalry among the British, the Dutch, and the Swedes to his advantage, for these rivals sought to gain the friendship of African rulers or those with wealth and political sway. In fact, the combined real powers of Jan Hennequa and Jan Claessen might have surpassed those of the ruler of Fetu in the late 1640s and 1650s.[70] African traders and officials such as Hennequa and Claessen learned European languages such as Portuguese or Dutch and were astute enough to take advantage of European competition when the (perceived) odds were in their favor and often played one European nation against the other. In 1663 the Royal Adventurers eclipsed the EIC as they entered the Guinea trade with an explicit focus on participating in the international enslavement enterprise, for this trade was certainly lucrative. Between August 1663 and February 1664 the Royal Adventurers delivered 3,075 enslaved Africans to Barbados—a primary sugar-producing colony in the British Caribbean and one of several destinations of captive Akan persons—and the emptied vessel carried sugar and plantation goods back to England.[71]

Noting the engagement of the British and other Europeans in the Guinea trade, the entry of the Brandenburgs of Germany into the West African trade of the seventeenth century occurred on account of Friedrich Wilhelm's interest in overseas trade and his appointment of Benjamin Raule, a Dutch merchant, as director general of the Brandenburg navy. Raule proposed Brandenburg involvement in the "Guinea trade" to Friedrich Wilhelm, and, after two attempts, he persuaded Wilhelm but at Raule's "own cost and risk, and [agreed] that His Highness the Elector [Friedrich Wilhelm was] playing no further part beyond providing the necessary license and twenty men, ten for each ship."[72] The two ship were instructed by Wilhelm to "sail to the coast of Guinea and Angola, to buy gold, ivory, grain [malaguetta pepper], slaves and... also half a dozen young slaves aged between fourteen and sixteen, handsome and well-built, to send them to Our court."[73] The Dutch captured the first of the two ships near Assinie—a trade nexus for the Portuguese between the coast and the gold and ivory of the interior in the late sixteenth century, though little of its early history is known due to its sparse population and lack of navigable waterways. The second vessel landed between Cape Three Points and Dutch-controlled Axim and concluded a provisional treaty with "three caboceers" for "an approximate site for erecting a fortification" a year before the Brandenburg African Company was founded in 1682.[74] Such treaties were usually drawn up by Europeans and presented to Africans to sign.

A Brandenburg presence had been established on the Gold Coast in the late seventeenth century, but the Brandenburgs were seen as rivals to rather than replacements of the Dutch. The Brandenburg fort of Gross Friedrichsburg at Pokesu, slightly different from the initial site of 1681, was built in 1683 on top of a hill in front a marshy plain and largely in the midst of a rainforest and swamps. The Akan peoples of the area cultivated maize, yams, and rice and engaged in fishing. In 1684 an additional trading post was established at Akwida (or Akoda), some 7.5 miles southeast of Pokesu, and another post at Takoradi, which lay some 12.5 miles east of Akwida.[75] Takoradi, the principal Ahanta port, possessed a bay and access to large canoes, while Akwida was a small peninsula in a bay. Gold and to a lesser extent ivory were primary commodities on the western Gold Coast ("upper coast" to the Dutch), and gold was the more important of the two. Since the Gold Coast was a highly competitive region for enslaved persons—contextualized by a temporary drop in enslaved persons and declining gold production in the 1690s—along a coast littered with almost fifty European trading posts and forts, the Brandenburgs turned to Ouidah, Calabar, Aného ("Little Popo"), and "Great Popo" on the Slave Coast (Bight of Bénin) for enslaved cargo in the late seventeenth century.[76]

The Caribbean holding of St. Thomas became the Brandenburg base and entry point for enslaved persons through a Danish treaty signed in 1685 for a thirty-year license that permitted the Brandenburg African Company to import such persons and reexport them to other islands. The treaty expired in 1716 and was not renewed, perhaps due to Brandenburg's lack of a strong navy in the face of European competitors who had greater naval power, internal and financial issues of the Brandenburg African Company, and the high mortality on Danish ships, which benefited Brandenburg ships in the Danish Caribbean. In 1711 the Dutch joined their British trading rival, seemingly having suppressed their differences, and fought against John Konny (Jan Conny), local African leader and merchant of Komenda, over the seizure of Gross Friedrichsburg and trade on the western Gold Coast. However, Konny's well-armed and disciplined force of nine hundred defeated the combined Dutch and British forces.[77] As a result, Konny is remembered as a defender of Brandenburg interests against competing British and Dutch forces, though he actually pursued his own interests, which involved indigenous conceptions of land tenure and coastal politics.[78] By 1720 Friedrich Wilhelm III (or Friedrich Wilhelm I of Prussia) received final payments from the Dutch and relinquished his claims to Gross Friedrichsburg, Takrama, and Akwida.[79]

As the trade in gold and enslaved persons intensified during the mid-seventeenth century, Accra remained a key but contested Gã terminus, for the Gã were notionally ruled by the Akan polities of Akwamu, Akyem, and Asante between 1681 and 1750, thus reinforcing their Akanization.[80] By 1702, Akwamu had come to control many of the ports and thus a substantial amount of coastal trade from the eastern Gold Coast to Ouidah. After Akwamuhene Ansa Sasraku's death around 1688 or 1689, Basua (Bansiar) and Ado, Sasraku's sons, assumed the leadership of a shared yet divergently led Akwamu in that Basua sought to focus on consolidation, while Ado, the younger of the two, followed in his father's footsteps and sought continued expansion.[81] When Basua died in 1669, Ado assumed full leadership of Akwamu. However, it was not during Ado's reign but during that of his successor, Akwonno, that Akwamu reached its full extent in 1710 with its farthest northern extension to Kwahu and its eastern extension in Ouidah, though Dahomey came to exercise control over Ouidah a quarter-century later. Akwamu's quest for empire from Kwahu in the north, Akyem in the west, Ouidah in the east, and to the coast came through a political-military union of contiguous polities and settlements under its leadership. Osei Tutu and ɔkɔmfoɔ Anokye used this political-military organizational model to forge the Asanteman (Asante nation) centered at Kwaman (Kumase), and a two-hundred-year-old Akwamu-Asante alliance remained intact until Akwamu became part of the Gold Coast colony in 1888.[82] The presence and aggression of the forest polity of Akyem to the west and the military strength of the coastal Fante to the southwest (second only to that of Akwamu) prompted Akwamu to move its capital to the east at least twice. The Akyem factor was omnipresent among the Akwamu even after the former defeated the latter in 1730. The combined forces of Akyem Abuakwa and Bosome overpowered Akwamu in 1730, and this victory was reminiscent of their 1717 victory over Asante, which included the death of Osei Tutu, the cofounder of Asanteman.[83] Akwamu was able to develop a friendship based on mutual interests with the Fante from the second half of the seventeenth century until 1730, but even such an alliance was not able to forestall a convincing Akwamu defeat by Akyem. After its defeat by Akyem in 1730 and the revolt of the tributary polity and provinces that year and the year before, Akwamu consolidated the remainder of its polity on the eastern bank of the Volta River. Its political and military prowess of old, like its previous empire, could not be resurrected, though some of its peoples who had been exported to the Danish Caribbean attempted to do just that.[84]

On the coast, the Fante were able to secure firearms and ammunition in pursuit of regional conquest and control of trade routes in the seventeenth century. In the eighteenth century, the Fante became a key trade factor between the coast and Asante and its hinterlands—since the Fante economy was based largely on the sale of enslaved persons to coastally based Europeans but procured from Asante and its hinterlands—during its transformation from disparate and loosely organized societies into a centralized, politico-economic unit. In the mid-eighteenth century, Thomas Melvil at Cape Coast Castle referred to the "Fantee nation" as an "avaricious unruly people" whose main ɔbosom, "Bura Burum [Borbor] Weiga," provided "Oracles and Govern's that otherways licensious [sic] People" but sought "the God's assistance" to facilitate British trade interests.[85] The role of this ɔbosom (Weiga or Wergan), located at the sacred grove of Nananom Mpow, is significant, for, at least by 1750, Weiga united the informally organized Fante groups into a sort of "federal Union," wrote Melvil, "founded on Manners, Customs, & religion, for they are under the same Subjection to the Father (or God) of Fantee as the Western Fantees are."[86] Mankessem was the base of the federal assembly of Fante settlements, wherein elected "braffoes" were agents and servitors of the authority represented at Mankessem, as well as the Nananom Mpow ancestral shrine and ɔbosom (Weiga) of the Borbor Fante, who came from Takyiman.

The braffo (ɔbrafoɔ) at Mankessem was a military leader who served the ɔbosomfoɔ for the Nananom Mpow ɔbosom, which rose to political prominence in the 1740s. The process of forging a centralized politico-economic unit among the Fante was internally shaped by the cultural and political role of the ɔbosom at Nananom Mpow and externally by rise of Asanteman and its efforts to control the passageways and ports of trade.[87] As production costs of firearms fell in the eighteenth century, sales rapidly increased, and African trade volume rose in that century perhaps due to the fact that European demand for African exports was stronger. In the eighteenth century, the Fante discontinued their policy of conquest and sought to secure firearms for trade and defense of their control of trade routes west of Accra since Asante controlled those to the east and north of the Fante. The Fante then assumed a greater role as middlemen for and consumers of enslaved persons, gold, and European trade goods between Asante and European parties, while pursuing an internal policy of not enslaving their own "full citizens" unless for crimes or debt.[88] As a result, the Fante did not suffer from depopulation, as did other West African societies ravaged by the international enslavement enterprise, and possibly increased its population through domestic forms of unfree labor.

THE ASANTEMAN ("ASANTE NATION") FACTOR

In the first decade of the eighteenth century, Fante and Asante traders dominated much of the trade to and from the coast earlier conducted by the Akani, whose caravan traffic had lapsed and with whom the Dutch at Elmina had hoped trade would continue. The Dutch often referred to gold traders of Akani origin or not as *akannisten* (i.e., professional Akan). The Dutch came to the Gold Coast in the late sixteenth century in the latter stages of a supposed and emergent Asante agrarian order, as argued by Ivor Wilks and repeated by others, that occurred in the fifteenth and sixteenth centuries, wherein successful agriculture was established by clearing the forest with enslaved labor imported from the north (through the Juula) and the south (through the Portuguese) in exchange for Akan gold, which satisfied the demands of an equally emergent global economy.[89] According to Larry

Yarak, a former student of Wilks, "It may be concluded then that the clearance of the forest and the establishment of a viable system of agriculture, the importation of slaves and their assimilation into the matriclan form of social organization, and the emergence of small-scale ɔbirɛmpɔn-dominated polities, were in fact all part of a single process which can be dated to the fifteenth and sixteenth centuries."[90] Such a conclusion, however, is misplaced. Our discussion in chapter 2 argues that such processes began much earlier in and around Kumase and the data does not exist to support Wilks's model, and thus that "standard" narrative about Akan sociopolitical order in the southern forest requires an alternative scenario and a clear distinction between Asante people, Asante the "empire state" (Asanteman), and Akan sociocultural formation.

The early history of Kwaman (kwae, forest; ɔman, nation, cultural group), which later became the Asanteman capital of Kumase, lacks explication by way of archeological and scribal sources, though oral accounts provide some clues that can lead to a greater apprehension of its nascent developments. Several Asante stool histories speak of the role of key hunters such as Adu Nyame Bofuo (bɔfoɔ, hunter) and Nana Baah Kumah of the Oyoko abusua (family, clan), but little can be gleamed beyond these names. Recall our discussion on hunters and their omnipresent roles in the founding and formation of Akan social orders; in that context, it is quite instructive that Kwaman has the settlement-marking suffix -man (nation) and that one of its early settlers carried the name bɔfoɔ (hunter). That "the Kumase area had a long occupation of human settlement" is well supported by the archeological record (as detailed in chapter 2).[91] On the issue of human settlement, Akwasi Boaten argues, "gathering was the most important economic activity" in the eighteenth century among an Asante people who were once "mainly hunters" but whose (earlier) subsistence farming was tempered by the tools they used, the sacredness of several kinds of large trees, and low population growth, perhaps on account of malaria and the rigors of forest settlement.[92] The early history of what would become the Asanteman capital, which awaits more extensive research, should prompt us to distinguish rather than conflate proto-Asante society with Asanteman of the eighteenth and nineteenth centuries.

Often, particularly for those who study the Asante, the history of Asante is also inappropriately conflated with the Akan in general; narratives of the general and the specific—with overlap and distinct origins and trajectories— are presented in interchangeable terms, when, in fact, Asante history and practices are not an unproblematic synonym for Akan counterparts. In what became the Asante polity of the early eighteenth century, the most powerful ɔbirɛmpɔn consolidated chiefdoms and small-scale states into a larger and unified political unit, Asanteman, over which the ɔbirɛmpɔn of Kumase presided as Asantehene and was sanctified by the spiritually ordained *Sika Dwa Kofi* ("Golden Stool"), to which the divisions (*aman*) of Asanteman gave their political allegiance.[93] The specific manner and meaning of these developments in the formative process of Asanteman did not occur in any other Akan society; there are no parallels among the Bono on the forest fringe, Dɛnkyira to the west of Asante, Akwamu and Akyem to the east, or the coastal Fante. This is not to say that proto-Asante experiences in cultural and political development were wholly unique; the matter is precisely how Asanteman gave particular shape to extant and preexisting Akan structures and cultural norms. Thus, for example, national oaths, stools, festivals, and the *abosom* were of some antiquity, but the "[n]ew national oaths and festivals [of Asanteman] centered on the supremacy and glorification of the Asantehene's ancestors, and Akan deities [*abosom*] symbolized the creation of the novel political order."[94]

In Asante thought, existence in temporal life continued in the spiritual—as the former paralleled or was extended into the latter—and the Asantehene remained an Asantehene in life and in temporal death.[95] In addition, the annual *odwira* festival (held nationally and locally), *adae* ceremonies (held twice every forty-two days), *kra da* (soul day) and *ntorɔ* observances with dietary restrictions, and *afahye* (festivals) for the *abosom*—with shrine officials that supplemented their spiritual work by small-scale trade and farming—all affirmed the culture of the social-political order and its leadership. Indeed, these occasions were important for all Asante and, thematically, for most Akan. In the process of empire building for Asanteman, warfare became the means of accumulating wealth, subduing and consolidating peoples (rather than polities) to the south and north of Asante—key sources of enslaved labor—and rearranging existing obligations within conquered territories so that those subjects not only gave their political allegiance but also served Asanteman through labor, the production of commodities, and the fulfillment of military and tax obligations. Those obligations were linked to specific "stools" (as symbols of political authority and custodianship of land), and a growing number of stool holders for such offices required labor, the use of land, and trade opportunities from which to generate revenue for wealthy and "royal" individuals (see figure 3.2). The Asante trade in people and products remained unbroken from the seventeenth century into the late nineteenth century, when gold, enslaved persons, kola (after 1820), and rubber (of the late 1880s) were key commodities.[96] In the latter part of the eighteenth century, Akan and Asante reluctance to export gold and the intense competition for "high-quality" captive persons led to increases in the cost of such persons and reversed the flow of the gold trade by their demands for gold in most barter transactions for enslaved persons.[97]

Plantations surrounded Kumase, and enslaved persons of Kumase officials worked on them and provided the necessary vegetables, fruits, and

Figure 3.2. Engraving of Asante "Prince Adoom" and his son, ca. 1820. Adoom (or Adom) was likely an *ɔdehyeɛ* (member of the ruling family or clan) and an individual of some social standing in terms of wealth and authority and by way of the European monarchal notion of "prince." William Hutton, *A Voyage to Africa*, Yale Center for British Art, Paul Mellon Collection.

foodstuffs. For the most part, those serving the same stool lived in the same ward and thus were not organized by clans; prominent persons, however, lived in separate areas. Kumase also had a "zongo" section close to the main market area (*dwaberem*), which included a trading center for imported and locally made goods and foods. Because markets in outlying *aman* (divisions of Asanteman) were held on specific days, one would move—as trader or buyer—to different markets on different days. The seventy-seven wards (*abron*) of Kumase (similar to Bono-Manso), which were separated by twenty-seven streets, provided the spatial and architectural setting where people lived, various interest groups operated, political changes related to authority and wealth occurred, and maneuvers along traditional and kinship lines were carried out. However, every Asante belonged to a village—the fundamental politico-economic unit—headed by an *odekuro* (village head). Administratively, the Kumase division of Asanteman was organized into nine (and, by the nineteenth century, ten) units populated by key officeholders and headed by one such officeholder, who was indicated by the suffix *-hene* (e.g., *krontihene*). The ten administrative-military units were and are the Kronti, Akwamu, Nifa, Benkum, Adonten, Kyidom, Oyoko, Gyaase, Ankobea, and Manwere. Into the eighteenth century, the Asante polity was managed through these units, in addition to councils presided over by the Asantehene, and, at the end that century, "Greater Asante" came to include territories in what are now northern Ghana, western Togo, eastern Ivory Coast, and the Atlantic seaboard, connected to Kumase by four southerly and four northerly "great roads."

Asante established its hegemony in the northern region in a period that witnessed the emergence of a territorially expansionist polity, and, under this political aim, Asante officeholders depended on externally generated rather than internally produced surplus through commoners and free producers in metropolitan Asante. Expanding trade was subordinated to the needs or interests of Kumase and *amanto* (divisional officeholders), and externally generated surplus came through militarily prowess in that "Asante territorial expansion was predicated upon the military revolution," which involved new forms of military organization, modes of conducting wars, a mass rather than an elitist army, and the use of muskets "as the main arm."[98] The urbanization of crafts prior to the seventeenth century became ruralized, "and the unity of craft and agricultural production at the village level was established," which, along with other transformations, allowed eighteenth-century communities of commoners to accumulate the surplus they produced and have greater control over the conditions under which they were governed.[99] In the eighteenth and nineteenth centuries, unfree laborers acquired through war or trade were incorporated into commoner families as *odonkɔ* (pl. *nnɔnkofoɔ*; i.e., persons of northern origin characterized by facial scarification) and contributed to the demographic and economic expansion of the agrarian village system in Asante and beyond. However, unfree labor in the sixteenth and seventeenth centuries was used less in gold production and more in food-crop production, including land clearance, since such persons were imported and gold was the principal overseas export commodity, while in the eighteenth and nineteenth centuries gold was imported, and unfree laborers were the main export.

Asante relations with the Dutch remained constant through the tenure of the Dutch and the Danish on the coast and Asante as a sovereign entity. Thematically, the Dutch, like other Europeans, strategically made, ended, and reestablished alliances with shifting coastal and inland friends and enemies alike, once the opportunity presented itself. Dutch interests shifted more intensely from the procurement of gold to enslaved persons in the eighteenth century as competition from other Europeans on the Gold Coast increased in the context of a heightened international enslavement enterprise, a declining though persistent gold trade, and the establishment of relations with Asante—a major source of gold and enslavable peoples. After the defeat of Dɛnkyira, with whom the Dutch had traded and are likely to have provided arms in its conflict with Asante, the Dutch immediately dispatched David van Nyendael to Kumase to congratulate "Asjante Caboceer Zaij" (Osei Tutu), establish trade relations, and request that Asante reestablish peaceful trade conditions from the interior, particularly against Twifoɔ and Adom, to the Dutch ports.[100] Van Nyendael was instructed to present a list of goods awaiting prospective traders on the coast and to keep a journal "so that when the time comes we may use it as a guide."[101]

Unfortunately, Nyendael died before he could submit a report on his mission, but it initiated a Dutch Asante relationship that ended when the Dutch left the coast and bequeathed their possessions to the British in 1872. The Dutch enterprise on the Gold Coast, however, had shown signs of decline much earlier in the eighteenth century, when the Dutch decided to abandon a number of their forts, and certainly in the nineteenth century due to internal and external issues.[102] The Dutch West India Company (WIC) lost its trade monopoly in 1735, and, once the WIC went bankrupt and was liquidated in 1791, the Dutch republic assumed administration of WIC forts. The management of these forts was left to various bodies formed and dissolved between 1795 and 1813, until the newly formed kingdom of Netherlands (in 1813) placed those responsibilities under a ministry for colonial affairs.[103] Dutch and British talks of abandoning Dutch possessions on the coast began as early as 1824, though the Dutch had internally pondered the situation since 1819, perhaps influenced by Dutch abolition of the slave trade as a condition of British diplomatic recognition of the new kingdom of Netherlands, following Britain's lead. In the years between those discussions and the Dutch relinquishing of its possessions to Britain, several Dutch schemes involving the use of its forts were attempted. Dutch attempts at gold mining at the Ahanta village of Dabokrom failed in 1849, and efforts of Dutch governor Daendels to establish plantation agriculture near Dutch forts and export cotton grown in Asante in the early nineteenth century also failed.[104] Finally, a similar outcome resulted when the Dutch East Indies army attempted to recruit coastal and Asante "volunteers," who turned out to be enslaved persons rather than "volunteers," as some were given money by the Dutch to pay for their freedom into Dutch enlistment. Pawns (dependant persons because of debt) and others were secured in that manner, but free Africans refused to volunteer, and even French and British forces found it difficult to secure African volunteers for their respective colonial armies.[105] The Dutch decision to cede its possessions to Britain was influenced by all of these factors, in addition to resistance from Wassa, Dixcove, and Komenda to Dutch authority and the costs thereof.

The Danish experience on the Gold Coast lasted almost two centuries (ca. 1658–1850) until the Danish government, like the Dutch, handed over its possessions to the British. Danish sources provide relevant information on every year of the eighteenth century up until 1778; between the 1770s and the 1780s, Danish slaving exports reached their peak. Thereafter, Danish sources shift their concerns to disputes between Dutch and Danish interests on the Gold Coast. Before 1730, these sources focused primarily on Akwamu (Aquamboe) and their main rivals, the Akyem, in addition to smaller polities on the coast such as the Gã settlements.[106] The Danes had close contact with Akwamu as a political and trading necessity, and at the beginning of the eighteenth century Akwamu were the main suppliers of enslaved persons to the Danes, who concentrated on them as the main export commodity and soon became concerned about the gold trade from Akyem and the slave trade from Akwamu due to wars between the two. In 1725 Akwamuhene Akwonno (Aquando) died, and his death signaled, according to Danish sources, a decline of Akwamu. Akwonno's successor, Akwamuhene Ansa Kwao (Ensangquau), had to keep a close watch on Akyem after the death of Akyemhene Ofori (Offorie) and forestall immediate responses from coastal villages under Akyem rule.[107] These coastal villages noticed the internal challenges of Akwamu and their conflict with Akyem and formed an alliance. During the Akwamu wars with Akyem, the Danes replaced the Dutch in Ada, which the Dutch had settled in 1730. After convincingly defeating Akwamu in 1730, Akyem secured a position between them and the coastal ports of Accra, where the Dutch, British, and Danes were stationed. After 1730 the Danes introduced guns and shifted their concern to Akyem and the possibility that Asante might conquer that polity.[108] After its defeat of Akwamu, Akyem remained in fear of an Asante attack as is evident in its request for "Danish guns" and its engagement of the coastal Fante on friendly terms. However, some "caboceers" (officials) in Akyem sided with the Fante, and some with Asante, culminating in a 1738 battle between Akyem and Fante; both Akyem and Fante were fearful of an eminent Asante attack.

The Asante defeated the Akyem in 1742, and in May of that year, the Asante army arrived on the coast as Danish reporting of Asante took center stage. The Danish records first mention an Asante "king" in July 1743; the Danes called him "Oppocu" (i.e., Asantehene Opoku Ware) and reported that he died seven years later. It appears that Opoku Ware's attack on polities south of Asante, especially the coastal villages, who had formed an alliance in anticipation of an Asante assault, was aborted for unspecified reasons; Danish sources indicate he went northward instead. The alliance of coastal states closed off routes to the coast in the southeast and then in the southwest after fruitless attempts by Opoku Ware to break the alliance formed by Fante, Akyem, Wassa, and Dɛnkyira. Dɛnkyira, prior to its defeat by Asante, had controlled Wassa, Twifoɔ, Sefwi (Great Inkasa), Assin (southern part of Akani), and the gold-endowed Aowin.[109] However, the Asante, in defiance of the alliance, continued to trade east of Tema, just west of Ada on the Volta River, and at Ningo—an important trading center in gold and enslaved persons in the eighteenth century. The Danes' fears of a peace between Asante and the anti-Asante alliance was realized, not so much because of what was rumored to be peace talks between Asante and Akyem but because the Fante had taken Asante trade away from the Danish forts. Paradoxically, neither conflict nor peace between Akan polities benefited Danish trade interests.[110]

The fierce rivalry between the Danes, the Dutch, and other European forces on the coast included the exploitation of indigenous political animosity for their own interest, that is, competition for markets and trade partnerships based on mutual advantages. Where such obligations remained unsatisfied, as in the case of Ada and the Danish-Dutch conflict, a number of African groups sought better offers and often exploited European rivalry in doing so.[111] Ada leader (or official) Tetteh Djabaku seized an opportunity to strengthen Ada and his own economic and political position and therefore broke the Danish trade monopoly in taking advantage of Danish-Dutch rivalry by aligning himself with the Dutch-Accra connection. Djabaku stuck to this policy until February 1777, when he reverted to the Danish due to internal and external pressure.[112] As competition intensified between European nations on the coast, so did European involvement in local politics through diplomatic maneuvering, as well as instigating and exacerbating real or imagined local rivalry among the indigenous polities on the coast.

That said, several eighteenth-century observers stationed at the Christiansborg fort at Osu in Accra left us accounts that focus less on politics and more on cultural dimensions, thus providing some (external) insights into Akan culture and society. The minister Johannes Rask (1708–1713), the merchant L. F. Rømer (1739–1749), the medical doctor and botanist P. E. Isert (1783–1786), and the minister H. C. Monrad (1805–1809) were all primarily based at Christiansborg and shared similar observations on the Gold Coast separated by an average of twenty-six years among all four.[113] Rask, like Lutheran minister Johann Müller, recorded the lack of interest in a Christian God among the Akan, and while Rømer and Isert understood that these Africans believed in a "Supreme God with lesser gods," Isert was very suspicious of the motives and practice of the ɔkɔmfoɔ. Rømer, though a secular trader, made religious interpretations that are similar to those by the two ministers and faulted the Africans' "evil nature" and hence provided the rationale for a civilizing and Christianizing mission.

All of these observers situated in one area over a period of time consistently recorded the rapid recovery and strength of Akan women after childbirth, and Monrad noted the disgrace women suffered for being infertile. In addition, a woman would be denied burial if she died in childbirth before the child was born. Isert, on the other hand, observed that most of the crimes were concerned with debt or adultery, rarely robbery or murder.[114] Monrad noted that married couples did not show public affection but stated that happiness, love, and friendship existed among them and among ordinary peoples; interestingly, he wrote that the "blacks" spoke of a "happier time before the arrival of the Europeans." Rask, as did Isert, noted their aptitude for learning several languages quickly, found the people healthy and long lived, and admired their ability to heal and treat illness by their own methods, their generosity with food and drink, and their ability to meet and to allot land without conflict. These observations, in spite of their bias, allow us a window into the humanity of Africans on the Gold Coast and the forest interior. That humanity, however, was not expressed without conflict. Warfare as a sign of and a way to resolve conflict occurred in the context of considerable diplomacy and the very trade contestation that brought many captive Akan and "Akanized persons" to the Americas.

WARFARE, FIREARMS, AND THE ENSLAVEMENT ENTERPRISE

In the eighteenth century, the tropical rainforest covering the southern parts of the Gold Coast merged into its freshwater, swamps, and coastal sand dunes, and the Accra grassland extended south to a coastal strip. Certainly, the undergrowth and restricted visibility of the forest circumscribed movement and warfare. This rainforest and its environs provided the setting for Akan settlements on the coast and in the hinterland, which engaged in considerable diplomatic activity by way of couriers and representatives who were sent on diplomatic missions to other Gold Coast settlements and West African polities.[115] These activities occurred during a period of the increased scale and intensity of warfare, the militarization of Akan societies, and the equally heightened scale of the rapacious international enslavement enterprise in African peoples. The Akan in general and the Asante in particular were exemplary in their respect for the use of diplomacy, though there were several instances in the eighteenth and nineteenth centuries in which Asante complained of the ill treatment of its ambassadors by the Fante. Trade rivalries were the principal source of hostility between the Asante and Fante and in terms of intra-Fante conflicts.[116] The Asante-Fante clash was as much diplomatic as it was military, and Asante used diplomacy, in a largely consistent manner, as an alternative to war.[117] Nineteenth-century Asante used diplomatic communication with letters written in Dutch to Elmina, English to Cape Coast, Danish to Christiansborg, and Arabic to the northern areas. However, Asante exemplariness should not be misconstrued as exclusiveness, for Asante's former overlord, Dɛnkyira, for instance, had appointed and sent a coastal trade representative named Ampim to the British at Cape Coast; on Ampim's death in 1698, the British sent gifts to the Dɛnkyirahene.

Beyond the Akan-European exchange of gifts and the envoys' frequent visits to European trading headquarters (and occasionally to Europe), gifts were also exchanged among West African polities, as in the case of Asante and Wagadugu. Since gifts were meant to facilitate trade and the plethora of European nations on the coast sought to fulfill commercial interests, it is not difficult to imagine that the aims of war were generally trade, wealth, territorial expansion, and the desire for power over others. As such, strategies and tactics of warfare mirrored those aims through long-term planning and deliberation, preparation in diplomatic, political, and military terms, and careful choice of timing and place.[118] Up until the mid-nineteenth century, military activity appeared to have been confined to the dry season— November to March or December to April—on the coast and in the forest, and toward the end of the eighteenth century professional armies began to replace militia and became dependent upon expensive and externally supplied weapons and ammunition. Beyond guns and protective objects—such as the talismans provided by Muslims to the "pagan" armies of Gonja and Asante—convention or war protocol mitigated warfare. Those conventions, which imply concepts of honor and fair conduct in warfare, included the formal declaration of war, which did little for ambushes but gave parties time to prepare, deliberate, propose time and place, and send the women, children, and the elderly to safety.

In consideration of these intra-African conventions, war for Europeans who were principally interested in gold and enslaved persons—who were often used to procure gold—was both a facilitator and an inhibitor in the acquisition of either commodity. At the beginning of the dry season in November 1679, Dutch director general Abramsz wrote, "Slaves were very easy to get on the Gold Coast, because of war. In Arder [Allada], on the contrary, the slave trade was entirely stopped because of war."[119] Fourteen years later a conflict and potential war erupted between Twifoɔ and Komenda on account of trade with Europeans, and with regard to this the Dutch reasoned as follows: "Such a war would be to the great disadvantage of the trade, and if the passages were closed...we wouldn't make any money."[120] Calculating the damages and likely losses if war were to occur, Dutch officials provided the worth of the very merchandise that caused the conflict "in order to settle the difference." Finally, in the year Asante defeated Dɛnkyira, the Dutch director general Van Sevenhuysen noted, "At present the slave trade is in as bad a shape as the gold trade, although we thought that the present wars in the interior would rather promote the offer of slaves."[121] The year of the principal war was 1701, and that war involved Dɛnkyira and Asante, and an Asante victory dramatically shifted the balance of power in the forest interior, which lasted until the end of the nineteenth century.

Asante engaged in military campaigns throughout the eighteenth century, with concentrated periods in 1711–1723 and 1744–1749, an average of two years of warfare each decade except 1710–1720 and a sixteen-year period of no warfare (1781–1797). The highest numbers of Gold Coast captives—at an average close to 111,000—were exported in the first half of the eighteenth century (ca. 1721–1740), with less than half that average from 1741 to 1750.[122] Notice the lack of congruency between Asante periods of concentrated warfare and much of the first half of the eighteenth century and the fact that an average of 117,000 exported captives for the last four decades of that century coincides with relatively little Asante warfare between the 1760s and 1800. For the nineteenth century, Asante fought for a total of twenty years the first three decades, and, with the exception of the 1870s (when warfare claimed the entire decade), the remaining decades of the century averaged less than two years of warfare each. Here, two observations are significant. First, these campaigns were linked to trade fluctuations since gold and ivory trade required peaceful conditions (up until the early eighteenth century), but warfare facilitated (or inhibited) the availability of enslavable peoples, and, thus, the gold and slave trade were incompatible. Asante's omnipotent role in the international enslavement enterprise needs revision, however, and particularly in arguments that claim warfare as the common denominator for nonconsensual African exportation to the Americas. Second, according to these tabulations, a military campaign occurred every decade in both centuries, but there were intervals of up to eight and sixteen years without war or a warlike conflict. Several key instances in the eighteenth century should illustrate the interplay of Asante diplomacy and the (in)frequency of Asante military campaigns. In the eighteenth century, Asante maintained tribute-collecting residents in both Dagomba and neighboring polities, as well as trade representatives in Accra, Akuapem, and Cape Coast, while Gonja and Dagomba maintained representatives in Kumase as the *kunkuma*—an official of the Ya Na's court in Dagomba—who protected Asante interests in Dagomba. Around 1714 an Asante delegation settled a dispute between Twifoɔ and John Kabes, a prosperous merchant and leader of Komenda, and this was significant, for the "advent of Asante in coastal trade patterns after 1700 helped make Komenda a major trading point [on the western Gold Coast] and Kabe's middleman role was enhanced commensurately."[123] The Dutch reported that Asante army officers also settled disputes in the vicinity of Axim in a political rather than military manner in the early eighteenth century. Yet, the faces of diplomat, negotiator, and warrior were often worn almost simultaneously, and some were unreceptive to diplomatic means of resolution.

The Asante-Aowin war of 1715 began in September and concluded in an Asante victory in December, but its military campaign against Amanahia lasted from that year until 1721.[124] During that period, the Asante people were in conflict with officials from Akyem, while a band of Aowin and Wassa reportedly raided Kumase and seized booty; apparently, at least for Aowin, this raid was retaliation for its rather quick defeat. Parenthetically, some of the gold ornaments as a part of that booty might have found their way into a pirate ship, the *Whydah*, wrecked near Cape Cod, Massachusetts, since Akan or Asante gold pieces dated to 1717 were found in the wreckage.[125] Nevertheless, an Asante ambassador was pelted with stones for asking the Fante to withdraw their protection from Wassahene Ntsiful, who was exiled in Fante in 1726. Wassahene Ntsiful (ca. 1720–1752) was installed by Asante but rebelled against Asante authority in 1725, and in 1730 he evaded capture by an Asante army with Fante assistance. On both occasions, Asante expeditions sent to address the matter were less than fully successful.[126] In 1744 Ntsiful again revolted, enlisting the support of Twifoɔ (whom he had attacked and annexed earlier), a portion of Akyem, and the Fante, and formed an anti-Asante coalition for some twenty years in the interest of controlling and profiting from trade that passed through his area since Wassa had replaced Twifoɔ as a key point on the route to Dutch Elmina. The Elmina route—Elmina was one of the wealthiest and most populous towns—was used between 1744 and 1816 more for diplomatic than trade purposes since Asante preferred the longer, Accra route, which ended in importance at the end of the international enslavement enterprise on the Gold Coast. A year after three Asante officials were dispatched to the

Danish, Dutch, and English quarters of Accra, Asantehene Osei Kwame deployed ambassadors to the Wassahene to ask whether the Fante accepted gifts on the occasion of a ruler's death in 1777. Meanwhile, Asante pushed toward the sea with much vigor, and Asante access to firearms increased, with greater quantities of arms available on the coast.[127]

The Portuguese had armed Africans living near their forts in order to protect them against local hostility. Those in Elmina exchanged guns for gold with the Portuguese and became adept in their use well by the sixteenth century, though the Portuguese were prohibited from selling guns to Africans due to papal decree.[128] Firearms were imported around 1550 by primarily British and Dutch traders and were widely used on the Gold Coast by the end of the seventeenth century, when there was a direct correlation between heightened enslavement enterprising, increased intra-European competition, and greater quantities of firearms in the region. In the seventeenth century, the Dutch, British, Brandenburgs, and Danes began selling muskets, and by the mid-seventeenth century, musketeers emerged as both the principal military option and a specialized form of infantry, and Asante access to these arms on the coast remained a key issue until the early eighteenth century. For instance, Wassa ambassadors, on behalf of their ruler, succeeded in creating a league of coastal polities from Cape Apollonia to the Volta River in order to prevent gun supplies from reaching Asante in the early eighteenth century. Nonetheless, the Dutch soon thereafter became the major exporters of firearms, particularly flintlock muskets produced in Holland, which were paradoxically named "Dane guns," to the coast, and, in the mid-seventeenth century, it appears that both enslaved persons and gold were used to procure these arms.[129]

The Asante introduced guns into Dagomba perhaps in the late eighteenth or early nineteenth century, but an earlier date is likely since the Dagomba cavalry fought with musketeers secured from Asante in 1744 and 1745. Asante's invasion of Dagomba included the seizure of a number of Arabic texts that passed into the hands of the Danes at Christiansborg and reached Denmark, specifically the Royal Library in Copenhagen.[130] This Asante attack, which resulted in a treaty, compelled Dagomba to find new sources of captives and send two thousand prisoners annually to Kumase. In 1772 an Asante military campaign against Dagomba led to the capture of Ya Na, the Dagomba sovereign, who was ransomed for one thousand enslaved persons.

Beyond their obvious use for military purposes, firearms were also used for hunting, protection of crops, and firing salutes in a variety of ceremonial acts. Most of the gunpowder was imported, particularly from the Dutch and the Danes, and was always in demand but usually in times of war. Locally made gunpowder supplies, however, also existed among Gold Coast polities despite the shortage of sulfur.[131] After 1650 the Dutch reportedly sought to sell guns only to those with whom it had military and commercial agreements; the British sold to any interested party.

Political alignments among Africans and Europeans and between the two were flexible and provided few short- or long-term guarantees, and such relationships were never one sided. For the African part of the equation, Asante engaged in diplomacy first and continued to do so up until the last moment, just before military confrontation, and hence had no standing army. Asante went to war either to conquer neighboring peoples and polities in the eighteenth century or to suppress rebellions in the nineteenth century. Enslaved captives of war—of which more were required of northern provinces (paralleled by gold in the southern provinces)—were more political assets of Asanteman and individuals to be acquired and exchanged, and thus killing large numbers of the enemy would not accomplish this goal.[132] Enslaved captives had cash, labor, and tributary value, and European merchant-slavers knew that that value was transferable to kin, even after death, via their wills.[133]

On the topic of slavery and Akan society, many of the English observations come from Asante rather than other Akan societies and focus on Kumase and not the larger Asante union (Asanteman). In Asante, there were several categories of servile labor: *akoa* (subject), *domum* (captive), *odonkɔ* (foreigner, enslaved person of northern origins), *akyere* (slaves intended for sacrifice and often condemned criminals), and *awowa* (person pledged or given as surety for the debt of a kin).[134] All free citizens of Asante were *nkoa* or "subjects" obligated to an officeholder, but an *akoa* (pl. *nkoa*) was also an enslaved person of Akan origin, while the female *akoa* was called *afana*. The international enslavement enterprise fostered domestic enslavement, at least on the eighteenth- and nineteenth-century Gold Coast, and the meaning of people and land as sociopolitical entities up until the nineteenth century shifted to economic resources in the twentieth-century concomitant with a cash-crop economy and the meaning of *nkoa* as "subjects" irrespective of origins.[135] The varied categories of servile labor and status, as well as their changes in meaning over time, were and are often left undifferentiated under the rubric of "slave trade" and "internal African slavery" in West Africa. In the context of European competition for West African commerce, national trading companies of European origin were created and chartered by their respective nations and were given a monopoly over that nation's trade in West Africa. To these companies, "slaves" were human cargo irrespective of either their cultural origin or their importance in the society from which they came. Companies such as the Dutch West Indies Company or the Royal African Company of England emerged in a period that anticipated the height of the international enslavement enterprise in the late seventeenth century. Private ships of European countries, or "interlopers," circumvented the monopolies of national trading companies and therefore came to conduct a substantial part of the trade.

Recently it has been argued that a little more than 10 percent of the total population of Western Africa was exported as enslaved persons between 1680 and 1860.[136] This estimate raises several questions: ten percent of how many people per society and over what spatial and temporal range? How does one quantify the factors of disease, mortality in the quest for captives and after the capture, the scrupulousness of merchants who discarded or undercounted captives to evade fees levied upon them, or those Africans who used abortive measures or suicide over those centuries? In studies of the international enslavement enterprise, the research is largely driven by economic and statistical models that focus, almost religiously, on volume, prices, supply, cargo, expenses, profits, losses, competition, and partnership without much attention to the human dimension of the primary subjects of such studies—Africans. For instance, the parameterizing use of the term "slave trade" in the titles of books and articles on the subject connotes a business venture, whereas "holocaust," a concept descriptively applicable and indicative of a "crime against humanity," is almost exclusively often used in non-African contexts. Indeed, a marked preference for the former in academia suggests the precariousness of African life in African studies as an acute subtext.[137] Recent scholarship in African studies fails to fully excavate an African humanity embedded in the varied responses to enslavement and hegemony, as well as the ways in which those responses shaped the Americas and other places where exported Africans found themselves in appreciable numbers.[138]

The human responses of Africans to enslavement included attacks on forts, and at least sixty-one recorded attacks occurred on ships by land-based Africans in the seventeenth and eighteenth centuries. In addition, there are 388 recorded cases of enslaved African uprisings on board vessels close to African waters or en route to the Americas.[139] As Europeans fortified their barracoons and forts to protect themselves, Africans built fortresses, fortified towns, resettled in hard-to-find places, transformed habitats and the ways in which they occupied land, diverted rivers, and burned down European factories. In addition, these Africans also employed young men in militias to protect and defend communities; spiritual specialists; medicinal plants for camouflage, ritual cleansing, and protection; poisonous plants and thorny trees and bushes for general resistance, all of which led to rising costs, which in turn factored into the decline of the trade. Thus, enslaved and potentially enslaved peoples employed protective, offensive, and defensive strategies irrespective of their origins in West Africa, including resistance to capture and deportation, but such resistance was interlinked with accommodation to, participation in, and attacks against enslavement itself. Gold Coast societies, however, were less organized (compared to the Europeans) to specifically exploit the international enslavement enterprise. Varied European industries and port cities were created by "slave trading"; without those industries and port cities on the African side of the equation, the "slave trade" could not have been integral to African societies that functioned within a confluence of competition and commerce.[140] And so, the argument that some coastal and inland African rulers or individuals willingly, even enthusiastically, entered the international enslavement enterprise is fully compatible with the devastating effects of that enterprise on African socioeconomic structures and lives via European demands for African rather than European or white captives. Indeed, as the Gold Coast captive Ottobah Kobina Cugoano, once sold in Grenada and then in England, succinctly argued in his 1787 narrative, "if there were no buyers there would be no sellers."

It was reported that a ruler of Dahomey said to a British governor, "Are we to blame if we send our criminals to foreign lands? I was told you do the same."[141] Indeed, medieval Europeans bartered their own, and the idea of enslaving the British poor in the mid-eighteenth century—a notion concomitant with the height of the international enslavement enterprise—was passionately defended by key British intellectuals and businessmen. A number of European nations exiled and forced into labor their prisoners and minor politico-religious segments of their country, but they did not use a system of hereditary enslavement with its deculturing and racist pillars, nor did they enslave their European enemies or Jewish communities. The international enslavement enterprise that was built upon an African labor force was hereditary, and racism did exist in Europe prior to that enterprise, which may explain why Muslim enemies of Christian Europe were enslaved along with Africans, but this was not the case for domestic or political enemies in Europe or for religious foes such as European Jews.

Joseph Inikori argues that international trade was crucial to the key sectors of a rapidly industrializing British economy—the industrial revolution unfolded in northern England, while its agricultural revolution was a southern phenomenon—and to its success in trade with Africa and the Americas. Africans were central as both consumers and producers of goods involving large shares of the international trade. Britain shipped a substantial number of Africans to the Americas, and the growth of its shipping and related industries was largely dependent upon this trade. Without this international trade, there would hardly have been as much innovation and investment during the Industrial Revolution and the domestic technical transformations caused by overseas demands: Innovation required the selling of products produced on the demand side in order to generate innovation on the supply side.[142] Before industrialization and a considerable presence on the Gold Coast, the British tangled with the Dutch, who had enjoyed some success in the gold and then slave trade, after ousting the Portuguese from from the region and creating overseas colonies in need of African laborers.

4

"The Most Unruly"

The Akan in Danish and Dutch America

Yefiri aman firi aman na ɛyɛ ɔman
(We came from nations from nations and create a nation.)
—Akan proverb

Quabena (Kwabena), an enslaved person held by the Danish, escaped captivity sometime in 1703. He was not in the Danish Caribbean but rather on the Gold Coast. Quabena was seized and returned to the Danish fort of Christiansborg in the town of Osu (Accra) on 13 October 1703 by an Akwamu person who received "1 ounce of gold after the fashion of the country" for his services.[1] Why would Quabena and others like him think a successful escape and avoiding recapture and exportation to the Americas were possible? Those like Quabena might have miscalculated the predatory nature of the eighteenth-century Gold Coast—the height of the international enslavement enterprise to the Americas—or thought they, too, could receive freedom or a letter of freedom like Asameni, a Danish company "slave" who ran away to the Akwamu capital and who attempted to capture Fort Christiansborg in December 1687 but was later granted his "freedom letter" by Erick Tilleman.[2] A year after Asameni attempted to seize Christiansborg, the fort experienced a "slave riot," when a number of "chained slaves had broken off their irons and planned to overrun the fort, but they were unable to agree" with reportedly only six whites left to man the fort.[3] Of the fourteen freedom seekers, four "jumped over the walls and batteries...and ran off."

The fate of the other 10 remains unclear, but it might have been similar to that of others who revolted—such as the "Fantee Negro" who killed a Danish soldier in freeing other captives for export and leading a revolt but was "pinched with 3 hot tongs," broken on the wheel, and "his head and hand severed and placed on a stake, as a deterrent and example to others"—or Quabena, the runaway.[4] Asameni died on 20 October 1703, only thirteen days after Quabena's recapture and likely exportation to the Americas on board the *Christianus Quintus*, which left Christiansborg with 145 captives, not including 13 procured at Cape Coast and 150 from "Popo" (Hula

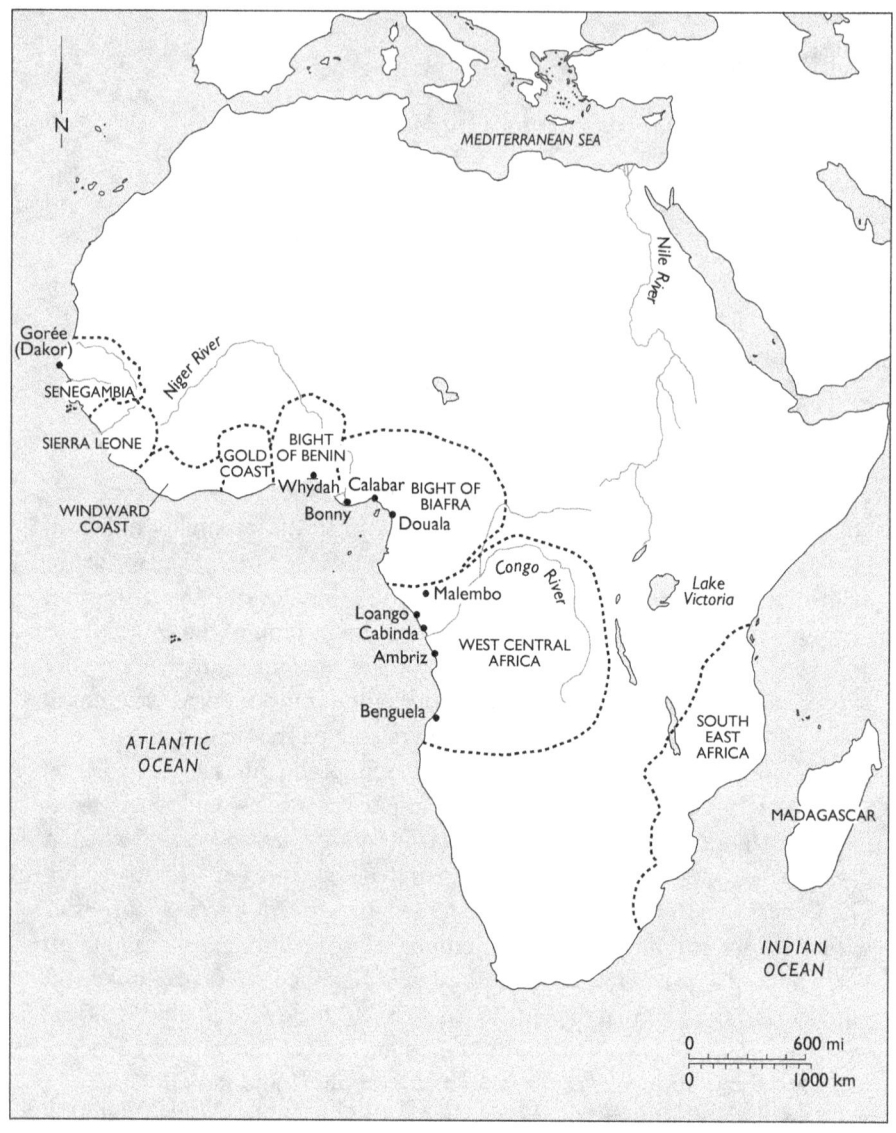

Map 3. Eight principal regions of the international enslavement enterprise during the eighteenth century. In these clusters of embarkation, key ports should not be confused with the actual places or peoples from which Africans left for the Americas; many traveled to those ports from great distances in the interior and across contemporary national borders. Reprinted by permission of the Omohundro Institute of Early American History and Culture from the *William and Mary Quarterly*.

[or Aného, if "Little Popo"]) or Ouidah on 28 October 1703.[5] The vessel on which Quabena was likely transported arrived in the Danish Caribbean holding of St. Thomas in May 1704 with 295 captives. For the Danish West India and Guinea Company, St. Thomas was not only its primary entrepôt for the international enslavement enterprise but also the site of an early seventeenth-century Maroon settlement largely occupied by "Amina" (Akan) freedom seekers in the forests and mountains of that island and St. John. Thematically, the Akan were thus Maroons, runaways, collaborators, forgers of culture, and seekers of polities of their own making on the Gold Coast and in the Americas, and Danish and affiliated vessels carried an aggregate total of at least 25,000 to the Danish Caribbean, or 5 percent of the total number of captives transported on the 2,128 recorded voyages from the Gold Coast to the Caribbean between 1696 and 1806. The Dutch Caribbean and Guiana more than doubled that percentage by a combined importation of 11.6 percent of those total voyages, accounting for at least 72,000 disembarked Africans between 1663 and 1807. These Danish and Dutch vessels, including their European partners, carried not only Akan peoples from one of the principal regions of the international enslavement enterprise but also a composite Akan culture to the Americas (see map 3).

AKAN POLITY AND CULTURE IN THE DANISH COLONIES

The islands of St. Thomas, St. John, and St. Croix constituted the Danish Caribbean colonies. The first Danish settlement on St. Thomas failed in 1665, but the Danish position of relative neutrality between competing French, British, and Dutch forces in Europe and the Americas allowed for other attempts at settlement by way of the Danish West India and Guinea Company in 1671. Two years later, the West India and Guinea Company assumed responsibility for trade on the Gold Coast and for the Danish forts (specifically, its Frederiksborg fort in Fetu and its Christiansborg fort at Osu in Accra) but came into only limited contact with Akan polities, granted the transfer of its headquarters to Osu in 1685 and the corresponding focus of its commerce on the eastern Gold Coast and across the Volta River into the Bight of Bénin. The Danish sources reflect these developments since, prior to 1685, they focused primarily on Fetu but thereafter concentrated on Akwamu and its subjugated coastal settlements, Akyem (after 1730), Asante, Fante, and those between Accra and the Volta River (or across the river into Popo and Ouidah) after 1742. These areas and their overwhelmingly Akan and Gã-Adangme peoples, including an Akan diaspora in the Bight of Bénin, formed the bulk of that gross but estimated sixty thousand captives disembarked at the entrepôt of St. Thomas, which became a plantation colony in the late 1680s. In 1675 St. John was colonized, and plantations were firmly established after 1715, whereas St. Croix, the larger and more fertile island, was acquired in 1733 for the development of sugar plantations. Most planters and merchants who invested in these plantations were of non-Danish origin, and while Danish was the official language, English, Dutch, and French were used in ordinary conversation. Throughout their tenure as Danish holdings, St. Thomas remained a major entrepôt engaged in the international enslavement enterprise, augmented by the slave-driven and sugar-producing economies of St. John and St. Croix, which were considered appendices to St. Thomas until St. Croix became the primary colony in the mid-eighteenth century.

The Danish West India and Guinea Company established plantations for the production of sugar, cotton, and other provisions by way of enslaved African labor supplied through its Gold Coast trading posts in West Africa and other sources. Environmental factors, rebellions against enslavement, and various laws intended to curtail those activities plagued the plantations of the Danish Caribbean. The Danish colonists imported one thousand or more Africans on an annual basis (see table 4.1), but the enslaved population remained relatively low compared to those of other sugar-producing colonies and because of high mortality and low fertility rates among the enslaved. Moreover, the plantation economies of St. John and St. Croix were especially prone to persistent revolt, even after emancipation in 1848, and its costs factored into the larger cost analysis of sustaining enslavement and the price of importing Africans. Resistance began on the African coast and continued after Africans entered the colonies and endured the public auction (abolished in the late 1830s), the branding, the march to the plantation, the "seasoning" process of acclaiming new arrivals, and regimented life in and around the plantation. The African population in all the Danish colonies included newly arrived Africans, Africans born or with long residence in the colony, those in Maroon settlements, "free" but landless Africans not from the colony, and those manumitted. This social configuration, ambiguously distinguished by levels of freedom and unfreedom, was a key source of white anxiety, given the imbalance between the number of enslaved Africans and the number of freed persons of African descent. The relentlessly severe "slave code" of 1733, promulgated by Governor Philip Gardelin, sought to address that imbalance, but it, including a series of natural calamities that resulted in famine and starvation, contributed to the St. John revolt of that year. The spring of 1733 included some of the driest weather ever. This was followed by a long and destructive hurricane season in the summer, which led to an increasing scarcity of provisions. As a result, more and more Africans marooned themselves in the forest interior to escape the famine. These Maroons avoided capture, and their presence created anxiety

Table 4.1. Select Danish Voyages from the Gold Coast (Christiansborg) to St. Thomas, 1698–1753

Year	Voyages
1698	The *Københavns Børs* embarked with 470 captives (148 men, 238 women, 55 boys, 24 girls, 5 infants) in the first half of the year and disembarked in September 1698 with 258 or 280 captives. A mutiny on board took the lives of many, though some jumped over board. Thirty-seven died upon landing, probably from an outbreak of scurvy.
1704	The *Christianus Quintus* embarked with 145 from Christiansborg, 13 from Cape Coast, and 150 from the Slave Coast on 28 October and disembarked with 295 or 333 in May 1704.
1705	The *Kronprinsen* embarked with 460 male and 382 female captives on 1 September after 16 had died of smallpox at the fort and 6 captives had run away. The ship blew up at Príncipe and never made it to the Caribbean.
1707	The *Christianus Quintus* embarked with 447 captives, including 211 from Aného and Ouidah, on 6 June and disembarked with 393 or 403 in May 1704.
1717	On 3 April, 171 captives embarked, and 153 disembarked in June.
1718	On 19 March, 216 captives embarked, and 164 disembarked in July.
1722	The *Håbet Galley* embarked with 206 captives in February and disembarked with 201 or 195 in April.
1724	In March, 405 captives (190 men, 117 women, 88 boys, 10 girls) embarked, and 351 captives disembarked in June. The *Christiansborg* embarked with 416 captives, not including 9 who died before the departure in March, and disembarked with 357 in June. The *Håbet Galley* embarked with 250–252 captives on 16 August and disembarked in October.
1726	On 28 September, 281 captives embarked, and 207 disembarked in February 1727.
1727	The *Christiansborg* embarked with 207 in February. The *Håbet Galley* embarked with 238 captives on 6 March and disembarked with 217 in May. The *Denunge Jomfrue* embarked with 51 captives on 11 September and disembarked with 32 in January 1728. A Zeeland vessel with 18 also embarked this year.
1729	The *Håbet Galley* embarked with 126 captives (63 men, 45 women, 14 boys, 4 girls) on 28 May and disembarked with 120 or 126 in July.
1733	The *Laarurg Galley* embarked with 443 captives (82 from Christiansborg) in February and disembarked with 242 or 244 in May. Reportedly, 199 died of a virulent form of dysentery.
1736	The *Jomfruen* embarked with 150 captives (55 men, 72 women, 18 boys, 5 girls) in April and disembarked with 108 in June.
1739	The *Laarurg Galley* embarked with 45 captives in November and disembarked with 44 in January 1740.

(continued)

Table 4.1. Continued

Year	Voyages
1742	The *Grevinden af Laurvigen* embarked with 53 captives in April and disembarked with 51 in June.
1744	The *Williamina Galley* embarked with 82 captives in March.
1746	The *Williamina Galley* embarked with 154 captives in August.
1753	In July, 271 captives embarked; the *Patientia* embarked with 275 on 30 July and, after an onboard mutiny between Cape Coast and Elmina, which resulted in a serious loss of life and cargo, disembarked in December with 146. The *Kronprinsens Ønske* embarked with 255 captives in October 1754.

Sources: Ole Justesen, ed., *Danish Sources for the History of Ghana, 1657–1754*, 2 vols. (Copenhagen: Royal Danish Academy of Sciences and Letters, 2005), vol. 1, 118, 181, 187, 199, 210–211, 249, 269, 313, 320, 327, 345, 357, 364, 370, 395, 470; vol. 2, 513, 559, 571, 593, 686, 918, 951; Per O. Hernæs, *Slaves, Danes, and African Coast Society* (Trondheim: University of Trondheim, 1995), 251–256; Waldemar Westergaard, *The Danish West Indies under Company Rule, 1671–1754* (New York: Macmillan, 1917), 146, 320–326.

and difficulty for the planters—but not enough to prepare them for what began around 3 o'clock in the morning on 23 November 1733.

The first and most successful revolt by enslaved peoples in the Danish colonies occurred on the island of St. John. In 1733 "Amina" or "Mina" (Akan) peoples from the Gold Coast revolted and ruled St. John for several months before French forces came to the aid of the Danish planters. The French hoped their intervention in the Americas and the sale of St. Croix to the Danes would translate into a French-Danish alliance in Europe. To a lesser extent, they also took into consideration the fact that French Huguenots were part of the planter elites on St. John. Between November 1733 and June 1734, largely Akan insurgents, in addition to Gã-Adangme participants, of the Gold Coast polity of Akwamu staged a revolt and controlled St. John in an effort to overthrow the white planter regime and establish a polity of their own, with the Akan as perhaps the new planters.[6] In the wake of the Akwamu polity's collapse in 1730, a pool of enslavable Akwamu peoples was created, and the uprisings by oppositional forces and neighboring polities who allied with them led to the capture and exportation of some of Akwamu's women and men. A large number of the insurrectionists were newly arrived Africans from the Gold Coast, specifically those from Akwamu. These Akan persons, who were skilled in the use of firearms, remembered the structure and the fall of their polity in Akanland and likely sought to re-create it (see table 4.1). The principal leaders and participants, according to the historical sources and a fictional account, included King June (Jama or Gyamma, ɔbirɛmpɔn, member of the royal court, and commander in the Akwamu army), Aquasshie (an Akwamu royal), King Claes (King of Adampe [Adangme]), two persons named Quassi (Kwasi), Coffy (Kofi), Kompa (good akɔm practitioner?), Asa (medicine man), and Aquashiba (an Akwamu royal).[7] Jama (Gyamma) was a servant of Akwamuhene Ansa Kwao and had his own account with the Danish at Fort Christiansborg. He, along with others, probably arrived in the Danish Caribbean on board the *Laarurg Galley*, which embarked with 443 captives, including 82 from Christiansborg, and disembarked with 242 or 244 in May 1733.[8] The 82 from Christiansborg might have included a tightly knit group that included most of these leaders and participants of the revolt. If this were so, Jama (King June) as the leader of the revolt and the architect of an impending Akan-based polity would not have been surprising.

The goal held by these insurrectionists, however, was seemingly to replace the existing slave society with one of their own, in which the sugar-cotton economy of the former was to be left intact and in which the white planters would be killed or driven out. The revolt would extend to other Danish island colonies through Amina forces on those islands.[9] But not even that vision and an Amina network or their defeat of Danish and British forces would compensate for their lack of firearms, ammunition, and wide support from diverse segments of the enslaved and "free" African community. According to Ray Kea's analysis of the 1733 revolt, almost none of the "free" population and few of the Maroons joined the insurrection, and only 10 to 30 percent of the enslaved population actually participated in the revolt.[10] French forces soon came to the aid of Danish planters and restored planter rule in June 1734. Almost all the leaders and a number of other insurrectionists committed suicide and, in their mind and spirit, returned to *asamando* ("where the ancestors dwell"). Suicide in Akan culture was and is considered acceptable only if due to a state of war or an attempt to remove dishonor and ridicule; otherwise, the spirit of that person is barred from *asamando*. As for Aquashie, he and a small group remained marooned for several months until they surrendered to authorities based on a promise of pardon. Most of these returnees were tortured, burned at the stake, or sawed in half; their leader, Aquashie, was decapitated.[11] In the midst of disbelief and revenge (realized through these executions), the whites on St. John and the other islands remained fearful of the Amina, who were, in their minds, the "most unruly and barbaric," "unfaithful and warlike," "so wicked and lazy," and yet the "strongest of all the Negroes" with "witch doctors among them who are so powerful."[12]

The 1733 insurrection was not only the first revolt in the Danish Caribbean but also the first successful one (albeit limited to six months) by African captives against white colonists, and that historical moment predated the North American and the Haitian revolutions—both of which were based on principles similar to those behind the St. John insurrection. Unlike the Haitian uprising or the late eighteenth-century rebellions in Grenada and St. Vincent, the Akan of St. John sought to preserve the mechanisms of production rather than destroy the sugar and other estates so as to economically suffocate enslavement and those who held the Africans in captivity. In the wake of the St. John revolt, planter repression followed there as it did elsewhere in the Americas, but the ownership of the colonies was transferred to the Danish monarchy in 1755. In the mid-eighteenth century, the Danish colonies had a total enslaved population of 14,877 and a total "free" population of 1,979, and St. Croix accounted for almost 60 percent of that enslaved population (8,897). Christian Oldendorp maintained that the Amina were most numerous in St. Croix and St. John in the latter eighteenth century. If that observation is accurate, the Akan accounted for a sizable number of St. Croix's large share of the total enslaved population. This demographic reality and the planters' deep anxiety, which was no doubt inflamed by the 1733 St. John revolt, led to the sheer brutality those planters employed in the alleged 1759 uprising, which they justified on the basis of information gleaned from rumors and "confessions" gathered through torture. Of the 89 Africans accused of conspiracy to revolt, 58 were acquitted, 10 were expelled from the colonies, 7 escaped and remained at large, and the rest were hung, strangled, burned alive, and gibbeted. Indeed, large numbers of Akan persons were implicated in the successful St. John uprising in 1733, as well as the so-called 1759 conspiracy, where it seemed, in this instance and in others throughout the Americas, that perceptions of the Akan were reified in the minds of planters and colonial officials and made them mistaken targets for real or imagined agency.[13]

The alleged plot of 1759 to burn the plantations and kill the whites during the Christmas holiday unraveled from an argument between Cudjo (Kwadwo) of Søren Bagger's sugar plantation in Prince's Quarter and two white men, Benjamin Bear and Peter Hyde, wherein Cudjo threatened to kill Peter Hyde. Bear and Hyde informed Merrik Turnbul, the burgher lieutenant and a planter in King's Quarter, who told the captain of the town, Major de Nully, who in turn informed the governor. After the "conspirators" were swiftly rounded up, the testimony of several enslaved Africans who had heard Cudjo's remarks and the voluntary testimony of Cudjo's brother, Quamina (Kwamena), sealed Cudjo's fate.[14] According to Quamina's testimony, Cudjo planned the uprising; Cudjo, however, named William Davis, a "free negro," as the one who proposed the idea, but the "trial" judge, Engelbret Hesselberg, believed the real leader was Qvau (Kwao) or Quaco (Kwaku), who had witnessed the 1736 Antigua revolt and whose father was hung therein because of his testimony (in order to save his own life). Of those executed, a few confessed, but most did not—even while being hung, strangled, burned alive, or gibbeted.[15] William Davis confessed but "cut his own throat" before execution; Cudjo also confessed and was "burned alive"; Prince Qvakoe (Kwaku) was broken on the wheel; and Qvau or Quaco "confessed nothing" and lived for forty-two hours in "a gibbet or iron cage." Qvau, Prince Qvakoe (Kwaku), and Cudjo were implicated as the principal leaders of the suspected, though not improbable, revolt, and since Qvau or Quaco was banished from Antigua—and probably traveled with planters who relocated to St. Croix after the 1736 Antigua revolt—it is likely that he designed the uprising, if indeed there was one, based on the kind of Akan statecraft, oaths, and culture disclosed by the alleged Antigua conspiracy.[16]

A decade after the 1759 conspiracy, Christian George Andreas Oldendorp, a Moravian clergyman, concluded his visit to the Danish colonies. He described the Amina as a Gold Coast "nation" and stated that the people were noble, belligerent, courageous; they also used firearms (unlike their enemies), and spoke an Akan language similar to that of the Akkim (Akyem). The Amina's Gold Coast provenance can be confirmed by their apparent wars with the Fante, Akkim (Akyem), Akkran (Accra/Nkrãn; Gã), Asseni (Assin), Kifferu (Twifoɔ), Atti (Etsi), Okkau or Okkan (Akani?), and Adansi (Adanse).[17] Other "nations" of Gold Coast origin included Quahu (Kwahu), Akripon (Akropɔn, capital of Akuapem), Assanti (Asante), and Tambi (Adangme). Oldendorp's text is significant since he interviewed (precisely, "interviews with baptized slaves") a number of Africans in general and Akan from the Gold Coast in particular and thus provides an invaluable snapshot into their late eighteenth-century world in West Africa and in the Danish Caribbean. Oldendorp notes that the number of "kingdoms," and this included his own inventory of "nations," was often exaggerated, for when the Africans were asked the name of their "nation," they provided the name of the location or pronounced it differently from other Africans of the same or different "nation." Most of Oldendorp's Akan or Gold Coast informants were multilingual in that they understood Akan (Twi), Gã, and Ewe, and Oldendorp's impressive linguistic data demonstrate that the Amina were indeed Akan in the Danish and perhaps other colonies and were certainly not Gbe-language speakers, though the former may have understood some Gbe languages since the Akan language and Akan names did spread along the Slave Coast.[18] Akan or Akan-derived names found along the former Slave Coast (among "Papaa" and its constituents) included the following male and female names (in that order) recorded by Oldendorp: Sunday-born (Quaschi; Quaschiba), Monday-born (Kotjoh; Atjuba), Tuesday-born (Akuh; Akuba), Wednesday-born (Jau; Jaba), Thursday-born (Kommena; Abramma), Friday-born (Koffee; Afiba), and Saturday-born (Quammi; Amimba).[19]

As a clergyman, Oldendorp, like others before and after him, was deeply concerned about indigenous African beliefs and practices and, simultaneously, convinced of Christianity's converting powers and indivisible claims to the "right God." Nonetheless, his Gold Coast informants, clearly of Akan origin, referred to their Creator as Jankombum (*Onyankopɔn*), Borribori (*Bɔrebɔre*; an appellation for the Akan Creator), and Quereampum (*Tweadeampɔn*) and noted that this Creator was called on each morning and during "prayer" (*apaeɛ*, libation) for protection, assistance, healing, strength, and victory in wars.[20] They, he said, "consider Jankombum the greatest God and creator," "pray" in sacred places, eat together, have "a priest called Sofo [*ɔsofoɔ*], who performs the burial ceremonies and is paid with gold and food for it."[21] Although Oldendorp was attuned to the language of his informants when they made references to concepts of the soul or spirit ("Unsumsum [*sunsum*] in their language") and to the use of talismans (*nsuman*) for war or stated that they had a "sorcerer in [their] country [who] is called Konfu [*ɔkɔmfoɔ*]," he complained much about the continuity of Akan culture from the Gold Coast to the Danish islands in the form of "superstitious" beliefs among these "pagan Blacks."[22] In addition to observations on Akan spiritual concepts, Oldendorp also made significant notes on Akan cultural practices and language, and these notes support some of our contentions about the idea of Mina discussed earlier. Though Oldendorp's attention to clothing ("cloth they used is called Attama"; *ntama*), matrilineal succession, marriage ("it is taken as a disgrace if they do not marry each other"), polygamy, and responses to crime is noteworthy, it is his cultural notes on scarification and the efficacy of Akan medicinal knowledge and practice that provide clues to further clarify the Akan experience in the Americas.

On Akan scarification, Oldendorp wrote the following: "They had on each side of their heads three incisions, one beneath the other, from the ear to the eye. They said that they had these because *they considered it beautiful and also to distinguish themselves from other nations*. Their mothers made these [incisions] when they were children. The skin is cut with a knife and palm oil mixed with coal [i.e., *mɔtɔ*, a composite, powdery black medicine] is rubbed into it, so that it cannot grow shut again."[23] These horizontal cuts on the temple, according to Oldendorp, were at odds with a description of Akan peoples from John Stedman, a contemporary of his stationed in the Dutch colony of Suriname. Stedman wrote that the "Coromanti," who were "the most esteemed," had three to four long slashes on each cheek, which actually resemble the so-called country marks of the Yorùbá (Nago) rather than the Akan.[24] For the Akan, an incision is made on the right cheekbone and is filled with a powdery black medicine (*mɔtɔ*) to prevent convulsions (*ɛsoro*) through a "cutting beneath the eye" ritual called *aniasetwa* (*ani*, eye; *ase*, beneath; *twa*, cut); this "cut beneath the eye" was given to all Akan children and thus served as a cultural identifier.²⁵ The "country masks" of Oldendorp and Stedman are inconsistent with the general and singular Akan mark, which is usually situated below the left eye and on the cheekbone, but, at least in Oldendorp's case, his description does suggest that some of those he interviewed from the Gold Coast very likely had in their families spiritual specialists (e.g., ɔkɔmfoɔ or ɔbosomfoɔ) or were specialists themselves who usually had specific markings on the body as an indicator of their vocation. Some of those markings on these specialists included three lines on the temple, and this line of thinking may explain how Oldendorp was able to gather the kind and quantity of information on Akan spiritual concepts and practice that he did.

Those same spiritual specialists were also skilled herbalists and practitioners of indigenous psychic and physiological healing. Thus, the high praise for Akan knowledge, skill, and efficacy in indigenous medicine was not surprising since, as Oldendorp himself observed, "the physicians of these people are most often also priests."²⁶ In the Danish colonies, that praise continued but was part of a particular ambivalence among broad segments of whites that, paradoxically, supported and encouraged the use of medicinal plants linked to the same "obeah" they simultaneously discouraged and suppressed for its real or imagined ties to poisoning. The planters' concern with *obeah* provided for its legal prohibition and made its practice punishable by death.²⁷ As was the case in the British colonies of the Americas, legal proscriptions against *obeah* in the eighteenth-century Danish colonies and increased Christianization in the nineteenth century might have contributed to the disappearance of *obeah* in print and its largely demonic connotation among whites and diasporic Africans alike. However, in reality—even among those large numbers of African converts by the mid-nineteenth century in St. Croix—the healing and spiritual practice did not cease to exist or to play an active role in the lives of African-descended communities.²⁸ To be sure, many Akan persons who envisioned their homeland as a space of residence for the soul still had to deal with the exigencies of plantation life and the spiritual convictions of the Akan people, and their progeny may very well have attempted to alleviate the dislocating trauma of the capture, voyage, and resettlement in foreign lands, where they could not control the mechanisms or modes of production. Much of that trauma was reflected in the life stories of Amina or Akan captives brought to the Danish colonies, and, here, a few that Oldendorp recorded (and in a form close to the original German text) will suffice. Unfortunately, the names and, by extension, a significant part of the Akan or Akanized person's identity were not preserved in Oldendorp's account.

Oldendorp interviewed an "Amina black" who, in spite of his being the brother to a local sovereign, was captured by his own countrymen in a local war and brought to the Danish fort (of Christiansborg) on the Gold Coast. Another Amina had the same fate. He was wealthy and "a cousin of the subking," and in war he commanded three thousand men. He went to a part of the coastal Fante area with two little boys who carried his currency and an older boy who carried his rifle. There he gambled away his money and the three boys. The victors seized the two little boys, but the older one, still carrying the subking's weapon, escaped and, instead of capturing the latter boy, who ran, they overpowered the once wealthy war commander and took him to "the fortress of the whites." With gold dangling from his arms and legs, the subdued gambler arrived. His brother came to bail him out for the amount of three sheep, but the white governor did not accept this and sent the commander-turned-captive to another fort, where four Africans and six sheep arrived as bail for him. The governor at the new fort did not want this bail, sent the commander aboard a vessel for enslaved persons, and told those who came to bail him out that the captive was not there at the fort. Nonetheless, the commander's brother sent the captive a message stating that he had not yet been able to free him but that this would happen within the next eight days (*nnawɔtwe*, eight days, that is, the seven-day inclusive Akan "week"). However, the vessel sailed off the following night, and the commander was made an enslaved person.

Oldendorp also tells us about another Amina, one who had been a wealthy merchant on the Gold Coast and had owned and sold enslaved persons and who came to be himself enslaved in the following manner. When he was a young adult, his parents had given him, "according to the custom of Guinea," a small female child as a bride. He later fell in love with another woman and had sex with her because his child bride was still too young, despite her showing dissatisfaction with their relationship. When the first bride reached the age of womanhood, the wealthy merchant set out to meet her with eight male and female servants who carried gold, ivory, three rifles, and other items, but he first stopped at a European fort to sell some of his commodities in order to procure the best gifts for his bride-to-be. However, those at the fort arrested him and all of his people, and this was the doing of the friends of another woman with whom he had also had sex. His relatives sent the governor of the fort four sheep as a present to allow him to remain at the fort until they arrived. He watched them arrive but was sent to a ship, aboard which he and his servants shared the same fate as the commander and became enslaved persons.[29]

The governor of the fort told the captain of the ship to treat the once wealthy Amina merchant with respect and not to "put iron on him" since he was from "a high-class family and [was] a law-abiding good man." And so it happened. He was not put into restraints, kept his clothes, drank with the whites, and, upon arrival in St. Thomas, was not sold publicly with the other "newly arrived Africans" but bought separately. Afterward, several of his father's enslaved persons or servants arrived. They looked him up, still respecting him in his "slave status," and viewed him as their "low-ranking master." Because he had to help them to obtain some clothing, they therefore had to help him by sometimes working on his small plantation. Above all, he was a "diligent [and] faithful black" who—aside from all of the heavy work he did for his owner with the utmost care—was able to also acquire something for himself by his diligence.

Finally, Oldendorp provides us with an account of a "black from Akkran [(Accra; Gã) who] also became enslaved." During a great famine, he was traveling with his friends to the coastal Fante area to purchase corn (maize) and was captured by human traffickers who intercepted travelers on the road and brought him to "the fort of the whites." His friends, who were of "high class," made every effort to obtain his release by providing "two blacks" for his return. However, they came too late. A captain who arrived at the fort before the "two blacks" demanded that he have his entire load of enslaved Africans since he had promised to arrive and retrieve them and was dissatisfied with the governor because the governor had already sold most of the enslaved persons in the fort to others. The governor sent all the enslaved captives he had, including the "Akkran" man in question, on board his vessel. The friends of this man cried out and lamented on the bay, but it was in vain as the ship was ready for the voyage and sailed off to the "West Indies."[30]

Between the 1733 and the alleged 1759 revolt, African resistance to the international enslavement enterprise elevated its costs—this includes an insurrection on the *Patientia* that reduced its human cargo to half on its way to the Danish Caribbean in 1753. That cost, however, did not immediately affect the value of sugar, which was the primary export commodity, approximately 90 percent of which (followed by cotton, rum, and tobacco) went to Denmark. The production and population growth of St. Croix made it the primary and most important sugar-producing Danish colony. Most of the plantations had shifted to sugar production beginning in the 1760s, and windmills, which facilitated the crushing of sugar cane, were prevalent in many flourishing plantations on the island, which was divided into six quarters.[31] The St. Croix population at the end of the eighteenth century reached 23,000 enslaved Africans and 1,000 "freed" persons of African descent, compared to 2,000 whites, as Gold Coast Africans continued to be imported to St. Croix. One 1789 slave auction notice in the *Royal Danish American Gazette* read in capital letters: "Two Hundred and Forty-Nine Gold Coast Negroes."[32] Between 1781 and 1790, the Gold Coast exported its highest documented number of Africans—more than 135,000 to the Americas.

For those in the Danish colonies, a continuous Akan presence factored into the material culture of the enslaved, and Akan architectural design evident in the eighteenth century facilitated their ideational culture of contiguous clans and their political culture of revolt in the grouping together of their houses. This method included the "big yard" (compound) concept, in which houses were built around a compound and where socialization, cooking, and clothes washing occurred.[33] Until the twentieth century, most of the enslaved and their descendants lived in wattle-and-daub houses roofed with grass or sugarcane leaves. These houses were clustered to resemble small villages and were usually placed on the least usable land and almost always situated west of the principal estate residence. Sugar estates with an extensive "slave village" included a sugar factory and wind- and horse-powered mills triangulated in the center. Moving clockwise, one found the refuse located in the northeast, the cattle pen and extended agricultural plots with mule stables to the east, a crushed cane shed and watering well to the southeast, the slave village to the south, the sick house for the enslaved and the servants' houses, besides the planter's or manager's house, to the west, and the kitchen gardens to the northwest.[34] Such estates and their enslaved labor forces produced large quantities of sugar; in fact, much of the 18 million pounds of sugar produced in 1773 came from St. Croix, wherein close to half of the island's land was devoted to sugar production and its profits.

However, St. Croix's prosperity declined with British occupation of the Danish colonies between 1801–1802 and 1807–1815, as sugar production diminished due to competition from beet sugar in Europe and cane sugar from other Caribbean islands between the 1800s and the 1840s. Unrest, economic despair, and mass insurrection in St. Croix compelled Governor General Peter von Scholten to abolish slavery on 3 July 1848 in spite of planter opposition.[35] The planters soon demanded "just and equitable compensation" for loss of property on account of the governor general's ordinance "to abolish Negro slavery in the Danish Colonies."[36] Here and elsewhere in the Americas, emancipation was a refashioning of socioeconomic relationships, wherein the church and the state were the principal agents of social control in urban and plantation contexts rather than freedom from the control or power of another. Those emancipated became part of a thirty-year sharecropping program governed by stringent labor laws amidst worsening economic conditions, high mortality, poor housing, and protest and labor strikes. In fact, it was the labor revolt of 1878 that ended serfdom.

Better economic opportunities elsewhere in the Caribbean led to immigration as an option for some African descendants at the end of the nineteenth and the start of the twentieth century, while the Danish Crown decided to cut its losses and sold its Caribbean holdings to the United States in 1917. The Danish colonies in the Caribbean came to harbor Akan persons who crafted their own political destiny and sought to create a polity of their own preceding the Haitian revolution. The Akan also became skilled artisans: for instance, Cuffy the tailor, who also played the violin, or servants like Cudjoe, who was the caterer for a "freeman negroe" [sic] named John Messer, whose wife was also enslaved; forgers of Maroon settlements independent of the planters' government but a coexisting force in its racialized and exploitative social order; and those who envisioned freedom by running away (e.g., Coffe [Kofi] Smith in 1775), striking, protesting, or seeking manumission initiated by the colonial state, which was only rarely granted.[37] The case of Quamina was one such rare manumission, and the colonists looked upon him favorably on account of the evidence he provided in the alleged 1759 Akan-led conspiracy. However, those whom he betrayed in testimony and those many thousands more who toiled on the islands saw him and their lot in a much different light.

MAROONAGE AND AKAN CULTURE IN THE DUTCH COLONIES

Much like the Danish possessions in the Caribbean, Dutch colonies also included key island holdings such as the Curaçao Islands (Curaçao, Little Curaçao, Aruba, Bonaire, and Little Bonaire), St. Martin (shared with the French), St. Eustatius and Saba, but with the mainland exception of Suriname. Curaçao, Aruba, and Bonaire were too arid, and precipitation was too irregular for any genuine plantation economy to develop. Here, again, Suriname was the exception, for it became the principal "slave society" of the Dutch in the Americas. The most populated of the islands was Curaçao, with its small, millet-producing plantations. These plantations were unable to produce large quantities of sugarcane and tobacco or even enough food, like the sizable sugar-producing colonies that dominated much of the landscape in the Americas. Curaçao, however, experienced revolts by enslaved persons similar to those in the sugar-producing colonies in 1716, 1750, and 1795. Curaçao's climate and soil remained formidable, and food production became a major underlying cause of conflict and theft. Thus, Curaçao was mostly a place of transit rather than one of the destinations for enslaved Africans, and many were sold to British, French, and Spanish colonies and even southern states in the United States. The Dutch Caribbean, of which the Curaçao Islands were central, received at least 27,000 Africans from the Gold Coast. Those not destined for transshipment settled the islands, whereas the Dutch Guianas, of which Suriname was key, received at least 72,000 from the Gold Coast—more exports than any other West African region.

By around 1700, Curaçao had approximately 4,000 enslaved Africans. Although slaveholders underreported the enslaved population to avoid head taxes, and most of the latter were said to be of Kôngo-Angola origin, Africans from the Gold Coast had arrived in Curaçao well before the Dutch West India Company leased plantations to private persons in 1715 and before the international enslavement enterprise became a private enterprise in the 1730s.[38] From as early as 1680, Akan persons from the Gold Coast were shipped to the islands: On 15 April 1680, arrangements were made for 250–300 "Negro-slaves from El Mina to Curaçao," and in 1710 more captives from the Gold Coast were sent aboard a vessel named the *Elmina* bound to Curaçao.[39] These persons from the Gold Coast region and specifically through Elmina, Accra or other Gold Coast ports came to be known as "minase negers" (Africans who purportedly embarked at Elmina), were considered "good house slaves," and formed part of an enslaved population organized into three groups: domestic servants, craftspersons, and field laborers.[40] The regional or port origin of the Africans that constituted the population of Curaçao can be gleaned from the place names found largely on the eastern part of the island: Amina, Popo, Kongo, Calabari, Mandinga, and Africa (a burial ground for the enslaved located on the San Juan plantation).[41]

The plantations established on Curaçao and in Suriname might not have been radically different—and were certainly created and sustained at a much higher overall cost—from those proposed by the Dutch on the Gold Coast. The key difference—and the fundamental reason that proposal failed on the Gold Coast—was that Africans remained on their own soil and in their historically situated culture and ecology. Moreover, the Dutch were unable to control the theft of goods by the local population and sustained heavy costs in recovering runaways.[42] The Dutch envisioned and initially began cotton, indigo, and sugar cultivation along the banks of Gold Coast rivers in Shama, Butri, and Axim, but officials noted the difficulty of the last, for "much of it is stolen by the Negroes themselves," and they lacked the "experienced Negroes...who could teach the ways of cultivating sugarcane to the slaves here [i.e., on the Gold Coast]."[43] Twelve "experienced Negroes" were requested from Suriname, and, though the Dutch plantations on the Gold Coast failed, their plantations in Suriname flourished; we can be certain those twelve individuals were valued for their skills and that they could be controlled as seasoned captives.

The seasoning process for the Africans who entered Suriname did not differ much from that in Danish or other European colonies in the Americas. John Stedman, a Dutch soldier writing in his journal in October 1773, described the process (which he called a "Ceremony") of African entry into the Suriname colony. After arrival and inspection, "the new bought Negroes [were] imediately [sic] branded on the breast or the thick of the Shoulder by a Stamp made of Silver with the inicial [sic] letters of the Masters [sic]

Name... No sooner is this Ceremony over and a new name given to the newly bought Slave than he or she is delivered to an old one of the same Sex and sent to the Estate, where each by this Guardian is properly kep'd clean, instructed and well fed, without working for the Space of 6 Weeks, during which Period from living Skeletons they become Plump and fat with a beautiful clean Skin till disfigured by the lash of the cruel Whip, which too generally follows from the hands of the too relentless Overseers."[44] This must have been part of the experience of the nine hundred combined souls procured at Accra, Apam, and Senya Beraku and who came to Suriname on the *Peynenburgh* and the *Christina* in the latter part of 1705. From the Africans' perspective, the other part of that experience in 1705 or any other year we may never know, though the nature of Suriname's slave society allows us to discern some of those feelings and thoughts.[45]

Carved out of a small space between the sea and the dense forest, the British established the Suriname colony in 1651. A century later, Suriname was a flourishing colonial paradox of plantation and paradise: opulence among the planters and acute misery and brutality for the enslaved. The British ceded the colony to the Dutch in exchange for New Amsterdam (New York) in 1667, and hundreds of British planters, accompanied by some 2,000 enslaved Africans, left Suriname between 1668 and 1680 and many relocated to Jamaica. By the mid-seventeenth century, Suriname was producing more revenue than the other Caribbean colonies, and Africans vastly outnumbered the colonists by a ratio of 65:1 in the plantation districts during the latter half of that century.[46] The enslaved population increased from 4,200 in 1684 to 10,000 in 1701 and to 50,000 by 1765, all dispersed among 591 plantations situated on rivers and adjacent to swamps and forested lands. Prior to 1725, close to half of the enslaved population came from the Bight of Bénin (Slave Coast). For the rest of the century, half the Africans came from the Sierra Leone–Senegambia region (labeled Gangu), 25 percent from the Gold Coast (labeled Kormantines or Coromantin) after the Dutch position on the Slave Coast declined, and the rest came from the Loango-Angola region (labeled Loangu people). The low numbers of Gold Coast exports to Dutch colonies may have been due to the cumulative effort of a series of key events: the Komenda wars of the 1690s, the war of Spanish succession (1701–1713), Anglo-Dutch antagonism on the Gold Coast (1704–1711), and the economic crashes in London and Paris. Nonetheless, an average of 100,000 captives left the Gold Coast between 1721 and 1800, which may account for their increase after 1725 and their numerical contribution to an enslaved population, of which 90 percent was born in Africa by 1740 and largely adult male.

Richard Price suggests that the years 1675–1725 constituted the formative period of the Saramaka society, one of the principal Maroon groups in

Suriname, but the core processes of coalescing—its central motor an "inter-African syncretism" of distinct yet overlapping African cultures with little input from European and Amerindian sources—unfolded in a period of twenty-two years (i.e., 1690–1712).⁴⁷ For Price, the three principal groups intimately involved in those processes of building institutions and structures in a context of war were those from the Bight of Bénin, the Gold Coast, and the Loango-Angola regions. In his account, John Stedman listed Africans of "different Nations or Casts [sic]," which included Congo, Loango, Nago, Papa, and Coromantin.⁴⁸ The Coromantins (Gold Coast), Papas (Bight of Bénin), and Loango (Kôngo-Angola) played together, as they did among Jamaican Maroons, using distinct yet shared verbal and musical registers, engaged in communal divination, and made all these resources accessible to each Saramaka who learned and transmitted the melodies to their progeny. For Price, the Komanti (Akan) input to Saramaka society contributed to its warriors' rites, militarily and spiritually served all villages for warfare, and included the central use of the Apínti drum and Anasi-tóli (Ananse story), though we must include an Akan spiritual and expressive culture as well. In many ways, Akan processes of cultural development in the West African forest and river environs may have been a "historical rehearsal" of infinite proportion for similar settings, including the Americas, since we find parallel thematic processes of forging culture in like environments with the same or different actors (if we include ancestry as a "living" resource among those forgers of culture). The Coromantin were "the most esteemed," argued Stedman, and we can confirm that Africans in this category of identification were Akan or Akan culture bearers from Stedman's servant Quacco (Kwaku), who spoke to Stedman in "Coromantyn" and was probably typical of other Coromantin. Indeed, Quacco did share samplings of a clearly identifiable Akan language with Stedman: *Co fa anyso na baramon bra* (go to the river and bring me some water) and *me yeree, na comeda mee* (my wife, I am hungry).⁴⁹ What Stedman heard and apparently understood was very close to the Akan original: *kɔfa nsuo na ma me bra* (go bring water for me and come) and *me yere, na kɔm de me* (my wife, hunger possesses me [i.e., I am hungry]).

Since the founding and transfer of the Suriname colony, Akan persons and other Africans contributed in discernable ways to the African cultural dynamic of the colony and its centuries-old culture of resistance and Maroonage. In the hot and humid tropical climate of Suriname and in one of the most brutal slave societies, Maroon bands and settlements were formed in the late seventeenth century and still exist, like their Jamaican counterparts, even today. Maroonage continued uninterrupted until Suriname abolished slavery in 1863, though extant groups persisted thereafter. Maroonage as a natural response to Dutch enslavement was often inevitable, given a favorable topography and the imperatives of the human spirit in those who escaped before or shortly after the initial "seasoning" (the "ceremony" described by Stedman) and thus thwarted efforts to negate their humanity through institutionalized brutality. John Stedman's very presence in Suriname in 1773 owed itself to these Maroons since he was merely one person among hundreds of European soldiers sent to the colony to help fight the new Maroon groups, which emerged after the colonists made treaties with the two largest Maroon bands, the Djuka and the Saramaka, in the early 1760s and as Maroon raids on plantations increased in the late 1760s and early 1770s. A bevy of Maroon attacks on plantations were part and parcel of the tradition of resistance and subsistence independent of planter authority as revolts and uprisings punctuated the late seventeenth century and much of the eighteenth century.

In the eighteenth century, that tradition also took place on board several slaving vessels at sea or not far from the Gold Coast: Slave insurrections occurred twice on the *Agatha* en route to Essequibo and Suriname in 1715 and 1717 under the same captain, the *Vrijheid* in 1732, the *Vrouw Johanna Cores* in 1763, and the *Guinese Vriendschap* and the *Willemina Aletta* in 1771. Almost half of all vessel-based uprisings occurred between 1751 and 1775, and undoubtedly the Akan played a significant role, for the Gold Coast recorded some of its highest annual exports during those years.[50] Of the close to seventeen hundred who disembarked in Suriname in the aftermath of these voyages, some of them likely joined existing or new Maroon communities. In 1760, when 75 to 80 percent of the enslaved population was Africa born and the colony was pregnant with new Maroon groups, the Djuka launched another attack on the plantation of Onoribo, and peace was soon sought between the leader of the Djuka and his six chiefs (Mafunage, Titus, Kwauw [Kwao], Kwaku, Kofi Semprendre, and Boston) and Governor Wigbold Crommelin. Governor Crommelin sent a letter by way of two enslaved Africans, Kofi and Charlestown. Boston, a "captain" who was literate and acutely aware of the British treaty with the Maroons of Jamaica in 1739, received the letter from Kofi and Charlestown.

The Djuka armed forces were led by a "captain" named Kormantin Cojo (or Coromantyn Codjo) and another named Kofi, who was perhaps Kofi Semprendre. These captains led an assembly and dance that ushered in the negotiations of 13 October 1759, which were concluded the following year by a "blood treaty" (a ritual in which the blood of the treaty makers was mixed with other ingredients and consumed).[51] In their negotiations with the Dutch colonists, the Saramaka employed a similar ritual, and the same process of oath making (linked to Akan political culture) was used for forging alliances among Maroons and non-Maroons alike. This approach to oaths was also found among the Maroons of Jamaica and in other parts of the Americas.[52]

The Saramaka concluded their peace treaty in 1762. Once the Djuka and the Saramaka had received their "freedom" and were reduced to "watchdogs" for the colony via their respective treaties, other independent Maroon groups in Suriname joined forces. Some even raided the smallholdings of "free men" such as Quassi (Kwasi). Others shot a Curaçao *bomba* (slave driver) named Cadjo (Kwadwo) in revolt, while groups of "Negroes of Coromantin, the most formidable of all these Africans, revolted and killed their master[s]."[53] Another Maroon group with no ties to others was led by a "chief" named Kwami (Kwame) in the late eighteenth century, while the Kwinti Maroons situated west and southwest of Paramaribo and in the Para region fell under the leadership of *gaanman* (paramount chief) Kofi-maka between 1770 and 1827. A "chief" named Jermes, "a Negro of Coromantin," who led an earlier Maroon group in Para during the period when Suriname was under British rule, preceded Kofi-maka.[54] Unlike other Maroon groups that originated in the Dutch colony of Suriname, such as the Saramaka and the Djuka (also known as *Okanisi*; cf. ɔ*kanni*, an Akan person), the Aluku or Boni Maroons who came to settle in French Guiana near the Maroni and Lawa rivers did not create a lasting treaty with either the Dutch or the French colonists, though oaths of peace were made with French colonial authorities or persons claiming to act on their behalf. The French, on their part, did not pursue peace in the latter years of the eighteenth century since they did not view the Aluku as a threat; after the late 1770s, the majority of the Aluku remained in French Guiana, and in 1860 a treaty was finally negotiated with the French and the Dutch.

Although the Djuka and the Saramaka were among the largest Maroon groups in Suriname and French Guiana, all Maroons groups shared basic constituents in terms of society and culture. All Maroons irrespective of numerical size or geographical location shared a similar political and agrarian structure, and the primary social unit was the matriclan (*lô*) and its divisions. Among the Saramaka, most of the *gaán-óbias* (major spiritual forces) were vested in clans and said to have been brought from Africa.[55] A leader headed each matriclan, and succession (in principle) occurred by way of being "the eldest son of [the male leader's] eldest sister."[56] Certainly this social configuration mirrors the matriclan (*abusua*) structure of the Akan and the *abosom* (spiritual agents) vested therein, and settlement patterns and the names thereof provide further evidence of an Akan influence on the African cultural dynamic in Suriname and French Guiana. Among Aluku Maroons, for example, some of their settlements were named Kofi-hay, Kwamigron (Kwamekrom), and Kormantin-Kodjogron (Kwadwokrom); the last of these was said to harbor mostly Kormantins who fled from plantations and were led by Kormantin Cojo (Kwadwo). The names of settlements differed from those of matriclans in Suriname, for those who left the plantations to form Maroon communities named many of their matrilineal clans after the plantation from which the initial group(s) of Maroon ancestors had come.[57] When plantations were sold, enslaved families were not separated, which might have allowed for greater identification with one's plantation community rather than their African "ethnic" or clan identity, though Akan Maroons clearly stamped their culture on their settlements.

The Akan of the West African forest marked their towns with the affix *kurom* or *krom* (i.e., *kuro-mu*; *akuro*, town; *mu*, inside), and the Akan used personal names for settlements spawned by those who found new land and became its custodian. Thus, we can rightly suspect that the suffix *-gron* was no more than a slightly distorted phonetic recording of Akan town-marking suffixes used to demarcate Akan-led settlements. We might even rightly suspect that these settlements carved out sacred spaces for Akan and broader African spiritual practice. According to one late eighteenth-century source, the Maroons referred their Creator as "Nana," and after two centuries of Christian proselytization, many of the larger Maroon groups remained unaffected, and only some of the numerically smaller groups had converted, with the exception of the Saramaka leader, Alabi (Johannes Arrabini), and the small contingent around him.[58] The de facto leader of the late eighteenth-century Saramaka, Antamá, immediately protested the baptism of Alabi, the German missionary's first Saramaka convert in 1770, and led an antiwhite effort for months thereafter. Antamá is a central figure, however, because he was one of the most powerful *obia* men or spiritualist healer among the Saramaka and had a "Tonê shrine" like his father, spent a great deal of his time healing, and practiced a spirituality disengaged from the Christianity of Alabi and the minority of people who followed him.[59]

For Antamá and the majority of the Saramaka, in addition to other Maroons, the Creator was realized as Gaan Gadu and Nana Kediama Kediampon (i.e., Nana Tweadeampɔn Kwame), and, for many Maroons, the most important and powerful spiritual entity after the Creator was and still is Tata Odun. According to Kenneth Bibly, "Tata Odun is said to have come over from Africa along with the ancestors and to have led them safely through the forest to their present location"; Tata Odun's principal custodian was the *gaanman* (paramount chief).[60] Bibly was of the opinion that the *odum* tree of contemporary Ghana was the source of name "Odun" in Tata Odun. The Herskovitses claimed that "Tata" meant "father" and that the "river gods" went under the generic name "Tonɛ" (Tanɔ?), whereas Richard Price regarded Tonɛ or Tonê as a "river god from Africa," one of which Antamá's father, Gweyunga, had brought from Africa to Suriname. Based on these suggestions, Tata Odun would be a forest "god" who was embodied by the *odum* tree and was senior to other such entities.[61] Their suggestions have some plausibility, but a stronger argument can be made for another reading of the Herskovitses' material, collected in the first half of the twentieth century, and

Richard Price's and Kenneth Bibly's fieldwork data if these sources were further grounded in the spiritual concepts and language of the Akan.

Among the Akan in West Africa, the Tanɔ River is the most sacred river and the source of all Atanɔ-derived *abosom* and is thus regarded as one of the first offspring of the Akan Creator in Akan oral archives and its indigenous spiritual-cultural praxis. Tata could connote seniority or "father," which is the meaning of the term *"tata"* in Kikôngo. However, perhaps unbeknownst to the Herskovitses and Bibly, the term "Tanɔ" was (and still is) often contracted to "Ta" (as in Ta Kofi, that is, Tanɔ Kofi). Moreover, reduplication is a salient feature in the Akan language (e.g., *asaase* or *asase*, earth, is the reduplicated *ase*, under, beneath).[62] Moreover, what the Herskovitses referred to as "Taki Taki" words among Africans in Suriname and what others have collected among Maroons in Suriname and French Guiana include a significant number of Akan lexical items.[63] The following inventory is but a sample of that corpus, and, here, the Akan equivalents (in parentheses) precede the Maroon lexical items (see table 4.2).

The lexicon in table 4.2 includes largely concepts related to Akan spiritual culture and then those related to ideational culture (e.g., *Anansi tɔri, ɔpete, abɛrewa*) and material culture (e.g., *ofana, odan, asikan*). The notion of *abɛrewa* is a foundational idea in the constitution or basis of Akan matrilineality and cultural identity, for children are rooted in and thus belong to their mother's matriclan, and this integral principle was not missed by the Herskovitses in Suriname: "When separation occurs, the children remain with the mother. If she is unable to care for them herself, her mother, if living, takes all or several of the children, or a sister or a maternal aunt cares for one or more of them."[64] This observation mirrors earlier accounts by European observers on the Gold Coast who made significant notes on Akan motherhood, particularly (in their mind) how quickly Akan women recovered from childbirth. This practice continued in eighteenth-century Suriname, where Stedman noted among the qualities of the "Coromantyn" that they took "mothering seriously" and to the point where new mothers did not cohabit with their husbands for two years after giving birth.[65] When these concepts are considered as a reflection of a composite Akan culture, we can see that Tata Odun was likely to have been an alternative or additional embodiment of the West Africa Tanɔ or ɔse Tanɔ. This Tanɔ would have remained senior in a Suriname setting among a host of Tanɔ *abosom*, such as Tanɔ Yao, who was also second to Nana Kediama Kediampon (Nana Tweadeampɔn Kwame), a position the Tanɔ of West Africa maintained as one of the first offspring of an Akan Creator. Two songs collected by the Herskovitses in Suriname further clarify the meaning of Tata Odun and its Akan basis. The refrain of the first song sung by a "priestess," *Yu mu yɛpi mi*, the Herskovitses translated as "you must help me." Its words are as follows:

Table 4.2. Select Akan Lexical Items among Maroons in Suriname and French Guiana

Abɛrewa/Abálawa (*aberewa*) – earth mother, old woman; ancient ancestress linked to Akan matrilineality
Adjá (*aduro*) – medicinal plants
Adjaini (*gyahene*, lion [f. *gyata*, lion]?) – jaguar spirit called Kwao
Ahuá (*ahuaha*) – medicinal plant
Akéma (*ɔkyerɛma*, drummer) – drum[mer]
Akra/akaa (*ɔkra*) – soul; supernatural force that governs one's destiny
Anansi (*Ananse*) – spider; Anansi *tori* (*anansesɛm*) are stories or folktales ("cuenta di nanzi" in Curaçao)[a]
Antamani (*ntaban*) – wing
Anumá (*anoma*) – bird
Apínti (*mpintin*) – "talking drum" used at major council meetings and rituals, wherein its rhythms open proceedings, invoke and greet the spiritual entities, and so on. The bulk of *apínti* messages are of Akan origin.
Asêmpê (*asɛmpa*, good word, righteous cause?) – process brought from Africa and used to extract confession
Asikán (*sika*) – money
Asamaká (*asaman*, deceased person, skeleton of a man) – skull of a deceased man
Asúmani (*asuman*) – charm or talisman
Awali (*ɔware*) – board game (cf. *aware*, a term for marriage)
Boofó (*borɔfo*) – white people
Bosum or Abosomo (*abosom*) – children or spiritual extensions of the Akan Creator, often inappropriately referred to as "shrines" or "gods." In the "*winti* songs" of the Kromanti language in Suriname, the word *bosum* (*ɔbosom*) is used for *winti* or "god."
Busuú ([*o*]*bosu*, dew) – water or rain
Doku/dokonu (*dɔkono*) – dish of cornmeal wrapped and cooked in banana leaves
Goon uwii (*nwi*) – cornrow hairstyle (*nwi*, hair)
Inikóko (*okokɔ*, domestic fowl; *akokɔbere*, hen) – hen
Kediama Kediampon (Tweadeampɔn Kwame) – "Supreme God," a synonym for Nana. Nana is also found in drum rhythms related to the leader of the Saramaka and probably other Maroons.
Komfo/Konfó (*ɔkɔmfoɔ*) – priest or spiritual specialist
Kotoko (*kotoko*, crested porcupine) – a sinister name for a gun but more likely a link to Asante and their skill in warfare, for their national symbol was (and still is) the porcupine. There are several songs and proverbs with "Asanti kotoko," such as *Asantí kotoko bu a dú okáng, kobuá, o sá si watera djan de, djantanási*.
Kromanti (*Kormantin*) – name of village and port on the former Gold Coast, which became an interpolated category of identity for those exported. Among the Saramaka, the Komanti are the ultimate warriors, healing spirits, and quintessence of the term "obia."
Nana Nyanwé (*Nana Onyame*) – "Great God"
Nyam – glory (cf. *nya*, to get, capture; *nyam*, to eat [found in Africa and the Americas])

(*continued*)

Table 4.2. Continued

Obólodiê (oborɔdeɛ) – plantain
Odani (odan, house, room, or building) – house
Ofana (afana, sword; cf. akofana or akofena, sword of war/state) – machete
Okókolo (okokɔ; akokonini, rooster) – rooster
Opete (ɔpetɛ, Onyankopasakyie) – vulture (cf. stories of "John Crow" and "King Buzzard")[b]
Osai Tando (ɔse Tanɔ) – "Father" Tanɔ, that is, Ta or Tanɔ Kora, offspring of the Akan Creator, embodied by the sacred Tanɔ River and source of all Tanɔ-derived *abosom*. Ta Kora is often referred to as the "father" of these *abosom*.
Otoló (otuo) – gun
Ponsu (po, ocean; nsu, water) – community fishing event
Susa (sasa) – avenging spirit (of an animal)
Tando (Tanɔ) – Komanti god from Africa
Tata Yao (Tanɔ or "father" Yao) – *ɔbosom* named Ta or Tanɔ Yao; also known as (Tanɔ) Ananka Yao and as a "river Komanti [spirit]"
Yao (Yao, Yaw) – name of a male born on Thursday

a. Allen, "Social History," 179–180, 209n8, 251. Called *nanzi* or *kompa nanzi*, this "small spider" remains the main figure of stories and a hero. Allen's study suggests these stories archived historical events and struggles against enslavement and its postemancipation forms.
b. Stories of John Crow in Jamaica are akin to the vulture Carrion Crow in Guyana, and both resemble narratives of "King Buzzard," an African ruler who sold his people to white slavers, who then decided to enslave him as well; upon his death, he could not go to heaven or hell, for his soul was condemned to wander alone forever in the form of a great buzzard. See Monica Schuler, "Liberated Central Africans in Nineteenth-Century Guyana," paper presented at the Harriet Tubman Seminar, York University, 24 January 2000, p. 18. This paper was later published under the same title in *Central Africans and Cultural Transformation in the American Diaspora*, ed. Linda Heywood (New York: Cambridge University Press, 2002). Though my references are to the unpublished paper presented at York University, the published version is relatively the same in content and organization.

Yu mu yɛpi
Yu mu yɛpi
Yu mu yɛpi mi
Yu mu yɛpi
Yu mu yɛpi
Yu mu yɛpi o!
Yu mu yɛpi, Osai Tando [ɔse Tanɔ]
Yu mu yɛpi, Abɛrewa [ancient ancestress]

The second song sung in the "Kromanti tongue" by that same unidentified but now "possessed priestess" went as follows:

Sa komanda, na kromanti Akua	*Sa-kɔm-anna, na "kromanti" [korɔmante] Akua*
Sa komanda, achawa-o, achawa-a	*Sa-kɔm-anna, atwa wo ho, atwa wo ho a*
Dati na kɔmfo	*Dede na Kɔmfo*
Akɔmfo na me ba[66]	*Akɔmfo na mɛba*

"The Most Unruly" 117

The Herskovitses did not provide a translation for the preceding text in the left-hand column; however, the intelligible Akan words, including some of lexical items in table 4.2, allow for a transcription and the following translation: *Sa-kɔm-anna, na "kromanti" [korɔmante] Akua* means "one who dances *akɔm* and has not slept, korɔmante Akua," while *sa-kɔm-anna, atwa wo ho, atwa wo ho a* would be "one who dances *akɔm* and has not slept, spin yourself in a circle, spin yourself in a circle" (the motion and context for *akɔm* dancing). Dede or *ɔdede* is a Guan rather than an Akan term, but it carries the same meaning as the Akan *ɔkɔmfoɔ*: *Dede na kɔmfo* refers to "dede (Guan spiritualist) and kɔmfo (Akan spiritualist)," and *akɔmfo na mɛba* means "*akɔmfo* [sg. *ɔkɔmfoɔ*], and I will come."[67] In our efforts to clarify the identity of Tata Odun and other important *abosom* among the Maroons of Suriname and perhaps French Guiana, we also elucidate the Akan contribution to the continuity and transformation of an African cultural dynamic in the Americas. What is remarkable is the marked similarity of Saramaka spirituality and culture, for example, between its present form and the one encountered by German missionaries after the 1762 peace treaty. In addition, like indigenous African spiritualities, Saramaka "religion" had no name (as far as the outsiders were concerned), for it was not a separate realm of life.[68] These Maroons and others were able to simultaneously forge and maintain culture and a spiritual practice that halted much of the missionary proselytization. They did this on account of their relative isolation, a high African-to-European ratio, an internal dialogue among African cultures shaped by diasporic experiences, by war and independence, and by nonnegotiable convictions that were the composite fruits of that dialogue. Indeed, the picture we can draw of early and extant Maroon communities, particularly of those who rejected or delayed their treaty signing, is not that "traditional African institutions" could not cross the Atlantic, as Richard Price argues, but that those institutions were knowledge intensive and were constituted by the very "immense quantities" of knowledge and beliefs transported in the hearts and minds of those who survived the temporally one-way voyage and escaped captivity shortly after arrival.[69]

Further evidence for the contribution of a composite Akan culture to the African experience in Suriname is found in the material or expressive culture, which is itself often linked to or rooted in a spiritual culture and practice. In a photo of a garden camp included in *Maroon Arts*, Richard Price and Sally Price have captured a small settlement of three houses, four open-sided structures, a so-called menstrual hut, and, apparently unbeknownst to its photographer, who had made no mention of it, an *Onyame dua* (Creator's tree) positioned in what appears to be the center of this camp (see figure 4.1).[70] An *Onyame dua* is often referred to as "God's alter," and, in this photo

Figure 4.1. A Saramaka Maroon garden camp on the Upper Pikílío, Suriname, 1968. Note the appearance of an *onyame dua*, which can be made of either the three- or four-pronged tree of the same name, in the middle of the camp. Photo courtesy of Richard Price.

and as was typical in Ghana, a calabash vessel was situated between four sticks that acted as prongs with what appears to be some (unrecognizable) items inside a vessel that usually contained eggs, herbs, rainwater, and other ingredients and where people make offerings or say "prayers." The *Onyame dua* in the Akan homeland might have three or four prongs, but they were usually part of the tree that was known by the same name.

Other material culture included cloth, stools, and drums that resembled Akan types with variations in style from the original Akan forms. The Saramaka *apínti* drum, for example, was used by Aluku drummers at funeral rites—perhaps also nine-night wakes held in Paramaribo and elsewhere—and was beaten with sticks held in an upright position. This drum is identical in name and function to the Akan *petia* or Asante *mpintin*, both of which were also played with two sticks in an upright position and form part of the drums of the *fontomfrom* orchestra.[71] This orchestra is also found among the Saramaka in the form of five drum types: the *apínti, deindein, agidá, apúku doón,* and *lánga doón*. The *deindein* resembles the Akan *adukurogya*, and the *agidá* directly corresponds to the *fontomfrom* (also known as *bomma*), and both the Saramaka and the Akan of West Africa play the latter horizontally with one stick and one hand.[72]

"The Most Unruly"

A number of these drums were not only used in funerary rites but also in outdoor spiritual ceremonies that scholars have described as "play" among the Djuka and other Maroons. Incidentally or not, this "play" (also found among the Maroons of Jamaica) mirrors the outdoor scene of an Akan *akɔm* spiritual ceremony where the *abosom* are invoked and manifest themselves through the *akɔmfoɔ*. In both Suriname and Ghana, the *akɔmfoɔ* in spiritual communion with an *ɔbosom* have their face and upper body covered in white clay (*hyire*) and are surrounded by attendees in a circle and they dance counterclockwise to the drums.[73] These ritual spaces of invoking the *abosom* (and in some instances the ancestors as well) were premised on community-based resolutions to challenges related to life and living, which often came down to social, biological, psychic, and spiritual healing. As in the Danish colonies, high praise for the efficacy of herbal medicines employed by Akan persons and consumed by many, including Christians and Jews, continued in Suriname. In the area of indigenous medicine and healing, one of the "most renowned priestess[es was] a Negress called Dasina." Dasina was likely an *ɔkɔmfoɔ*, for she had a corner in her house with a "large earthen pot filled with water" and other ingredients, wherein "she consult[ed] her pot and her figures [('idols...made of earth')]...[and gave] the sick persons some water that is in the pot to drink."[74] That special vessel is generically called *asuo yaa* and is used for divination; its waters can be used for spiritual baths, among other purposes (see figure 4.2). In addition to Dasina, one of the most famous healers was "[t]he Negro Quassy" (Kwasi), though he also served as the colony's "healer-diviner" and as the principal intermediary between the colony and the Maroons.[75] He was respected "as a priest" among whites and some Africans and called "Loacouman ['diviner'] Quassy" until his fame among the colonists reportedly eroded after he failed an experiment designed by one Monsieur Pichot.[76] Quassy, described as an opportunist, continued his anti-Maroon activities and served the colony faithfully into his nineties or until he died in 1787.[77] Quassy was also a practitioner of what Stedman described as "obia," and the latter even observed a "rebel negro" Coromantin wearing "a superstitious obia or amulet tied about his neck, in which case he places all his hope and confidence."[78] In Suriname and largely among Maroons, "obeah" remained positive as a form of spiritual power, healing, and protection unlike in the (former) British or Danish colonies of the Americas in the nineteenth and twentieth centuries.[79] *Brua*, a concept akin to "obeah" in Curaçao, had a similar connotation.[80]

In postemancipation Curaçao, the vast majority of the African-descended population had limited access to valued resources controlled by white elites before and after enslavement. For Suriname, the plantocracy remained a powerful force until the beginning of the twentieth century and evolved a racialized social order and hierarchy based on color. This meant Africans

Figure 4.2. Spiritual healer woman in Paramaribo, Suriname, ca. 1839. Such spiritualists formed an integral part of the therapeutic resources available to enslaved and newly emancipated Africans. Some whites also often praised the efficacy of their medicinal preparations. Pierre Jacques Benoit, *Voyage à Surinam*, Beinecke Rare Book and Manuscript Library, Yale University.

were positioned at the bottom, beneath the Chinese (Westernized, Christianized, and Dutch speaking), who trailed the Javanese, Hindu, Dutch, and other Europeans, while the Maroons and Amerindians were peripheral to the political economy of the country. Ironically, the meaning of prior "blood treaties" between the Maroons and the Dutch colonists and their supposed sovereignty meant little if anything when the national army, led by former military dictator Desi Bouterse, fought all Maroon groups in a brutal civil war during the 1980s.[81] Freedom for those manumitted during the nineteenth century and during formal enslavement was also precarious, for, in Curaçao and perhaps in Suriname as well, "sometimes both the freed and the enslaved ended their lives lying by the side of the road."[82] During the period of manumission in Suriname (1832–1863), rarely were enslaved children under twelve or adults under forty manumitted before 1849, and between 1832 and 1848 only 882 enslaved men and 1,399 enslaved women were manumitted—a total of 2,281 manumissions that occurred almost exclusively among persons forty years old or older.[83] The reason for the greater number of women compared to men is that manumission usually occurred through concubinage with white men, as offspring of such an arrangement, and as a result of faithful service toward and labor for one's owner. This was certainly the case in Curaçao, where the number of manumissions increased after 1850 and where many converted to Catholicism under increased proselytization and social control by the state. Between 1832 and 1863, a total of 2,489 men and 3,875 women were manumitted across all age groups in Suriname, and, out of 6,364 manumissions during the nineteenth century, only 5 persons were manumitted six years after slavery was legally abolished on 1 July 1863.

In postabolition Suriname, 45.4 percent of the formerly enslaved men were "too young," suggesting that at least one-third of the manumitted were children and possibly of African European parentage, while others worked as house servants, craftspersons, farmers, and shoemakers.[84] For women, 41 percent of the 2,993 manumitted women labored as house servants, while 32 percent were listed as "too young," and the rest were seamstresses and farmers. Those who were manumitted assumed new family names and either kept or relinquished the name given to them during slavery. One example is a women registered within the (black) Jewish community of Suriname named Adjuba (Adwoa, "Monday-born female"; Atjuba is the version found east of the Volta River). Adjuba was manumitted on 20 December 1841 with her three children—one carried the first name of her (former) slave owner, Daniel Jessurun Lobo—but she could not assume her owner's last name as a family name, and so she took "Lobo" (wolf) in translation and became known as Adjuba Sara Wolf. In all likelihood, Adjuba and her immediate ancestors shared a similar story as to their entry into the slave society of Suriname, a story that mirrored those of many, including Stedman's Quacco, who disclosed what might be called an "autobiography."

Along with two younger brothers, Quacco was stolen from his parents, who lived by hunting and farming when he was very young. He was carried off in a bag and soon became the "slave of [a] king on the coast of Guinea" with many hundreds more who, like him and his siblings, were given as gifts to captains of the "king's army." His new owner sold him again to a captain of a Dutch ship for "some [gun] powder and a musket." Then he was transported to Suriname and at some point became the "Black boy" servant for Stedman in the latter half of the eighteenth century.[85] The layered narratives of those manumitted and of the Maroons in Suriname differ little from other accounts of Akan and African peoples' lives in the Americas and, in Quacco's case, autobiographical accounts found largely in the British colonies. The next chapter takes up the Akan experience in the British Caribbean.

5

The Antelope (*Adowa*) and the Elephant (*Esono*)

The Akan in the British Caribbean

Esono kokuroko
(The elephant is bigger)
Adowa na ɔman wɔ no
(It is the small antelope to which the nation belongs)
—Akan drum text

To the Akan, the elephant (*ɛsono*) has tremendous size and force, and its tail remains a key symbol of wealth and leadership in Asante, but the small antelope (*adowa*) is clever and versatile. Because it is wisdom (*nyansa*) rather than brute strength has greater communal value, then it is to the antelope the "nation" belongs. The Akan in the Americas personify this antelope, for although their gross numbers were relatively small in relation to the bights of Bénin and Biafra and certainly the Kôngo-Angola region, their ability to influence and even transform the course and context of their lives and those of others has fittingly made some of them national symbols of leadership in the (British) Caribbean. For this chapter on the British Caribbean, I want to make it clear the Akan on the Gold Coast or elsewhere did not create the interpolated identities of "Mina" or "Coromantee"—even if some were identified with these trademarks as proxies for "nations" in European travelogues—nor did they root their identity in the small fishing village of Kormantin (phonetically distorted as "Coromantee" and its variants), since "some [scholars] go as far as to refer to a Kormantse [or 'Coromantee'] 'nation'" in ways that seem facile and baseless in the culture history and language(s) of Gold Coast peoples.[1]

The British established their Gold Coast base at Kormantin in 1631 through former Dutch merchant Arent Groote, who persuaded Ambro Braffo of the Fante to sign an agreement that would allow the British to build a lodge near the Kormantin village. The lodge was built but then destroyed by fire in 1640, and the British withdrew from Kormantin thereafter; surprisingly, Akan and non-Akan persons from the Gold Coast found primarily in British America and through British-registered vessels continued to be recorded widely as "Coromantee." The brief importance of Kormantin was eclipsed by the key British coastal holdings and embarkation ports of Anomabu and Cape Coast during the eighteenth century as the focus of the international enslavement enterprise on the Gold Coast shifted westward away from Accra and the area divided by the Volta River. It was also during this time that the "Mina," who spoke Akan rather than the Gā-Adangme language, were brought to the Americas in numbers enough to constitute a distinct group there. However, those Africans from the Gold Coast who were transplanted to the Americas through largely British-controlled ports and on British vessels still carried the designation of "Coromantee," and it is highly doubtful whether a "nation" under the "Coromantee" rubric ever existed at all.

The general characterization of the Mina in the Danish and Dutch Caribbean mirrored that of the Coromantee in the British Caribbean: They were prominent in Maroon communities, conspiracies, and revolts against slavery in pursuit of sovereignty, and they formed spiritual-healing practices (based on indigenous medicinal knowledge), kinship networks, and mutual aid societies as ways to reconstitute family and community in foreign lands. The Dutch capture of Kormantin from the British in the mid-1660s was part of a series of events in which the Dutch and the British vied for trading supremacy on the Gold Coast, and though both were on peaceful terms, they nonetheless interfaced with one another's operations, captured one another's ships and Gold Coast bases, and competed for the favors of coastal leaders and merchants through gifts and bribes.[2] During this period, the Dutch had almost driven the British from the Gold Coast, while the Royal Adventurers faced heavy opposition to their "slave trade" monopoly in England, and British planters in the Caribbean objected to the large number of enslaved Africans that were sold to Spanish colonies. The successor of the Royal Adventurers, the Royal African Company, faced similar criticism, and when its monopoly ended in 1689, British merchants obtained licenses from the company and paid taxes to company officials.[3] The Dutch and British war of 1665–1668 resulted in the Dutch seizure of Kormantin and the British capture of Cape Coast Castle, supplemented by its holdings at Komenda, Winneba, Fort Royal, Accra, and Anomabu. The Dutch capture of Kormantin, however, meant a virtual end to the role of the coastal village in Britain's slaving activities on the Gold Coast, but it did not translate into an equally rapid decline in the use of "Coromantee" as a marker for most Africans exported from the Gold Coast; the term remained in wide circulation beyond the British colonies. In eighteenth-century Saint Dominique (Haiti), for example, there were references to "Coromantees" and "Minas," which supports the continued use of the former. It also suggests that distinctions were made between the enslaved Africans from various locations on the Gold Coast who were brought to Saint Dominique via British ships since the term "Coromantee" was commonly used on British vessels and in the American colonies.[4] But the Akan presence in the Americas was less considerable in what became Haiti than in other parts of the region, such as the wider British Caribbean.

Between the mid-seventeenth century and the first decade of the nineteenth century, 61.4 percent of the recorded 2,485 voyages from the Gold Coast to the Americas occurred on vessels registered to the British. The remainder went to North American (12.8 percent), Dutch (9.8 percent), French (5.6 percent), Portuguese-Brazilian (5.9 percent), and Danish (4.5 percent) colonies.[5] Thirty-six percent of the 2,128 recorded voyages from the Gold Coast to the Caribbean went to the British colony of Jamaica, while remaining voyages went to other parts of the British Caribbean, including but not limited to Barbados (15.1 percent), Guyana (4.5 percent), and Antigua (3.6 percent). The Gold Coast figured prominently in the minds of planters and merchants in the British colonies of the Americas. The British controlled key Gold Coast ports and possessed an institutional or industrial framework built crucially upon and sustained through transatlantic slaving, made it so that Britain's colonial reach facilitated the passage and settlement of Akan peoples outside of their homeland. British records list 86,703 Gold Coast captives having been exported to the Americas (presumably the British Caribbean and North America) between 1758 and 1775 under British registered vessels, but the Trans-Atlantic Slave Trade Database lists a slightly lower number of exported captives—82,794—using the same criteria.[6] Merchants, planters, and officials raved over the "superior quality" (read: laboring capacity and low mortality) of these captives embarked principally from Anomabu and Cape Coast, and many, considering the risks, paid higher prices to secure them during the eighteenth century.[7] Table 5.1 provides a sample of voyages from the Gold Coast to the late eighteenth-century Caribbean.

The inspector general at the custom house in London noted the irregular transmission of data from the "West Indies" and (we should trust) that the number of voyages and persons in table 5.1 does not constitute most or all "cargoes" imported to the British Caribbean. Of the fifteen known autobiographical accounts left by Africans shipped to British colonies in the Americas, Jerome Handler found that six out of the ten that contained details about areas of embarkation listed the Gold Coast. Of these, three disclosed "Asante" or "Fante" as their "ethnicity," while one mentioned being from what is now northern Ghana. Several of these Africans were transshipped to North America during the period when Britain was the primary slave-trading nation.[8] Consistent with accounts shared by Akan persons in the Danish colonies or persons like Quacco (Kwaku) in Suriname, many of these Africans who shared "autobiographies" were captured as

Table 5.1. Gold Coast African Imports to the British Caribbean, 1789–1795

Year	Vessel	Gold Coast Port	Embarked	Deaths	Disembarked
1789	Mary	Anomabu	232	1	231
	Alert	Anomabu	276	11	265
	Chambers	Anomabu	238	4	234
	June	Anomabu	357	25	332
	Lovely Lass	Anomabu	408	10	398
	Diana	Anomabu	357	6	351
	Fly	Anomabu	239	1	238
	Molly	Gold Coast	428	18	410
	Hind	Gold Coast	203	1	202
	Ruby	Gold Coast	175	5	170
	Concord	Gold Coast	211	3	208
	Marian	Gold Coast	225	4	221
1791	Mermaid	Anomabu	140	4	136
	Mercury	Anomabu	310	10	300
	Golden Cage	Anomabu	541	5	536
	Venus	Anomabu	239	13	226
	Young Hero	Anomabu	197	—	197
	Jupiter	Cape Coast	299	28	271
	Ellis	Anomabu	404	15	389
	Ariel	Anomabu	164	—	164
	Lovely Lass	Anomabu	380	12	368
	Abigail	Winneba	106	—	106
	Gely	Anomabu	131	1	130
	John	Anomabu	200	3	197
1792	Speculator	Anomabu	58	1	57
	Eliza	Anomabu	122	3	119
	Rio Novas	Anomabu	467	53	414
	Fly	Anomabu	239	2	237
	Jelly	Anomabu	132	—	132
	Venus	Anomabu	236	—	236
	John	Anomabu	201	1	200
	Ann	Gold Coast	206	8	198
	Talbot	Anomabu	131	1	130
	Alice	Anomabu	341	6	335
	Frances & Harriott	Anomabu	339	73	266
	Royal Charlotte	Anomabu	101	—	101
	Queen Charlotte	Anomabu	70	1	69
1793	Flora	Cape Coast	116	1	115
	Rio Nova[s]	Gold Coast	573	4	569
	Dutch Portland	Cape Coast	100	2	98
	Molly	Anomabu	391	4	387
	Talbot	Anomabu	131	—	131
	Iris	Anomabu	341	3	338

(continued)

Table 5.1. Continued

Year	Vessel	Gold Coast Port	Embarked	Deaths	Disembarked
	Martha's Goodwill	Cape Coast	46	4	42
	London	Anomabu	251	7	244
	Express	Gold Coast	126	1	125
1794	Countess de Galvez	Cape Coast	342	12	330
	Golden Grove	Gold Coast	412	3	409
	Express	Anomabu	128	1	127
	Bird	Anomabu	286	13	273
	John	Cape Coast	222	7	215
	Mercury	Cape Coast	373	31	342
	Fly	Cape Coast	238	4	234
	Iris	Cape Coast	256	15	241
1795	Mary	Anomabu	453	11	442
	Experiment	Anomabu	238	7	231
	Commerce	Anomabu	233	—	233
	Queen	Anomabu	523	5	518
	Gambia	Cape Coast	278	5	273
	Bud	Anomabu	281	6	275

Source: "An Account of All Cargoes of Negroes Imported into the British West India Islands from the Coast of Africa [...]," *House of Commons Sessional Papers of the Eighteenth Century: Forces, West Indies, 1795–96*, vol. 100, 27 November 1795–6 May 1796, 183–190. Vessels to the Volta River, which formed the eastern part of the Gold Coast, included the port of Whydah (Ouidah), but, for that reason, these voyages were not included in the table. The source does not explain how the deaths occurred, and the custom house officers in London who completed this list noted that the data for 1790 were "so defective, that the Inspector General can render no Account of that Year." Most of these slaving voyages departed from Liverpool.

children during warfare, kidnapped by slave raiders, duplicitously enslaved, or torn from home and family as a result of debt owed by a relative. The six that identified the Gold Coast as an area of embarkation, as well as two others, are summarized as follows, scattered across British America.

- Ashy, a Fante woman who was transported to Barbados and lived most of her life on the island, had her story recorded in 1799 in "English creole."
- Abu Bakr was born in Timbuktu around 1790, captured in warfare, and then exported on a British vessel from the Gold Coast to Jamaica, where he spent thirty years. He wrote his account in Arabic around 1835.
- Belinda (Royall) was born near the Volta River in northern Ghana (perhaps the Black Volta River, just above the edge of the forest). At the age of twelve, she was shipped possibly to Antigua before she arrived in Massachusetts. Belinda was seventy years old in 1782,

which would give us a birth year of 1712 and would mark her departure from the Gold Coast in the year 1724. While her parents were praying at a shrine in a sacred grove, Belinda recalled as a child, an armed band of "white men" captured her people and detained them in chains. Either these "white men" were lighter-skinned Africans from the Sahel region who raided settlements such as Belinda's in northern Ghana or Belinda's capture took place on the coast proximate or via the Volta River, where her family would have had an increased likelihood of seeing armed white men.
- James Albert Ukawsaw Gronniosaw was from Bornu but exported via the Gold Coast on a Dutch slaver to Barbados in the 1720s. He was transshipped to New York, where he was freed in the 1760s and then relocated to England, where he composed his account (published in 1772) around the age of sixty.
- John Joseph, an Asante and prisoner of war (along with his sister), was transported directly to New Orleans in the early nineteenth century and worked in Louisiana, South Carolina, and Virginia. He moved to England in 1843 and related his account.
- Ottobah Kobina Cugoano, a Fante, was kidnapped around the age of thirteen and sent to Cape Coast Castle and then shipped to Grenada or other parts of the Caribbean and finally to England at the end of 1772. He published his account at the age of thirty.
- Venture Smith was born around 1729. He was kidnapped and taken to the fort at Anomabu on the Gold Coast and transported to Barbados around 1737 but was taken to Rhode Island shortly thereafter, where he lived as a farmer and a married man with his family. He lived in Connecticut and New York as well. Smith was freed at the age of thirty-six but narrated his story at sixty-nine years of age.
- William Unsah Sessarakoo (William Ansa Sasraku?), "young prince of Annamaboe" (Anomabu) on the Fante coast, was duped, shipped, and sold to a planter in Barbados around 1744 but was later liberated and taken to London in 1749. He returned to his family on the Gold Coast a few years later.[9]

THE CULTURE OF CONSPIRACIES AND REVOLTS: THE AKAN IN BARBADOS, ANTIGUA, AND GUYANA

The preceding eight accounts in abridged form are instructive, for these snapshots plot out those geopolitical points where Akan persons were transported in the Americas (map 4)—that is, Barbados, Antigua, Jamaica, South Carolina,

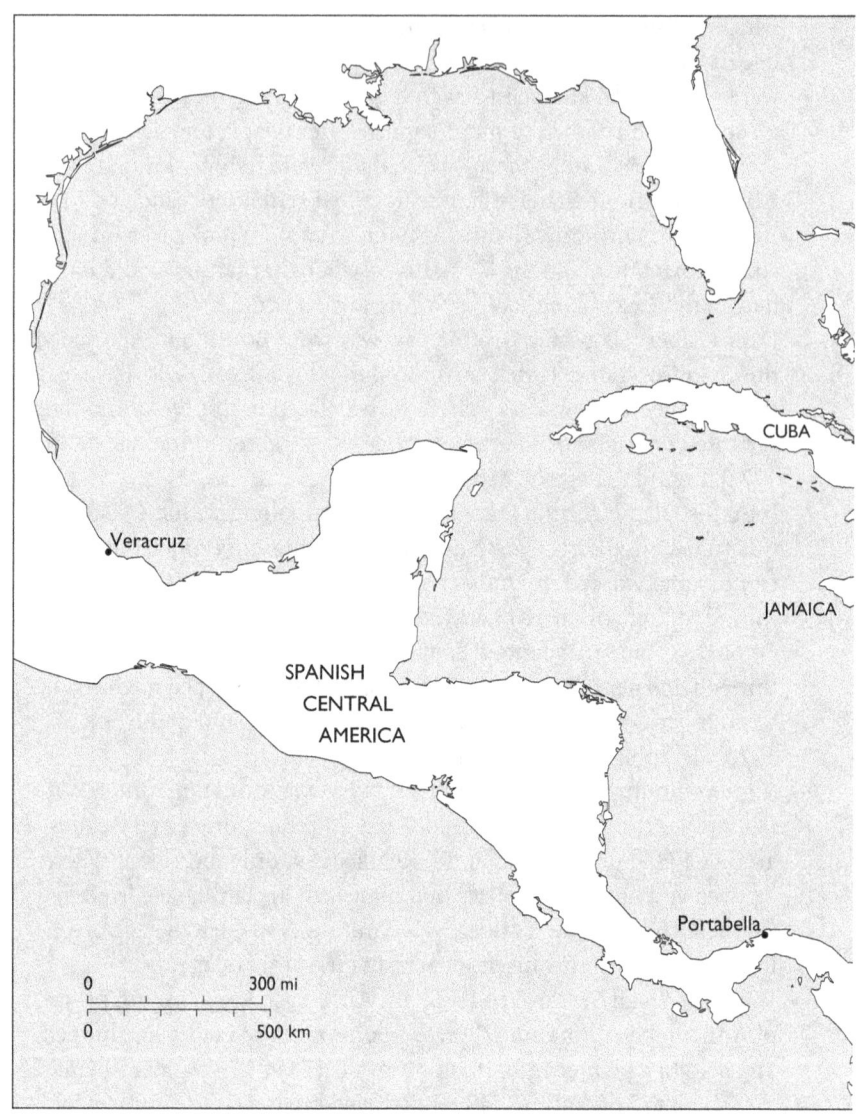

Map 4. The eighteenth-century Caribbean region during the international enslavement enterprise. Reprinted by permission of the Omohundro Institute of Early American History and Culture from the *William and Mary Quarterly*.

ATLANTIC OCEAN

BAHAMAS

SAINT DOMINGUE

PUERTO RICO

LESSER ANTILLES

CARIBBEAN SEA

CURAÇAO

BARBADOS

Cartagena

Caracas

TRINIDAD

GUYANA

Virginia, New York, and elsewhere—and affirm some known anomalies about the Gold Coast as an area of exclusive or mostly Akan exportation. As these sketches of individuals exported from the Gold Coast show, some were not from the Gold Coast region (e.g., Abu Bakr, James Albert Ukawsaw Gronniosaw) or of Akan cultural origin (e.g., Belinda). More than likely they were clustered—with Akan persons—under the category of "Coromantee," a category that could simultaneously apply to a preponderant or minority Akan presence in the same Caribbean society, on the same plantation, and within the same Maroon group or kinship network. Thus, knowing the port of embarkation is a necessary though insufficient criterion, but that piece of information suggests that we need to employ additional evidence from Akan spiritual, ideational, and material culture augmented by the historical data and the demographic patterns of Akan importation into the Americas. British records internal to the international enslavement enterprise observed at Anomabu that "all nations trade [here] without interruption" in that 20 to 25 ships at one time could be found on "Annamaboe Road." But, in spite of and because of the evident demand for captives, ship captains often noted the common practice of sending small vessels from Anomabu to procure captives from Bénin and Lagos and then selling them as Gold Coast captives, though one captained admitted, "the Slaves of the Gold Coast are easily distinguished."[10] Thus, we must temper the urge to equate "Coromantee" with "Akan" based on a literal reading of the sources and instead consider a composite Akan culture in specific historical contexts. We know that most if not all of the people featured in the eight patently abridged biographies departed from the Gold Coast in general and specifically the British headquarters at Anomabu and Cape Coast. However, at least half of these persons spent some time in Barbados, the first, large-scale, sugar-producing British colony (established in 1627), and so we turn to Barbados and begin our consideration of a broad Akan experience in the British Caribbean.

"The Grand Conspiracy of the Negroes": The Akan Moment in Barbados

As the easternmost island of the Lesser Antilles, Barbados had, by the mid-seventeenth century, become Britain's wealthiest and most populous colony in the Americas through Dutch intervention in the 1640s. To the English planters, the Dutch introduced sugar and related technology developed on plantations in the Brazilian state of Pernambuco and provided a significant number of Africans to grow and process the sugar.[11] That sugar was, in turn, not only used to procure more Africans but also received as payment by the Dutch and sold in Holland. In 1675 the colony held its breath as the alleged Akan-led "grand conspiracy" to revolt unfolded. The supposed plot, however, was uncovered from what might have boiled down to betrayal from within. The "True and Faithful Account of the Grand Conspiracy," published a year after the alleged plot, claimed that the plan had been in the works among the "Cormantee or Gold-Cost [sic] Negro's [sic]" for three years and that its aim was to install a "King, one Coffee [Kofi,] an Ancient Gold-Cost [sic] Negro, who should have been Crowned the 12th of June last past in a Chair of State exquisitely wrought and Carved after their Mode; with Bowes and Arrowes to be likewise carried in State before his Majesty."[12] Trumpets were to be made of elephants' teeth, gourds sounded on several hills to announce their "general rising," the sugar cane fields were to be burned, and the conspirators were to cut the throats of their captors. These activities would be preceded by sacred oaths and perhaps a political plan of action (the "grand design") on how to manage the postinsurrection colony based upon the ideational (centralized politics), spiritual (oaths and rituals), and material (wooden stool as symbol of leadership) culture of Akan polities. We can be assured that in this instance "Coromantee" referred to a sizable Akan presence, granted the foregoing cultural evidence. Demographically, an average of 40 percent of the Africans imported to Barbados came from the Gold Coast between 1650 and the 1710s, and a historical aggregate of at least 136,000 Africans came from the Gold Coast—only Jamaica had a higher total in the British Caribbean.

The Africans from the Gold Coast were seemingly preferred, at least up until the late eighteenth century, but before then, "The negroes most in demand at Barbados, are the Gold Coast, or, as they call them Cormantines," wrote officials to the Royal African Company in 1692 or 1693.[13] The voyage of the *James*, which unfolded during the year of the alleged plot of 1675, and the publication of its account in 1676 provide one of many examples of the African experience on board vessels that left London, procured captives on the Gold Coast, and disembarked at Barbados, as one of several possible landings, to meet the demand for such captives.[14] After the British had secured gold and a number of captives, one "neagger-man" died suddenly on 6 September 1675 near Assinie. At Axim, the vessel procured water, wood, and food for the enslaved, and while anchored at Winneba, Sekondi, and Kormantin, it secured more gold and captives from Anomabu, which included the losers at the conclusion of a battle between Wassa, Fetu, and the Akani. The *James* then proceeded to Cape Coast with a total of sixteen captives around 9 December. In the (European) New Year, the vessel took on more captives and washed them with water. Thereafter and on a daily basis they ate fish with corn and, on at least two occasions, were given "tobacco and pypes." The *James* reached Barbados on 1 May 1676. On 24 May the captives were shaved and washed with water, smeared with palm oil, and given tobacco.

The next day, 103 were sold; the following day, 70; and on 27 May, 118, totaling 291, with some "refuse slaves." Five of the "refuse slaves" were sold on 31 May, with 17 (7 men, 10 women) remaining. Typically, Royal African Company agents or merchants in the Caribbean and elsewhere received company captives upon arrival, immediately boarded the vessel, checked the captain's journal and accounts, mustered the Africans, and sorted them in preparation for the sale, which sometimes took place on board. The *James* was then restocked with 224 new captives (taken from a vessel that arrived from Old Calabar) bound for Nevis: Each were sold, including the 18 that were described as "very bad," for 1,000 pounds of sugar, though one individual sold for 1,400 pounds of sugar. Of the 20 that remained ("refuse slaves"), each was sold for 1,700 pounds of sugar, though marginal notes in the original documents state that the Gold Coast captives sold at 3,500 pounds of sugar a head.

The crew and vessel then sailed for England on 8 July and anchored at Downs on 12 October 1676. At the end of this voyage, a total of 28 men, 19 women, and 4 boys died on board the *James*. Some departed this world in moments of convulsions or fevers, after refusing to eat, or as a result of dropsy (edema), leaping overboard, or swellings of the face and head. We can be sure that the incongruence between African diets and the food supply used by slavers contributed to African mortality and morbidity, for corn and tobacco might have been disastrous for yam-consuming peoples via gastrointestinal disease.[15] Such a disease even contributed to cases where new life died within the dying: One woman "[m]iscarryed and the Child dead within her and Rotten and dyed 2 days after delivery."[16] Most of these Africans either were from or only departed from the ports of Anomabu and Winneba on the Gold Coast and were, without question, procured to feed an almost insatiable demand.

That demand was more real than imagined, and the thinking that the Akan were "habituated from infancy to war," brought "with them into slavery lofty ideas of independence," and were "dangerous inmates on a West-India plantation" must have framed a "Cormantine" conspiracy in Barbados.[17] An actual plot seems doubtful, though not improbable, for the "conspiracy" and the false "Tryal at a Court" was based on the bold talk of a "Young Cormantee Negro" indirectly overheard and reported by another enslaved African, Anna, to her owner. After that "Cormantee Negro" implicated several others (of what is uncertain), the hunt was as swift as the executions: Seventeen were initially burned alive and beheaded, and then twenty-five more were executed. Many probably maintained their innocence, including the five who hung themselves, and in one courageous moment in which confessions were sought from "one of those that were burned alive being chained at the stake," another chained "Cormantee" named Tony insisted, "Are there not enough of our Country-men killed already?"[18] The former, who was not named, "would not speak one word more" thereafter.

In the end, we gain the these insights into Akan cultural thought and behavior at the expense of the more than one hundred Africans implicated, the close to fifty persons that were executed, and the few that committed suicide on account of a conspiracy that might not have been real. After this alleged plot, there were a few revolts, such as the one in 1649, though those revolts did not include insurrections on board vessels that left the Gold Coast for Barbados—that is, the *Adventure* in 1696, the *Dorothy* in 1708, the *George* in 1727, and the *Hare* in 1731. On the whole, Barbados did not "experience any truly successful slave revolt, most likely because it was too small and lacked an interior that would sustain a Maroon colony and guerrilla warfare."[19] One could argue that Akan culture lent itself to and its peoples were active participants in revolts and conspiracies throughout the Americas. However, our understanding of a composite Akan culture in the region would be better served by using those moments of insurrection or plot not as ends but rather as means to examine the cultural window they offer in order to better approach these Akan people and their experiences.

"Conspiracy of the Negroes at Antigua": The Akan Cultural Factor

In ways similar to the alleged Barbados plot of 1675 and related conspiracies and insurrections in the Danish and Dutch colonies, the Coromantee-led conspiracy to revolt in Antigua during 1736 provides another historical macromoment to enlarge our understanding of the Akan experience on a community and personal microlevel. The 1736 conspiracy to revolt also reveals much about (the potential of) intra-African alliances and about strategies of forging operational unity using Akan cultural practices. These aspects contrast with the lack of broad support among distinct segments of plantation-based Africans (born in Africa) and freed and unfree artisans (those born in the Americas). These artisans were mobile in an urban setting and interacted with a greater cross-section of Africans via their profession. Unlike the popular stereotype of Akan persons in the Americas as unskilled and as having been procured for their strength and ability to labor with little "seasoning," most of the Akan "conspirators" who were executed were skilled individuals: One of two men named Cudjoe (Kwadwo) was a sugar boiler, while the other was a carpenter and fiddler; one of two men named Quash (Kwasi) was a cooper, while the other was a carpenter; one of two men named Secundi (Sekondi) was a driver, while the other was a suspected leader of a revolt in the aftermath of the plot; one of two men named Quaco (Kwaku) was a cooper, while the other was a driver; and Cuffee (Kofi) was a mason. A number of these Akan men were carpenters and coopers, but there were more drivers, including Secundi, Cuffy (Kofi), Cudjoe (Kwadwo), and Quashee Cumma (Kwasi Kuma).[20] According to the available records, these individuals were mobile and had access to arms and other resources, and a few apparently had acquired some wealth, given the magnitude of their feasts and other celebrations.

The 1736 plot to revolt began in an urban setting, much like the 1733 Akan-led revolt in the Danish colony of St. John. As the alleged brainchild of a sizable group of skilled Coromantees that had enstooled as "king" another Coromantee named Court (Great Takyi), this group of a few hundred in total were implicated in planning to blow up a ballroom where a coronation ceremony for the British crown was to be held and with much of the plantocracy in attendance.[21] This plot, like the alleged Barbados conspiracy of 1675, is questionable in both its existence and the extent of its design, though it is not improbable for the very same reasons, and it offers another well-documented instance of the Akan cultural practices in the Americas. John Thornton argues that the so-called *ikem* (ɛkyɛm or ɔkyɛm, shield) or "shield ceremony" in which Court was made "king" and which Antiguan officials (and several historians) interpreted as a declaration of war was actually an ennobling ceremony—used for Gold Coast merchants and for Court as one of the richest enslaved persons in Antigua—disguised as a coronation.[22] Thornton notes the circumstantial "evidence" or "confessions" secured by torture, as well as the rumors against Court, who maintained his innocence, while Philip Morgan, who relies on Thornton's interpretation, is convinced that the Antiguan judges misinterpreted the "shield dance," the courts procured "evidence" by inflicting pain through torture, and key witnesses accused others who were tried in closed sessions.[23] David Gaspar constructed a detailed account of what he claimed was an *actual* plot but who disclosed how the courts secured "confessions" and that we have only their version. Gasper argues that the *ikem* dance was "in fact [an] Akan ceremonial that prepared participants for war against the whites."[24] Gaspar's account demonstrates the depth of the archival sources available and their explications of Akan cultural practices—much better than the Barbados plot of 1675—but the Barbados and Antigua cases are too similar in their origin and outcomes to simply say there would have been a revolt by the supposed "conspirators" in question.

In the Antiguan trial records, there are only a few omnipresent and key witnesses, the testimony of those accused and those trying to avoid torture or execution are inconsistent, there were disputes about confessing to the magistrates and spies in the prisons where the accused were held, and those on trial had no legal representation, in contrast to the 1712 Akan-led revolt in New York, where some counsel was provided in the Supreme Court cases.[25] These considerations cast doubt not on the possibility but on the extent of a real conspiracy, as Gaspar argues, for the alleged plot was uncovered before it could take place, and there is no evidence to suggest that there was a revolt, such as in the 1712 case in New York or the 1733 case in the Danish colony of St. John. For Thornton and Morgan, an ennobling ceremony might be one interpretation of the so-called shield dance, but there are others. Thornton relies on Dutch merchant Willem Bosman's account of such a ceremony, which employed a horn and a shield to convey "nobility" among "commoners," but Bosman does not provide an Akan or a Twi name for this ennobling ceremony (the judges in Antigua had recorded a specific ceremony called the *ikem* dance). He also raises additional questions about Thornton's interpretation, for Bosman was fond of using the Gold Coast settlement of Axim (because of its relationship with the Dutch) for examples of local sociopolitical rank and mobility when they were atypical. Thornton argues that Court was ennobled because of his riches, which allowed him to move from the rank of "commoner" to that of "noble" since Court was not of "royal blood." However, if Bosman concludes that those who possessed "the greatest *Riches* receive[d] also the greatest *Honour* without *Nobility* being mixed in it to the least," then why would an ennobling ceremony be performed for one of the richest enslaved persons in Antigua?[26] Certainly, one could become wealthy and wield some political power in Antigua or the Akan homeland; however, *wonya wo ho a, wonyɛ ɔdehyeɛ!* (if you become rich, you will not be a "royal" [or "noble"]).

It would seem that something might have been missed in the evidence and in not placing the cultural data extrapolated from those sources into perspective. Certainly, the alleged Akan male conspirators and the women, such as Obbah (Aba, Yaa), were involved in oaths and in rituals held at gravesites by a silk cotton tree and whose feasts served purposes other than gathering. Similar rites that connected imperatives of the temporal world with resources of the spiritual one were also present in the supposed Akan-led plot on St. Croix in 1759, but there was no revolt or real conspiracy. The oath ceremony performed in Antigua involved "drinking the *abosom*" (*yɛnnom abosom*, we should drink *abosom*); that is, this oath taking was a process of initiation and solidarity before witnesses that included spiritual entities such as the *abosom* and to whom one would be accountable. But such oaths were used in nonmilitarized situations in order to integrate a "stranger" into relatively sovereign communities, and this was certainly the case for Akan persons who formed or joined Maroon societies in Suriname, French Guiana, and Jamaica. Thus, the oath ceremony (*ntam*) preceding Court's enstoolment or installment. During the enstoolment he sat in state wearing a green silk or velvet cap with gold ornamentation (which he had worn before), all of which would appear to be a diasporic version of the annual *odwira* festival, which marked the harvest season, the start of the indigenous Akan new year, a culmination and expression of a composite Akan culture, and a time to install a new or pay homage to the leader of a settlement or polity.

In those polities or settlements, a matrilineal group of "king makers" chose potential leaders from among their own clan members; upon approval, the candidate had to make a sacred oath (*ntam*, "the great oath of kings") to his community, to the ancestors (of whose land and its peoples he became custodian), and to the *abosom* with attendant ritual sacrifices for several days before assuming office. As we shall recall, Court was chosen by a community of Coromantee, he took the oath before his "coronation," and he consulted Quawcoo (Kwaku), the "Old Oby [*obeah*] Man," on the finer points of the foregoing process. Then Quawcoo made sacrifices for Court (as he did for Secondi), showed him how one used or "played with the Ikem [shield]," used a ceremonial sword (*akofena*) in the form of a wooden cutlass, and blew an "Oben" (*abɛn*, horn) made of "Elephants Tooth."[27] Bosman observed that the *obirɛmpɔn*, a man of "great reputation by [his] riches" and third in social ranking, used small elephant teeth and one or two shields, "intimating that he will not be afraid" in war or to "divert [i.e., entertain] himself" during an eight-day festival. These men (*abirɛmpɔn*), referred to as nobles by the seventeenth-century compiler Olfert Dapper, were, "in reality," not so. According to Bosman, "because no Person can Enoble himself, but must be so by Birth, or by Creation of another: In both which they [i.e., the nobles, in Dapper's mind] are deficient."[28] Bosman could not have been any clearer. All of the key paraphernalia (e.g., shield, sword, horn) and the rituals (e.g., oath, sacrifices) used with Court would have been in line with an *odwira*-like festival suited for the Antiguan environment, for here, not unlike on the Gold Coast, leaders of settlements and polities recognized their subordination to larger political configurations (e.g., the Antiguan plantocracy in Court's case), used those paraphernalia in wars and ceremonies, and thus had to know how to "play" with them, as well as to be well versed in and representative of the language and composite culture of the society. Indeed, when it came to Court's installation, the "Language and Ceremonies used at it [were] all [in] Coramantine," though it took place among a large crowd of white, Coramantee, and other African spectators.[29] This was relatively no different from the *odwira* that Thomas Bowdich witnessed in 1817 among the Asante, wherein the Asante sought to "unite the various nations by a common festival" that hosted Akan and non-Akan peoples from tributary and visiting polities, but the "Language and Ceremonies" were then in Akan in spite of the diverse audience.[30]

In actual fact, the idea of an *odwira*-like festival—and not an ennobling ceremony or a shield dance as a prelude to war—seems more probable. When Court was in state, he had next to him Gift, the "braffoo" (*ɔbrafoɔ*, enforcer of law), with white clay (*hyire*) on his face and wearing a cap with feathers; Quashey (Kwasi), the "asseng" (*ɛsɛn*, herald), with an "Elephants Tail" (symbol of wealth in Asante and a key ceremonial object for its leader, the Asantehene); officials of varying rank; and probably speech intermediaries (*akyeame*). This arrangement of personnel and their actual and symbolic meaning would have been wholly consistent with the institutional framework of an Akan policy and the way in which an ɔhene (ruler), existing or newly enstooled, would position himself at an *odwira* or analogous event. On a Sunday, about 2 p.m. in the afternoon, Court was installed as "King of the Coramantees" in the presence of more than a thousand enslaved persons and whites in a public show or "coronation," and though Court's owner was certain this was an innocent act that had its roots in Court's country, the important date for this event is not clear. The judges and a witness mentioned Thursday or Sunday (twice) on 3 October (twice) or 6 October, but 6 October was a Saturday, and 3 October was a Wednesday, which suggests 30 September since Sunday was named twice and 30 September provides the closest Sunday to 3 October (also named twice).[31] If this concession is accurate, then 30 September 1736 takes on additional meaning, for it was an Akwasiadae or *adae kesee* (large resting place or moment) for the Asante, a day and a moment that signaled the end of one Akan calendrical year and opened a new one marked by the *odwira*, which took on specific meaning for the Asante. Though other Akan societies observe *odwira* or analogous (harvest) festivals, the Asante *odwira* came to be structured more elaborately and served as a forum for allegiance to the Asante polity, as well as annual plenary sessions on the state of Asanteman (Asante "nation"); in addition, Asantehene (male leader of Asante), in consultation with political and spiritual advisors, determined *odwira* in nineteenth-century Asante. During the nineteenth century, the Asante *odwira* fell between the European months of August and early October, and there is no reason this would not have been the same for the prior century since it is held that the first *odwira* marked the temporal inception of Asanteman in 1701.[32]

Court's consultations with Quawcoo, his spiritual and political advisor, and the design and timing of the so-called coronation, including the rituals and preparations in material culture, could not have better matched an *odwira*-like event unfolding in front of a diverse crowd of more than two thousand. Nonetheless, how would Court have known about the *odwira* or its analogous forms if he was in Antigua in 1701, the same year the Asante *odwira* first began? Besides Quawcoo's guidance as one source of Court's knowledge, Court had ample opportunity to have witnessed or participated in an *odwira*-like festival, for he came to Antigua at about ten years of age, which means he probably came there aboard the *Falconberg*. The *Falconberg* was a Royal African Company vessel that left the Gold Coast on 24 March 1700 with 606 captives and landed on 18 May in St. John (Antigua) with only 376 Africans after a fifty-five-day voyage and amidst death tolls of up to 40 percent.[33] According to the edited version of the judges' general report,

Court was called "Coquo Tackey," that is "Great" Takyi, and we can be confident this name meant that Court embarked as an Akan from an Akan-speaking area rather than as a Gã from the Gã-inhabited Accra region.[34] Most scholars have deduced a Gã identity for Court based on the name "Tackey," though the Gã name is actually "Taki" and "Tacky," as found in the records for Antigua and the Gold Coast, and, when written, is often reduced to "Tecki" or "Tacki." In fact, Bosman, who witnessed the well-known and protracted "Komenda wars" (ca. 1694–1700) between the British and the Dutch and no less than nine Akan polities, recorded several key individuals named "Tecki" (e.g., Tecki Ankan, Takyi Kuma), and the timing and scale of those wars and Court's arrival in Antigua strongly suggest he was exported from one of those Akan-speaking polities as a consequence of the Komenda wars.[35] At the end of the wars, Takyi Kuma was made "king" of Eguafo (of which Komenda was the port town); Court, unlike Takyi Kuma, was recorded as "King Tackey [Takyi]" not because of military prowess but rather because of his *obirɛmpɔn* status, the likes of whom Bosman ranked third in the Gold Coast or Axim social order and who begat "great reputation by their riches," much like Jama of the Danish colony of St. John (Jama or Gyamma was an *obirɛmpɔn* in the Akwamu court and also called "King June," according to the records of the St. John revolt in 1733).[36] In fact, Court is representative of those individuals, such as John Kabes of Komenda, who acquired power and prestige by trading for themselves in an increasingly precarious, militarized, and commercialized Gold Coast of the seventeenth and eighteenth centuries, but the synergy between Court and Quawcoo paralleled the political savvy and wealth of Osei Tutu and the spiritualist *ɔkɔmfoɔ* Anokye, cofounders of Asanteman in 1701.

The story of Court is also significant beyond his role as "king" and leader of the alleged plot. Except for Court, who was about ten years old when he arrived in Antigua in 1700 or 1701, the rest of the principal leaders of the alleged plot were Antigua-born Africans, including Court's close associate Tomboy. The forged alliances between those born in Africa or Antigua and were not of Coromantee origin (e.g., Ibo Oliver took the Akan oath) suggests the concrete potential of Africans in general and the Akan in particular to create a coalition of distinct segments in ways similar to yet predating Denmark's attempt in early nineteenth-century South Carolina.[37] Like the storyline of Denmark's alleged plot and the real or imagined designs of so many others, the 1736 conspiracy in Antigua would have been betrayed from within, given the apparent fragility of operational unity (between the followers of Court and Tomboy) and, in part, by factors beyond the insurrectionists' control, such as the postponement and rescheduling of the British coronation ceremony in the ballroom. These betrayals, however, have larger implications for the study and the aims of operational unity in the Americas since, even though Court was able to forged horizontal leadership alliances and perhaps with other Akan in vertical command, the alleged plot was uncovered through (and death sentences were pronounced after) confessions from other Coromantees such as Cuffee (Kofi) and Robin.[38]

Like Quamina (Kwamena), whose testimony betrayed the alleged Akan-led plot of 1759 in St. Croix, Cuffee and Robin were rewarded in the end as voluntary witnesses, and both were emancipated in 1739 and granted monthly allowances for as long as they stayed in Antigua. Cuffee's and Robin's voluntary testimonies and reward were certainly in the interest of the white planters who viewed both witnesses with favor, but how the enslaved community viewed these two was certainly a different story. Indeed, those who were betrayed at the level of personal relationships rather than as co-conspirators, and were either executed or exiled by way of Cuffee's and Robin's testimonies, would have thought or articulated this proverb: *ɔfatwafo akatua ne owuo* (The payment for a traitor is death). Other testimonies included that of Quamina, who said he knew Quawcoo (Kwaku) in "Cormantee country." Quamina testified in terror because of his knowledge of Quawcoo's powers as an old "oby man" (*obeah* man); Quawcoo's reputation preceded him, for in a postconspiracy response to the executions of Court and Tomboy, Secundi had used his services in a plot with others to poison their owners.[39] After the deaths of Court and Tomboy, the group led by Secundi, who employed the spiritual services of and spoke Coromantee to the "oby man" Quawcoo (i.e., "chawa worra terry" or *twa owura tiri*, cut off [your] owner's head), perhaps conspired to revolt—as in the case of the Akan insurrections on board the *Mary* (1708), the *Two Sisters* (1758), the *Black Prince* (1763), and the *Othello* (1765) en route to Antigua—after the alleged plot and the execution of its implicated leaders. Freedom fighters under Secundi's leadership, such as Cuffey (Kofi) and Quashey (Kwasi), were condemned, beheaded, and burned, while Secundi was gibbeted.[40] These punishments were consistent in other neo-European colonies of the Americas during the eighteenth century (e.g., "conspiracies" of 1712 and 1741 in New York City). In all, five enslaved Africans were broken on the wheel, six were gibbeted alive, and seventy-seven were burned at the sake. Those banished included three individuals named Quaco, two individuals named Cudjoe, two named Cuffee, two named Quash, two named Quamina, two named Cubinna (Kwabena, Kobina), two named Cuffy, and Quawcoo, the "oby man." At least one of these persons, Quaco, turned up on the Danish island of St. Croix and, ironically, was implicated among the leadership of the alleged 1759 Akan-led plot.

Undoubtedly, a large part of the spirituality in the form of rituals and *obeah*, names, and specimens of language related to the historical moment of 1736 was Akan in origination. Though the transparent Akan names and instances of Akan language are less questionable, the idea of "obeah" in largely the Caribbean and its Akan origins has come under criticism, and several writers have put forth the Igbo "dibia" as a more likely source.[41] What became known as "obeah" or "obia" had divergent meanings for enslaved Africans and Europeans, and the term was widespread throughout the Caribbean and South America (i.e., Guyana and Suriname) as it came to be employed by both the enslaved and the whites. The force that the practitioner used was essentially neutral, with positive ends (including the force directed at owners of the enslaved) and negative ends, though it was only in the nineteenth and twentieth centuries—concomitant with missionary expansion and the entrenchment of hegemonic colonial values—that the term assumed a wholly negative, pejorative meaning, except in Suriname.[42]

The term "dibia" might be the source of "obia" or "obeah" but not necessarily the practices subsumed under that terminology since Quamina knew Quawcoo the "oby man" and his powers on the Gold Coast, and this would locate Quawcoo's "obia" in a largely Akan context. The term "obeah" (and its variants) is found in Barbados, St. Kitts, St. Vincent, Suriname, Jamaica, Guyana, and Antigua—places of known and sizable numbers forming an Akan presence—but relatively absent on the North American mainland, where the Akan were less numerous, except in specific states such as South Carolina (in which "obeah" was used), and where the practices thereof were largely referred to as "voodoo" and "hoodoo."[43] Antiguan planters preferred (as first choices) Africans from the Gold Coast and then Ouidah, especially "Caramantee, Fantee, and Poppa," and, of these three, the first two groups were Akan, and the third consisted of Africans, including Akan settlers, east of the Volta River on the so-called Slave Coast.[44] All Leeward island planters placed Coromantees at top of their list, and many Gold Coast Africans arrived in Antigua and were a dominant group among the enslaved in the 1720s and 1730s. This presence and strong cultural dominance of the Akan suggest that the "Obia" used by Quawcoo and others derived from *bayi*, a concept linked to the optimistic utterance εbεyε yie (it will be good or well), made to provide hope to those who need to consult the *ɔbayifoɔ*—the one who does or uses the neutral force of *bayi*—and, in the Americas, the suffix *-foɔ* might have been dropped to produce *ɔbayi* or "oby."[45]

"An Insurrection of the Negro Slaves": The Akan
Experience in Guyana

In former British Guiana (contemporary Guyana), the idea and practices associated with *obeah* underwent similar transformations in meaning as described earlier. Whatever the term's origins, *obeah* remained relevant in the lives and revolts of many Africans in general and Akan in particular and as a potent force marshaled toward cultural resistance in the late eighteenth and nineteenth centuries (see figure 5.1). Between 1661 and 1810, approximately 70,000 to 80,000 captives from the Gold Coast arrived in the Guianas, and in 1795 British Guiana (Guyana) came to include the former Dutch colonies of Essequibo, Demerara, and Berbice, when these colonies surrendered to a British fleet from Barbados. That crude approximation of captives, however, might have been augmented by Africans from Barbados, who accompanied their owners to British Guiana shortly after the Dutch surrender. As these Africans joined an Africa-born population that represented three-fourths of an enslaved community, "liberated" Africans and Africans from Suriname flowed into Guyana after its 1834 emancipation of those enslaved. The second half of the eighteenth and first half of the nineteenth century was a crucial period for African revolts against the plantocracy and to freedom that was left unrealized in the postemancipation period. Though the demographic pattern of the African population shifted by the

Figure 5.1. Prisoners serving sentences for "obeah" at an Antigua jail, 1905. Five of these prisoners were from Nevis, three from Dominica, and one each from St. Kitts, Montserrat, and Antigua. Reproduced by permission of the National Archives at Kew.

mid-nineteenth century, with a large West Central African input, the Akan (described as "Kormantines" or "Kramanti") made significant contributions to the processes of sovereignty and cultural autonomy well beyond their sheer numbers. Notwithstanding the preservation of Akan cultural elements archived in Ananse stories, Akan names (e.g., Quarquo [Kwaku], Quaminah [Kwamena], Quoffie [Kofi], Afibah [Afia], Quamini [Kwame], Quashie [Kwasi]), spiritual practices clustered under and often associated with *obeah,* and ceremonial "dances" such as "Komfo," the Akan were most remembered and perhaps revered for their leadership in the quest of freedom—the national hero of Guyana is named Kofi (Coffy), and this was not an arbitrary decision.[46] Between 1763 and 1764, a widespread revolt resulted in the seizing of the sugar colony of Berbice, wherein almost the entire enslaved population took control of the colony under the leadership of Coffy (Kofi) in ways very similar to the 1733 Akan-led revolt in the Danish colony of St. John.

Most plantations in Berbice were privately owned, including a few Berbice Company plantations, situated along the Berbice River, and a few along the Canje River, due to the fertility of the soil. The mouth of the Berbice River—with its coastal tide, flats, and swamps—provided the only way to enter the colony by water. Fort Nassau, the socioeconomic and administrative center of the colony, was built on the upper part of the Berbice River, while the governor and the court of justice resided on the Daagrad plantation.[47] The Berbice Company granted land to planters who had considerable capital, and most planters had estates of five hundred acres for the production of cotton, coffee, cacao, and sugar—the company devoted nine out of its eleven plantations to sugar. In 1762 the colony had approximately 125 plantations and a population of about 5,000—3,833 enslaved Africans, 346 Europeans, 244 enslaved Amerindians, and the remainder were enslaved persons, workers, and officials of the company.[48] If an epidemic, food shortage, and rumors of revolt based on the intensely brutal treatment of those enslaved were not enough for Governor Wolfert Hoogenheim, his relatively new administration was welcomed by the gravity of a revolt that erupted on the Magdalenburg plantation on 23 February 1763—the end of the short rainy season.[49] The plantation was on the western part of the Canje River, and soon others followed in revolt, including plantations on the upper part of the Berbice River, with close to 4,000 individuals wielding six hundred guns under the leadership of an Africa-born cooper named Coffy (Kofi).

During the first week of March, the freedom seekers killed sixty or more whites at the Peereboom company plantation and continued on that path. Rather than assist their colonial counterparts in Berbice, Dutch officials in Essequibo and Demerara (south of Berbice) mustered large contingents of Amerindian forces to prevent the revolt from extending into their respective colonies.⁵⁰ As some reinforcements from St. Eustatius arrived between March and May (part of the long rainy season), reports of internal conflict among the freedom seekers circulated: alleged disagreements between the Africa-born and the Berbice-born captives about tactics and leadership. Coffy and his leadership core sought to create a sovereign polity based upon Akan statecraft and demanded or attempted to negotiate with Governor Hoogenheim a cession from the entire colony. Though similar in its ultimate aim, this act was unlike the strategy pursued in the St. John case, and it, consequently, proved fatal as Coffy was now faced with internal dissent, as well as inventive excuses used by Governor Hoogenheim to stall the revolt via a chain of correspondence.⁵¹ Like a confluence of the St. John revolt and the alleged plots by Denmark in South Carolina and Court of Antigua, Coffy proposed a division of the colony into an independent African confederation of distinct cultural groups in the south—consistent with the phenomenon of Gold Coast confederations—and a colony of an enslaved population ruled by planters already positioned in the north.⁵² Thus, on the one hand, there was the quest for a polity based upon operational unity among distinct groups and interests who shared at least the recognition of the value of freedom and self-rule. On the other hand, there was also support for freedom for some and unfreedom and exploitation for others in contiguous yet smaller colonies.

What happened next is murky. Some accounts note a split in the leadership between two Africa-born groups: the "Delmina" (Akan), led by Coffy, and the "Angola-Congo," led by Atta, who deposed Coffy and his followers. Others note that a rival Coromantee leader under Coffy, Akra or Akara, pushed for all-out war without compromise in response to Coffy's proposal. In either case, treachery and internal strife took their course, and the rebellion fell apart from within (about a year after the revolt), which allowed for Dutch military reinforcements to arrive.⁵³ Coffy committed suicide—thus allowing him to return home or to *asamando* (where the ancestors dwell) as suicide on account of war was culturally acceptable—and the Dutch military forces overwhelmed the other leaders and participants. The fractured group led by Atta was less cohesive than under Coffy's leadership, and though Coffy's group had stored enough food through an effective division of labor, this was not the case for Atta and others, who faced a long rainy season, food scarcity, and an ongoing epidemic. When further Dutch reinforcements arrived in November, a number of the insurrectionists had already surrendered on account of colonial appeals having to do with fair treatment, illness, and starvation. By February 1764, the end of the short rainy season, more than 1,000 voluntarily ended their resistance, and approximately 2,600 were recaptured and kept alive. A total of 124 were hung, broken on the rack, burned at the stake, or put to death by slow fire, and most of these were suspected ringleaders that the "famous Captain Boobie and another (Quaco [Kwaku])" had helped to retrieve.[54] Atta, the "chief captain" of the fractured group, was put to death by slow fire and after being pinched with "red hot pinchers." He "owned his crimes and often prayed to God and the Governor... He gave terrible cries and seemed more sensitive of pain than all the others, but in general they showed so little concern, were so little moved."[55]

In the end, Atta blamed some of the planters for their "cruelty and inhumane treatment" as the cause of the revolt. Akara and Gousari, two former leaders under Coffy, were part of the group that surrendered, and they offered their services as scouts and "rebel" catchers, each eventually earning a pardon and serving in the colonial army of Suriname to fight against the Maroons. For those many thousands who participated in the Coffy-led revolt and now found themselves returned to captivity but left with the memory of a potentially successful overthrow of the Berbice plantocracy, life must have been tense, painful, and bitter in the late eighteenth and early nineteenth centuries. This may not have been the case for new and incoming Africans to the colony, but "new negroe" or not, Akan men and women continued to appear in newspaper advertisements for runaways in the first decade of the nineteenth century when Berbice, Essequibo, and Demerara formed British Guiana. In February 1807 Coffy and Quamina were listed among the "Runaway and Arrested Slaves," along with Adjuba (Adwoa), who was listed for at least three months (February–April) and might have found her way to Suriname and become part of one of many Maroon groups.[56] Another "Negro Woman by [the] Name Amba [Amma], well known in the Colonies of Essequebo and Demerary," also ran away, and, unlike North America, the Guianas had large groups of Maroons who had relatively independent and self-sufficient communities that needed women as healers and midwives and thus offered Amba or Adjuba concrete possibilities.[57] In sum, the year 1807 not only marks the British abolition of the international enslavement enterprise but also offers the best snapshot of patterns among Akan runaways over a longer period. Categorically, some, such as the "Tall Negro Man named Codjo [Kwadwo]," escaped individually; others fled in small groups, as was the case for "A Negro woman, Yaba [Yaa]," Quaco (Kwaku), and Quimina (Kwamina) or the eight individuals named Quamina and the three named Quacoe (Kwaku), who left their estates in the month of January, several on the same day.[58] The inhumane treatment that Atta held responsible for the Coffy-led revolt of 1763 did not end after Coffy's suicide or after these women and men seized their opportunities and pursued a course, though on a smaller scale, fitting to Coffy's memory.

The memory of the Coffy-led revolt and temporary occupation of Berbice might very well have influenced the 1823 uprising in Demerara (part of

British Guiana), which was led by Deacon Quamina (Kwamena) and included thousands of reportedly Christianized Africans across more than forty-five plantations (see figure 5.2). The uprising might be considered a "labor strike" in that many of these persons were responding to new and stringent British regulations that affected their work and the practice of "their religion," but it might also have been reflective of rumors that the British parliament had ended slavery. The insurgent force led by Quamina was part of a tradition that included Coffy of the earlier century. John Smith of the London Missionary Society (LMS) wrote in his journal entry for 25 July 1823 that Quamina, likely Deacon Quamina, had inquired whether he "had heard the report that 'the King had sent orders to the governor to free the slaves.'" Smith informed Quamina that such a report "must not be believed because it was false."[59] Quamina, however, "was sure there was something in agitation, and he wished to know what it was," and he received little satisfaction from Smith's response that the report was likely a government regulation "for the benefit of the slaves, but not to make them free."[60] Ironically, on the day of the revolt, 18 August 1823, Smith says nothing about the uprising in his journal, which was his last entry.[61] Thousands of Africans in the uprising were massacred by British troops, and the failed

Figure 5.2. Retreat of British colonists during the 1823 uprising in Demerara (British Guiana), 18 August 1823. The second and largest revolt against enslavement in what is now Guyana, the uprising included appropriately 12,000 enslaved Africans, whose sheer insistence was a factor in Britain's decision to abolish slavery in its colonies. Courtesy of the Chaplin Library, Williams College.

uprising ended in carnage, including the death of John Smith, who was sentenced to hang in 1824 on the charge of inciting the revolt.

The Act of Emancipation was passed that year, and the expansion of LMS activity in Guyana and the Caribbean and among the formerly enslaved was a direct outcome of that emancipation. Emancipation or not, labor strikes continued, and the one in 1848 also failed, for it lacked the effectiveness of the labor strike of 1842, which was suspected of "obeah man" intervention juxtaposed with a reportedly Christianized and Christianizing ex-enslaved population. If the 1848 strike had the support and participation of the "obeah man," then it might have been more successful.[62] Between 1848 and 1860, there was an upsurge in the popularity of *obeah* and other African spiritual and healing recourses, and these were also tools of effective cultural resistance to white cultural and political hegemony.

One of the most popular rituals of West African origin was "Komfo" or "Cumfo." "Komfo" derived purportedly from "[the] Dahomean [concept of] Komfo" and was a "syncretism of West African religious beliefs" associated with rivers, argues Brian Moore, and both "Creoles" and Africans engaged in its widespread practice.[63] Monica Schuler has written about enslaved narratives of "flight" back to Africa and the "Komfo ritual" in Guyana—a ritual at rivers in hopes of going back to Africa through a sort of crossing the cosmic divide represented by water or the grave. This ceremony was witnessed in 1920, with the added feature of "dancing by a self-described Obeah man dressed in a white gown," which may be linked to the practice of enslaved "Kramanti" (Akan) dancing back to back during the "pre-flight ring dancing."[64] It is doubtful the term "Komfo" is of Dahomian origin, for it is not found in Gbe languages (e.g., Ewe, Fon) spoken in the former Dahomey or contemporary Bénin, but the factors of "Kramanti" dancing, *obeah*, and language strongly indicate that Komfo was linked to the abilities of the Akan *komfo* (i.e., *ɔ-kɔmfoɔ*), one who was skilled in traversing the spiritual-temporal world and calling upon or marshaling its resources and powers. Be that as it may, practitioners of Komfo and *obeah* resisted missionaries who sought to suppress the Komfo ritual, and some suggest that this ritual might have been most strongly entrenched in Berbice—the site of Coffy's now famous 1763 revolt—though it was practiced throughout Guyana.[65] Some "cumfo men" practiced *obeah* as well. In the nineteenth century, the Komfo ritual and *obeah* were pervasive and deeply rooted in African communities; however, an ambivalence within those communities developed toward both. This ambivalence was both understandable, given the severe hostility and scorn that emanated from white authorities and missionaries, who translated those practices as demonic and proof of barbarism. This was unfortunate for those Africans who were seduced by that interpretation since Komfo and *obeah* provided powerful counterweapons against such preemptive cultural strikes. If greater numbers in nineteenth-century African communities had resisted the stringent laws and flogging, which did not deter the *obeah* men, who continued their practice even after being jailed and beaten, then Komfo and *obeah* might have developed into more than symbols of cultural resistance and become mobilizing cultural practices in the nineteenth and twentieth centuries.[66]

By the mid-nineteenth century, the results of the international enslavement enterprise and "liberated" African immigration between the 1840s and 1860s allowed for the gradual eclipsing of a West African majority by a Central African one, at least in Berbice, where the Akan were second to Bakôngo and related West Central African groups.[67] Many "liberated" West Central Africans settled into "ethnic" quarters into which plantation villages were organized, but many also died in transit at depots, while others were hospitalized, blinded, or deeply depressed by their longing for home and succumbed to "mass baptisms" and proselytizing during the "liberated" African experience.[68] The idea of being "liberated" did not, however, mean that Africans went home; many were actually conscripted into the military of neo-European states and apprenticed to their governments, indentured as laborers, and often transshipped throughout the Americas, where they were coerced into "free" labor contracts in places like Brazil without an opportunity to leave.[69] Very few Akan were a part of these experiences, given the British abolition of the slave trade and their presence on the Gold Coast, the internal and external forces operating on the nineteenth century Gold Coast, and its shift to domestic unfree labor. The last wave of Akan probably came in the last decade of the eighteenth and the first few decades of the nineteenth century, when the Guianas constituted a key slaving frontier.[70]

The abolition of enslavement created a labor crisis that was solved by importing a quarter of a million indentured workers from India and China between the mid-nineteenth and early twentieth century, and this demographic transformation foreshadowed the political and racial tensions of the twentieth century. In that context, most African descendants remained at the bottom of the social hierarchy, and their culture did not provide for cohesion and group consciousness due to an imperialist and racialized domestic order that made African culture the demonic inverse of white or neo-European culture. Imperialism took the form of a largely white elite who controlled the print and other media, the schooling system and its curriculum, and the churches, and thus these institutional arrangements reinforced the powers of the elite. Assimilation was imitation of the culture, language, and values of the white elites. The Chinese who entered Guyana in the late nineteenth century converted to Christianity en masse and made the greatest accommodation to the host society, and those who self-consciously identified themselves as Africans, as well as "liberated" Africans and their progeny, were encouraged to do the same, following the example of a small number of "Creoles" who sought partnership with those in power. Most Africans and their descendants, however, were situated in rural areas from the mid-nineteenth to the early twentieth century, and their status after emancipation in 1834 and throughout the next century "was nothing more than slavery in disguise."[71]

MAROON MELODY AND AKAN CULTURE IN JAMAICA

We began our thematic examination of the Akan experience in the British Caribbean with Barbados, the first large-scale, sugar-producing British colony, and so it is fitting to conclude this chapter with the sugar-producing colony that replaced Barbados in the mid-eighteenth century and one of the most "rebellious" islands shaped by Akan culture—Jamaica. Merchants from London to Rhode Island thought Coromantees were suited best for the Kingston (Jamaica) market, and, for British planters in Jamaica, the Coromantee or "Kromanti" were at once most prized but intractable, as rebellions led or inspired by them occurred in the first two decades of their entry in the colony (1670s–1680s). From that period to the latter part of the century, Jamaica was one of the largest markets for British enslaved imports. A large number of enslaved Africans came from the Eastern Caribbean (particularly Barbados) to Jamaica, and these numbers augmented the broader African and specific Akan presence on the island. Estimates of imports from the Gold Coast to Jamaica reveal the following patterns: In the periods 1670–1700 and 1701–1750, approximately 6,000 and 45,000 captives, respectively, were sent to Jamaica, and both accounted for 19 to 20 percent of the total enslaved persons imported to the colony. In the periods 1751–1790 and 1791–1810, approximately 120,000 and 37,000 persons, respectively, accounted for more than 19 percent of the total import.[72] In total, a little more than 35 percent of the Africans exported to Jamaica between the mid-seventeenth century and the first decades of the nineteenth century came from the Gold Coast region and its hinterlands, and Jamaica's share of those who embarked from the Gold Coast equaled the total Gold Coast exports to the rest of the British Caribbean. Though Africans from the Gold Coast account for an average of 19 percent in these key intervals, there were peak clusters of importation that may change our understanding of "Kromanti" (and its variants) as a synonym for Akan persons and thus the latter in Jamaica and the Americas.

The Gold Coast accounted for 31 percent of the Africans imported to Jamaica between the 1670s and 1710, years that witnessed the following: a conspiracy to revolt in 1675, reports of revolting and martial law in 1678, a conspiracy that was uncovered in 1683, a rebellion suppressed in 1685–1686, and a major rebellion in 1695. One-third of the sixty-two recorded insurrections on board slaving vessels traveling from the Gold Coast to the Americas took place on voyages to Jamaica between 1704 and 1807, six of which unfolded in the 1720s and two on the same ship. In the crucial fifty-year period of cultural dialogue (ca. 1675–1725) among the various African groups to settle Jamaica, 46 percent of a population sample of 56,000 captives between 1701 and 1725 came from the Gold Coast, and we can be sure they shaped the previous rebellions as much as did the cultural dynamic on the plantations and in the Maroon communities. Between the 1670s and 1710, Gold Coast importation corresponded to increased European competition and firearms on the Gold Coast and conflict among Akan polities, as the next four decades would include confrontations with non-Akan polities above the forest belt to the north and northeast, while during the mid- to late eighteenth century, Jamaica received an average of no fewer than 20,000 Gold Coast captives. Between 1780 and 1790, these imports constituted almost half of the total population that entered the colony. The latter part of the eighteenth century also witnessed increased raids and wars between Akan polities on the Gold Coast and in its hinterlands and to a lesser extent between non-Akan people (e.g., Dagomba) to the north of the forest belt. We should recall, however, that many of the peoples north of the forest had been culturally influenced by the Akan, and thus the question for us is not whether Akan people categorized as "Kromanti" or "Gold Coast" came to Jamaica and the Americas in large or insignificant numbers, but rather, in what ways did an identifiable Akan culture settle and interact with other African and non-African cultures in places like Jamaica?

Few would question that the Akan influence in Jamaica has not been preponderant, with contributions to the processes of cultural reconstitution and continuity from other Africans. However, if the Akan and non-Akan persons from the Gold Coast—that is, its coastal societies and those north of the forest—were Akanized through the processes detailed in the previous chapters, then we may have to rethink our thinking about the Akan presence in the Americas. The Akan never constituted a majority among other African cultural groups shipped to varied parts of the Americas, including Jamaica, in most of the intervals outlined earlier. However, because of their leadership skills in war and political organization, as well as the contours of their presence as archived in the musical traditions, language, and patterns of life in Jamaica and other parts of the Americas, we should look no further than Akan culture for an explanation. In other words, Akan culture reached the Americas by way of Akan and non-Akan persons who were decidedly shaped by Akan cultural institutions (through adoption or hegemony or both), and it was preserved or reconstituted over the course of several centuries in West Africa and the Americas. A key area of cultural transformation and continuity—fashioned through transatlantic experiences—is the relation between musical traditions and cultural formation and consolidation in Jamaica, with implications for other parts of the Americas.

Richard Rath has examined three African songs (named "Angola," "Papa," and "Koromanti") transcribed by Hans Sloane in 1688 since Sloane's musical descriptions "provide a unique glimpse into [what Rath calls] the process of creolization [and cultural transmission] among enslaved Africans of known ethnicity."[73] Rath argues that Sloane's descriptions preserve "a cultural record of first-generation transatlantic slaves from several distinct African regions" and that Sloane's "evidence tells of Koromantis, Papas, and Angolans creating identities as Africans under the bonds of slavery in a new world."[74] The melody, rhythm, instrumentation, and language of the songs, particularly the Angola and the Koromanti, converged through an intra-African conversation in that the lyrics to "Koromanti" were Akan and the instruments belonged to Angola. Thus, in "Angola," two distinct cultural groups are combined, but the cultural boundaries are maintained in each (e.g., the upper register is of Akan origin, and the lower register is of Angolan origin). In contrast, the "Koromanti" song represented to Rath "a creolized ethnic identity" fashioned in the Americas in that more blending and crossing of cultural boundaries existed in the "Koromanti" song. This, according to Rath, suggests that Africans in the Americas "may be thought of as the unraveling of a number of individual twines from different ropes and their recombination into new ropes."[75] The implications are that Africans engaged in a "syncretism" among themselves prior to and during their interactions with non-African cultures and that if "ethnicity" gave way to "race" as a broader construct (of external import), that idea of "race" was complicated by the fact that African cultural groups held on to their specific cultural universes.

The lyrics of the "Koromanti" song transcribed by Sloane and examined by Rath are largely Akan, and that language allows us to further examine the processes detailed by Rath, as well as elements of Akan material and spiritual cultural found in the Maroon musical styles of Jamaica. The Maroons have preserved many of the cultural elements of Akan origin, more so than those Africans and their descendants in the larger planter society. Arguably, the oldest and most pronounced sources of African musical styles in Jamaica are archived in the Maroon settlements of Moore Town, Scott's Hall, and Accompong, and this, in large part, holds true among other Maroon societies of the Americas. The Moore Town Maroons spoke the "Kromanti" language until the 1930s and possess the most elaborate Kromanti tradition, and included in that tradition are "recreational songs" and "nation songs" (e.g., Kromanti, Papa [Ewe-Fon], Ibo [Igbo], Mandinga [Manding], and Mongola

[Angola]) that reflect the distinct African cultural groups that constituted early Maroon communities and the ancestors of whom manifest themselves during Kromanti ceremonies.[76] Outside of a ceremonial or ritual context, cultural differentiation and its identities do not exist outside of a Maroon identity, though many accept that their ancestors were the convergence or coalescing of distinct groups, which makes it currently impossible to disaggregate. Categories of Maroon music reflect those currents that flowed in a composite African cultural stream. Those currents included the Tambu (Bakôngo), Sa Leone (Sierra Leone), Mandinga (category of song and drumming style that uses a special stick called an *abaso* or *akani* stick), Papa (considered among the most powerful songs and used to open serious Kromanti ceremonies), Ibo (Igbo), and Kromanti (the pinnacle of Maroon music, wherein the drum "talks" while the singers sing—a combination still found among the contemporary Akan). Tambu is another example of convergence of the Kromanti tradition of Maroons (particularly Akan) and nineteenth-century Central African immigrants (Bakôngo) inasmuch as key and official Maroon instruments like the abeng (*abɛn*), which is an Akan term for the horn of an animal, and the *gumbe* drum represents the Bakôngo.

In the Kromanti category of Maroon music, one song is called "Anabo Yedeng," and the words are all in Kromanti. If Akan is the source language, the words would be *nea aba o (na) ayɛ dɛn* (that which has come is what?). This transcription and translation may be instructive, for the song tells the story of a "fete man" (Kromanti dancer and spirit medium) who encountered and was challenged by an *obeah* man. In one Kromanti song recorded in a similar context by Kenneth Bilby, though without the following transcription and translation, the fete man sang the following:[77]

O kumfo nyaba-ee, yo-ee	ɔkɔmfoɔ nya ba (when the ɔkɔmfoɔ has come)
Poor nanabeti, yo-ee	Poor Nana bɛte (poor Nana [elder or spiritualists] will hear)
Kumfu nyaba-ee, yo-ee	ɔkɔmfoɔ nya ba (when the ɔkɔmfoɔ has come)
Bin a nyaba-ee, yo-ee	Abena nya ba (when Abena has come)
Poor nanabeti, yo-ee	Poor Nana bɛte (poor Nana [elder or spiritualists] will hear)

Maroons have also preserved the concept and practices of the "kumfo man" (*ɔkɔmfoɔ*) as "ritual specialist," but only fragments of indigenous spiritual practice can presently be found in the Maroon town of Accompong, unlike the Maroons' eastern counterparts. The Kromanti healing and spiritual ceremonies (called "play") were prime occasions for the fete man and kumfo man, both of whom may engage in *obeah*, as was the case in Guyana and other parts of the Americas. However, those who did not share Maroon blood were typically not privy to these ceremonies as Maroon identity was

Figure 5.3. Accompong Maroons singing and making music at the annual January 6 celebration, Jamaica, 2001. Photo by author.

and is still rooted in the unique cultural element of Kromanti dance. The instruments in these Kromanti ceremonies include drums (*printing* [*ɔprenteng*], used also for drum language), machetes struck with iron or *adawo* (*dawa*, an iron or metal object), bamboo tubes played with two sticks (*kwat*), and the *abeng*. The drummer is still called "okrema" (*ɔkyerɛma*, drummer) or "printing man." Drum language was used at the beginning of each Kromanti ceremony to call the ancestors and other spiritual entities involved and also during the ceremony to invoke them for the benefit of the community and the "yarifo" (*ayarefoɔ*, sick persons). In Charles Town, the Kromanti tradition is fragmentary, though there are extant songs that are used to invoke spiritual agencies in Kromanti and are thus powerful; in Scott's Hall, the Kromanti tradition continues from earlier times, and the most powerful songs there remain those in the Kromanti category, yet this tradition is in decline.

In Accompong, there are few practicing ritual specialists, and the Kromanti songs are not used to invoke the ancestors and other spiritual entities or to accompany ceremonial dance. Instead, during grave digging and burials, gravediggers will pause, pour libations to Yankipong (Onyankopɔn), Assasi (Asase Yaa), and the ancestors and sing Kromanti songs.[78] One such Kromanti song was recorded in 1986, and I recorded the same with slightly different words of Akan import in 2002, which are as follows (see figure 5.3):

The Antelope (Adowa) and the Elephant (Esono) 153

A min-ny wah oh, a min-ny wah oh, sa-key a bra nay
Ye-ko te-ko, ye-ko te-ko, yam bam say eh
A a yeh, a a yeh, oh say oh, ye-ko te-ko, yam bam say eh

Amene-awɔ (?) o, amene-awɔ o, san 'kyi a, bra nnɛ
(Raven-like savanna bird, raven-like savanna bird, come back, come today)
yɛko te ko, yɛko te ko, yɛbɛsa ɛ
(we fight and fight, we fight and fight, we will fight)
aye, aye, ɔse o, yɛko te ko, yɛko te ko, yɛbɛsa ɛ
(aye, aye, leader of a polity [ɔhene], we fight and fight, we fight and fight, we will fight)

This war song is a staple among the Maroons. Its content and tenor are confirmed by the historical record in terms of the fights between the Maroons and the British colonists, and they may also correspond to the idea of a "true Maroon," as represented by the term *yenkunkun* (*yɛnkɔko*, let us go fight). The meaning of this and many sacred Maroon songs have been lost among those in Accompong, though extant "grave-digging songs" (called Kromanti songs) are performed in a version of Akan among those who preserved these songs to communicate with early Africa-born ancestors of the Maroon, but without the accompanying meaning. This fundamental problematic of cultural transmission in Accompong and perhaps elsewhere may be due to the signing of its 1738–1739 treaty with the British only a decade after the critical fifty years (ca. 1675–1725) of intracultural dialogue among the Africa-born ancestors, as well as to the subsequent Westernization and missionary activity with a British resident monitoring Maroon behavior on site. This arrangement for Accompong was not unlike the Maroons of Suriname, but the critical difference is that the latter signed their treaties in the 1760s and had at least another generation or two to institutionalize and protect its composite melody or culture. If this interpretation is close to what happened, then it would appear that the generations that played specific and shared cultural roles in the songs Sloane recorded were living in a plantation setting similar to that of the Maroons; however, the composite culture shaped by early Maroons outside of the plantation and in a state of war was invariably distinct from that shaped by those who spent more time on the plantation and later joined or formed a Maroon group. This variance and even the ideological fallout between Cudjoe and other Maroons over the signing of the treaty in 1738–1739 had important cultural consequences into the late eighteenth and early nineteenth centuries.

By the start of the nineteenth century, when British slave vessels were still transporting Africans from the Gold Coast to Jamaica, the Kromanti language was on the verge of extinction and bound to those African-born Maroons who used it and were passing away while the last ships of captives arrived on the island. In 1793 or 1794, several vessels from London left

Annamabou (Anomabu) on the Gold Coast carrying 1,367 Africans in total on four ships: The *Union* held 530 captives, the *Golden Grove* 400, the *Countess Galvez* 300, and the *Express* held 137, most or all en route to Jamaica.[79] This shipment was not unusual since captives from the Gold Coast to Jamaica constituted almost half of the imported population between 1780 and 1790, and from 1791 to 1795 almost 18 percent, or 17,300, of the total African import from the Gold Coast. A number of Akan persons who were part of these waves of importation left some autobiographical information (presumably narrated), while others left biographical fragments through runaway advertisements, such as those for a "New Negro Girl of the Coromantee country," Cuffee ("a Coromantee" of Westmoreland), Yeabah ("a Negro woman of the Coromantee country"), Cudjoe at the Black River jail, and Quaco of the Spanish Town workhouse.[80] On Bryan Edwards's estate, there were several representative Akan persons—that we assume were typical of other plantations such as Thomas Thistlewood's estate in Jamaica—such as Clara and her two brothers, who arrived in late 1784 from the Gold Coast.[81] Clara was born in a village named Anamoa near Anomabu, and her parents and her nine siblings were enslaved and sold to pay the debt of a "great man" (*ɔbirɛmpɔn*) upon his death. Her brothers might have been Quaw (Kwao) and Quamena (Kwamena), as the Fante version of their Akan names suggests the Fante coastal area, of which Anomabu was a main port of embarkation.

Located on the same plantation as Clara, Quaw and Quamena were born the property of a man named Banafou (*batafoɔ*, long-distance merchant?), who sold them to a captain on account of his debt, who in turn brought them to Jamaica at a young age. A bit younger than the twenty-year-old Quaw and the eighteen-year-old Quamena, Afiba (Afia) was the property of a man named Quamena Yati as well, though her place of origin is difficult to discern. Finally, for Oliver ("country name Sang") and Cudjoe (Kwadwo), both were from Asante, and whereas Oliver was captured at a young age during a nighttime Fante raid and sold for "sica" (*sika*, piece of gold, currency), Cudjoe, fifty years old in the late 1780s, lived during the reign of Asantehene Opoku War (ca. 1720–1750). Cudjoe was captured and sold at the age of sixteen to pay for the adultery infraction of his elder brother.[82] These biographies resonate with those that opened this chapter, but here the use of Akan lexical items (and in translation) is noteworthy, for Akan language use, concomitant with sustainable and influential Akan demographics, suggests a greater use of that language in the non-Maroon settings of Jamaica and might explain the historical and contemporary level of Akan vocabulary found in Jamaican English (Patois or "Patwa"). John Thornton estimates that, around 1750, 40 percent of Africans in Jamaica spoke "Coromantee" as their mother tongue, and if this suggestion is close to the reality, then the Akan input into the African-based culture in Jamaica not only went beyond their sheer numbers and their presence in Maroon communities but also underscores the theme of Akanization in West Africa and the Americas—even if some or many of those speakers were bilingual.[83] However, these Coromantee speakers did not constitute a distinct "nation" of Gold Coast origins, as John Thornton has argued for some time, and the nature of the conflicts between and within the Coromantee on the plantation and in Maroon societies exposes the idea of a singular or distinct "nation" and the relative diversity of Coromantee speakers.

In 1760, a thousand or more enslaved Coromantee under the leadership of Tacky or Takyi killed sixty whites and engaged in a "reign of terror" (from whites' perspective) during a rebellion that reportedly employed "obi" (*obeah*) via elder Coromantee in the parish of St. Mary.[84] Tacky's revolt was reportedly part of an islandwide phenomenon, with similar uprisings in other parishes. Yet, as irony and history would have it, the Maroons of Scott's Hall were the ones who hunted and killed the freedom-seeking Tacky—some of these Maroons were Coromantee as well—and thus ended the revolt. Though, here, the Maroons were joined by enslaved Coromantee such as Cuafee (Kofi) and Quaco (Kwaku), who were both "set free paid £5 and £5 a year hereafter for being loyal in [the] slave rebellion" of 1760.[85] Thus, Akan or Coromantee persons inhabiting a world regulated by the rhythm of a plantation or a Maroon society were rewarded for their loyalty to whites and the plantocracy. What might appear as a surprising act of betrayal was, in fact, the outcome of a treaty between the Maroons and the colonial authorities, and one of its clauses included the return of all Africans who attempted to become maroons themselves or threaten the state via revolt. These clauses were largely upheld since the Maroons feared deportation.[86] What is not surprising is that many of the leaders of the Tacky rebellion were *obeah* practitioners, and this confluence of spiritualists and political strategy was also the case in the alleged Akan-led plot of Antigua in 1736 (e.g., Coromantee Quawcoo, Caesar, and John "Obiah"), revolts in Guyana, and elsewhere.[87] Indeed, Jamaica went hardly a decade without a serious revolt that threatened the slave society throughout much of its history—for instance, Cuffee's yearlong rebellion in 1685–1686 and another Cuffee-led Maroon attack against slavery in the 1720s. We can suspect that spiritual traditions such as *obeah* and *kumina* played integral roles in the planning and execution of many insurrections, though *obeah* is distinct from a *kumina*, which was introduced during the nineteenth century by "liberated" Central Africans.[88]

Mirroring Deacon Quamina's (Kwamena) 1823–1824 uprising in Demerara (Guyana) of thousands of supposedly Christianized Africans who were massacred by British troops, Sam Sharpe's "Baptist" rebellion of

December 1831—organized through the institution of the church—led not only to the destruction of hundreds of sugar estates and properties but also the death of some 500 enslaved Africans.[89] In 1830 Jamaica had approximately 311,000 enslaved Africans across a constellation of plantations, and though we can imagine the anxiety of the white planters, the brutal repression of Sharpe's contingent might have reflected a larger psychosis of African self-assertion with a rebellion in Antigua and the 1831 Nat Turner-led revolt that killed whites in Virginia. Sharpe's decision to not employ the services of *obeah* practitioners perhaps was the same as Deacon Quamina's a decade earlier, but both cases turned violent, and protesters were massacred in ways that even Christianized Africans could not reconcile with the prescriptions of Christian theology. Perhaps if Sharpe or Deacon Quamina had strategically employed *obeah* or another African-derived spiritual recourse, the outcome might have been favorable, for we have seen the successful control of entire colonies by Akan-led forces and the effectiveness of *obeah* in protest movements in mid-nineteenth-century Guyana. To be sure, it was not Sharpe's initially nonviolent, Christian-based revolt but rather the almost uninterrupted tradition of (spiritually and culturally based) resistance and maroonage and then the obsolete political-economy of chattel enslavement that ushered in emancipation in 1834.

In fact, the year following Sharpe's revolt, 6 percent of enslaved Africans formed part of the "jobbing" groups that were hired out to do the planters' most demanding physical labor, and a number of enslaved Africans were imprisoned for crimes ranging from burglary, assault and battery, harboring a runaway, to rebellions and rebellious conspiracy, in which case many were sentenced to death and hung.[90] But the climate in 1832 was such that first an announcement to "rebellious slaves" was issued in January and then a proclamation in February of that year, denouncing the actions of "the most flagrant outrages and destructions of property" of those enslaved "under the pretense that orders have been sent out by His Majesty for their emancipation."[91] The proclamation assured those in protest pardon for being misled and requested that they surrender within ten days of the proclamation to a military post or return to their respective plantations. Governor Sligo's letter to the "apprentices" in 1834 sought also to appeal to some of the same people in rebellion in 1832 and to the newly freed, but this time he argued, "I am your friend...The people of England are your friends and fellow subjects" in hopes that the newly emancipated would labor diligently under "former owners" to prove "deserving of all this goodwill" of apprenticeship.[92] Those who behaved poorly, such as by running away, were supposed to be retrieved by the Maroons or the police and serve a longer term of apprenticeship.

The apprenticeship system began in August 1834 and ended in 1838, and its failure owes much more to continuous agitation by those formerly enslaved than from the governor or the assembly of Jamaica, who often equivocated in their debates on emancipation and the "slave codes" of 1816, which allowed for greater missionary activities among the enslaved. These debates between 1816 and 1830, for example, were characterized by intense struggles against emancipation, paralleled by reports of discontent, rumors of emancipation, predictions of rebellion, and the ultimate feeling that it would be "a lapse of ages before the Negroes can even participate of the blessings of freedom, the very name African must cease to exist in their memories before their customs are obliterated."[93] Evidently the 1832 proclamation, apprenticeship, and emancipation meant little in the midst of continued protest and the later Morant Bay rebellion of 1865, led by Paul Bogle in the sugar-producing parish of St. Thomas. The highly organized Morant Bay uprising sought to redress the social injustices of the Jamaican authorities and not of the Queen of England, but Bogle's ambivalence toward the British authorities in Jamaica and Britain and his attempt to enlist the support of the Maroons became a large part of the uprising's failure.[94] Like Tacky's revolt, it, too, was brutally suppressed by the colonial army, which had significant Maroon assistance.[95]

One can argue that the Maroons, since the signing of their treaties with the British colonial authorities in 1738–1739, were more traitors than liberators in view of their complicity with the clauses of those treaties. Moreover, their memory or legacy as freedom fighters is questionable in light of all the revolts and runaways they helped to suppress. This is not to suggest that Maroon history, accumulated knowledge, and sovereignty (for them) are insignificant but rather that the well-known Accompong celebration of 6 January that commemorates Cudjoe's (Kwadwo) birthday and the treaty of 1738–1739 is ironic, for the very treaty to which Maroons ascribe a key role in the consolidation of their identity as Maroons also marked the social death of many would-be Maroons and African sovereignty seekers, who were reduced to residues of the memory. Many of their names might have been etched among the national heroes of Jamaica (see figure 5.4). Maroons in Accompong and elsewhere, including Nanny, did not view the 1738–1739 treaty with reverence, and the strategic and ideological issue this caused during the 1740s must have been substantial, for Cudjoe had some Maroons and a number of enslaved Coromantees executed for their attempted coup.[96] Despite the ways in which eighteenth-century and contemporary Maroons view their leadership and the treaty of old, the memory of Cudjoe and Nanny reverberate throughout the Caribbean and take on specific meaning, for instance, on the island of Carriacou. The culture of the island has been rooted in the ancestry of specific African "nations" via the "big drum" ritual dance, wherein the "Cromanti" are the most important group and referred to as the "first nation," though they were not the

Figure 5.4. Illustration of the encounter between Maroon leader Cudjoe and a British officer, ca. 1738. Cudjoe (Kwadwo) had signed a concessionary treaty with the British after years of warfare, and this illustration was meant to capture the meeting that shortly preceded the treaty-signing process. Robert C. Dallas, *The History of the Maroons*, Beinecke Rare Book and Manuscript Library, Yale University.

first African group on the island.[97] The "big drum" songs, like the Maroon songs of Jamaica, place great value on the Cromanti category of sacred songs, where "Cromanti Cudjoe" and Nani (Nanny) are archived and invoked, and these icons probably came to the island with enslaved Africans from Jamaica when the British took control of Carriacou from the French.[98] All "nations" are a part of the "big drum" ritual, but the ritual was likely established by the Cromanti (Akan)—the largest and most influential of those enslaved on Carriacou—and the oldest and most important songs are found in the Cromanti, Igbo, and Manding categories.[99] Some of these Cromanti songs include and are titled by key characters such as Sai Amba (Osei Amba?), Anancy (Ananse), Ena (ɛna, mother), Ahwusu (Owusu), and Cromanti Cudjoe.

In ways similar to how those Cromanti songs of Carriacou are held sacred and imbued with historical personages such as Cudjoe and Nanny, contemporary Maroons continue to view their treaties as sacred covenants that authenticated their identity as distinct, sovereign people within Jamaican society, and it was that "historical act of oath taking, consecrated by both Maroon and British blood, that created a permanent bond between themselves and the British monarchy" in the Maroons' eyes.[100] However, since the Maroons became "free" according to treaties that the Maroon signers probably did not read, European influence in Accompong, for example, was significant even after the Accompong treaty was signed. Of all Maroon settlements, Accompong was the most shaped by Western culture. Maroons tracked down enslaved Africans who escaped from the plantations, white superintendents were resident in each town and supervised its administration, a number of villages were divided, and Christianization and the stamping out of African spiritualities have produced ambivalence in Maroon identity since it was defined by cultural practices (e.g., Kromanti dance) that are at odds with Christian patterns of behavior. Conflict within Maroon societies and with the colonial authorities continued and escalated into the eight-month war of 1795–1796. Those who surrendered were deported to Nova Scotia, and, in 1800, large numbers were sent to Sierra Leone—deportations that many feared and because of which they had complied with the colonial government.[101] The irony is clear.

Those Maroons who were eventually deported to Sierra Leone were joined by "rebellious" enslaved Africans from the British Caribbean, particularly Jamaica and Barbados, among other Africans from England and North America. Some "African immigrants" left Jamaica for Sierra Leone as late as 1861.[102] In 1799 the British Crown granted the Sierra Leone Company a new charter that gave it the right to govern Freetown (capital of the colony), and the company officials believed Westernized Africans were superior to indigenous Africans (yet culturally inferior to Europeans) and had the capacity to govern themselves and become civilized. The latter expectations were evident when Maroons became employees of the company as jurymen and constables and held low-ranking appointments within it.[103] The Maroons, according to Thomas P. Thompson, the Crown's first governor of Sierra Leone, were fearless and headstrong but honest and vigorous—"a savage half-reclaimed." British colonial policy created "ethnic" and somewhat binary cleavages between schooled and unschooled Africans, "liberated" and settled Africans, Maroons and "liberated" Africans and propagated the idea that "West Indians" would civilize their African siblings. The Trelawny Maroons assumed military positions that mirrored their role in Jamaica, and, not surprisingly, they were used to suppress rebellions in the colony.[104] The Maroons were characterized as polygamous, non-churchgoers who created their own rulers, laws by which to live, and a military social organization, and many hoped to return to Jamaica and regarded Sierra Leone as a temporary place of residence. Their spirit of independence and distrust of Europeans—as a result of many broken promises—fueled the prospects of returning (by some Maroons) to an independence they had enjoyed before deportation.

Groups of Maroons petitioned the colonial government of Sierra Leone, and a number of them did return to Jamaica between 1837 and 1841. The majority of the Maroons, however, stayed and eventually married "liberated" Africans and Africans from Nova Scotia.[105] By the first half of the twentieth century, Maroons, at least those in Accompong, continued to emphasize their rights and appealed to British officials via the 1738–39 treaty between Colonel Guthrie and Captain Saddler and "Colonel" Accompong and "Captain" Cudjoe. The Accompong Maroons, in a memorandum of 1938, argued, "This treaty has not been violated and holds good until today," and they provided a précis of the history of the treaty in their request for development aid from the British government.[106] The Maroons, led by "Colonel" H. A. Rowe, regarded the "church and school [as] valuable institutions" and listed their service "in time of rebellion" among the reasons for requesting development aid. They mentioned that they had quelled "the Morant Bay rebellion by capturing Paul Bogle," and in March 1938 the bicentenary of the treaty was celebrated. Such efforts in the service of the British did not help the Maroons, for, as Mavis Campbell argues, by the 1790s a significant number of enslaved Africans had grave misgivings about these and other Maroons. In the Trelawny Town war against the British plantocracy, the Trelawny Maroons' closest allies sided with the colonial authorities and the enslaved. The support in supplies and human resources the Maroons had received in earlier times was no more.[107] Thus, their plea for development aid (e.g., paved roads, medical assistance) from the British is telling, for that memorandum ended, ironically, with the idea that "the Maroons are...good citizens," a puzzling contrast to their continuous and adamant claims of a separate identity outside of the then Jamaican colony and the current nation-state.

In earlier and contemporary Jamaica, the Akan experience became archived in names, stories, foods, language, proverbs, music, spiritual practices, as well as numerous Maroon settlements.[108] Yet, that experience was not without the memory of violence and victories in the colony of Jamaica. Many in Jamaica self-consciously identify with "Africa" and as children of Africa, some identify as Akan via the Asante ("Ashanti") but none use the Coromantee trademark as an identity marker. Colonial slavery figures into any talk of cultural identity or non-trademark consciousness, making their fate that of children losing their mother. In "The Narrative of the Son of a Slave Woman," an unnamed child in nineteenth-century Jamaica talks about his mother who was "from a part of the Gold Coast called Anamabo [Anomabu]" and worked as a house cook in her owner's home from the time she was about fifteen years of age until she was sold to a man from Barbados for a hundred guineas.[109] The day after her departure, the son felt "grief like all the African Race." Analogously, the Akan who were trans-shipped from the Caribbean to the North American colonies were that mother, and Barbados signaled North America, while that son symbolized Akan cultural forms at the intersection of "mother" and foreign lands, as he simultaneously confronted the ruptures of diasporic experiences in the Americas. The next chapter tackles the Akan experience in North America.

6

"All of the Coromantee Country"

The Akan Diaspora in North America

> *Korɔ-akyirikyirikyiri ne*
> (The one who went far, far away)
> *Korɔ dadadadadadada ne*
> (The one who went long, long ago)
> *Korɔe-ansa-na-obi-aba*
> (The one who went before someone who arrived)
> *Opanin ne hwan?*
> (The elder [i.e., the first or most significant] is who?)
> —Akan drum text

On the Akan experience in North America, Michael Gomez has argued that their contribution to African cultural transformation in the United States was "a perspective intimately concerned with land and the ancestral realm" and that Akan desirability in U.S. colonies "appears to have been founded upon their reputation as unskilled and vocational laborers" since physical strength and a capacity to work were the "principal characteristics by which the Akan were known to whites."[1] To some whites and African descendants who experienced or carried memories of racialized enslavement, the Akan would have been classified as "Guinea niggers" who left the Guinea coast of West Africa for the Americas and who were largely remembered as "small and black" unskilled laborers for "De Guinea nigger don't know nothin' 'cept hard work."[2] But these so-called "Guinea niggers," a geographically racialized category that could have easily included the Akan, were much more than unskilled "good workers" who knew "nothin'"—almost all Africans were commodified and ultimately seen as laborers of varying skill sets. For the Akan, one typical case should suffice. A formerly enslaved African (descendant) of Mobile, Alabama, recalled a certain "Uncle" Louis, who "was a 'Guinea nigger'" and whose "ancestors had been brought from the Guinea coast of Africa," a synonym for, at times, the Gold Coast. Uncle Louis was described as "short, strong and very black, with heavy neck, thick lips, flat nose and eyes like those of a hog. He had great knowledge of wild plants, claimed to understand the language of birds and beasts. He prided himself on his powers as a hunter and also claimed intimate friendship with ghosts and spooks."[3] Uncle Louis, in spite of his old age, was also prone to run away. Nonetheless, his region of embarkation, physical description (though stereotypic with some caricature), intimate knowledge of medicinal plants and animals of the natural order, self-assured pride as a hunter who was conversant with the spiritual order of things, and propensity to abscond provide the best synoptic profile of the Akan in West Africa and the Americas embodied in one person.

The substance of Gomez's argument—part of a larger statement on African cultural continuity and transformation in the southern United States—is a useful one, for it speaks to select elements of Akan culture and desirability in North America. However, that argument is weakened by a misreading of Akan cultural development in West Africa and the ways it informed a composite Akan-based culture in both captivity and postbellum North America. Certainly, the physical and cosmic voyage across the Atlantic and its rapacious circumstances might have contributed to the trauma and feelings of displacement experienced by many Africans brought to the Americas, including those "liberated" Africans of the nineteenth century, but the suggestion that this feeling of displacement ruptured the Akan connection to land and their personality may not have been so. As the previous chapters show, Akan persons who left a record of some sort envisioned a spiritual return to their homeland and seem to have invested in the idea that *asamando* (where the ancestors dwell) was a space where all could gain entry in spite of immediate geographical places of birth and death, and what was critical was not necessarily a connection to land but to ancestors and spiritual agencies that would facilitate that entry via the appropriate rituals. Furthermore, Akan cultural ties to their Creator were linked to principal, water-derived *abosom* (e.g., Tanɔ and Bea rivers, Lake Bosomtwe, Bosompo or Bosonopo [the ocean]) rather than land- or forest-based manifestations of that Creator. Thus, wherever there was water, there was the possibility of returning to or connecting with the spirit and memories of home, though rituals were concurrently done at graveyards for those who passed away in home or foreign lands.

In this chapter on North America I use runaway ("slave") advertisements and other records to examine the lives of some of those who lived in captivity and complied with the order of things, as well as of those who sought to temporally and spiritually transcend captivity in various ways. The Akan experience in North America was much more than scholars' characterization of them as unskilled, physical Akan laborers who were traumatized by the Atlantic crossing owing to their connection to the land. The Akan and their genetic and cultural progeny formed a spirituality premised on water-derived spiritual agencies, including rivers and other such bodies, pointing to the relative importance of land in Akan cultural formation in West Africa and an embedded spirituality that understood the transition to ancestry as "crossing the waters." In the temporal dimension, Akan influence in their own lives and that of other Africans far overweighed their small numbers, and that influence, based on a culture and a skill set formed in West Africa, lent itself to the politics (e.g., slavery), diasporic culture (e.g., naming pattern, language), and spirituality (e.g., rituals) of Africans in North America. Here I focus initially on names and naming as one of the most significant and enduring cultural practices in the Caribbean and North America—and some in the Caribbean still possess first or last names of Akan origin—in order to establish an Akan naming pattern and method of name transmission in Georgia, Virginia, Maryland, and South Carolina. I employ runaway advertisements to identify those names and some of the lives behind them, which include themes of flight and slavery in Maryland, the role of language acquisition in struggles against slavery, and the numerical importance of Africans and the Akan in South Carolina in terms of cultural transmission while in captivity, though some communities, such as the Gullah, developed in relative isolation from whites. In North America, the Carolinas (primarily South Carolina) received the most Gold Coast shipments, with 102 direct voyages, followed by Virginia (32), Georgia (12), and Maryland (7), though these do not include the large number of transshipments from the Caribbean or elsewhere in the Americas. The chapter, therefore, focuses on the lived experiences of Akan persons imported to and in the history of Georgia, Maryland, Virginia, South Carolina, and certain parts of the northern United States.

NAMES, NAMING PATTERNS, AND THE AKAN PRESENCE

African names were more commonly found in British colonies—where even Africans with Anglo names gave their progeny African names—more so than in Portuguese and Spanish colonies since, in the latter cases, Africans were usually baptized and given Christian names prior to their departure from Africa or upon their arrival in the Americas. Akan "day names" were a very early African naming pattern uncovered in documents related to the past few centuries of the Americas, and these names often occur in their Akan form in plantation inventories and runaway advertisements.[4] The structure of Akan names followed the seven-day week with male and female versions: Monday (Kwadwo, Adowa), Tuesday (Kwabena, Abena), Wednesday (Kwaku, Akua), Thursday (Yaw/Kwao, Yaa/Aba), Friday (Kofi, Afia/Afua), Saturday (Kwame/Kwamena, Amma/Amba), and Sunday (Kwasi, Akosua/Esi). Some African and Akan persons, however, carried Akan names in translation (e.g., Monday) or in Anglo form, but even among these Africans, owners had little control over what enslaved Africans called themselves and others in the slave quarters, fields, and other places out of the general purview of whites. To be sure, many owners recorded African names in general and Akan names in particular in varied types of documents. One example of an Akan name in translation is found in the case of Louisa Gause of South Carolina, one of more than two thousand formerly enslaved persons interviewed by Federal Writers' Project workers in the 1930s. Louisa was technically not a "slave" if her father had documented her "age in de Bible" and, in doing so, noted that she was born "de first year of freedom."[5] Louisa's father was named Cudjo (Pa Cudjo), and her grandfather was named Monday, an English translation of Kwadwo ("Monday-born male").

Runaway advertisements and other documentary sources that contain Akan names and bits of personal data provide invaluable opportunities to reconstruct some of the lived experiences of the Akan and their descendants, though, as with all documents, these should be used with caution. Runaway advertisements were first and foremost catalogs of objectified African bodies, and there was a great deal that was not or could not be recorded in these sources, including planter's accounts and plantation inventories, about the emotional, traumatic, and interior corridors of African (descended) life in North America. That notwithstanding, a careful reading of runaway ads does give us fragments with which to work, for they were ubiquitous in the eighteenth century during the height of the international enslavement enterprise and provided descriptive details that reflected more of a yielding to some of the empirical characteristics of the African than the relative weight of the planter or his agent's biases and erroneous perceptions. These ads, however descriptive, are marked with limitations and fraught with some error, and this disclaimer is critical, for our argument is based, in part, on the Akan naming pattern. In some cases, enslaved Africans not of Akan cultural origin were listed with Akan names, and in other cases Gold Coast Africans were listed without less ambiguous identifying factors (e.g., place or port of origin, "country marks") or apparent Akan names such as Quash employed as surnames not only among the enslaved but a very few owners as well. For example, Quamina (Kwamena) and Cudjoe (Kwadwo) of South Carolina were, respectively, described as "a short thick Ebo fellow" and "an Angola Negro" when both had transparent Akan names in the midst of a significant Akan or Gold Coast population in that state.[6]

Usually, runaway advertisements were conceived with enough identifying details—based, certainly, upon the planters' perceptions of and widely held notions toward the Africans—to enable the capture of valued and productive laborers, which presupposed a certain level of detailed accuracy on the owner's part, given that the average runaway was a twenty-five-year-old male who escaped during the most demanding agricultural seasons. In addition, skilled persons such as Quamina the cooper and Cudjoe the bricklayer also formed part of the escaped profile. In terms of abilities that departed the plantation or urban setting with each escapee, the Akan held a range of key skills, which brings into question the idea that they were sought after by white planters because they were unskilled laborers. In colonial and postantebellum North America Akan persons were agriculturalists or farmers, blacksmiths, bricklayers, carpenters, coopers, cooks, firemen, goldsmiths, hammermen, musicians (e.g., fiddlers), tailors, sailmakers, and "watermen," who worked in and around port cities. We should recall that the Akan came from agrarian, goldmining, and coastal seafaring societies, whose production units included not only blacksmiths and goldsmiths but also artisans such as woodcarvers, musicians (e.g., drummers, horn players, flute players), cloth producers and dyers (e.g., *adinkra, kente, kyɛnkyɛn*), and others, suggesting a continuity of roles between the homeland and areas they came to occupy in North America. Though some of the foregoing vocations continued, many in Georgia and other parts of the southern United States became tenant farmers and sharecroppers in the postemancipation period, whose social context gave birth to a musical genre called the blues, which appropriately reflected the beauty and the betrayal of the hopes invested in emancipation and reconstruction. African-descended persons with Akan names employed as first or last names—a phenomenon also found in the Caribbean—continued into the early twentieth century. Federal census records for that period reveal numerous instances of Cuffy (Kofi) and Cudjoe, some of whose fathers carried the same name, preserved in African communities and families mostly in South Carolina, Georgia, Virginia, and to a lesser extent other parts of the southern United States, such as Tennessee, Texas, Mississippi, and Alabama.[7] For Alabama, one well-known example is the story of Cudjo Lewis, who said that the sovereign of Dahomey and his troops had captured him when he was nineteen years old and that white slavers had brought him aboard the *Clotilde* to Mobile, Alabama, in 1859.[8] When Zora Neale Hurston interviewed Cudjo in his late nineties, she referred to him as (and he called himself) Kujjo (or Kossola) and located him between contemporary Ghana, Togo, and Bénin. This relative location may be accurate if the captain of the *Clotilde* went to the Slave Coast, specifically Ouidah, to acquire the Africans that included Cudjo. When he and other shipmates brought to North America were emancipated in 1865, they settled a community that became known as African Town. Cudjo and the other Africans wished to go home, for in the postemancipation era they saw themselves as simply "free, without country, or home."

PRESENCE AND PROGENY IN THE SOUTHERN UNITED STATES: THE AKAN EXPERIENCE IN THE HISTORY OF GEORGIA AND MARYLAND

The same year the Akan in the Danish colony of St. John staged their successful revolt against the plantocracy, the city of Savannah was established.

Less than two decades later, the increase in unfree African labor matched the increased number of large plantations and profits yielded from rice and cotton production on the mainland and islands divided by the salt marshes of Georgia. Initially, Georgia officials prohibited the importation of "Black Slaves" with an act in 1735, but with intense pressure for these captives from the late 1730s an additional act of 1750–1751 repealed the former act.[9] In the coastal areas and river swamps, rice was exploited around 1750 with the importation of Africans into the colony and in the Lowcountry as this grain contributed much to the economy and social order. However, planters from the Carolinas and to a lesser extent Virginia would control much of the Georgia Lowcountry when they moved into Georgia as owners of enslaved Africans skilled in rice cultivation and other vocations and with a disease tolerance critical to survival in the colony. Georgia would become a key exporter of indigo, rice, and forest-derived products such as lumber, but the key commodity of rice would be eclipsed by cotton during the latter eighteenth century and into the nineteenth century (hence, the notion of "King Cotton"). In 1775 Africans constituted approximately 45 percent of Georgia's population, and the shift from rice to cotton, tobacco, and sugar cane was clear by that year (see table 6.1). The rise of cotton was bolstered by the use of types of cottonseed effectively grown and cultivated on the Sea Islands and the coast and by the implementation of Eli Whitney's cotton gin, patented in 1794; the economic prosperity occasioned by the cotton gin meant a further entrenchment of enslavement for Africans in Georgia and other colonies.

For much of Georgia's history, agriculture remained the core of its economy and social organization, and the busiest seasons of that agricultural cycle occurred in the spring, summer (e.g., weeding tobacco in the heat and harvesting rice at the end of August), and autumn (e.g., harvesting and drying of tobacco; sowing of winter wheat). It was during these cycles, when African labor was needed the most, that the vast number of Africans escaped the plantations. Newspaper advertisements for such runaways provide some insight into the experiences of the African population in general and Akan (descendants) in particular. A profile of the average runaway suggests that the majority were twenty-six- or twenty-seven-year-old males, "native black" or "nonnative black" who sought freedom alone or with one or two associates during the peak seasons of the farming year. Some spoke English fluently, and this aided their escape, as well as distinguished (as part of a set of factors) those born in Georgia and those from the Caribbean or Africa; owners advertised a month after the escape, and rewards were fixed in accordance with the qualities of "native black" and "nonnative black" runaways.[10] Runaway advertisements for Africans from Georgia mention the term "mulatto" far less than do those for Africans from Maryland, which tentatively suggests lower levels of miscegenation, especially with regard to those

Table 6.1. Estimated African and White Population in Georgia, 1751–1870

	1751	1754	1760	1765	1773	1787	1790	1810	1830	1850	1870
African	420	2,000	3,578	4,500	15,000	23,500*	29,662	106,957	220,017	384,613	545,142
White	1,700	5,000	6,000	6,800	18,000	—	52,886	144,450	296,806	521,572	638,926

Source: Evarts B. Greene, *American Population before the Federal Census of 1790* (New York: Columbia University Press, 1932), 181–183; U.S. Department of Commerce, Bureau of the Census, *Negro Population of the United States, 1790–1915* (Washington, D.C.: Government Printing Office, 1918). The estimates before 1790 derive from conflicting sources, and thus these numbers are in no way precise, though they provide some sense of the demographic changes throughout the eighteenth and nineteenth centuries. The long dash stands for "no data," while the asterisk (*) under 1787 represents an average of two estimates.

Africans on the Sea Islands and the coastal areas and in consideration of the fact that many nonnative Africans listed in the advertisements were from Barbados, Jamaica, Antigua, and, generally, the "West Indies," "Guinea," and "Africa." These places of origin or transfer are consistent with those from which Africans were imported into Georgia through the port of Savannah or Sunbury between 1755 and 1771, in which the majority came from West Africa (i.e., Senegambia and Sierra Leone), the Caribbean (especially Jamaica and St. Christopher/St. Kitts), and South Carolina.[11]

Most of the Akan came to Georgia not so much from the Gold Coast but more through South Carolina and Caribbean colonies like Jamaica, which received at least 119,120 Gold Coast captives between 1751 and 1790 and during a period when an average of 100,000 were exported to the Americas. In 1764 and 1765 the *Georgia Gazette* reported nine men "lately imported from the Gold Coast," ten "Gold Coast New Negroes, Just imported from the West Indies," "Seventy Prime Healthy Gold Coast Slaves" from South Carolina to Georgia, and 50 to 60 "Healthy New Negroes, Just arrived from the Gold Coast."[12] In June 1797, a year after an insurrection of Gold Coast captives destined for Savannah on board the *Mary*, the *Sally* arrived in Savannah from Anomabu with 149 Gold Coast captives.[13] Direct Gold Coast voyages such as those made by the *Mary* or the *Sally* to Georgia were not numerous, for most occurred in 1796, with no more than two thousand captives landing. However, when direct traffic provided relatively small number of captives, transshipments from the Caribbean and South Carolina consistently augmented or even surpassed those numbers. Thus, the Akan formed part of the "nonnative" and Georgia-born African population, and, in the case of both groups, the runaway advertisements confirm this pattern of importation and suggest that a number changed their names or were recorded with non-African names but insisted on the use of their Akan names. For example, an African of the "Coromantee country" named Bergen spoke very little English, but he insisted on calling himself "Affoa," and this thirteen-year-old with "country marks" was probably a recent arrival in the colony.[14]

Mercury, a tall and slender male "of the Coromantee country" escaped from Charleston, and the forty-year-old was probably Akan, if we can trust Christian Oldendorp's late eighteenth-century description of Akan "country marks" since Mercury had "three small marks like cut on his temples."[15] Another male "of the Cormantee country" was named Somerset, and this tall, "likely fellow" did not speak English well, was likely not born in the country, and had escaped from John Graham's plantation at Augustine's Creek. From this same plantation, Cuffy (Kofi), a tall and bearded man with red eyes, had escaped a year after Somerset, and he, too, could not speak English, for he had been in the province for only five months.[16] Unlike Cuffy,

Quamina (Kwamena) escaped from John Forbes's plantation in St. John's parish a month after Somerset, and he spoke "good English," but he was described as short, well made, and very black and with "country marks on his face."[17] These Akan persons also sought freedom in large numbers and with other Akan and African escapees. In May of 1765, four men—Quash (Kwasi), Quou (Kwao), Quamina (Kwamena), and London—ran away, and all were reportedly well known in Savannah.[18] Yet, another Quash of South Edisto Island, including Quamina and Cudjoe (Kwadwo), were part of groups of twenty and thirty-four Africans, respectively, whose escapes were reported on the same date from different planters or their agents.[19]

Runaway advertisements also provide a window through which to excavate some Akan experiences among married couples and families. Quash of Great Ogeechee escaped with his wife, Jenny; according to their owner, both were forty years old, about 5 feet tall, spoke "bad English," and had the general Akan "country mark" of a "large mark from cut under one of the eyes."[20] Venture, also of the "Coromantee or Guinea country," sought refuge among other enslaved Africans when he escaped, while three who were "all of the Coromantee country" and were "supposed to be related" escaped together; however, the fact that they were in their twenties and spoke very little English created additional challenges for their quest for freedom.[21] After legal emancipation and the reconstruction period, tobacco took a strong commercial foothold in the late nineteenth century. Like cotton and the cotton gin, this development led to a socioeconomic extension of chattel enslavement in the form of sharecropping and tenant farming. Nonetheless, many would have found meaning and participated in the (secretive) singing of "Many Thousand Go," a spiritual likely created after legal emancipation and one that captured most of the coercive forces in their lives:

No more peck o' corn for me, no more, no more
No more peck o' corn for me, many tousand [sic] go
No more driver's lash for me
No more pint o' salt for me
No more hundred lash for me
No more mistress' call for me[22]

Akan-descended families, like other African-descended communities, pooled limited resources within families and kinship groups and transmitted an intergenerational culture (e.g., naming patterns) to their descendants, who lacked the lived experiences of enslavement. Some of their offspring even disengaged from an African ethos, which was at odds with survival and existed in a subordinate partnership with the white republic. Cudjoe (Kwadwo) and his wife, Tena, had nine children in 1870, and that number included one daughter named Affie (Afia) and a son named Cudjoe—

presumably after his father and grandfather. The family lived in Williamsburg, South Carolina, but established bank accounts at the Freedman's Bank in Savannah and New York in 1870 and 1873, respectively.[23] The fifty-four-year-old Cuffee Cobbin (b. 1818) of Darien, Georgia, also followed this pattern by naming one of his three sons Cuffee (Kofi). However, there were also those like Quash Bolton, who neither inherited his name from his parents nor named any of his children after himself; this forty-six-year-old carpenter was born in Chatham and reared in Savannah, married Melissa after the death or divorce of his first wife, Margaret, but the only child of the latter union moved to Tallahassee while Quash and his new wife and nineteen-year-old son continued living in Savannah.[24] Quash's father died when Quash was twenty-one, and his mother passed away eight years later. Out of his two siblings, one brother named Spanish was sold away from the family, and the other, named George, was somewhere in New Orleans, if alive.

Women like Affie Johnson, Affie Grant, Ama Fields, and Ama Owens also formed part of the nineteenth-century Akan experience in North America. Twenty-six-year-old Affie (Afia) Johnson was married to Titus, and though an infant of theirs died, they had a fourteen-year-old daughter named Seraphina. Affie had three siblings, named Bole, Emma, and Quabner—the last named after their father, Quabner Noble. By 1870 Affie's brother and father had passed away, and though the brown-skinned Affie was born in Savannah, she and her family lived in Houston County, and she worked in the area of "trashing" sugar cane.[25] Affie Grant was thirteen years older than Affie Johnson, but she, too, was born in Georgia (precisely, Daufusky or Daufuskie Island) and married Alex Grant after her former husband, Billy Adams, passed away. She had four children and two sisters, named Mary and Elsie, and both parents were deceased by 1869; the brown-complexioned Affie lived on the Habersham plantation (about three miles from Savannah) and worked there for Robert Habersham by planting crops.[26] For Ama Owens (b. 1850), the dark-brown, twenty-four-year-old had one child, no husband, and six siblings and worked as a cook for Mayor Akins in Alabama. However, little information was preserved in the Freedman's Bank records for the 5-foot-tall, brown-skinned Ama Fields of Memphis, Tennessee. By the turn of the twentieth century, Akan descendants such as Quabner Wells, who was found in both the 1910 and the 1920 U.S. federal censuses, provide some limited insights. Quabner lived on the Sea Islands in Glynn County in 1920 with his wife, Celia. Having been born on the islands in about 1847, the seventy-three-year-old was the head of household in a rented home. Quabner could not read or write, but he spoke English and worked as a laborer in the area of local sanitation. We know nothing about his father from the census records, but his mother was also born in Georgia, most likely on the Sea Islands.[27]

The profile for the average runaway in Georgia was the same for Maryland and Virginia as well, though Maryland had more cases of so-called "mulattoes," or Africans with "yellowish complexion," which were not necessarily mixed-race persons.[28] Cuffee of Maryland, said to have a "yellow complexion," was not a tall man at 5 feet 6 inches, but he spoke "good English" and had a wife in Piscataway, New Jersey. More than likely he escaped in that direction, for he once lived there during the spring, one of the busiest seasons for farming.[29] Another Cuffy ran away from a plantation in Gravelly Branch two years earlier, also in the month on May. The thirty-five-year old Cuffy was described as tall and "well-made" and was thought to have run off with a blacksmith named William Robeson.[30] A decade younger than Cuffy but an escapee in 1783, Quash was originally from another state, and he, like Cuffee and Cuffy, ran away in the spring, during the month of April, and was last seen in Baltimore. The "very black" twenty-five-year-old stood at 5 feet 10 inches and spoke in the "dialect of Creole Negroes." This description related to language use was probably accurate if Quash originally came to Virginia from St. Eustatia or Statia (a small Dutch island in the Caribbean).[31] All of these runaway advertisements ran during June and July, and that Quash likely headed for the Baltimore harbor is not surprising, for African importation into Maryland occurred primarily in the summer months.

Maryland's plantation economy focused more on tobacco than cotton and, in some parts, wheat, with an attendant import-export trade via the Baltimore harbor. Through ports such as Annapolis or the North Potomac, Maryland received at least 1,500 Gold Coast captives from seven direct voyages between 1708 and 1762 (compare this figure with the population estimates in table 6.2). The Chesapeake Bay region, surrounded by parts of Maryland and Virginia, received at least 15,000 Gold Coast captives, and these largely Akan persons predominated in the northern Chesapeake more than elsewhere. Current research by Lorena Walsh shows that Gold Coast imports, in which she includes the Windward Coasts, account for an average of 26 percent of the approximately 17,000 Africans that arrived in Maryland between 1698 and 1773, with a peak of 83 percent from 1719 to 1730—a period in which at least 114,000 Gold Coast Africans were imported into the Americas—and no (recorded) imports between 1731 and 1745.[32] This pattern of imported Africans stands in sharp contrast to that of a century earlier, when Maryland procured most of its African population by way of Barbados, as did Virginia between the 1690s and the 1710s. By the first decade of the eighteenth century, Maryland was importing more than 5,000 per year, with large numbers coming from Gambia and the Gold Coast via London-based vessels in the hands of largely private merchants.[33] Though Maryland and Virginia had large numbers of Akan speakers, as evidenced by the sample runaway advertisements earlier, Michael Gomez's argument

Table 6.2. Estimated African and White Population in Maryland, 1710–1850

	1710	1719	1732	1748	1761	1782	1790	1810	1830	1850
African	7,945	25,000	21,000	36,000	49,675	83,363	111,079	145,429	155,932	165,091
White	34,796	55,000	75,000	94,000	114,332	170,688	208,649	235,117	291,108	417,943

Source: Greene, *American Population*, 124–27. See also U.S. Department of Commerce, Bureau of the Census, *Negro Population of the United States, 1790–1915* (Washington, DC: Government Printing Office, 1918); Donnan, *Documents*, 4: 17–18, 21, 35 n. 2.

that both colonies were more informed by Akan speakers or culture than were Georgia and the Carolinas because of their numbers is not wholly tenable in light of the Akan presence in the Caribbean and South America. In those locales, Akan input into the African cultural composite was far more significant than their actual numbers would suggest over a significant period of time.[34]

Indeed, even in Gomez's argument for a transition from ethnicity (as Akan) to race (as African) engendered by a common servitude, attitudes toward white, and conversion to Christianity, these processes occurred as African cultural practices continued and yet ultimately divided the converts from the unconverted and facilitated competing visions of African-descended survival in North America. Many, however, resisted "creolization" and the imposition of a racial construct. Granted an uninterrupted internal, cultural dialogue among Africans, that resistance was most evident among Akan descendants in Georgia through a continuance of Akan naming patterns and the fragments of a corresponding culture.[35] We also find evidence of these processes in the colony of Virginia, where, as in Georgia and other colonies, African servitude and a sense of racialized inferiority helped to facilitate white solidarity, economic exploitation and inequity, and contested attempts at social and legal control of that African labor force. The implication here is that "race" was not a framework around which Africans and their progeny could have clarified their cultural identity, addressed political and cultural hegemony, or facilitated cultural continuity. Rather, they accomplished these things around a composite culture and an attendant identity. This failure of "race," as an imposed construct derived from a society demarcated by racialized identities, may explain the divergent visions in Gomez's ethnicity-to-race model and the inability to develop a sustained and unambiguous racial consciousness across segments of the African and African-descended community.

COMMUNITY AND CULTURE: THE AKAN EXPERIENCE IN THE HISTORY OF VIRGINIA

As in Georgia and Maryland, runaways were an omnipresent challenge to and a problematic for planters and colonial officials of Virginia—the latter two were often one and the same—and Virginia laws of the time support this contention. The years from 1640 to the 1660s witnessed the relative freedom exercised by African communities on Virginia's eastern shore through ownership of labor and land, but this would change in the 1660s as Virginia's racialized laws became less ambiguous, and enslavement became more narrowly defined in those laws and the actions based upon them in social practice.³⁶ As Virginia's white indentured servants served short-term needs and became planters themselves, and as formerly indentured servants temporarily overturned the sociopolitical order during Bacon's rebellion, white elites turned increasingly to enslaved African labor and created, out of that social tension, a sense of white cohesion to control the enslaved as a permanent, servile group, prevent their revolts, and translate blackness as the demonic inverse of whiteness. This process of greater white solidarity in the face of an internal enemy took on greater shape as the supply of indentured servants declined after the 1660s and the importation of Africans increased. All the while, the rising prices for the former, coupled with high white mortality, put into perspective continued planter demand for those servants. Certainly, the racism that those imported Africans encountered existed before Bacon's rebellion, for the thirty-two Africans in the 1619–1620 Virginia census were considered "slaves" without the kind of legal and social framework that would become more explicit during the next four decades.³⁷

Between 1660 and 1772, a period that marked direct importations from Africa and their decline, most of the acts passed concerning slavery and the maintenance of this social order focused on runaways and outlying enslaved Africans (some of whom pursued maroonage) and articulated punishments and the suppression of both as a major concern of the colony's leadership. For example, William Byrd II of Georgia wrote to Lord Egmont of Virginia in July 1736 that "they [Virginia] import so many Negros hither, that I fear this Colony will some time or other be confirmed by the Name of New Guinea." Noting the recent cost in lives and money expended on the Maroon wars of Jamaica, Byrd uncomfortably surmised, "we have mountains in Virginia too, to which they may retire as safety, and do as much mischief as they do in Jamaica."³⁸ Such fears shaped the strategies of maintaining the established colonial order, and those strategies included defining all enslaved Africans as property, requiring a pass for interplantation travel, stipulating that neither enslaved nor "freed" Africans could bear arms, prohibiting engagement in commerce without permission, placing restrictions on movement and meetings (e.g., for "holy days," feasts, and burials), and capturing or killing runaways and outlying Africans. These steps were informed by the loss of labor and other services, as well as the fear that Africans would leave the colony through the assistance of unscrupulous ship captains, poisoning, conspiracies (e.g., 1687, 1710, 1723, and 1730), and revolts. For example, a pivotal act passed in December of 1662 stipulated that the child of an enslaved mother inherited the mother's enslaved status for life, unlike the English tradition from which these planters came, in which children received their status from the father. This act might have also enabled African mothers to become more influential in the socialization process than fathers.³⁹ Another important act, passed in September of 1667, noted that baptism did not translate into freedom for enslaved Africans born in Virginia, and some Africans were undoubtedly under that impression, as white owners were encouraged to Christianize their African captives.⁴⁰

It is in this broader context of socioideological control via Virginia's legal instruments and in which Africans were cast as the internal enemy of the colony that the majority of Africans, who were largely from the Gold Coast, Angola, Senegambia, and the Bight of Biafra, found themselves. Before the end of the seventeenth century, most of these Africans had come to Virginia via Barbados, which itself was second only to Jamaica in terms of Gold Coast importation into the Americas on British vessels.⁴¹ Virginia planters such as Robert Carter and his kin also procured a large number of Africans from domestic sources (e.g., Maryland, the Carolinas) to evade import duties, but this pattern changed in 1759 and continued into the 1770s, when owners had to produce a list of all those enslaved and cost by gender to the county courts within twenty days of purchase.⁴² Between 1676 and 1773, the most active period of the Royal African Company, more than 5,000 Gold Coast Africans arrived in Virginia by way of thirty-two Atlantic voyages and, unlike elsewhere in the Americas, there are no recorded insurrections among any of these voyages to the Virginia colony.⁴³ The bulk of these Virginia-bound voyages were clustered between the 1720s and the 1760s—the peak period of Gold Coast importation into the Americas, which witnessed at least 100,000 arriving each decade—and the Akan arrivals entered the colony largely through the Rappahannock, York, and James rivers.

The mouths of these rivers, and of the Potomac as well, are all on the west side of the Chesapeake Bay in a southerly direction as the bay starts in northeast Maryland and runs toward southeast Virginia and then to the Atlantic Ocean. The York district had a consistent Akan and Bight of Biafra presence from 1704 to 1774, with the Akan accounting for 13 percent of the total African importation, but with a peak of 81 percent between 1761 and 1774, whereas the South Potomac had an overwhelming Senegambian presence but no recorded importation from the Gold Coast.⁴⁴ Based on the incomplete records of imports into Virginia between 1727 and 1769, most Africans came from "Africa" (18,300), Angola (3,572), "Guinea" (3,328), Gambia (2,724), Barbados (2,712), "Bonny of Africa" (1,453), "Callabar" (1,441), St. Christopher/St. Kitts (876), Jamaica (440), "Coast of Africa" (417), Antigua (385), and other parts of North America (384).⁴⁵ Ambiguous places of origin such as "Africa" or "Guinea" were often nonexclusive synonyms for the Gold Coast or under which Gold Coast was subsumed, for, in June 1739, the *Black Prince* arrived at the York River with 112 Africans from "Affrica," but this vessel actually "arrived from the Gold Coast, with a Cargo of choice Slaves."⁴⁶

Around 9 July 1772, 250 "fine healthy Windward and Gold Coast Slaves" arrived on the *Nancy* to be sold on the James River beginning, Wednesday, 29 July, and a month later the *Union* arrived with 280 "fine healthy Gold Coast Slaves" scheduled to be also sold on the James River on (Wednesday) 26 August.[47] Both sales continued until all of the captives were sold, and there was probably overlap between the Africans' arrival, preparations for sale, the auction, and the continued need to liquidate these commodified Africans. It seems that Wednesday held some significance, for this pattern of selling captive Africans on Wednesday continued into the next summer— as most vessels arrived in the summer months—when a "Small Cargo of Choice Gold Coast Slaves, well assorted and healthy," were scheduled to be sold on Wednesday, 9 June, not on the James River but rather at Alexandria on the Potomac River. For at least one Virginia planter, "Gold Coast Slaves [were] Esteemed the most Valuable and Sell best," and this 1763 sentiment, certainly shared by other planters, coincided with relatively high rates of Akan importation into Virginia.[48] Between 1761 and 1774, the Upper and Lower James and Rappahannock districts received high numbers of Akan persons (26, 82, and 40 percent, respectively) for all of these naval districts, suggesting a marked influence of Akan culture in Virginia south of the Potomac River during that period. In sum, the Akan and those from Senegambia and the Bight of Biafra remained the most consistent in presence and provided a cultural input that shaped the lives of Africans in eighteenth-century Virginia. Most of these Africans' lives were transacted on the agricultural fields in the Tidewater region, which produced wheat, rye, oats, corn, and forest products; on basin plantations for the lengthy and labor-intensive cultivation of tobacco; and on some upland plantations. As natural increase among them fostered Virginia-born offspring, the trade into the York and Rappahannock districts began to decline around the 1740s or 1750s.[49] The adults and not their Virginia-born children, however, made decisions about culture. Thus, whether the social and succession organizational principle in these regions of African importation were patrilineal, matrilineal, or a (fluctuating) resort to either of the two, extended kinship grouping was common and central to all, and this feature provided a nexus for forging survival strategies, culture transmission, community, and belonging.[50] Many who came from West Africa shared a good deal in the spheres of language, economies, and cultural patterns, and, under the demands of a racialized and dehumanizing oppression, they forged a composite fabric that still recognized the distinctive strands that constituted the whole cloth.

By the 1730s, only one-third of Virginia's enslaved population had been born in Africa, and of those entrants into the colony and their predecessors, the Akan and the Igbo were the most numerous imports into Virginia

Table 6.3. Estimated African and White Population in Virginia, 1624–1850

	1624	1648	1715	1743	1774	1782	1790	1810	1830	1850
African	22	300	23,000	42,000	200,000	270,762	300,213	413,790	500,427	503,279
White	1,253	15,000	72,000	88,000	300,000	280,000	391,524	463,893	543,627	616,069

Source: Greene, *American Population*, 136–142. See also U.S. Department of Commerce, Bureau of the Census, *Negro Population of the United States, 1790–1915* (Washington, D.C.: Government Printing Office, 1918).

(see table 6.3). Most enslaved households were multigenerational, with community gardens (i.e., mechanisms that facilitated earth relations) and extended family ties or kinship networks that developed and maintained a culture inclusive of naming practices, which, arguably, sought to carve out a space for identity and ancestry when enslaved Africans were ascribed racialized identities in a foreign idiom. Ironically, it was large estates, such as the Pharsalia plantation and those along the James and York Rivers, that allowed enslaved families to be maintained more so than did smaller holdings due to the large crops and wealth they yielded. The well-documented Pharsalia plantation of William and Thomas Massie, located at the foot of the Blue Ridge Mountains in the piedmont region of Virginia, provides a case not unlike others. It has shown that the "most common [naming practice among Africans and their descendants] was for a daughter to name one of her own daughters after her mother."[51] Certainly, this practice has been shown to be the case for the Akan and their descendants in Georgia, and the context of family and its extensions within and across plantations and the urban settings of major cities became means of cultural preservation, socialization, and the protection of individuals. Yet, if the constitution and the functions of family were primary concerns for pre- and postemancipation Africans, and if spouses were the most frequently mentioned relatives that runaways in Virginia sought during the eighteenth century, then newly arrived Africans encountered additional difficulties running away. Though hiding others, whether related by blood or not, was common among the enslaved, those new to Virginia lacked kin or friends to harbor them.

Another factor was language. Many Africans were bi- or multilingual even in the European languages (e.g., French, Spanish, English, Dutch, German, Portuguese, and possibly Hebrew) spoken in the colonies and as found in several colonial and antebellum newspapers, and this skill either aided or hindered chances of survival or the prospects of escape. A large number of Akan persons described in runaway advertisements for Virginia spoke one or more European languages, and those who spoke "very good English" included not only Virginia-born Africans, such as twenty-seven-year-old Quash, but also others born elsewhere, such as Jamaica-born Cuffey (Kofi), who arrived in Halifax from Duplin County, North Carolina.[52] The slender twenty-five-year-old Cuffey was described as a "very sensible fellow" who spoke "tolerable good English," but his English language competency was a matter of place and proximity since he would have had enough contact with the language departing from a British port on the Gold Coast, aboard British registered vessels, and coming from the British colony of Jamaica.[53] Those born in the Virginia colony covertly achieved literacy through English-based religious literature—as would those in an Islamic society via the Qur'an—and this was certainly the case for individuals like George's father,

Quash, who "read de hymn book and Testament to [his children] sometimes," and more than likely this was not out of a certain religious fervor since George could "not remember ever goin' to church durin' slavery days."[54]

Others who were subsumed under the category of "new Negro," such as twenty-five-year old Quash (Kwasi), who spoke no English but may have learned some after his departure, also spoke another language in general and "middling good French" in particular.[55] Quash was described as "very black" with numerous cuts on his backside from whippings. He, unlike the "Gold Coast Negro" with a pleasant countenance named Brumall or George of Albemarle County and "marked in the face as the Gold Coast slaves generally are," was apparently more defiant in character.[56] That spirit of nonconformity to dehumanization included the "outlandish Negro" named Quash, who sometimes called himself "John Quash" or George Quacca—this first name possibly derived from his owner, George Hope—and the stout and tall twenty-four-year-old "appear[ed] very proud and stately" with his "masterly speech."[57] Yet, it was individuals like Quamina (since most runaways were men, especially if alone) who demonstrated the boundaries of courage beyond those of enslavement and its shackles: The thirty-year-old Quamina escaped in Wilmington with an iron collar with two prongs marked "GP" around his neck and with leg irons on both legs in August, one of the busiest times of the agricultural cycle, which included weeding the tobacco and harvesting rice in the heat.[58]

These biosketches provide a fragmented glimpse into the lives of some Akan individuals who formed a significant segment of a composite cultural group imported by Chesapeake slaveholders in large numbers and who shaped African and African-descended cultural development in the colony by way of its marked matrilineality and communitarianism. Bolstered by the creation of gardens, courtyards, and cabins designed to facilitate these ideas of matrilineality and communitarianism, the Akan also imparted their material culture as is evident in what appeared to be *adinkra* symbols on cemetery stones, textiles, and other artifacts such as waist beads, which were found in antebellum Virginia. Some of these *adinkra* symbols, especially the Sankofa symbol, were found in early Virginia and the African Burial Grounds in New York City.[59]

Between 1790 and 1830 the enslaved population in Virginia remained at 39 to 40 percent of the total population (see table 6.3), including a very small group of "freed" Africans. The former population might appear more numerous if we include those who moved to the Midwest and beyond with large numbers of Virginia slaveholders in the mid-1760s. By the nineteenth century, the "freed" population had increased via self-purchases and manumissions at a rate that matched the wider net cast by evangelical proselytization, and it is possible that those who became "free" between the wars of the 1770s and the 1860s accepted the slaveholders' articulation of liberty and Christian articulations of a transcendent freedom as a singular voice rather than a fundamental contradiction. To the majority of the enslaved, the latter conclusion was probably truer than not, for many witnessed the organized terror of Christian church groups, the double standard toward African-descended converts, and the distance between the violence of those who controlled the social order and the Christian doctrine they preached and claimed to live by. Nonetheless, those "freed" could be easily kidnapped, reenslaved (if emancipated under the owner's will in order to settle outstanding debts), and have their rights forfeited, for officials became concerned about their numbers, and an 1806 law required those emancipated to leave the state within twelve months or be reenslaved. For white commoners, the fear of an impending "slave revolt" was also a real concern until the second half of the nineteenth century.[60] Compared to Virginia, South Carolina's enslaved population rose from 43 to 54 percent in the late eighteenth to the nineteenth century, while its "freed" population was less than 8,000 by 1830—Virginia had approximately six times that number.[61] In 1860, South Carolina's "freed" population was just under 10,000, whereas its enslaved population was 402,406, which marked an enslaved-to-free ratio of 40:1, and this gave South Carolina officials even greater and continued reason for concern than those in Virginia had.

THE SIGNIFICANCE OF NUMBERS AND NAMES: THE AKAN EXPERIENCE IN THE HISTORY OF SOUTH CAROLINA

Between two permeable worlds of unfreedom and emancipation and of the enslaved and "freed" populations, Louisa Gause of South Carolina was born ambiguously in the "first year of freedom," which could have been the end of the civil war in 1865, the passing of the Fourteenth Amendment to the U.S. constitution (1868), which granted citizenship to those of African origin, or perhaps it was neither. Belonging in the United States was an unstable condition for African descendants since they were no longer legal but rather social chattel marked by a disdain associated with their ancestry and circumscribed by the paradox of emancipation that did not provide true freedom. Two centuries prior to the Fourteenth Amendment, Africans from largely the Caribbean (i.e., Jamaica and Barbados) accounted for approximately one-third of the South Carolina population. In addition, as in the case of Louisa, the normative coexistence of freedom for some with its absence among that one-third meant that they were not part of "we the people" but rather the skilled and knowledgeable labor force that cultivated staple crops such as rice for "we the people." In the late seventeenth century, the cultivation of rice helped to resolve pressing economic questions that made the plantation economy viable, and this was crucial, for rice growing was a pursuit or skill outside of the English experience.[62] By the early eighteenth century, rice cultivation on swamplands was creating greater demands for Africans, who produced the rice that paid for the importation and sale of other Africans. For instance, a "Parcel of Gold Coast Slaves" was imported from Barbados in 1732 and "sold for rice or Currency on Credit."[63] Most rice was produced on inland swamp rice plantations of limited size; the shift to tidal rice cultivation in the Lowcountry led to an abandonment of the former due to the innovation of dams, irrigation techniques, and increased profits (see figure 6.1). The success of rice—a crop augmented by products created by Africans skilled in woodcraft, raising livestock, fishing, and sailing—soon led to an increase in an African population (from the Caribbean and Africa) that came to constitute a majority in the early eighteenth century, especially in the Lowcountry.

Many Akan persons brought to South Carolina in the seventeenth century came by way of Barbados and Jamaica (as "parcel[s] of Coromantees from the West Indies"), while others, in the eighteenth century, came directly from Gold Coast fishing communities and its hinterlands. These Akan captives labored in a fierce malarial environment, but this was perhaps

Figure 6.1. A South Carolina rice field. The arduous task of rice cultivation began usually in the spring, and mortality was high among those enslaved Africans procured for this kind of labor in malaria-infested environments. Used with permission of Documenting the American South, the University of North Carolina at Chapel Hill Libraries.

to their benefit in terms of survival in the swamplands, given their centuries-long exposure and adaptation to the malarial parasite in the West African forest. A minimum of 17,000 Akan persons or persons fluent in Akan culture settled the ports and coastal areas of South Carolina as a result of 102 recorded voyages from the Gold Coast. The majority of these captives were men (63 percent), and about 13 percent of the 19,000 exported from the Gold Coast died en route to South Carolina. For those 2,500 persons who passed away while in transit, their lives and stories remained archived in ancestry. Much of the importation into South Carolina occurred between 1711 and 1807, when large numbers arrived from the mid-eighteenth century to the early nineteenth century, with peaks periods for 1751–1775 (8,700 captives imported) and 1801–1807 (5,500 captives imported). Throughout the eighteenth century, a number of vessels—such as the *Neptune*, the *John*, the *Friendship*, the *Fanny*, the *Mary*, the *Nancy*, the *Gambia*, and the *Factor*—made multiple and unsanitary roundtrips to and from the Gold Coast with the terror and stench of captives embedded in their bowels.[64]

The Akan who endured the voyage and arrived via Charles Town (Charleston) or another port formed part of an African majority that encountered an intensification of anxiety in the whites, who feared rebellion and engaged in increased legal stringency, which facilitated runaways and the Stono rebellion of 1739—a year in which approximately 40,000 Africans and 20,000 whites inhabited the colony (see table 6.4).[65] Though the Stono rebellion does not appear to have involved a significant Akan presence, South Carolina planters had ample reason to suspect them, for only a decade earlier the *Clare*, presumably on its way to South Carolina, experienced an onboard insurrection as it left the Gold Coast. The Africans seized the firearms and gunpowder, drove the captain and crew off the vessel, brought the vessel ashore, and made their escape some miles away from Cape Coast Castle.[66] In the aftermath of the Stono rebellion, heightened repression came in the form of a comprehensive slave code, or Negro Act of 1740, which legally circumscribed African movement and assembly; eliminated prospects for subsistence through food production, wage labor, and literacy; limited the ratio of planter-to-African to 1:10, and even empowered planters to murder "rebellious" Africans. In fact, enslaved Africans from other North American colonies were often sent to South Carolina when accused of misconduct. The Negro Act of 1740 was followed by a tax that led to slow sales and little importation during the next three years; in response to this tax, South Carolina merchants such as Henry Laurens, one of the mainland's wealthiest, turned their sights on Georgia and Florida.

The restrictions articulated in the Negro Act of 1740, however, did little to delimit runaways or the contact among and relations between Africans isolated from whites along the coast and on the "islands" of the colony.

Table 6.4. Estimated African and White Populations in South Carolina, 1715–1850

	1715	1720	1741	1763	1773	1785	1790	1810	1830	1850
African	10,500	12,000	40,000	70,000	110,000	80,000	108,895	200,919	323,322	393,944
White	6,250	9,000	5,000	35,000	65,000	108,000	140,178	214,196	257,863	274,563

Source: Greene, *American Population*, 173–175. See also U.S. Department of Commerce, Bureau of the Census, *Negro Population of the United States, 1790–1915* (Washington, D.C.: Government Printing Office, 1918).

Many coastal peoples exercised high levels of social independence and cultural cohesion. One distinct outcome of intra-African cultural dialogues in the Lowcountry, where Africans lived in relative interaction with yet greater isolation from white culture, was the birth of the Gullah language and culture that extended along a coastal strip 30 to 40 miles wide and 250 miles long from Cape Fear, North Carolina, to St. Johns River, Florida. In *A Peculiar People*, Margaret Washington examined the process of culture formation among Gullah-speaking people of the coastal South Carolina region and argued that religion formed the core of an African American nationalism and political resistance to slavery and to white America.[67] Though some might debate the scope of that argument, the processes of culture formation, language creation, and the extended family arrangements facilitated by related people in clusters of contiguous houses and who often purchased land and attended social functions collectively were undoubtedly the product of their relative isolation and concentration on large rural plantations.

The Gullah language reveals much about the origin and dynamic input of its composite strands. Approximately 44 percent of Gullah names derived from peoples around the Bight of Bénin and on the Gold Coast, each of which accounted for 4 percent and 13.5 percent, respectively, of those imported throughout the eighteenth century. The Kôngo-Angola region led in the frequency of conversational words as the area with the highest percentage of importation (39 percent), while 69 percent of the words in stories, songs, and prayers were from the Mende and 29 percent from Vai, both accounting for a little more than 23 percent of Africans brought to the colony during that century.[68] Interestingly, key syntactic features and central parts of Gullah speech derive from the Akan language, and, according to William Pollitzer, "Twi [Akan] appears to be moderately influential in all linguistic features."[69] The wider influence of the Akan language beyond the Gullah and Charleston areas must await further research, but the results of that endeavor would certainly be significant since we have evidence of African language use well into the late nineteenth century, when some of the enslaved would "talk half African, and all African" in places like Spartanburg, near the North and South Carolina border.[70] Beyond Akan, the language of Africans from the Bight of Bénin had the greatest effect on sounds and grammar, but these peoples represented the lowest percentage of importation into the colony, in large part because South Carolina slaveholders sought Africans from the Gold Coast, Senegambia, and Angola but held a particular disdain for those from the bights of Biafra and Bénin. Be that as it may, the enslaved population was more or less centralized in the Charleston district, which is situated between Myrtle Beach and Beaufort along the coast, and Charleston remained a key port as evidenced by the British capture of Charleston in 1780, at which time many planters and their enslaved captives fled to North Carolina and Virginia. Large numbers of Africans also landed in Charleston from Barbados, followed by those from St. Kitts, Antigua, Jamaica, and other Caribbean islands.

Cuffe (Kofi), "being a Gold Coast Negro" of Charleston, was only one of many Akan names (as markers of Akan persons) found in that port city and in other parts of South Carolina, particularly Beaufort County and Colleton County in general and Hilton Head, St. Helena Island, and Butler Island in particular (see map 5).[71] Eighteenth-century names found in Charleston include Quamina and Cromantee Pero, both of which were names of "negroes sold unto Alexander Rose, esq. . . . in the month of April 1779," in addition to the following names excavated from Butler Island Plantation records: Cudjo (Kwadwo), Cuffee/Cuffy (Kofi), Minda (Mina?), Quacco/

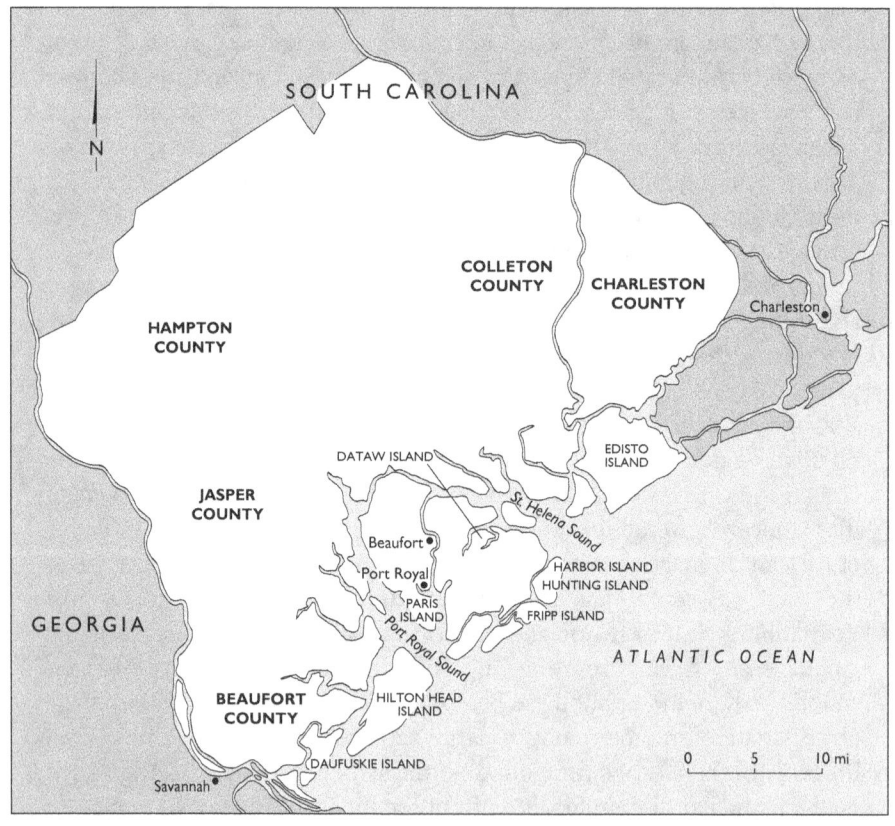

Map 5. Map of the South Carolina Lowcountry. The heart of these coastal counties has always been the city of Charleston. Akan persons lived in and around the port city of Charleston, in Colleton and Beaufort counties, and on Daufuskie Island, Hilton Head Island, St. Helena Island, and Edisto Island.

Quaka (Kwaku), Quamen(o/a)/Quomeno (Kwamena), Quamma (Kwame), Quash (Kwasi), and Aff(i/ee)/Affy (Afia).[72] A large number of these Akan persons were well known in and around the Charleston district and certainly included the likes of Quash and Cuffee, both of whom were listed to be sold by Dr. Jacob Martin. Cuffee had a wooden leg when he ran away, and this may have hindered his escape, while Quash was described as an "old Negro" and a gardener with a mark like a cross on one of his cheeks, which suggests that he had lived in the colony for some time and may have been cut or branded on the cheek or wrongfully ascribed an Akan name (or phonetic variant) if the cross was a "country mark."[73] Cudjoe, in the spirit of Cuffee, yet more like Quash and Jenny of Georgia, escaped with his wife, who (though unnamed) was young and tall and spoke "good English," "Chickesaw," and perhaps French, for the "Chickesaw" (Chickasaw) acquired her from a French settlement in Mississippi.[74] The Chickasaw were an indigenous North American group who settled across the Mississippi River (a county in Mississippi bears their name). Another couple of an intra-African form and from St. Helena Island consisted of the forty-five-year-old Cudjo, a "sensible Coromantee Negro," and his wife, Dinah, an "Ebo [Igbo]" who spoke "very good English." They escaped—less than a decade after the Stono rebellion—with their eight-year-old son and eighteen-month-old daughter.[75] York "of the Coromantee country," who also escaped from St. Helena Island and whose identity is confirmed by "country marks down his temple," was brought to North America at a young age, and perhaps a combination of contact with English speakers on the eighteenth-century Gold Coast and transport to an English-speaking colony provided the well-built, twenty-year-old the wherewithal to speak "good English."[76] One could argue that York was named and preserved in the historical record as such because of his young age, but that factor alone is insufficient, for we have seen other instances in which Akan persons were defined in a foreign idiom but claimed a name closer to home. This was certainly the case with thirteen-year-old Bergen of Georgia, who called himself "Affoa" in defiance of his Anglo name.[77]

A woman named Chloe maintained her "country name," Agua (Akua), and we know that she was Akan, for, like others already named, "her country marks [were] three short strokes on each Temple." At 5 feet 5 inches, Akua was probably sick when she escaped, for the advertisement reports that she walked a "little lame," had "Guiney worms" in her legs and thighs, and was slender with a "big belly."[78] Beyond declaring and maintaining one's name and thus securing an integral part of their humanity, other Akan persons were more insistent without apparent consequence. Seventeen-year-old Quamina was one such person, and though he was born in South Carolina and had no "country marks," the carver and chairmaker was known in and around Charleston for his "impudent behavior." According to his owner, John Fisher, "he has told me to my face, 'he can go when he pleases, and I can do nothing to him, nor shall I ever get a copper for him.'"[79] In the year after the British captured Charleston, Quamina escaped, and in February of 1781 Fisher offered a reward of two guineas for his capture and return. Among a list of individual men and women, families, kin, the sick, and those with a wooden leg, even those who were elderly sought freedom. This was true for a number of Akan, including the short and elderly Cuffee, a minor merchant who "used to sell things around town."[80] Not only does this *opanin* (elder) add to our survey of the different types of Akan persons in colonial South Carolina, but his name suggests a preponderance of the name Kofi (and its variants) throughout the Americas, as the previous chapters point out. Thus, the many Kofi found in various records make a strong argument for the town and the creek that bear the name Cuffee in South Carolina. Throughout the nineteenth and early twentieth centuries, the name Cuffee remained in use, and, as shown earlier, the cultural pattern of naming a child after one's parent, grandparent, or ancestor continued. In fact, the vast majority of Akan names encountered in the historical record were (in order of frequency of occurrence) Cuffee/Cuffy, Cudjoe, Quash, Quamina, and geographical and cultural designations such as the Gold Coast and Coromantee (and its variants). The reoccurring presence of the name Quamina is revealing, for this is the specific Fante version of the broader Akan name Kwame (Saturday-born male). Thus, the frequency of the former in the Americas in specific clusters of time concomitant with the international enslavement enterprise provides some insight into the types of Akan persons transported to the region.

Born in 1802 in some part of the Caribbean, seventy-year-old Cuffee Davis was brought to Hilton Head after the abolishment of the international enslavement enterprise, and there he farmed and lived with his wife, Peggy, and their five children. Cuffee's father, Cuffee Telfier, died in the "West Indies" and more than likely was born in West Africa.[81] A year after Cuffee Davis's birth, South Carolina resumed its involvement in the international enslavement enterprise until the federal government made such activity illegal in 1807. The South Carolina General Assembly prohibited the enterprise in 1787, and a number of other Southern states did the same during the last three decades of the eighteenth century. Key state legislators at Charleston had argued that the rice industry could not survive without African skill in rice cultivation, and both Lowcountry and Upcountry legislators held economic interests at odds with each other in the dispute about whether to end the "slave trade." The fear of insurrection was ever so present and proximate to the Haitian revolution and Gabriel's planned insurrection in 1800.[82] The conflict between the two legislative groups was thus fueled by the increased need for but also the fear of large numbers of African imports in order to maintain the rice industry. That need carried consequences that included real or imagined revolt, given important demographic considerations. In 1790 the enslaved and the white populations in the Lowcountry was 78,000 and 28,644, respectively; however, that imbalance shifted drastically in the Upcountry, where the enslaved population numbered 29,095, while the white population numbered 111,988.[83] The white population in the Lowcountry in 1800 and 1810 was 29,242 and 26,803, respectively, compared to an enslaved population of 95,015 and 102,024, respectively, for those years. The Upcountry told a different story: 166,561 and 187,393 whites for 1800 and 1810, respectively, and 51,136 and 94,341, respectively, for the enslaved population.[84] Between 1800 and 1810 the enslaved population in the Lowcountry accounted for at least 80 percent of the total population, while averaging only 34 percent of the total population throughout the Upcountry.

Domestic enslavement, in turn, increased with the decline of the international enslavement enterprise. Yet, as vessels from Africa and the Caribbean entered the port of Charleston up until the 1850s or 1860s, African and African-descended women, in particular, were being increasingly pressured in sexual relations, kidnapped, or sold—in which case they were often forcibly torn from kin, friends, and communities—with greater emphasis placed on domestic enslavement during the first half of the nineteenth century. During that period, several Akan descendants provide us with important, albeit brief, insights into their interior lives. Quabner (Kwabena) Wright, a farmer married to Molly, was born about 1835 in Blake Township in Colleton County, South Carolina, and lived there up until the time of the 1880 federal census. Wright's wife, Molly, was born in chattel enslavement, and she and her female kin probably experienced the additional stress placed on African-descended women during a period of heightened domestic enslavement. Forty-five-year-old Quabner had a five-year-old son, also named Quabner (b. 1875), following a cultural naming pattern that suggests some Africans held on to Africa as much as they could in the postemancipation era. It also suggests that the senior Quabner's father might have carried the same name as well. Unlike the younger Quabner Wright, Quabner Holmes, who was married to Betty, did not work due to his age but stayed at home. He and his parents were born in Blake Township, and he was eighty years old in 1880, which meant he was born in the year Gabriel planned his revolt in Richmond, Virginia. Quabner Washington was born about 1775, and at 105 years of age, he was still married to his wife, Judy—both living in Blake—but his (unnamed) parents were born in West Africa.

A consistent theme for all these men named Quabner was marriage, children, and family, regardless of their age, and this was also the case for others than those named Quabner. Cuffee Haywood was married to Abbie (Aba, Yaa?) and had five children, including a son named Cuffee. Cuffee was not born during Gabriel's planned insurrection but only two years before Denmark Vesey's (supposed) conspiracy in Charleston. He was fifty-three years old when he established an account at the Freedman's Bank in Beaufort on 5 March 1873 as a self-employed farmer in Port Royal, South Carolina.[85] Cuffee's parents were named Cuffee and Rose, but another bank account entry of 1869 gives his year of birth as 1827. Cuffey Rembleton, a contemporary of Cuffee Haywood and a resident of Charleston, was born in 1824 and was married to Patt; he had four children and seven siblings. The dark-brown-complexioned, forty-five-year-old was a waiter for a James N. Latson, and though his father was deceased, Cuffey carried his memory by bearing his name.[86]

AKAN PRESENCE AND EXPERIENCE IN THE NORTHERN UNITED STATES

Paul Cuffee, the well-known maritime entrepreneur and early African-descended nationalist, also carried the memory and example of his father by perpetuating a cultural naming pattern as others in the southern United States had done. Though Cuffee's mother was a Wampanoag christened Ruth, his father was reportedly an Asante individual captured on the Gold Coast and later enslaved in Massachusetts and remembered as Kofi.[87] We can be confident that "Cuffee" is but a phonetic rendering of the Akan name "Kofi," adjusted to the position of second name—this positioning is key, for the Akan, prior to the nineteenth-century Christian orthodoxy on the Gold Coast littoral, generally held two names, and, at times, either could be the first in position (e.g., Kwaku Kwao). If second names or surnames conveyed property, in that Cuffee's father was known locally as Kofi Slocum (after his owner), then Paul Cuffee's name and that of others in the Caribbean and North America take on added significance, for the positioning of "Kofi" as a second name translated into an ownership of one's self and a relationship to ancestry via an Akan father. Cuffee's father was brought to the state of Massachusetts, and there he worked diligently to procure his freedom and a farm of some one hundred acres for his family and himself. Paul followed in his footsteps, procured his freedom, and became both the owner of a vessel and an independent commercial trader with his own African-descended crew. Paul, however, was not the only one entrusted to carry on his father's memory; his brothers, one of whom was named John Cuffee, were also. These men did so into the nineteenth century, and the continuance of that naming pattern and tradition for Paul Cuffee and others is remarkable, for very few Akan were imported into Massachusetts from the Gold Coast, though some arrived in the state via domestic transshipments.

On the whole, states like Massachusetts shared an ironic fact with Paul Cuffee: Neither apparently had direct connections with the Gold Coast, but both were influenced by Akan persons and culture. Though Cuffee's father was from the Gold Coast and Cuffee was probably made aware of this, he instead chose Sierra Leone for commercial reasons. At another level of irony, there was much commercial activity and Christianity among the Gold Coast intelligentsia at the time Cuffee, a Quaker, made his West African voyages in the first two decades of the nineteenth century. At the start of the eighteenth century, Boston had an African (descended) population that numbered in the hundreds, most of whom came from the Caribbean, especially Barbados and Jamaica, and notices of "slave sales" in Barbados and Jamaica support this contention.[88] Since at least 1720, a small number of Gold Coast Africans formed a part of the African community in Boston, and notices in the *Boston Gazette* demonstrate that this continued into the 1760s. For example, a notice dated 1720 lists a "Gold Coast negro woman"; "several choice Gold Coast Negroes lately arrived" appeared in a 1726 notice; and the arrival of "a Few prime Men and Boy Slaves from the Gold Coast" was advertised in November 1762.[89] It is unclear whether these captives came directly from the Gold Coast or via the Caribbean. Massachusetts had only one recorded voyage from the Gold Coast in 1748—approximately eleven years before Paul Cuffee was born—and it is tantalizing to imagine that Cuffee's father was one of the 126 captives who landed in the state, but Kofi (the father) had spent considerable time in slavery, and Paul was one of his youngest children.[90]

Yet, that one direct voyage is questionable, for the London-based Committee for Trade and Plantation reported that, in 1775, no fewer than thirteen vessels from Boston and Rhode Island were dispatched from the Gold Coast, with approximately twenty-three hundred captives all procured with New England rum and traded primarily with the governor of the British forts.[91] If this report is correct, then there were more Akan persons in Massachusetts or its port city of Boston in the late eighteenth century beyond what one voyage could bring. In addition, this demographic consideration might help to contextualize the presence and role of a Quaco or Quock (Kwaku) Walker—whose 1783 legal cases were part of the process of abolishing slavery in Massachusetts—and the likes of Cuffee (Kofi) and Quamo or Quoma (Kwame), whose legal cases did not involve slavery per se but rather several accusations of theft in concert with a woman named Ann Grafton.[92] Quaco Walker was born in 1753 or 1754—five or six years before Paul Cuffee and would have been his contemporary—and his parents were named Dina and Mingo; his case was argued on the grounds that his deceased owner "said I should be free at 24 or 25." He ultimately won both his case and his freedom, though slavery persisted in Massachusetts even after his 1783 case.[93] For Cuffee and Quoma, their political fortunes appear to have been the opposite of Quaco's, for the two were tried for several thefts in the Boston area, but, in the end, both they and Quaco were arguably "black person[s] without a legal master," for little had changed in Quaco's social status, and little would change in the enslaved status of Cuffee and Quoma.[94]

Out of the New England states of Massachusetts, New Hampshire, Vermont, Maine, Connecticut, and Rhode Island, it was Rhode Island, the smallest of them all, that received the human cargo aboard at least fifteen Gold Coast voyages between 1736 and 1802—though the majority came in the 1760s—and landed about 1,000 out of 1,700 captives.[95] Close to 42 percent of those women and men who embarked for Rhode Island died en route, and since most Rhode Island vessels concentrated their slaving efforts on a finite area of the Gold Coast, it is very likely many of the deceased came from the same or contiguous areas and shared intimate family and community ties. Rhode Island merchants procured enslaved peoples, gold dust, ivory, and camwood at principally Cape Coast Castle, Komenda, Elmina, and Anomabu. At Anomabu, Rhode Island merchant Samuel Vernon or his agent traded with "Baddoe [Badu of] Saltponds" and with "Cabbashire Quomino [at] Annomaboe [Anomabu]" for gold and captives in exchange for rum and sugar.[96] The captives for whom Baddoe (Badu) and Quomino (Kwamena) traded for rum and sugar were sold as commodified human cargo in the British Caribbean (especially Jamaica), Virginia, and the Carolinas.[97] At a May 1774 town meeting in Providence, Rhode Island, officials agreed on a resolution to prohibit the importation of "Negroes," but this measure was short lived, for it did not restrict merchants engaged in the international enslavement enterprise, and in the 1790s a number of Rhode Island vessels were back on the Gold Coast. Indeed, Rhode Island vessels secured Gold Coast captives years after 1802 and attempted to sell them in South American markets because of the closure of markets in the Carolinas. One such example was the *Ann*, whose human cargo consisted of "Zanteen [Fante] Slaves" from Elmina and others primarily from Accra.[98] Rhode Island, like the ratio of Akan influences to their numbers, maintained an active engagement in the "slave trade" of New England and cannot be compared to places like New Hampshire, Connecticut, Vermont, and Maine, which received no direct shipments, though these states probably imported a few but numerically insignificant number of Akan persons. In this regard, Rhode Island compared well with the commercial activity and ports of New York, although New York had a shorter duration of direct importation (ca. 1715–1765) and much more Akan and African importation via the Caribbean.

Between 1715 and 1765, New York received seven Gold Coast voyages that brought a little more than five hundred persons, whereas New Jersey received no such direct voyages through its Perth Amboy port, and Pennsylvania had one recorded voyage that came from the Gold Coast in 1761 with 130 captives—22 died en route and 108 landed.[99] In the tri-state area, New York was the commercial and economic anchor, but before the former Dutch colonial settlement (known as New Amsterdam) became New York, it was built by enslaved African labor (e.g., roadways, wharves, and a fort on Manhattan island) that included some Gold Coast or Akan persons from the Dutch-controlled port of Elmina in 1663.[100] Between 1626 and 1664, Dutch-controlled New Amsterdam imported at least 467 enslaved Africans, some of whom came from the Gold Coast, while sheer imports to the port of New York between 1715 and 1772 included 66 percent from the Caribbean (28 percent from Jamaica) and 30 percent from Africa.[101] During the first quarter of the eighteenth century, Caribbean importation far outweighed "Negroes" imported into the province of New York from Africa: Between 1701 and 1726, 1,572 out of the recorded 2,360 African arrivals to New York came from the Caribbean.[102] According to incomplete entries for African importation into New York between June 1715 and January 1765, 1,379 came from Jamaica, 663 from Barbados, 577 from the "coast of Africa" (in nine voyages), 401 from Antigua, 313 from Africa, 182 from domestic sources (e.g., Rhode Island, South Carolina), 105 from Curaçao, 91 from St. Kitts/St. Christopher, 85 from St. Thomas, 66 from Bermuda, and smaller numbers from the rest of the Americas.[103] Though these figures are fraught with missing entries and listings of vessels with no cargo, they do point to a consistent pattern in terms of African importation into North America: the prominence of the Caribbean, particularly Jamaica and Barbados, and other islands with a significant Akan presence. This pattern for North America and for eighteenth-century New York in particular was almost the same for New Jersey between 1718 and 1757, though on a smaller scale of importation.[104]

New York City came to have one of the largest enslaved populations north of Maryland (see table 6.5), and in April of 1712 it also became the site of perhaps the first enslaved African uprising in British North America. In 1712 the province of New York was inhabited by 1,775 enslaved Africans (called "Negro slaves") and 10,511 "Christians" (i.e., whites), according to E. B. O'Callaghan's tabulations, wherein the city's population was bifurcated into "Christian" men and women on one hand and "Negro slaves" and "Indians" of both genders on the other.[105] Africans from the Gold Coast entered New York City toward the end of Dutch rule and throughout the remainder of the seventeenth century.[106] In the eighteenth century, the bulk of Africans shipped directly to New York came from Senegambia,

Table 6.5. Estimated African and White Populations in New York, 1698–1850

	1698	1715	1731	1746	1758	1776	1790	1810	1830	1850
African	2,170	4,000	7,231	9,107	13,542	21,993	25,978	40,350	44,945	49,069
White	15,897	27,000	43,058	52,482	83,233	169,148	314,142	918,699	1,873,663	3,048,325

Source: Greene, *American Population*, 136–142. See also U.S. Department of Commerce, Bureau of the Census, *Negro Population of the United States, 1790–1915* (Washington, D.C.: Government Printing Office, 1918).

Kôngo-Angola, Madagascar, and other regions, with approximately 20 percent from the Gold Coast; the Gold Coast presence was augmented by about 14 percent Akan and other Africans who were born on the Gold Coast (clustered under the category of "Coromantee") and were brought to New York City as part of the imports transshipped via the Caribbean.[107] In fact, a large number of Gold Coast Africans came to New York with their owners from the Caribbean in general, and New York and Perth Amboy–based merchants acquired Africans from Jamaica, Barbados, and Antigua—three principal colonies inhabited by significant numbers of Akan persons who were known for their hand in real or imagined conspiracies to revolt. Africans from the Gold Coast and the Bight of Bénin contributed to an African cultural dynamic composed of Kwa language speakers in New York City in the first half of the eighteenth century. However, by the mid-eighteenth century and in the following decades, greater numbers of Africans from the Bight of Biafra and Africans who were Mande language speakers were present. In the first four and a half decades of the eighteenth century New York City had a preponderance of Akan language speakers. A famous enslaved revolt in 1712 and a conspiracy to revolt in 1741 both implicated Akan persons. An amazing synergy between political action and Akan spiritual culture was present in the revolt of 1712 and the alleged plot to revolt in 1741 in the form of rituals, burial rites involving chanting and drumming, blood oaths, and the ritual use of white clay (*hyire*).[108]

Even though gaps exist in the historical record and the claims in some reports are inconsistent, the general pattern of the events that marked the 1712 revolt is less complicated.[109] On 1 or 6 April 1712, about 23 armed Africans gathered at midnight with guns and hatchets, and in the middle of town, Cuffee (Kofi) and John set ablaze their owner's outhouse in the East Ward of New York City. As the fire spread, Africans and white colonists engaged in a confrontation that left at least 9 whites dead and 6 wounded; colonial militia units responded and captured 27 Africans. About 21 Africans were executed (e.g., hung, burned alive, beheaded; their remains were left as deterrents), 6 committed suicide (e.g., shot themselves or cut their throats), and about 12 others were not indicted or acquitted, including Cuffee (Kofi), who was sentenced to be hung but pardoned by Governor Hunter on account of insufficient evidence.[110] The fate of Cuffee, who was a key witness on behalf of city officials, was different from that of his fellow Akan defendants. Though Quashi (Kwasi) and Amba (Amma) were part of the small cohort that received acquittals, the likes of Quasi (Kwasi) and Quacko (Kwaku) were hung, and Quaco (Kwaku) was "burnt with fire until his bo[dy was] dead and consumed."[111]

Interestingly, there is no evidence in the trial records of any confessions made by those accused and eventually executed. We can be certain some were "Condemned on Slender Evidence in the heat of Peoples resentment," as argued by an eyewitness, who heard one of the accused "declare his Innocency [sic] with his dying breath" and "exhorted [another named Robin] to Confession" while hanging for three days in chains.[112] That eyewitness, the Rev. John Sharpe of the Society for the Propagation of the Gospel in Foreign Parts, saw some or all of the revolt and reported, "Some Negro Slaves here of the Nations of Cormantee & Pappa [Popo] plotted to destroy all the White[s] in order to obtain their freedom."[113]

The "Cormantee & Pappa," incorrectly called "subdivision[s] of the Akan" by Thelma Foote, did not represent actual people but rather were European trademarks for a coastal town (Kormantin) and a polity (Popo), respectively, from which largely Akan and other peoples embarked.[114] Sharpe claimed the group met on 25 March and engaged in a secret blood oath by "Sucking the blood of each Others hands, and to make them invulnerable as they believed a free negroe who pretends socery [sic] gave them powder to rub on their cloths [sic]," and with little Christianization among the enslaved he suspected no more than 10 percent attended church school.[115] Indeed, many enslaved Africans and Akan persons in and around New York City were non-Christian, bi- and multilingual (in African and European languages), and skilled laborers who worked or lived in proximity to "freed" Africans. The close to two hundred Gold Coast Africans that arrived in New York between 1710 and 1712 were part of the former enslaved community, and, in consideration of the role played by Cuffee and other Akan participants, as well as Sharpe's claim of a Cormantee plot, the Akan certainly did play an active (leadership) role in the 1712 revolt.

In reaction to the revolt, New York officials expended much effort to enact or extend a stringent set of laws such as "An Act for Preventing, Suppressing, and Punishing the Conspiracy and Insurrection of Negroes and other Slaves," which, when passed in December 1712, extended the "Act for preventing the Conspiracy of Slaves," which had been passed in October 1708. Soon the former was replaced by a similar act in 1730.[116] These enactments were made in an effort to proscribe proximity between segments of the African-based community: Movement among "freed" Africans was increasingly restricted; the scope of punishment was extended; gambling and the handling of firearms were prohibited and penalized by public whippings; manumission was discouraged; and those who were involved in a conspiracy or accused of rape were sentenced to death.[117] These strengthened pieces of legislation did little, however, to prevent another revolt. Indeed, rumors of a "slave plot" to burn down the city swept the region in 1741, as did tales of individuals who burned their owner's "barn and outbuildings" even though they were cognizant of the consequences, such as burning at the stake, one of which was witnessed by the "pious Methodist"

Quamino (Kwamena) Buccau of New Jersey in the late eighteenth century.[118] The laws extant throughout the eighteenth century, as well as those that were revised or created after the 1712 revolt, occurred in a context of socioeconomic disparities in a multiracial and urbanized setting in which 40 to 45 percent of white households in New York City held enslaved Africans, whites of varied economic and social standing lived in proximity to Africans, and many Africans were mobile, articulate, and assertive in and around New York and parts of New Jersey.

Consistent with the patterns of those who escaped the plantations of the southern United States, most runaways in New York and New Jersey were males between sixteen and twenty-five years of age, and these escapes occurred largely in May, June, and August among housekeepers, servants, and musicians who spoke English and Dutch well. Most Africans labored as farmers, vendors, construction workers, dockworkers, sailors, shipbuilders, and household servants, and the large bulk of runaway advertisements that list these kinds of Africans provide some insight into their lives, however fragmentary and inconsistent in detail the notices might be. Moreover, the appearance of Akan (named) persons from the Caribbean or West Africa and those mentioned in the eighteenth-century advertisements provide evidence of a continual, though rather small but influential, Akan presence in colonial New York. These notices also give us a glimpse into the interior corridors of their lives in captivity and their various responses to it—some sought freedom among busy markets and taverns, some found momentary solace among the community networks and spaces used by the enslaved and those freed, and a few changed their names and carried real or forged baptismal certificates as "freedom" papers and passes.

Those skilled and multilingual Akan persons imported from Africa or transshipped from the Caribbean included the likes of Quash (Kwasi), who escaped from his owner in New York City in 1730, and Quaw (Kwao), a tall young man who was born in Jamaica and described as cunning and sensible but stuttered very much after being brought to New York.[119] Quaw's runaway advertisement was printed in 1746, and he was accused of stealing money upon his escape in New York City.[120] Whether or not theft was the case, he and a number of Akan found some semblance of freedom in fleeing to or using the urban setting of New York City as a means of escape via networks and places (e.g., African Burial Ground, shops, and societies), where they lived beyond the surveillance of slaveholders and city officials. It was probably here that twenty-six-year-old Cuffee (Kofi) was sought and subsequently jailed "on suspicion of running away" in Philadelphia a year after Quaw escaped.[121]

These Akan men included those with greater occupational and physical mobility in a climate of great socioeconomic inequities and racialized restrictions in law and custom, and many sought life and liberty on their own terms and through opportunities that approximated freedom. The 1751 insurrection by seventy-five captives against the captain and crew of the *Wolf*, which left the Gold Coast bound for New York, was no more remarkable than the act of Quaco (Kwaku), who escaped captivity with an "iron collar with two hooks to it and round his neck" and a pair of handcuffs with a 6-foot-long chain secured to it.[122] Some such as Quaco left New York and sought access to a port or aligned themselves with one of the main factions in the North American colonies' cession from Britain in the 1770s as ways to seek a modicum of freedom. Twenty-six-year-old Quash (Kwasi), a cooper by trade, escaped and was thought not only to have changed his name to "Yerrah" but also to have gone either to Philadelphia or "the American Camp" since "he is fond of the soldiery." Reportedly, he carried a large bundle and no pass; his owner, John Jones, requested the help of "American gentlemen," officers, and soldiers to apprehend Quash, and for this he offered a reward of twenty dollars.[123]

Quaco (Kwaku), who also called himself William Murrey, did not have a pass either, but, according to his owner, "he [had] a certificate of his being baptized, which he shows as a pass, and says he is a free man."[124] These measures were part and parcel of the pursuit of freedom attempted by Cuff (Kofi) Dix, who was described as "a smart well set fellow" that spoke and understood English well and was a "most excellent hammerman." He was also "always chang[ing] his name, and den[ying] his master," and he escaped with an iron collar around his neck as Quaco had done a decade before.[125] The dark-complexioned Cudjoe (Kwadwo), at 5 feet 6 inches, escaped from on board a vessel named either the *Emanuel* or the *Hercules*, and he might have been successful since he spoke "good English" and French.[126] Cudjoe had good reason to seek freedom in this manner, for a few years earlier, the twenty-year-old Cuff (Kofi) of Cecil Country, Maryland, had run away several times, and each time— except the last—he was found aboard a vessel in the Philadelphia harbor, demonstrating the possibility of escape and of obtaining a modicum of freedom at sea.[127] Five years later, in 1775, Cuff, who was then twenty-five, was still missing. He might have been recaptured and resold, or he may have found refuge among Africans who harbored runaways like Cuff, and language might not have been a barrier for integration into different African communities, for he spoke "a little in the Negroe dialect" and some English.[128] The same would have been true for those like Cuffey (Kofi), a "well-set fellow" and tailor who spoke "pretty good English," though he came from a Danish colony. Cuffey and other Akan persons came from St. Croix to New York less than two and half decades after the island's alleged Akan-led plot of 1759 and during the same century in which the Akan were implicated in the New York revolt of 1712 and the city's alleged plot of 1741.[129]

In the alleged 1741 plot to revolt, confessions from persons such as Quack (Kwaku) were gathered at the stake; his "confession" implicated several individuals named Cuffee (Kofi), and, if we can trust the veracity of that testimony, he did not even trust his wife, who was the governor's cook, enough to share the supposed plot with her.[130] Cuffee, one of those whom Quack named, also confessed at the stake. He reportedly said that a white shopkeeper named John Hughson was the main contriver of the plot and that he and others had sworn an oath to Hughson. Of this Cuffee, David Horsmanden, the city recorder and a chief judge, tells us that he was "one of the principal negroes who was first initiated into this detestable enterprise" and that Hughson entrusted him with "a greater share of this internal secret than others of his colour."[131] Both this Cuffee and the other named in Quack's "confession" were burned at the stake a day after their conviction; Quack, along with another person named Quash (Kwasi), was burned at the stake, while John Hughson, the purported architect of the plot, was executed. Another Quack was hung, and others such as Quamino (Kwamena) confessed but were soon transported to Madeira, along with another Quash. This "plot" and the so-called confessions thereof reveal several characteristics that have come to define the Akan experience in the Americas in general and New York in particular, but scholars have paid insufficient attention to the implications of linking the Akan to this and other plots.

The 1712 revolt is less complicated since it, according to the records, actually occurred. But this is no certainty, for there was no "official report" produced and no evidence of trial records or questions put to the accused in the court transcripts. Furthermore, very little evidence—John Sharpe's letter notwithstanding—actually exists to convincingly state that a revolt took place in 1712. Nonetheless, these issues raise more serious questions about the alleged 1741 New York conspiracy because no revolt actually occurred. In addition, this conspiracy shared much in common with the 1675 Barbados conspiracy, the 1736 Antigua conspiracy, the 1759 St. Croix conspiracy, and even the well-publicized 1822 Denmark Vesey conspiracy to revolt in Charleston, South Carolina. We have already discussed the conspiracies in Barbados, Antigua, and St. Croix. Thematically, the Denmark Vesey conspiracy to revolt in Charleston differed little, though it reveals much about the 1741 New York conspiracy. In the Denmark Vesey case, Quash Harleston, "a free black man," was among those imprisoned but acquitted—unlike Denmark Vesey, who was hung—"for their guilt not being fully proved" while they maintained their innocence. Denmark Vesey also maintained his innocence, but he and others who were implicated on the basis of coerced testimony were executed, and some, including the "free black man" Quash (Kwasi), were sent out of the country.[132] Cuffy (Kofi), another Akan person or descendant, was also arrested for his involvement in the alleged Denmark

Vesey-led conspiracy, but he, too, was discharged on account of insufficient testimony against him.[133] The uneven fates of Cuffy, Quash, and Denmark Vesey point to the real problem of determining what constitutes a conspiracy to revolt, which suggests that we need to rethink the nature of revolts and conspiracies in the literature on resistance to enslavement. In this way we can begin to distinguish between the courage of liberation seekers (however they conceived of freedom) and the likes of Denmark Vesey, who protested their innocence without confession, and the incrimination of those who confessed and accused others as ways to escape execution or banishment in the face of white hysteria.

In the cases of the Denmark Vesey and the New York conspiracy of 1741, Akan persons, in varying degrees, were implicated in what would have amounted to attempts to address the injustices of a racialized plutocracy sustained by enslavement and its mechanisms. However, this aim may not have been their intention, and those that claim the 1741 plot was an Akan conspiracy support a questionable contention, for the actuality of a "conspiracy" was itself based on dubious evidence and the testimony of a white indentured servant named Mary Burton, who testified under duress from David Horsmanden. In the end, Burton was monetarily rewarded and then paid for her freedom with more than enough to spare, but the value of her testimony in the "official report" rapidly deteriorated once she began to implicate prominent whites in the alleged conspiracy.[134] Subsequent to Burton's testimony, the large number of Africans rounded up without guilt or charges were sentenced to death or deportation. More than a hundred persons were brought to a dungeon beneath City Hall and forced to confess and supply names, many of which included the thirty-one Africans hung or burned at the state. More than seventy Africans were transported from New York to Suriname, Curaçao, Madeira, Hispaniola (Dominican Republic and Haiti), and St. Thomas. The "Negro Burying Ground," whose southern portion was part of City Hall, was the resting place for those put to death after the 1712 revolt and probably those executed in the alleged plot of 1741.

Arguably, the confessions procured through torture and in closed sessions, prisoners who were denied legal counsel as part of the proceedings, Horsmanden's "official report" of the proceedings, the brutality of the executions, and the idea of the (alleged) plot carried out by Akan and other Africans who supposedly sought to seize the town, burn it, and kill all the whites served another purpose. In fact, the "official reports" produced in the New York City and Charleston cases served kindred goals. In ways similar to the conundrum in which South Carolina legislators were at odds over the need for but fear of increasing numbers of racialized African bodies and the imperatives of forging "whiteness" among Europeans with African "blackness" as its internal enemy, officials in New York, including

Horsmanden, sought a similar mobilization. Those officials attempted to configure Africans in the foregoing manner and as a threatening focus away from glaring social tensions and class inequalities, which rested largely on their shoulders and which the Africans were acutely aware of. This political framing may have been the real conspiracy, if any, for "blackness" was resurrected as the demonic inverse of "whiteness" and as a synonym for a permanent and servile labor group made to serve whites and white interests.

At another level of framing, Horsmanden tells us, through Mary Burton's "testimony," that Africans such as Quack (Kwaku) and Cuffee (Kofi) had sought to kill all the whites and install another white person by the name of John Hughson, the supposed mastermind of the plot and at whose tavern Burton was indentured, the "king" of the city.[135] Though Burton's testimony is highly questionable and laden with self-interest, it seems even more odd that Quack and Cuffee would want to install Hughson as "king" when in the Americas the general pattern was to install an African, one usually—though not exclusively—with an Akan name when Akan persons were implicated or involved in a plot or a revolt. Thus, it was quite possible that Akan persons at the stake "confessed" or told the white colonists of New York City what they wanted to hear: that a nonelite white man whose tavern entertained a cross-section of "lower classes" was the architect of a conspiracy since the whites of New York feared an African uprising. However, officials knew these "internal enemies" could be used to mobilize white solidarity more than the fear of a Spanish takeover.[136] The 1741 plot was indeed "a gruesome figment of the imagination of whites," but that fiction had very real implications for those executed and for those African descendants who had to live in captivity and in an environment of an increasing number of socioeconomic clashes and escalating legal stringency.[137] The only nonfictive element of the alleged plot was the implication of an enslaved African named Will, who might have been an Akan, for he participated in the St. John uprising of 1733 and the alleged Antigua conspiracy of 1736 and was deported to New York some time thereafter. Be that as it may, Will confessed at the stake and was burned as a result of his pursuit of momentary freedom via confession. At least so he thought on July 4—a date on which those who denied Will's freedom later proclaimed and immortalized theirs.[138]

7

Diaspora Discourses

Akan Spiritual Praxis and the Claims of Cultural Identity

> Nnεemmaafoɔ se tete asooe yεnsoɔ hɔ bio. Na adɛn nti na yɛntu tete-muka mmiɛnsa mu baako na ɔnka mmienu?
>
> Children of today say we should not do things in the ways of our ancestors anymore. So why is it that they do not take out one of the three stones used to hold up the cooking pot and just leave two?
>
> —Akan proverb

Born in 1930 in Augusta, Georgia, under the name Augustus or Gus Edwards, Nana Yao Opare Dinizulu entered a world marked by the Great Depression. During this interim between two world wars, Augusta was home to one of the oldest, African-descended Baptist churches, which Augustus and his parents probably attended. Proximate to the Georgia–South Carolina border, Augusta is divided by the Savannah River. Just as the Atlantic Ocean separates North America and Ghana, so the Savannah River could have divided Georgia and South Carolina—states, particularly the latter, that had a historic Akan presence—for Nana Dinizulu would cross both ocean and river and become transformed. In so doing, Nana Dinizulu helped to transform the landscape of Akan spirituality and culture as practiced in North America. The phenomenon of African-descended persons and their historic engagement with Akan culture and spirituality form the parameters of this chapter, and herein I telescope this concern by focusing on the efforts of the late Nana Dinizulu of New York, Nana Kwabena Brown of the District of Columbia, and two significant issues they raised for the study of the African diaspora in the Americas.

One issue is an imperative for internal dialogue on both sides of the Atlantic Ocean since most opportunities for both dialogue and the interrogation of diaspora in context and content are left to osmosis rather than seized by diasporic Africans and Akan migrants, who have now become part of an extending and unfolding diaspora beyond the confines of Ghana. Unfortunately, even scholars (of Akan cultural origin) that attempt to examine the "new African diaspora" in North America fail to grasp the significance of the parallel practice of indigenous Akan culture and spirituality by relatively few Akan from Ghana and a growing number of diasporic Africans. These scholars are more concerned with the immigrant narratives of Africans who have made North America their new "homeland" and the latter's perceptions of African descendants. Another issue is that many diasporic Africans have traveled to and studied in the Akan homeland since the 1960s and have problematized the "slave castles" of Ghana, wherein they became contested sites of meeting and reinterpretation at a crossroads where diasporic Africans are adopting Akan cultural institutions and spiritual practices. At the same time, Akan persons in Ghana are becoming increasingly Christianized and are leaving for North America and parts of Europe. As the Atlantic ocean becomes a path frequently crossed and re-crossed by both groups, these phenomena associated with the Akan diaspora strongly suggest that the study of a composite African diaspora must be one of ongoing movements and transformations in specific and shared dialogue among Africa-based and African-descended communities.

COMPARATIVE HISTORIES AND THE AKAN LENS

The Akan experience in the Americas and West Africa during the nineteenth and early twentieth centuries provides a very important "diasporic" lens for, in comparative perspective, that experience linked North America and West Africa and revealed similar processes that were unfolding among African and African-descended communities. New York became a nexus for these experiences and the similar paths pursued by converging, Westernized, and elitist segments of both communities. In Manhattan, the significant number of businesses and churches owned by prosperous families of African descent contrasted with the pomp and quasi-pageantry of those Westernized families and the poverty of the larger number of formerly enslaved persons, who worked as waiters, domestic workers, and dockworkers around the port districts in Manhattan. In North America the nineteenth century began with the gradual abolishment of the international enslavement enterprise, though domestic enslavement increased—New York abolished slavery in 1827. As "freed" Africans and their descendants shifted from chattel in the homes of former owners to wage laborers situated in cellars, and as competition for jobs and survival escalated in a period of heightened industrial transformation in New York City, violence and acute racism affected the lives of many. In fact, a decade after the Dutch attempted to restore the "slave trade" in the 1850s, many of the foregoing issues continued into the late nineteenth century. When the antidraft riots of 1863 forced

African descendants from Manhattan to independent African-descended communities in Brooklyn, they came to neighborhoods like Weeksville and Carsville, which had been established around the 1830s in the vast, semirural region of Brooklyn's Ninth Ward.[1]

These communities provided economic opportunity and charitable institutions, such as the African Union Society and its African School no. 2, which were established by and for African descendants; those institutions became a place of refuge for those who migrated to Brooklyn due the antidraft riots of 1863, in which poor whites blamed the hated Civil War draft on African descendants who resided in Manhattan. Determined to defend their lives and homes against an attack during these violent protests, the African descendants of Weeksville, for instance, took up arms and posted guards in an effort to protect themselves. The part of Manhattan that became known as Harlem, as well as sections of Brooklyn in its own right, became key cultural, political, and residential centers for African descendants from the South and the Caribbean in the late nineteenth and early twentieth centuries. With the "betrayal" of Reconstruction and Jim Crowism in the South, a nationalist spirit found expression in movements to establish all-African-descended towns and Oklahoma as an all-African-descended state. In 1879 Benjamin "Pap" Singleton's migration crusade from Tennessee toward the West mobilized as many African descendants in North America as in the movement led by Marcus Garvey in the 1920s, if not more. Those efforts to find strategic alternatives to injustice, violence sanctioned by custom and the law, and the need to protect the interests of families and communities in Oklahoma and Tennessee would foreshadow the appeal of the so-called back-to-Africa movements envisioned by Alfred Charles Sam (also known as Chief Sam) of the Gold Coast and Marcus Garvey of Jamaica, two Akan-related persons whose movements were based, not by happenstance, in Harlem and Brooklyn.

In addition to the sovereignty-driven movements within the political boundaries of North America, the nineteenth century also witnessed the emigration of thousands of Africans and their progeny from North America to Haiti. African descendants entered the twentieth century poised for a new political, cultural, and institutional vision beyond personalities such as Booker T. Washington, who opposed "going back to Africa" but sponsored programs and opportunities for those who desired a return to the African continent. Yet, it was Booker T. Washington who inspired Marcus Garvey to come to North America and whom Garvey wanted to meet; however, Washington died before Garvey arrived. The Garvey movement, with its focus on unification and ridding the African continent of colonial rule, and the Communist-oriented African Blood Brotherhood (ABB) influenced the contours of a Harlem renaissance. This revitalization drew the likes of

Langston Hughes, Countee Cullen, Alain Locke, W.E.B. Du Bois, Richard B. Moore, Arturo Schomburg of Puerto Rico, Hermina Dumont Huiswoud of Guyana, and Claude McCay of Jamaica. Cyril V. Briggs founded the African Blood Brotherhood in 1919 as a result of a split from A. Philip Randolph's *Messenger* publication over definitions of "radicalism" since the ABB momentarily leaned toward nationalism rather than socialism, which was advanced by the Communist movement. Members of the ABB included notables such as Richard B. Moore and Hubert Harrison, who originated the Harlem street-corner orator tradition that Malcolm X later embraced, fashioned the slogan "Race First," and provided an important platform for Marcus Garvey when he arrived in Harlem. While Garvey represented the sentiments of pan-Africanism and a nationalism that advocated Africa as the true homeland of diasporic Africans in the early twentieth century, his movement was preceded and can be better understood by the movement that Alfred Charles Sam initiated. In fact, Chief Sam's movement also anticipated the wave of diasporic Africans who settled in Ghana during the 1960s and thereafter and were primarily from the Caribbean and North America.

Born to Nana (James) Kwakye Sam and Akosua Twumasiwaa Buaa in 1879 or 1880, Alfred Charles Sam departed from the path of a missionary worker envisioned by his father and became a trader who inherited the chieftaincy of Apasu a few years after his first trip to North America.[2] In 1913 Alfred Charles Sam envisioned commercial and then diasporic voyages to the Gold Coast from North America through his Akim Trading Company Limited, which was incorporated in South Dakota. Alfred Sam served as its president after liquidating his interest in the previous Akim Trading Company, established in 1911 and chartered in New York. According to reports in the *New York Times*, Sam procured a vessel named the *Liberia* (formerly the *Curityba* and purchased for $100,000) with a capacity of five hundred passengers. Only those African descendants who held membership in the 130 "clubs of negroes" across the country could buy shares, and two of these shares (at $25.00 each) provided free passage to the Gold Coast for a husband, wife, and children under sixteen.[3] A nonshareholder, A. E. Smith, was "the only white man connected with the company," though he merely acted as its agent, but all officers of the trading company were "Gold Coast inhabitants" of Akyem, including Chief Sam, who was born and reared in Akyem and later schooled by the Basel Evangelical Mission schools at Kyebi and Akuropɔn, capital of Akuapem.

The idea for the voyage was based on Sam's purchase of land endowed with gold, rubber, and mahogany resources from ɔmanhene Kwame Dokyi of Akyem-Abuakwa and negotiated leases of additional lands from local Akan leaders. Those lands would be offered or rented to diasporic African settlers for an unstated amount. On the vessel's return, it would carry

African products (e.g., mahogany, cocoa beans, rubber, coffee) for sale in the United States.[4] Sam had had some success in commerce as a cocoa and rubber trader, and news of his aims, including the prospects of land, spread to the United States, particularly Oklahoma, which had a large number of African-descended towns and had sought black statehood in the late nineteenth century. The success of Chief Sam's message and interactions with prosperous African-descended businessmen and farmers in Oklahoma and other parts of North America was, in part, facilitated by the message of Bishop Henry McNeil Turner, who visited West Africa and South Africa. Here, the commercialist interests of Chief Sam converged with the emigration-minded aspirations of diasporic Africans, and, to that effect, the Akim Trading Company Limited urged the emigration of the best farmers and technicians among the diasporic Africans in North America to further the goal of greater autonomy for Gold Coast commercial interests vis-à-vis the British monopoly of Gold Coast imports and exports. Interestingly, as Chief Sam and sixty passengers departed on the *Liberia* for the Gold Coast via several U.S. states and Barbados, a group of nine African-descended men from Brooklyn—with no connection to Sam's project—formed the African Union Company to engage in business on the Gold Coast through a concession of land granted by "three of four native chiefs," as Sam had done in the effort to procure the same African products.[5]

Chief Sam and those who came to the Gold Coast eventually settled at Saltpond, near Kormantin (source of the term "Coromantee" and its variants) on the Gold Coast prior to being seized by a British warship and held in Freetown, Sierra Leone, despite the most obvious fact that the *Liberia* flew the British flag as a registered British vessel. The group of diasporic Africans were well received and cared for by several indigenous community leaders and their people—some of whom actually gathered monetary donations for the settlers and their stay—but a number of the former fell ill to malaria after inspecting and even clearing some of the land Chief Sam had purchased. The next year, however, Sam Chief's plan began to unravel with official restrictions and legal proceedings, debt incurred by the *Liberia*, and British authorities at Cape Coast Castle, who refused to provide Sam and his cohort with coal for the vessel. As a result of the cumulative effect of these barriers, the *Liberia* was abandoned and sold to the Universal Transportation Company, whose ship, the *Zealandia*, towed the *Liberia* from Cape Coast Castle to New York.[6] Amid a wave of discontent due to limited resources and a multitude of other issues mounted by opposition forces and after ten or more months on the Gold Coast, many of the emigrants, who were mainly prosperous male farmers and a few married couples, returned to the United States aboard the *Abosso*, while Sam became a cocoa buyer and abandoned the project on account of acute duress and the associated legal, political, and diplomatic costs. Chief Sam and his second wife, a diasporic African from North America, produced a child named Kwakye Sam—no doubt named after Chief Sam's father, Kwakye Sam, and in a manner wholly consistent with Akan naming patterns found in North America. Some diasporic Africans of Sam's expedition stayed and settled in Winneba, Accra, and Cape Coast and developed tobacco and rubber plantations, manufactured local gin (Gã: *akpeteshie*) and gunpowder, and developed engine-driven boats that were used along the coast.[7]

Many, however, were suspicious from the outset, and some, such as the British government and its Gold Coast colonial authorities, attempted to thwart Sam's efforts. In the United States, W.E.B. Du Bois warned readers of the *Crisis* about Sam and his "scheme" just as the local press on the Gold Coast did the same before its change of heart, a change occasioned by Sam's modified emigration plans to include sixty rather than five hundred would-be settlers after official British opposition, which forced Sam to do so once the British threatened to deny his vessel British registry.[8] In an unprecedented act, the British enacted an ordinance on the Gold Coast in order to "regulate those not born in any part of West Africa" and, in doing so, compelled "each Afro-American immigrant to deposit five pounds as a security bond."[9] Both the Gold Coast and the Sierra Leone press, including the nationalists who wrote for them, became fervent supporters of the "African movement" after Chief Sam modified his plans under British and Gold Coast colonial pressure. In spite of that pressure, Sam's African movement contributed to the development of pan-Africanism and nationalism in West Africa and the wider African world. It also anticipated Marcus Garvey's movement, though, as Sam and the movement's main intellectual proponent, Orishatuke Faduma, would admit, it was built upon the earlier efforts of Daniel Coker, Elijah Johnson, and Paul Cuffee (whose father was Akan and who advocated emigration and used his own money to repatriate thirty-eight African descendants to Sierra Leone in 1815), as well as nineteenth-century nationalists Edward Wilmot Blyden and Bishop Henry McNeil Turner.

Despite its apparent failures in the eyes of some, Chief Sam's movement and those that came both before and after it provide some very important insights. First, Chief Sam's efforts and those of his supporters and allies demonstrate the ways in which European or white sentiments and action functioned as a catalyst in the birth or reemergence of nationalist aspirations and strategies. Second, Sam's efforts provided a sense of the great measures that international and domestic European forces and their colonial agents took to proscribe African and diasporic African engagements and relations, especially those that threatened the former's capitalist hegemony and the global order of things. Such measures included the

British, North American, and Gold Coast campaigns and efforts by their ideological agents to discredit Sam's claim to land and chieftaincy, dissuade diasporic Africans from emigrating, compel Gold Coast shareholders in the *Liberia* to resign, and convince people that diasporic Africans would disrupt the so-called racial peace on the Gold Coast. Finally, African descendants in North America provided the most powerful lens through which to apprehend the deep, almost irreconcilable contradictions in a country governed by whites, who projected themselves as guardians of "civilization" and "freedom" though they engaged in and sanctioned racialized slavery and segregation, lynching, disenfranchisement, sharecropping or peonage, and an attendant psychological violence in print and visual media (e.g., caricatures, minstrels).

Faduma surmised that the African movement led by Chief Sam had precedent and that improvements in its administration—the establishment of provisions for the accommodation and welfare of the emigrants, thorough organization and periodic fiscal accounting of the Akim Trading Company—would have been the key to its success. Nonetheless, a decade after Sam's project, forty-nine-year-old Nana Amoah III of Cape Coast came to the United States to study the "progress of the Negro race" and "the centres of negro population," though, in actuality, he came as an entrepreneur seeking financial backing for cocoa shipping so as to enter the Gold Coast cocoa trade.[10] Nonetheless, he started with Harlem, one of the early bases of Chief Sam and his ideological successor, Marcus Garvey. After arriving in Virginia and then traveling on to New York on the *Aquitania*, Nana Amoah was scheduled to "visit Chicago, Philadelphia, and Baltimore [and other parts of the United States] to see what men of his race have accomplished...[and to help] bring about a closer understanding between the negroes of the two continents."[11] Nana Amoah was enstooled among a Fante community in 1914 (though the actual enstoolment occurred in 1919) and probably knew of Chief Sam and his African movement since Saltpond was within the Fante coastal territories and both men shared or at least supported pan-African ideals (Nana Amoah participated in the third and fourth Pan-African Congresses in 1923 and 1927).[12]

Nana Amoah and Chief Sam established or were part of a line of trader-nationalists who sought both economic support from diasporic Africans in North America and their technical assistance to combat the British commercial monopoly on the Gold Coast. They also hoped to bolster the status and institutions of the Gold Coast's "educated native elites." The *New York Times* noted, "the educated natives," of whom Nana Amoah was one, "dominate the thought and action of their people" although their numbers were small relative to the larger population, even in the urbanized areas.[13] At a lecture at the Episcopal City Mission Chapel of the Messiah in Harlem,

Nana Amoah was joined by "Prince Kojo Tovaluo-Houenou of Dahomey [Bénin]... and Dr. J. E. Kwegyir Aggrey" of Achimota College. That evening Nana Amoah not only urged his audience of African descendants to "cultivate racial pride... [as] African" but also referred to an 1897 treaty with the British that allowed for land to be held in trust for African descendants so that they could "claim land where their ancestors in Africa died intestate."[14] Whether such a treaty, in scribal or oral form, was actually made is unclear, though it would hold implications for those diasporic Africans who have returned to Ghana and engaged government and local officials about the very issue of land and the right to return to Ghana as one of several possible homelands.[15] Nonetheless, Nana Amoah's appeal to African descendants to contribute their technical knowledge and skill toward the "development" of the Gold Coast, as well as his and Chief Sam's suggestion of available lands and a homeland free from racism, was part and parcel of what Nana Amoah represented on the Gold Coast and of the meaning of his Westernized identity and commercial aspirations.

The identity of Nana Amoah is critical to our understanding of the purpose of his trips and the nature and intent of his orations to largely African-descended audiences while in New York. Nana Amoah, popularly known as Chief Amoah III but named Kwamina Faux Tandoh, became an entrepreneur in timber and import-export commerce after ending his medical studies in Britain around 1900, and it was he who "helped negotiate the concession that produced the Ashanti Goldfields Corporation."[16] The *New York Times* reported that Nana Amoah was a "member of the Church of England" and spoke English fluently, and Gold Coast authorities, who refused to fund his efforts, distrusted him as a "colonial" African. In the end, Nana Amoah was unable to secure the financing he needed and was deported to the Gold Coast after being found on the streets of New York by the police. He had collapsed from a brain disease in the winter of 1929, shortly before the breakdown of the European monetary system (Great Depression).[17] Nana Amoah, like Chief Sam, sought to break away from British commercial hegemony but failed largely because he appealed to the very entities that maintained foreign control and was part of the Gold Coast intelligentsia in the early twentieth century, who had been seduced by Westernization and Christianization. This intelligentsia had its roots in an insignificantly small, racially mixed community (called "creoles" by scholars, although the members of the intelligentsia did not apply this name to themselves) at Cape Coast since the seventeenth century. Westernization and Christianity allowed for a membership that saw itself as spreaders of Christianity and "civilizations" (see figures 7.1 and 7.2).[18] Many of its members were Wesleyan Methodists converts in the nineteenth century— a period when this community's impact increased—and their Cape Coast

Figure 7.1. Axim Wesleyan Methodist Church congregation, Gold Coast (Ghana), 3 August 1914. Copyright © The Trustees for Methodist Church Purposes. Reproduced by permission.

base was linked to other ports of Christian missions and the colonial authority of English-speaking whites in places such as Freetown (Sierra Leone), Monrovia (Liberia), and Lagos (Nigeria).

The likes of Chief Sam and Nana Amoah provide a significant backdrop for an Akan experience that is still unfolding, with more than ten thousand persons of Akan cultural origin in New York City and many diasporic Africans from North America and the Caribbean visiting, taking up residence, and forming relationships with the Akan homeland through New York airports and seaports. The Akan diaspora in the history of New York has been considerable as a metaphor for an unfinished process of earlier sovereignty seekers (e.g., the 1712 revolt and the alleged 1741 plot), political organization, intra-African (descended) community formation in Manhattan and Brooklyn, and ritual and culture in these processes. Their experiences form a part of and enriches the composite African diasporic narrative and provides a window into how they lived their lives in New York. The Akan experience also reveals how the broader yet similar processes of Westernization, Christianization, and elitist formation among segments of both African and African-descended communities of West Africa and North America, respectively, were unfolding during the nineteenth and early

Figure 7.2. Group portrait of "church girls" holding white dolls in Kumase, Gold Coast (Ghana), ca. 1910. Copyright © The Trustees for Methodist Church Purposes. Reproduced by permission.

twentieth centuries. From the mid- to the late-nineteenth century, even the most "creolized" and Western-educated in the Gold Coast colony displayed cultural ambiguity toward Akan culture in their quest to be buffers between the "native" and the colonial orders—antecedents of mid-twentieth-century political struggles between chiefs and educated elites. Consequently, these Gold Coast "buffers" turned to local institutions and became "traditional" officeholders since the colonial government incorporated traditional leaders as part of their policy of indirect rule. Thus, in their quest for partnership with British colonial authority and institutions, these elites sought the traditional in order to position themselves in the colonial regime as buffers. Toward that end, some even manipulated succession principles to be enstooled or did so through their *asafo* (paramilitary organization whose membership is based on a patrilineal principle) since these traditional offices provided status and financial rewards in the colonial order.[19]

That quest for partnership created factionalism among the elites and within their communities. As a patriarchal nuclear family began establishing itself (at the expense of existing kinship networks) since the nineteenth century, two divergent visions began emerging on the Gold Coast and among African-descended peoples in North America. Throughout the eighteenth and nineteenth centuries, Akan communities on the Gold Coast and African-descended ones in North America were largely non-Christian. In both cases, nineteenth-century converts split along "class" lines, and urbanized elites developed a Christian distaste for but an ambivalence toward indigenous African spirituality and cultural institutions, though this attitude was confined largely to Akan and non-Akan peoples on the coast, who were more exposed to European or white authority, values, and institutions. On the North American side of the equation, Michael Gomez argues that the foregoing process was evident by the first quarter of the nineteenth century, when "black elites" sought "admission into the club" (i.e., equal rights and full acceptance by whites), and while the majority of the African-based community saw racism and its insidiousness as deeply rooted in their fight for human and civil rights, the elites viewed slavery and discrimination as obstacles that prevented "their" progress and not necessarily collective advancement.[20] The parallels for both groups bridged by the Atlantic Ocean but bounded by shared concerns of a cultural and spiritual nature were more than striking at the turn of the twentieth century.

NANA DINIZULU AND THE REEMERGENCE OF AKAN SPIRITUAL PRAXIS

At the dawn of the twentieth century, close to 90 percent of African-descended peoples lived in the American South; however, a large migratory wave between 1910 and 1940 and again from 1940 to 1970 accounted for more than half of that once 90 percent residing in the northeastern region of North America and in major cities such as New York. Though next to nothing has been written about Nana Dinizulu's life as Gus Edwards, we can imagine, with some certainty, that he and perhaps his parents were a part of the first migratory wave to New York since he established an organization called the *Ghanas* in 1947, when he was seventeen. The Ghanas conducted classes in African singing, dancing, history, and culture and became the vehicle through which his Dinizulu African Dancers, Drummers, and Singers were established in 1947. These developments, however amazing for a seventeen-year-old, were consistent with Dinizulu's own account and the scant literature. Nana Dinizulu, in *The Akan Priests in America*, wrote, "I have been worshipping the Gods and Ancestors of Africa since the early forty's [1940s]. I became the first Akan priest and chief in America to worship the Gods and Ancestors of the Akan people of Ghana."[21] The claim of being the "first Akan priest" in North America may be reasonable in a certain context, but it is largely an inflated one, for Akan spiritualists were undoubtedly transported to the Americas since at least the seventeenth century, and even Dinizulu himself wrote, "Many great priests and noblemen were forced to come here [North America] during slavery."[22] Nonetheless, the constant contact and interaction with anyone from African heads of states to those in the cultural-artistic world afforded Dinizulu (through his dance troupe) ample opportunity to study and continue to propagate the cultures and dance traditions of Africa, particularly, though not exclusively, West Africa.

Nana Dinizulu became a part of Damballa Hwedo, the first recorded "religious" institution based upon Akan, Yorùbá-Fon, and Haitian (Vodun) traditions in North America and, in doing so, also became associated with Oseijeman Adefunmi, who is largely responsible for reestablishing the Yorùbá spiritual tradition in North America (see figure 7.3).[23] Upon Adefunmi's return from his initiation into the "priesthood" of Ôbàtálá in the Matanzas region of Cuba in 1959, he founded the Order of Damballa Hwedo with a Haitian associate in 1960 and then the Shango and Yorùbá temples. The Order of Damballa Hwedo was established in Harlem—where Dinizulu's wife, Alice Brown (Afua Owusua Dinizulu), settled at the age of ten and later met her husband—during the historical confluence of the civil rights and black power era. The Order of Damballa Hwedo, however, disintegrated in a few years, and when Oseijeman Adefunmi left New York to establish Oyotunji village (based on the Òrìsà-Vodun spiritual practices) in Beaufort County, South Carolina, Nana Dinizulu began forging the groundwork for the reestablishment of Akan spiritual practice through the Bosum Dzemawodzi organization based in Queens (Long Island City), New York.[24]

On Bosum Dzemawodzi (*dzemawodzi* is the Gã-Adangme synonym for the Akan *ɔbosom*), Nana Kwabena Brown recalls the following:

> Interesting enough, at that time there were not any Akan deities, at the time that I arrive[d], but there were gods [*abosom*]. There was a [Gã] priest... Almost 90 percent of the gods that were there were Yorùbá gods (Shango, Yemanya, etc.). The introduction of the Ghanaian gods was mostly Gã. It wasn't until Nana Yao Opare made his trip in 1969 (which probably was his second trip) that he met Nana Oparebea, and when he came back [to the United States] in late '69, that's when the Akan gods came... I think it was January 1970 Nana Oparebea [made] her first trip, and that was the full, full introduction of the Akan gods. Prior to that... most of the services of Bosum Dzemawodzi were Yorùbá (Shango, Ogun, Yemanja, etc.). That's because he had a very strong orientation with Baba Oseijeman [Adefunmi], chief of the Yorùbá culture for African Americans.[25]

By the 1960s, Nana Dinizulu had traveled to Ghana on several occasions. In 1965 a local official of the Ghanaian capital of Accra introduced Nana

Figure 7.3. Oba Ofuntola Oseijeman Adelabu Adefunmi at Oyotunji village, South Carolina, August 1979. Oseijeman, which is an Akan name (i.e., Osegyeman, Osei saves his people or nation), had as much to do with the reestablishment of Yorùbá spiritual practice in North America—though by way of Cuba and particularly among diasporic Africans—as did Nana Dinizulu for the Akan side of that equation. Author's collection.

Dinizulu to Nana Akua Oparebea, ɔkɔmfoɔhemaa (head female ɔkɔmfoɔ) of the Akonnedi Abena shrine in Larteh-Kubease, in the eastern region of Ghana. Larteh is approximately thirty-five miles north of Accra, on the Akwapem Ridge. Through consultations at the Akonnedi shrine, it was revealed that Nana Dinizulu was an ancestor of Nana Oparebea's family who had come to reunite the descendants of enslaved Africans with their people and culture in Ghana and elsewhere. Nana Dinizulu later wrote, "She [Nana Akua Oparebea] and I trace our ancestry to Nana Atwidan and Op[anin] Kwame Mensah of Nsaba, who are descendants from the Agona clan in [the] Ashanti [region of central Ghana]."[26] With regard to ancestry, Nana Dinizulu also wrote, "The Akans and Ga were brought to the new world and were first settled in such places as South Carolina, Georgia, etc., and in Jamaica and other British-owned West Indian islands."[27] As a child born in Georgia and to parents of African descent, he certainly had no reservations about the revelation of the Akonnedi consultation or his claim not only to Akan ancestry but also to the prerogatives of that claim.

Nana Dinizulu was given the titles ɔmanhene (male leader of the nation) and ɔkɔmfoɔhene (head male ɔkɔmfoɔ) of the Akan, that is, diasporic Africans who joined the "Akan movement" rather than persons of Akan cultural origin who migrated to North America with or without an association with that movement or adherence to Akan spirituality as practiced in the homeland. He was initiated into specific dimensions of Akan culture and traditions, and upon his return to North America brought the shrines or *abosom* known as Asuo Gyebi, Esi Ketewa, and Adade Kofi. One source indicates that "In the late 1960s Nana Yao [Dinizulu] founded the Bosum Dzemawodzi as a religious institution in America. He established the first temple in New York City [in 1967]. He established the first temple for traditional worship in Washington [D.C.] in 1971."[28] Nana Oparebea first traveled to North America in 1971 to help Nana Dinizulu with labors associated with the shrines and the training of the *akɔmfoɔ* (sg. *ɔkɔmfoɔ*, indigenous spiritualist) in New York. On later visits, Nana Oparebea established centers for the practice of Akan spirituality in New York, Philadelphia, the District of Columbia, California, and Toronto. Nana Oparebea was well known for having cured persons who suffered from spiritual complications, mental disorders, barrenness, impotence, epilepsy, stomach troubles, *abayi* (so-called witchcraft), pregnancy problems, and difficulties during childbirth. In 1962 the Ghana Psychic and Traditional Healing Association was established through the efforts of both Nana Oparebea, who was unanimously elected its first president, and Ghana's first prime minister and president, Kwame Nkrumah. It so happened that a high-ranking academician suffered from strange headaches but remained uncured even after both local and foreign biomedical treatments. He then came to the Akonnedi shrine through a friend's recommendation, and Nana Oparebea diagnosed and cured his disease. Thereafter, the academician initiated research into herbal medicine, and with the support of Kwame Nkrumah, who also consulted Nana Oparebea, the Ghana Psychic and Traditional Healing Association received full recognition from Nkrumah's government.[29]

Nana Akua Oparebea was the ɔkɔmfoɔhemmaa for Nana Asuo Gyebi in Larteh-Kubease and the primary ɔkɔmfoɔ for Akonnedi Abena, who was the principal ɔbosom of Larteh in particular and one of the best-known in Ghana. Akonnedi Abena, as the name suggests, was a feminine expression of divine origination "born" on a Tuesday, and Akonnedi trained only women to assume the role of akɔmfoɔ; however, this policy was modified to allow diasporic African men to undergo training as well.[30] Nana Oparebea was the primary spiritualist for and custodian of the shrine rather than its owner since Akonnedi belonged to the Asona abusua (clan, family) of Larteh.[31] As principal spiritualist, the power and prestige of Akonnedi rested squarely on Nana Oparebea, who inherited the position of custodian from Adwoa Ɔkɔmfoɔ and ɔkɔmfoɔ Amma Ansa. Nana Oparebea was born in 1900 as Akua Opare during the famous Yaa Asantewaa war against British incursion and reared at Anhuntem, in the vicinity of Ankwansu, near Adawso. Her father, Kwame Akuffo Mensa, was a prosperous farmer and abusuapanin (family/clan head) of Aboanum, Atweasin, in Aburi.[32] Nana Oparebea's mother, Aba Oyedi, was of the "royal" families of Amansore and Akantsane. Nana Oparebea followed in the footsteps of ɔkɔmfoɔ Ejo (first "priest" of Akonnedi, who died in 1800), ɔkɔmfoɔ Animah (Oparebea's grandmother), and ɔkɔmfoɔ Amma Ansa; she established her practice in her father's village of Nkumkrom (on the Aburi-Nsawam road) once she had graduated as an ɔkɔmfoɔ.

In Nkumkrom, Nana Oparebea rose to fame, and people from near and far came for consultations and healing. As principal medium for Akonnedi Abena, Nana Oparebea also "possessed" Nana Asuo Gyebi, the ɔbrafoɔ (shrine assistant) for Akonnedi; Nana Esi Ketewa, the ɔkyeame (speech intermediary) for Akonnedi; in addition, to that court structure of Akonnedi, she added Tigare and Adade Kofi, whom some regard as an offspring of Akonnedi. Her sacred stream remained the river Nsakye. This set of abosom reveals much about the composite strands that informed Akan spiritual practice in twentieth-century Larteh: Asuo Gyebi and Adade Kofi originated in the forested Asante region, Esi Ketewa was from the coastal Fante area, and Tigare emerged in northern Ghana. Originally of non-Akan import, Tigare went through a process of Akanization from a suman (talisman) to an ɔbosom in the Takyiman area of central Ghana. Furthermore, Larteh was also a Guan (non-Akan linguistic and cultural group) inhabited area, and when one combines this setting and the set of abosom that Nana Oparebea held and transmitted to North America, many who practice Akan spirituality on either side of the Atlantic Ocean may in fact adhere to a pan-Ghanaian or pan-African construct rather than one that is wholly Akan in constitution. As such, and granted the veneration of Akan *abosom* and Yorùbá òrìsà (e.g., Shango, Ogun) at Bosum Dzemawodzi, the claims that centered on an engagement in Akan spirituality and culture by diasporic Africans, especially those associated with Larteh via Nana Oparebea and Nana Dinizulu, are indeed questionable.

NANA KWABENA BROWN AND THE CLAIMS TO AN AKAN SPIRITUAL PRAXIS

William Brown is known to most in the District of Columbia and elsewhere as Nana Kwabena Brown. Born in New York City in 1944, Brown's grandparents, except for one, were all from the Caribbean. His maternal grandparents were from Antigua, and his paternal grandmother was from Barbados, while his paternal grandfather was born in Virginia. Antigua, Barbados, and Virginia all had significant numbers of Akan persons, a number of whom were spiritualists and leaders of key revolts. Nana Kwabena Brown was raised in New York City and in Westchester County but moved to the District of Columbia in 1961. He became a married man at the age of twenty-one in 1965. Nana Kwabena Brown remembered the following:

> [The period 19]65 to [19]70 was the height of the African cultural revolution, and it was during that period of time that I became immersed, which led to the study of my culture and my religion. I have had the pleasure of hearing Dr. King speak personally. I have had the pleasure of hearing Minister Malcolm speak personally. I have had the pleasure of hearing most of the luminaries speak personally (in their presence). And during that very, very intense time, it took us into a deep conversion, [an] emergent experience of Africanness.[33]

With the presence of Garveyites on his mother's side of the family, it is not surprising to find that Nana Kwabena Brown's mother was a family leader on account of her childhood environment with her father, which facilitated the connections her children made with their African cultural heritage. From an early age, Nana Kwabena Brown seems to have always been interested in spirituality. As a result of the cultural awakening of the 1960s, specifically, the cultural awareness in black pride, power, and self-awareness, he "began to seriously look for what God had created for the black man, in terms of spirituality."[34] According to Nana Kwabena Brown, this inquiry led to his investigation into and self-discovery through African cultural and spiritual practices. His cultural awareness was augmented by an equally strong desire to be "black, African, [and] independent," which led to the establishment of one of the District of Columbia's first African-oriented stores, called Zaro's House of Africa, which he, his mother, and his wife operated.[35] This level of independent economic and cultural activity became a vehicle for exposing many in the District of Columbia to African culture and art. Indeed, it was Nana Kwabena Brown's study of African art, the source of his livelihood between 1967 and 1968, which led him to uncover a profound spirituality that rested below the expressive surface of African cultures. Meanwhile, his mother, Iyalode Ida Austin, moved back and forth between New York City and the District of Columbia and did not settled in the latter until 1970 or 1971. Iyalode Austin was the driving force, as well as the one positioned at the forefront of her family's movement toward what Nana Kwabena Brown described as "the black cultural thing." Being a woman of some reputation in Harlem, Iyalode Austin came into contact with Nana Yao Opare Dinizulu and his Bosum Dzemawodzi through Ajaibo Waldron.

In 1969 Nana Dinizulu wrote, "Okomfo Ajaibo (Nkobeahene) began his training as a priest and graduated as my second Akan priest in America." Ajaibo's identity as "Nkobeahene" (Ankobeahene), which is confirmed by Brown's recollection that ɔkɔmfoɔ Ajaibo was a "big official" within Bosum Dzemawodzi, establishes this key encounter between Ajaibo and Iyalode Austin.[36] Not long after this encounter, Iyalode Austin recommended her son, Kwabena Brown, meet Nana Yao Opare Dinizulu in New York because of her own and her son's cultural activism and interest in African spirituality. Nana Kwabena would make subsequent visits to New York at least once a month. During the course of these trips to New York, he decided to develop a study group in the District of Columbia for those who were interested in the study and practice of African spirituality. The development of the study group was facilitated by monthly bus trips to New York, which strengthened the relationship between the two cities. Soon the study group invited Nana Yao Opare Dinizulu to the District of Columbia, and there he would reside and hold meetings at Nana Kwabena Brown's house. According to Nana Kwabena Brown, "essentially, that was the beginning of the Akan religious movement here in Washington, D.C. All the senior priests of the Akan religion here in Washington, D.C., by that I mean all those who have established a [shrine] house with which other priests trained and became priests, those senior priests all got their introduction to Akan religion here at this house."[37]

Some of those senior akɔmfoɔ include Nana Aba Nsia Opare, Nana Yao Odum Opare, and Nana Kofi Asinor Boakye. Nana Kwabena Brown asserts that "everybody else who is Akan came through them or came through somebody who came through them. That would be most of the priests here in [the District of Columbia]."³⁸ In 1971 two hundred and sixty individual persons went to Ghana to immerse themselves in Akan culture and its spiritual practice. To Nana Kwabena Brown, this trip "cemented the laying of the foundation for Akan religion here in Washington, D.C.," and, at this time, he was the official ɔkyeame for Bosum Dzemawodzi in the District of Columbia. Nana Aba Nsia Opare and Nana Yao Odum Opare became the first and second akɔmfoɔ of African diasporic birth, respectively, in the District of Columbia, and Nana Kofi Asinor Boakye was assigned the position of ɔbrafoɔ, or shrine assistant, to these akɔmfoɔ. Nana Kwabena Brown, however, had no real interest in becoming an ɔkɔmfoɔ; his energies remained in organizing study around the subjects of African art, culture, and spirituality. However, the trip to Ghana in 1971 had an unforeseen, life-changing effect. While in Ghana for six weeks, Nana Kwabena Brown witnessed probably thirty or more persons training at the Akonnedi shrine. To his amazement, there were akɔmfoɔ who were almost a hundred years old, and Nana Oparebea herself was in her sixties. For Nana Kwabena Brown, this experience in Ghana provided an "authentic view of what African religion meant, what God meant, what possession meant, etc.... [It] was really a lot for the nervous system."³⁹

While in Larteh-Kubease, Nana Oparebea and Akonnedi Abena began to take an interest in Nana Kwabena Brown. In fact, he tried to hide from Akonnedi. This turn of events caused problems. Nana Yao Opare Dinizulu had established his order in the District of Columbia, and in that order he had selected his akɔmfoɔ and given Nana Kwabena the position of ɔkyeame. Akonnedi, Nana Oparebea, and her ɔkyeame would have it otherwise and began to engage Nana Kwabena Brown in conversation. The result of these events was a split between Nana Kwabena Brown and Nana Yao Opare Dinizulu, whom Nana Kwabena Brown loved and considered a father. Nana Kwabena Brown revealed that "People whom I had brought into the culture went with the dad [Nana Yao Opare Dinizulu]... People [(referring to Nana Dinizulu) were] very unhappy with their plan not being the plan that was working, and [I found] myself being kicked out of the very group which I personally organized and developed."⁴⁰ In essence, Nana Kwabena Brown was effectively told that he was no longer a member of Bosum Dzemawodzi. Nana Kwabena Brown found himself isolated. It would take twenty or so years for the rupture between Nana Kwabena Brown and those persons who were once his close friends and associates to begin to heal. During the interim, however, everyone who came into the Akan spiritual tradition through Nana Kwabena Brown was separated from him, and though some rifts have healed, conflict still abounds between the various shrine houses on issues related to ideology, legitimacy, and sectarianism. In Larteh, attendant issues abound around the training of non-African-descended persons, demands for U.S. currency almost exclusively for spiritual and medicinal services, and North American–based trainees or affiliates offering shrine services via the Internet with online payment options.

Nana Kwabena Brown continued the study group and began having meetings wherein he taught the little he had learned while in Ghana. Nana Kwabena Brown also began to correspond with Nana Oparebea after a spiritually motivated experience at his home. In Nana Oparebea's correspondences with Nana Kwabena Brown, she noted that Akonnedi had followed him back to the District of Columbia so that he would be reminded that everything he experienced in Ghana was instructive. She also asked whether he would bring her to the District of Columbia for a second visit to the United States. The new study group was able to raise enough money to purchase four airline tickets. During Nana Oparebea's forty-five day visit, she began the training of both Nana Kwabena Brown and his wife (at the time) as *akɔmfoɔ* and four others within the District of Columbia. The African Cultural and Religious Society (ACRS), which evolved from Nana Kwabena Brown's study group and developed into his Temple of Nyame in 1978, was the organization that sponsored the second official visit of Nana Oparebea in 1973.[41] The ACRS, founded and registered in the District of Columbia in 1973, was one of the pioneer organizations in the promotion and practice of African spiritualities and culture in the area. When Nana Oparebea came to the District of Columbia in the 1970s, she established the second Asuo Gyebi shrine, along with Tigare, Esi Ketewa, and Adade Kofi, in the United States. On her 1973 trip to North America, Nana Oparebea posted one of her Lartehtrained *ɔkɔmfoɔ*, Akua Kyerewaa, at Bosum Dzemawodzi in New York and later the Ghanaian-born Nana Akosua Nsia Oparebea in the late 1970s.[42]

Nana Kwabena Brown was initiated into Akan spiritual practice as an *ɔkɔmfoɔ* and *ɔkɔmfoɔhene* (head *ɔkɔmfoɔ*) and, thus, the *ɔkɔmfohene* of the Asuo Gyebi and Tigare shrines of the District of Columbia and the representative of the Akonnedi shrine in that locality. Between 1973 and 1976 Nana Oparebea made several trips to the District of Columbia in order to continue the training of her *akɔmfoɔ*.[43] In 1976 Nana Kwabena Brown and his wife traveled to Ghana to complete their "priesthood" training and graduate. Upon their return, they continued teaching the spiritual practices and rituals they had learned and attempted to expose African-descended people to Akan culture in and around the District of Columbia. Over the years, Nana Kwabena Brown and members of the Temple of Nyame have continued Akan spiritual practices, exposing others to Akan culture, and have maintained a very high standard of (what they have come to know as) the culture and its traditions. In 1975 ACRS was incorporated as a 501(c)(3) not-for-profit religious organization, and Nana Kwabena Brown sought and obtained recognition as an official African clergyman. As the result of conducting research and discussions on the concept of "God" in Africa, Nana Kwabena Brown realized that *akɔm*—a multilayered concept and phenomenon of spiritual value but one that many in North America and Ghana have reduced to ceremonial dance and "possession"—was only a part of Akan spirituality but not its totality.[44] Many in Akan shrine communities in North America avoid the kind of scholarship Nana Kwabena advocates and thus continue to dogmatically view *akɔm* as a "possessional" ceremony around which their identity and "religious" life revolves.

After more than three decades, Nana Kwabena Brown and others associated with him realized that *akɔm* itself did not appear to be a stable enough basis on which to organize large groups of people. They expanded their umbrella organization, and Nana Kwabena Brown and members soon began calling themselves the Temple of Nyame Asuo Gyebi and Tigare shrines. In 1993 the Temple of Nyame, as a part of that expansion process, became affiliated with the Asuobɔnten, Bookyerewa, and Tigare shrines of Takyiman and Aboabo in the Brong Ahafo region of central Ghana. Nana Kwabena Brown's affiliation with Takyiman via the well-known Nana Kofi Donkor came, ironically, after Nana Kwaku Sakyi, a dear friend and colleague to whom Nana Kwabena first talked about Takyiman, traveled to Ghana and became an *ɔkɔmfoɔ* of an Tanɔ *ɔbosom*. Nana Sakyi became an *ɔkɔmfoɔ* during the late 1980s and early 1990s under the guidance of the late Nana Kofi Donkor, Nana Adwoa Akumsa, and Nana Kofi Effah. Nana Sakyi was born in Port of Spain (Trinidad) the year Ghana received its political independence from British colonial rule. He was introduced to Akan spirituality through Nana Kwabena Brown at the Temple of Nyame sixteen years after settling in the District of Columbia. After being adopted by Nana Donkor (in which he received the family name, Sakyi), Nana Sakyi became the first diasporic African to be initiated into and to graduate from the institution as an *ɔkɔmfoɔ* in Takyiman, the home of the sacred Tanɔ River and the ancient Tanɔ-derived *abosom* among the Akan. Presently, Nana Kwabena Brown promotes and presents "a system beliefs and practices which present God, the ancestors, and the deities as one holistic and interrelated system."[45] This perspective may explain why he continues to describe the "Akan system [as] very unique inasmuch as you can align it with every other non-African religious system in...[that] you have a Creator, the ancestors and the deities."[46] For Nana Kwabena Brown, Akan spiritual practice remains "a very wonderful [phenomenon]. The religion is one that is created by God and not by human beings, and so it is the most natural religion of mankind."[47]

In sum, Nana Kwabena Brown became involved with Akan spirituality "because [he] knew that God had something for the African," and he became a teacher of it "because it is very important for our completeness as a people that we are able to approach God in an African way."[48] Yet, for Nana Kwabena Brown, "[w]hether it's Akan or Yorùbá, it doesn't make any difference at all. The thing is where the people can connect to the spiritual world in a way that God created for us which feels natural and which makes us healthy and which we can use in very practical ways."[49] His claim to an Akan spiritual praxis embraces other such African-based spiritual traditions and also non-African belief systems that offer pragmatic approaches to life and living. Accordingly, Nana Kwabena Brown emphasizes that "religion and the [abosom] and the [other] spirits have got to assist you with your personal life, your family life, and with any kind of threat or just harmony within or around the side of you. And because of that I personally take a very proactive stance with the [Akan] religion in this country."[50]

In historical perspective, Nana Kwabena Brown's practice of Akan spirituality has become a "very liberating thing and not at all original because those of our people [who] remained free in the new world vis-à-vis in the mountains of Jamaica, vis-à-vis upriver in Suriname, vis-à-vis up in the mountains of Brazil, Ecuador, Columbia [have] been [able to do so]... because of their connection with their African religion."[51] Indeed, in the words of Nana Kwabena Brown, "The primary aim of [the] priesthood is to utilize the power of religion to help others to increase and improve the quality of their lives: physically, mentally, religiously, and socially. The aim is to provide a means for others to become more complete and whole individually and collectively."[52] The year of the Nana Kwabena Brown interview not only marked the 2001 visit of Asantehene Osei Tutu II, leader of the Asante people of Ghana, to the District of Columbia, where diasporic Africans held a reception and performance in his honor at Howard University, but also a past decade punctuated by two significant yet unconnected transitions unfolding among diasporic Africans and those from Ghana who had taken up residence in Harlem—a historic place of meeting in an unfolding African diaspora.

DIASPORA AND INTERNAL DIALOGUE

At a high school in Camden, New Jersey, Nana Dinizulu collapsed from a heart attack before a concert and made his transition to *asamando* (place where the ancestors dwell) in 1991. That same year, Otelia Oteng participated in her *bragoro* rite in Harlem, and this Akan ritual and ceremonial puberty rite signaled the transition from childhood to female adulthood. Although born in North America to parents from Ghana, Otelia tells those who inquire of her nationality, "I'm Ghanaian. That's my nationality."[53] Otelia's claim to an identity that is "Ghanaian" appears at odds with her American citizenship (which she did not claim here), but its roots are both cultural (via her rites) and political since Ghana grants dual citizenship to those born of Ghanaian parentage abroad. Among the approximately 10,000 Akan from Ghana in New York City, "the coming-of-age ceremony is rarely performed here [or in Ghana]." One participant, a doctor at Columbia Presbyterian Medical Center, commented, "This is not a pagan practice...This is a folk practice incorporating much common-sense wisdom."[54] Otelia and her family, including those in attendance at her *bragorɔ* rite, constitute a fraction of the 20,000 Asante people in North America and the 10,000 or more in the New York metropolitan area, all of whose concerns had to be attended to by Nana Opoku Asamoah, *Asantefoɔhene* (surrogate leader of Asante people in the United States) from 1989 to 1992.[55] The first *Asantefoɔhene* was enstooled in 1982, and in that line of leadership, the forty-one-year old Asamoah, who hails from a cocoa-farming family in Ghana, provides leadership to the Asanteman Association, which helps new Akan immigrants settle marital and legal challenges, those without kin create a sense of belonging, and Asante youth develop a full appreciation of their culture so as not to lose "sight of their culture in the melting pot of New York."

Unlike in Ghana, Nana Asamoah was chosen by way of an election in the association and ceremonially enstooled in May of 1989, with Ghanaians of distinct cultural groupings coming from Chicago, the District of Columbia, Los Angeles, and Canada to partake in the ceremony. Culture remained one of Nana Asamoah's top priorities, and, to that effect, the association under his leadership envisioned the establishment of a school so that the children would learn to "dress properly" and "master the Ashanti language, our dances and drumming." Interestingly, that apparent attention to indigenous Akan culture and Otelia's rare *bragorɔ* rite did not involve or consider involving those diasporic Africans who engaged in Akan culture and its attendant spirituality. In the places where the Asanteman Association has branches one finds a number of Akan shrine houses or organizations that base their existence on the practice of "Akan religion" and culture, and these organizations are located largely on the East Coast from Florida to New York, as well as in California and Canada. But there was no dialogue between two groups of people who claimed to engage in relatively the same cultural praxis. In fact, Onipa Abusia, "an Akan religious organization" based upon the founding philosophy of Nana Dinizulu and now led by two women founders of Bosum Dzemawodzi, were not a part of ceremonies like Otelia's, and it is highly unlikely they would have been invited as guests. However, during Nana Dinizulu's leadership of Bosum Dzemawodzi, quite a number of people from Jamaica, Puerto Rico, Haiti, Cuba, Nigeria, Ghana, and Sierra Leone came to and participated in Bosum Dzemawodzi activities and healing services, and some became official members, while others of Akan cultural origin were active in *akɔm* and other spiritual ceremonies in the 1970s and 1980s.[56] Most of these (diasporic)

Africans felt their participation in those activities and in the organization helped in the transition from their homelands to North America and fostered a substantive sense of family and community.

In South Florida, each of two Jamaican-born women became, according to one report, "a graduate Okomfo (priest) in the African religion of Akom" in 2007.[57] The two women, Akua Bakofoa (Nyoka Samuels) and Afua Fofie (Carol L. Miller), went through "three years of intense study and sacrifice" and were trained by Nana Mena Yaa, "chief priest for the Nana Adade Shrine in South Florida." One attendee at the women's graduation ceremony was Abenaa Mensah, who commented that her family was "very religious" and that her "grandfather was an Okomfo in Jamaica." In lieu of reports that say otherwise, we are left to conclude that Akan persons who recently settled in Florida and are perhaps one or two generations removed from Ghana did not participate in the *akɔmfoɔ* graduation ceremony. Particularly when we consider that the vocation of Akan spiritualists is premised upon service to one's community, the question is, whose community will be served? The opportunity for dialogue was left to osmosis rather than seized by both diasporic Africans and Akan migrants, who are now becoming part of an extending and unfolding diaspora beyond the confines of Ghana. Unfortunately, even scholars who are examining the "new African diaspora" in North America fail to grasp the significance of the parallel practice of indigenous Akan culture and spirituality by relatively few Akan from Ghana and a growing number of diasporic Africans. For example, in a recent edited collection titled *The New African Diaspora in North America*, one contributor who focused his discussion on the import of Asante chieftaincy in North America devoted less than a page to the singular phenomenon of diasporic African enstoolment in Asante communities in Ghana as "development chiefs and queen-mothers" with no attendant discussion of the latter's engagement with Akan spiritual practices or its larger cultural orbit.[58] These missed opportunities at the personal, organizational, or academic level, however, are not simply a North American failing. Those who live as and study the Akan in Canada suffer from a similar shortsightedness in social climates where both diasporic Africans and Akan immigrant communities shared experiences of institutionalized racism and occupy seemingly inflexible underclass positions.

Ghanaians, of which many were culturally Akan, came primarily to Toronto, Canada, in the 1960s, and although scholars who write of the "new African diaspora" claim the 1960s as an era of entry, those of that era were not the first Akan peoples to settle in Canada. After the British loyalists lost their cessionary conflict with the North American colonists in the late 1770s, thousands of African and African-descended peoples who fought alongside the former were evacuated to Nova Scotia (on Canada's southeastern coast) and the Bahamas. The "Book of Negroes" was created (in a North American and a British version) during the process of registering and evacuating those Africans largely through the ports of New York and St. Augustine in 1783—the year the British exchanged eastern Florida for the Bahamas with Spain.[59] Many Africans and African descendants rejected the climate and the unfulfilled promise of land, tools, and provisions in Nova Scotia and opted instead for Sierra Leone and the Bahamas. The Book of Negroes lists fifty-year-old Cuffie (Kofi) Bush of Connecticut, who boarded the *William and Mary* bound for Annapolis Royal (former capital of Nova Scotia) from New York in 1783.[60] Traveling to Annapolis Royal on the *Hope*, 22-year-old Quaco (Kwaku) was described as a "stout fellow," whereas 40-year-old Cudjoe (Kwadwo) Thomas (both of South Carolina) was deemed simply an "ordinary fellow."[61] Those bound for the Bahama Islands included 38-year-old Cuffy (Kofi) Lucas of Virginia, who boarded the *Nautilus* for Abaco, and 30-year-old Peter Quamina (Kwamena) of North Carolina, who left for Cat Island on the *Elizabeth*. Both Cuffy and Peter were described as "stout fellow[s]," unlike Quash (Kwasi), also a former resident of North Carolina but destined for Annapolis Royal in Nova Scotia, who was regarded as an "ordinary rascal."[62] Twenty-four-year-old Cuff Cummins (or Kofi Cummings) of Philadelphia traveled on the *Kingston*, bound for Port Roseway (renamed Shelburne), and, in the county of Shelburne, Cuffy Cumming was one of the heads of family at the Birchtown settlement—one of the largest "free" African-descended settlements in North America. Cuffy Cumming and others such as Cudjo François, Cuffy Miles, Cuffy Warwick and his wife, Lydia Warwick, and Cudjo Wilkinson came largely from places in the United States with a historical Akan presence, one related to the early Akan communities in late eighteenth-century Canada.[63]

The twentieth century witnessed a distinct wave of Akan persons in that they came not from North America but directly from what became the republic of Ghana. About 100 Ghanaians arrived in 1967. By 1991 that number had multiplied exponentially to 11,070, with more than 80 percent arriving between 1981 and 1991; most came to the Toronto metropolitan area. These numbers were the result of changes in Canadian immigration policies in the 1980s and of political and economy instability in Ghana; during this period approximately 69 percent of Ghanaian immigrants were admitted as "political refugees."[64] In the 1980s these broader Ghanaian and specific Akan persons began forming associations that were similar to other forms of (mutual-aid) associations among Africans in the Americas during past centuries, and in the tradition of rural-urban migrants in Ghana who formed associations, they thereby created "diasporas" in towns and urban centers. As was the case for Nana Opoku Asamoah of the Asanteman Association in North America, cultural concerns have been central to the existence of these Canadian-based associations. Those concerns include issues of socialization in a foreign land, language acquisition and maintenance, and the transmission of culture, traditions, and histories. Yet, it appears that "ethnic associations," which address those cultural concerns, wane as members become more economically mobile and seek partnership with the established order and its views and values. As a result, new immigrants and low-income persons who are more restricted find greater utility in ethnic associations and their networks, though that utility is seen largely as a means to becoming established and economically mobile.

In 1990 the National Congress of Ghanaian Canadians was formed as an umbrella organization for all "ethnic" backgrounds. It supported the idea of dual citizenship in 1993—the bill was ratified in 1997—and a change in the Ghanaian constitution on account of the strong family ties and fiscal contribution members made to the Ghanaian economy via remittances (official and nonofficial transfers of funds that represent close to 20 percent of Ghana's foreign exchange receipts).[65] In the early twenty-first century, more than three million Ghanaians were living abroad (*akwanufoɔ*, travelers, expatriates), and Ghana's brain drain of professionals trained in Ghana contributed to Ghanaian society and economy through remittances to families and governmental taxes on those remittances.[66] In this context, as Hein de Haas accurately concludes, "both European and African states have *little genuine interest* in stopping migration, because their economies have become dependent on migrant labour and remittances, respectively."[67] Most from Ghana emigrate on their own volition and remain within West Africa, and only 14 and 10 percent, respectively, make North America and Europe their destination—in Europe, many were registered as immigrants (in order of the highest populations) in Britain, Italy, the Netherlands, and Spain. As of 2006, approximately 56,112 Ghanaian immigrants resided in Britain, and 84,274 were living in North America, and these numbers formed the highest estimates of the Ghanaian-born population in non-African countries. In the places where Ghanaian immigrant communities, particularly those of Akan cultural origin, are located in North America and Britain one also finds recent and longstanding diasporic African communities—some the descendants of the Akan ancestors. It is not surprising that both types of community continue to encounter each other in places that profited from enslavement and the "slave dungeons" that marked the departure from homelands.

SLAVE CASTLES AND CLAIMS TO AN AKAN CULTURAL IDENTITY AND PRAXIS

Akan spiritual culture and political leadership in the Americas have contributed decisively to a composite and unfolding African diaspora since at least the seventeenth century, and that contribution has been facilitated by a largely internal dialogue among distinct and kindred strands of African cultural identities. Ironically, that conversation is recurring but on different terms as the "slave castles" of Ghana become contested sites of encounter and reinterpretation. While diasporic Africans engage in Akan cultural institutions and spiritual practices in their returns to Ghana, Akan peoples in their homeland are becoming increasingly Christianized—with the views and values thereof while claiming an "amputated" version of an Akan culture constituted by its spiritual values and institutions—and are leaving Ghana for North America and parts of Europe. While those outbound to North America in 2006 accounted for only 14 percent of all Ghanaian emigrants, the number of diasporic Africans who have entered Ghana as tourists, businesspersons, teachers, Fulbright and study-abroad participants, and repatriates have almost all found their way to the Elmina and Cape Coast castles at some point during their stay (see figure 7.4). Most often, these diasporic Africans encounter the Akan-speaking Fante peoples situated on

Figure 7.4. Cape Coast Castle, 2005. The castle was the former British headquarters on the Gold Coast and a major port of embarkation during the international enslavement enterprise. In recent times, it has been renovated and repainted white to boost tourism, but this "whitening" of the castle has caused outraged among diasporic Africans. Photo by author.

the coast and whose settlements surround an Elmina castle that embodies layered identities—as a trading post, dungeon for the enslaved, military fortification, colonial administrative center, prison, school, and office.

The Fante and other Ghanaians see diasporic Africans as tourists and tourism as primarily a path to "development" and generally are unconcerned with the international enslavement enterprise. An acute silence suffocates the topic in public discourse. Perhaps that silence is linked to specific Fante and larger Akan roles in the international enslavement enterprise. Diasporic Africans, however, view "the castles as sacred ground not to be desecrated," and, for them, confronting the castles is confronting lived histories and memories embedded in very real collective experiences.[68] It is, therefore, not surprising that many break down and cry not out of performance or pity but rather out of an equally real need to engage and embrace that history so painful—in order to heal. The contestation between diasporic Africans and the Akan over the meaning of the Elmina castle goes beyond a divide between the two. It is rather about vested interests in the interpretation of the restored castle and about whose story should be told: Dutch tourists are interested in the period when the castle was under Dutch rule, British tourists in British colonial rule, Asante persons in the room that housed Nana Agyeman Prempeh I, whom most Ghanaians see as a symbol of resistance to British colonialism, and diasporic Africans in all of these.[69]

For many diasporic Africans who come to Ghana and are not unilaterally concerned about slavery or its implications, they all, at some point in their visit or residence, are referred to as "oburoni," a term that is generally used as a synonym for "European" or "white man." Although that rendering is far removed from the idea of "lagoon person" (*buro*, lagoon; *-ni*, suffix for person) and the connotation of "foreigner" or "stranger" from beyond the southern extreme of the Akan world (i.e., lagoons and ocean), it has assumed pejorative powers, especially when applied to diasporic Africans. "Oburoni" is applied unevenly to refer to some non-Ghanaians and even children and adults born in Ghana but of light complexion or with curly hair, and even the Maroons of Jamaica use the term for non-Maroon persons. But, in all this, one wonders about the intent and frequent use of the term for diasporic African persons in contradistinction to efforts like the Joseph Project, spearheaded by the Ghana Ministry of Tourism and Diaspora Relations. The Joseph Project is rooted in the biblical character of Joseph and, according to Jake Obetsebi Lamptey of the Ministry of Tourism and Diasporan Relations, involves a series of activities and events that encourage diasporic African investment and missionary work in Ghana—the country that purportedly serves as the gateway to an African homeland. At the same time, those who work with the Joshua Project, a Christian fundamentalist organization that is premised on spreading passion for "God" through Jesus Christ and that monitors and strongly encourages the proselytization of those "unsaved" peoples of the world, would certainly find much support for their efforts in the Joseph Project.[70]

The Joseph Project and the efforts of the Ministry of Tourism and Diasporan Relations reveal that their efforts are not too dissimilar from those of Nana Amoah, Chief Alfred Sam, and others who sought the technical knowledge and skills of Western import through diasporic Africans. Ghana has translated few of its pan-African claims and quotes from Marcus Garvey or W.E.B. Du Bois into the long-awaited dual citizenship for those from the diaspora, institutionally revamped its curricula, broken the silence on slavery in the public discourse, or seriously engaged its own yoke of neocolonialism and evangelical fanaticism so that an internal dialogue among those concerned can actually occur. Recall that Chief Sam's movement of the early twentieth century, if nothing else, reveals that African descendants in North America have provided a powerful lens with which to apprehend the deep contradictions of black life in white-controlled societies, including the quest for partnership with and full acceptance by the latter. In that context, the governing views and values of Ghana (of foreign import) drive the country's quest for partnership and full acceptance in the global capitalist world while ignoring the global network of racism and how that network extends into the commonly held views of ordinary Ghanaians who employ "oburoni" without reservation or awareness of its implications.

Diasporic Africans do, however, find two layers of racism in Ghana through multiple encounters or even a single one: Certain Ghanaian proprietors will routinely serve or offer service to whites before diasporic Africans and, in doing so, will call the latter and not the former "oburoni," though both might be "foreigners." This situation reflects an overt and an internalized racism that diasporic Africans know all too well, and this knowing is compounded by payment of monthly fees, periodic stamping of passports, and other obligations diasporic Africans must fulfill in order to remain in Ghana, "the gateway to Africa." The diasporic African presence in Ghana also raises key issues of culture, for the enslavement experiences of both Akan and diasporic ancestors have become commodified as highly commercial spectacles for tourists, whose interest in indigenous culture may lead to the same among the local population, but that culture is largely performing arts and festivals, which disclose much of the deep-seated conflict between indigenous culture and Christianization. A number of "chiefs" and persons who benefit from these festivals in terms of exposure and some tourism revenue are Christians, and conflict arises when those who accrue and anticipate such benefits are required to engage in an indigenous culture of a non-Christian character, for example, pouring libations to the ancestors and the *abosom* and completing attendant sacrifices.[71] The predicament of these "chiefs" and others is no different from that faced by Westernized and Christianized intellectuals or merchants of the nineteenth- and twentieth-century Gold Coast who sought to partner with the colonial order through traditional offices and institutions but without a commitment to the cultural outlook and values that underpinned those institutions and without contradicting too many of their Christian claims.

These issues of culture and commodification provide an important background against which to examine the Ghanaian government's encouragement of diasporic Africans to think of Africa in general and Ghana in particular as their "home" to visit, invest in, and even to retire. As such, it has marketed this idea to its target audience without a concurrent sensitizing of Ghanaians, who regard many of their diasporic compatriots as "rich tourists," "white foreigners," or both in spite of official pronouncements to not treat them as "whites."[72] The irony of this pronouncement is that Europeans or whites, at least not explicitly or publicly, are not viewed in largely pejorative terms (e.g., *oburoni*) rooted in an internalized racism. In addition, beyond the diasporic Africans who visit Ghana as "tourists," there is an African American Association of Ghana and a Ghana-Caribbean Association, and thousands live in the country as neither "rich tourists" nor "white foreigners."

Perhaps the most recent outward display of Ghana's diaspora marketing occurred in 2007, when the country celebrated its fiftieth anniversary of political independence and the bicentennial of the British abolition of the "slave trade." Yearlong events, including rituals to ceremonially provide proper burial to millions of Africans who died during the international enslavement enterprise, marked a sort of euphoria for Ghana in 2007. These celebrations, designed and funded by the government and civic and business leaders, received their share of praise and criticism for how much of the national body was included and how distinct cultures were incorporated into the celebratory events, including the issue of ownership of "Independence Day." Few discussions or analyses, however, focused on how diasporic Africans in Ghana and in the American diaspora viewed the events and their meaning or the symbolism embedded in the literal "whitening" of the very "slave castles" that functioned as ports of nonconsensual departure and the seat of government. Here, the meaning of the restored Cape Coast Castle out of the interests of tourism and diaspora marketing is more than symbolic. Like Elmina castle, its Cape Coast sibling had been repainted white in a restoration process that produced similar kinds of contested responses as noted earlier in the Elmina case. Haile Gerima's film *Sankofa* is introduced and ends with pivotal scenes at Cape Coast Castle and features Akan, as well as diasporic African, actors in a journey of transformation, enslaved African rebellions, segmentation and hierarchy among enslaved African peoples, slavery as religiously sanctioned, intra-African violence sponsored by plantation owners and agents, rape of African women, and maroonage.[73] Gerima made the following statement in an interview:

> I, myself, have gone through an amazing spiritual transformation in doing this film. And most of the actors, too. To be sitting in the dungeon for hours to shoot a film and still smell the stench of the history of hundreds of years ago is not an easy experience.... I asked a Ghanian [sic] woman to pour libation [to help with problems associated with filming *Sankofa*], and this is something I had forgotten for years though we do it at home [in Ethiopia]... throughout the shooting in Ghana, the drummer, who is a high priest, continued to pour libation, and I feel there was more power for that reason to finish the film.[74]

For diasporic Africans, the castles and forts that line Ghana's coast bring to mind the composite of processes and experiences that a thematic part of the film *Sankofa* narrates and to which they and their ancestors were bound. Thus, as Obiagele Lake argues, "many diasporic peoples view themselves as parts of a larger African community in spite of and in resistance to political and cultural hegemony which represents these populations as bounded ethnic entities."[75] Most expatriates view themselves as Africans and as diasporic Africans, while they remain clear about "cultural differences and the consequences of these differences in everyday encounters."[76] In 1989 there were approximately 120 expatriates (mostly from North America and the Caribbean) living primarily in the Accra region and but also in Kumase, and some have been residents since the 1960s. Most have married indigenous spouses (with children integrated into both worlds), and the issue of their cultural acceptance (or not) is not especially dissimilar from that of other cultural groups in Ghana who do not originate in the American diaspora.[77]

Diasporic Africans such as Nana Dinizulu and others who root their cultural identity in an ancestral claim are no less (or more) "African" than those who have been historically called or self-identified as African and whose claims associated with cultural identity often reference a longstanding ancestry that emerged in Africa. African studies as a field of inquiry has yet to deal adequately with the calculus of how cultural development processes that span thousands of years have shaped not only identities in specific locales and among kindred and differentiated African peoples but also the meaning or supposed transmutation of those identities in their historically recent interactions with Europeans and others. A number of scholars have built careers on the term "Africa(n)" as a linguistic import or an invention, but few have moved us beyond that frontier without resorting to nihilistic and postmodernist jargon that is unintelligible and difficult to digest. It was of little consequence or meaning if an African was a Stone Age or an Iron Age person, a hunter-gatherer or pastoralist, Nilotic or Bantu, sub-Saharan or Congolese, Hottentot or Pygmy during the greater part of a relatively mapped human history. These racialized constructs and academic conventions came to be once the greater part of Africa had more pervasive and largely disruptive encounters with Europeans and Asians and once Europe "invented" the historian, who, in turn, did much to reinvent the world and others in it.

Arguably, diasporic discourses have forced an urgent reexamination of the African cultures and cosmologies that continue to place a far-reaching emphasis—across artificial borders and colonial languages—on ancestry as a powerful basis for cultural identity, clan constitution, the rights and privileges thereof, the construction of lineages and genealogies, leadership and contestation of power, and the like. This is certainly the case for the Akan, whose very cosmology, spiritual values, and ethos have always been deeply anchored in a dialogue between its indigenous conceptions of a Creator and an ancient ancestress, which in fact remains the basis of Akan matrilineality and the construction of a composite spiritual-ideational-material culture in Akan societies. Thus, Nana Dinizulu could claim Gã, Akan, and another cultural group or its spiritual values, as part of an African identity that is largely a composite identity formed not the least out of the convergences of varied clans and peoples over the vast African landscape, across time, and via sophisticated trade routes and networks, roadways, and waterways. One of the biggest historical fallacies is that such convergences occurred because of transatlantic slaving, a phenomena that supplants all other processes of disaggregation and reconstitution and wherein distinct African groups were forced to find commonality and interact in ways unknown before. This could not be so far from the historical record or the cultural self-understandings of African societies, counting Akan societies, as their cultures have moved moved their histories.

African movement is perhaps one of the most neglected dimensions of African history, and this is understanable by virtue of the very clear impediments that mitigate studying such movement in historical time-depth. Yet, we have sufficient evidence in the West African case of movements, interactions, convergences of lineages and spiritual practices, and the earlier formations of a composite cultural identity that predate the international enslavement enterprise and its aftermath. There is no reason, counterstudy, or evidence to unequivocally state or suggest that these processes could not have taken place much earlier in time in ways that they did—perhaps for the same or different reasons—in later centuries and are continuing to do during the present epoch. The movement of proto-Akan and Akan peoples in the West African forest and in interactions with savanna- and forest-based peoples began much earlier than what scholars have been willing to concede, but, unlike the peoples of the West African savanna who were Islamized in varying degrees, and the Christianized peoples of the Kôngo kingdom and the nineteenth-century converts of the bights of Bénin and Biafra, the Akan came to the Americas (and remained in West Africa until the early twentieth century) with a distinctively un-Islamic and un-Christian spirituality rooted in a composite culture of indigenous origination. As such, the most enduring and constant element of Akan culture has been its spirituality as a proxy for the identity of that composite culture and its bearers. Since the mid-seventeenth century, key constituents of a composite Akan culture and spirituality have been archived in the Americas in the form of cosmologies, rituals, sacred and publicly transmitted knowledge, and attendant social practices. These elements exist in the lives of diasporic Africans whose ancestors preserved memories and materials that some diasporic Africans renewed or built upon through a contemporary engagement with (what they understand as) Akan cultural forms and ideas.

CONCLUSION

Diasporic Africans possess archived and some layers of African culture, and some self-consciously continue to learn an Akan language, spirituality, and its composite culture in close approximation. They have embraced histories and engaged cultures worth preserving, yet the homeland parts of that equation might soon be on the endangered culture list. Most who are conversant with the history and contours of contemporary Ghanaian society in general and Akan peoples in particular cannot but notice the rapid erosion of the proverbial beauty and content of the Akan language to an elite-sanctioned Anglicization process, an evangelical and fundamentalist Christianity that assault the spirituality of a host culture and fulfill its quota for souls and proselytized converts, a parochial schooling system and missionary curriculum with far-reaching tentacles. Further, we find a host of contradictions between high personal hygiene and ecological degradation, the loss of voluminous indigenous medicinal knowledge and healers who are vilified for possessing this wisdom, the whitening of the "slave castles" and African womens' skin (see figure 7.5), and the selling of Ghana to foreign interests while marketing Ghana as the *gateway* for diasporic Africans to Africa. These exigencies have everything to do with the diasporic African, for, if nothing else and in spite of some of their own contradictions, they raise the necessity of another level of internal dialogue between diasporic versions of African or Akan cultures and the ongoing and yet vanishing parts of a cultural narrative rooted in Akan peoples of the forested West African region. That dialogue is a cultural one that has to be historically situated and free of performance or pretenses in terms of how African ministries of culture define culture, and tempered by critical understandings of composite cultures. However, there

Figure 7.5. In response to skin bleaching, this billboard declares, "Black is Beauty," Accra, Ghana, 2006. Photo by author.

is more to this composite culture: symbiotically, history is context, culture is content, where culture reflects a peoples' self-understandings and their spiritual or ideational references. Culture is what we do but it is more the philosophies that have worked for culture members and that underpinns actions and ideas over time and across geographies.

John D. Y. Peel once posed a critical question for the study of African spirituality, specifically, of Yorùbá spirituality and its historically situated interactions with religions or cultures external to Africa. He wrote, "Concretely, the [question] is whether 'Yorùbá religion' is to be regarded as whatever religion(s) the Yorùbá people choose to practice or as religious practices of distinctively Yorùbá origin and character, wherever or by whomever they are practiced. In the former case the defining unit of analysis is Yorùbá society, in the latter it is certain given forms of Yorùbá culture."[78] If we substituted "Akan" for "Yorùbá" the question would be no less valid. In West Africa, the identity of Akan culture and its spirituality was defined by distinct forms, and though it shared some of the views and values found in other African societies, it became "Akan," the trademark of pioneering, "first" peoples whose influence at home traveled the ocean and transformed soil, settlements, and souls. The conclusion is that Akan cultural identity was a composite in its early formation in the West Africa forest and in its interaction with other peoples who were assimilated into the Akan social order and gene pool through familial or clan arrangements, thereby engendering a localized "diaspora" in the Akan homeland. That cultural identity was constituted via a spiritual-ideational-material praxis that cohered in continuity and in transformation, as those Akan persons who made that one-way crossing of the Atlantic into the Americas disembarked with a fully-matured composite culture and engaged in an internal dialogue with other Africans as well as the contours of their environments. That dialogue framed and still continues to shape an unfolding African diaspora(s) in the Americas and around the globe. That small group in early nineteenth-century Jamaica might have known something of this dialogue when they planned and "told some of their shipmates, whom they solicited to go with them, they would proceed to the sea-side by night, and remain in the bush through the night, and the first canoe they found by the seaside they would set sail for their country."

Select Bibliography

Archival Sources

England
University of London, SOAS Library, Archives & Special Collections, London
CWM/LMS/West Indies and British Guiana/Journals/Box 1, John Smith Papers
The National Archives, Kew, Colonial Office (CO), Public Record Office (PRO), Probate Records of the Prerogative Court of Canterbury (PROB), Treasury (T), War Office (WO)

CO 1/17/60	CO 137/184	CO 879/67	T 52/26
CO 1/17/77	CO 137/192	CO 885/23/14	T 70/1463
CO 1/17/110	CO 137/356/25	CO 9/10	T 70/11
CO 1/17/111	CO 139/21/25	CO 950/167	T 70/1194
CO 1/19/5	CO 139/23/113	CO 96/358/26	T 70/1211
CO 1/22/20	CO 152/22	CO 96/358/26	T 70/1464
CO 1/3/2	CO 152/23	CO 96/677/12	T 70/1476
CO 101/78/5	CO 321/22/12	CO 96/785/3-4	T 70/1515
CO 137/154	CO 700/Georgia, 12	CO 96/813/12	T 70/29
CO 137/155	CO 879/120/6	CO 96/814/1	T 70/30
CO 137/160	CO 879/19	PRO 30/55/100	T 71/554–558
CO 137/167	CO 879/39	PROB 11/421	WO 97, 1715/14
CO 137/172	CO 879/45	PROB 11/916	
CO 137/181	CO 879/48	PROB 11/945	

West Yorkshire Archive Service
WYL250/3/West Indies/5

The Netherlands
Koninklijk Huisarchief (Dutch Royal House Archives), The Hague
No. G2/54/Ib

Portugal
Instituto dos Arquivos Nacionais/Torre do Tombo, Lisbon, Corpo Cronológico (CC)

CC, *parte* 1, *maço* 3, no. 119	CC, *parte* 1, *maço* 72, no. 38	CC, *parte* 2, *maço* 88, no. 137
CC, *parte* 1, *maço* 4, no. 32	CC, *parte* 2, *maço* 79, no. 25	CC, *parte* 2, *maço* 89, no. 80
CC, *parte* 1, *maço* 8, no. 45	CC, *parte* 2, *maço* 85, no. 200	CC, *parte* 2, *maço* 89, no. 82
CC, *parte* 1, *maço* 59, no. 89	CC, *parte* 2, *maço* 87, no. 30	CC, *parte* 2, *maço* 90, no. 13

Ghana
Public Records and Archives Administration Department of Ghana, Cape Coast
K. Sekyi, "The Downfall of Tekyiman and the Subsequent Emigration of the Mfantsis," ms.
Manhyia Archives, Kumase
"The History of the Immigrants from Takyiman," ms., n.d.

Jamaica
National Library of Jamaica, Kingston

MS 193	MS 613	MS 729	MS 769	MS 1344	MS 1681	MS 1873

Royal Gazette
Daily Advertiser

Guyana
University of Guyana Library, Georgetown
Journal of W. S. van Hoogenheim, 28 Feb. 1763–31 Dec. 1764, trans. Barbara L. Blair, ms.
Essequebo and Demerary Gazette

Canada
Nova Scotia Archives and Records Management, Nova Scotia
MG9, Shelburne Transcripts, 1782–1807

United States
Virginia Historical Society, Richmond
Keith Family Papers
Historical Society of Pennsylvania, Philadelphia
Butler Family Papers
Massachusetts Historical Society, Boston
William Cushing Judicial Notebook, 1783, ms.
Miscellaneous Bound Manuscripts
New York City County Clerk Archives, New York
New York Supreme Court of Judicature Minute Book, 6 June 1710–5 June 1714 (engrossed)
Court of General and Quarter Sessions of the Peace, 1691–1731
Schomburg Center for Research in Black Culture and Life, New York Public Library
Arthur A. Schomburg Papers, Sc micro R-2798, box 15
Melville J. Herskovits Library, Northwestern University, Africana folios
C. E. Aidoo, "History of the Denkyiras," n.p., n.d.

Newspapers
Daily Courant (Hartford, Conn.)
Gazette of the State of Georgia
Georgia Gazette
Georgia State Gazette or Independent Register
Maryland Gazette
Maryland Journal and Baltimore Advertiser
New Jersey Gazette
New York Gazette
New York Times
New York Weekly Post-Boy
North Carolina Gazette
Pennsylvania Gazette
Pennsylvania Journal and the Weekly Advertiser
Royal Gazette (New York)
Royal Georgia Gazette
South Carolina and American General Gazette
South Carolina Gazette
Virginia Gazette
Virginia Gazette and Weekly Advertiser

Databases
Afro-Louisiana History and Genealogy, 1719–1820 (http://www.ibiblio.org/laslave)
Freedman's Bank Records on CD-ROM. Salt Lake City: Intellectual Reserve and the Christ of Jesus Christ and Latter-Day Saints, 2000.
The Transatlantic Slave Trade Database (http://www.slavevoyages.org)

Select Published Primary Sources
[Anonymous.] *A Genuine Narrative of the Intended Conspiracy of the Negroes at Antigua*. Dublin: R. Reilly, 1737.

[Anonymous.] *An Account of the Royal African Companies Forts and Castles on the Coast of Africa*. N.p., n.d.

[Anonymous.] *Essai historique sur la Colonie de Surinam*. Paramaribo: s.n., 1788.

[Anonymous.] *The Trade to Africa Considered, and Demonstrated to the Improved to the Nations' Benefit*. N.p., 1707 [?].

Anonymous. *Great Newes from the Barbadoes or, a True and Faithful Account of the Grand Conspiracy of the Negroes against the English*. London: L. Curtis, 1676.

Awnsham Churchill, *A Collection of Voyages and Travels*. London: Messrs. Churchill, 1732.

Barros, João de. *Decadas da Asia*. Lisbon : Na Regia Officina Typografica, 1778.

Blake, John W., ed. *Europeans in West Africa, 1450-1650*. London: Hakluyt Society, 1941.

Board of Trade (Great Britain). *Journal of the Commissioners for Trade and Plantations, 1704-1782*, 14 vols. London: His Majesty's Stationery Office, 1925–1938.

Bosman, Willem. *Naauwkeurige Beschryving van de Guinese Goud-, Tand- en Slave-Kust*. Utrecht: Anthony Schouten, 1704.

Bosman, Willem. *A New and Accurate Description of the Coast of Guinea*. London: J. Knapton, 1705.

Brásio, António, ed. *Monumenta Missionaria Africana, África Ocidental*, 1st series, 15 vols. Lisbon: Agência Geral do Ultramar, 1952–1988.

Candler, Allen D. *The Colonial Records of the State of Georgia*. Atlanta: Franklin, 1904.

Christaller, Johann Gottlieb. *A Grammar of the Asante and Fante Language called Tshi based on the Akuapem Dialect with Reference to the other Akan and Fante Dialects*. Basel: Basel Evangelist Missionary Society, 1875.

Christaller, Johann Gottlieb. *A Dictionary of the Asante and Fante Language called Tshi*. Basel: Basel Evangelical Missionary Society, 1933.

Committee for Trade and Plantations (Great Britain). *Return from the Commissioners for Trade and Plantations, to the Honourable House of Commons*. London: Committee for Trade and Plantations, 1777.

Daaku, Kwame Y. *UNESCO Research Project on Oral Traditions: Denkyira, No. 2*. Legon: Institute of African Studies, University of Ghana, 1970.

Daaku, Kwame Y. *Oral Traditions of Assin-Twifo*. Legon: Institute of African Studies, University of Ghana, 1969.

Dantzig, Albert van. *The Dutch and the Guinea Coast, 1674-1742: A Collection of Documents from the General State Archive at the Hague*. Accra: Ghana Academy of Arts and Sciences, 1978.

Donnan, Elizabeth. *Documents Illustrative of the History of the Slave Trade to America*, 4 vols. Washington, D.C.: Carnegie Institution of Washington, 1930.

Durand, Jean-Baptiste. *Voyage au Sénégal fait dans les années 1785 et 1786*, 2 vols. Paris: Dentu, 1807.

Edwards, Bryan. *History, Civil and Commercial of the British West Indies*, 5 vols. London: T. Miller, 1819.

Edwards, Bryan. *The Proceedings of the Governor and Assembly of Jamaica, in regard to the Maroon Negroes*. London: John Stockdale, 1796.

Fynn, John Kofi. *Oral Traditions of Fante States*. Legon: Institute of African Studies, University of Ghana, 1974.

Gehring, Charles T., trans. and ed. *Correspondence, 1647-1653, New Netherlands Documents Series*. Syracuse: Syracuse University Press, 2000.

Grone, G. R., trans. and ed. *The Voyages of Cadamosto and Other Documents on Western Africa in the Second Half of the Fifteenth Century*. London: Hakluyt Society, 1937.

Hair, P. E. H. *The Founding of the Castelo de Sao Jorge da Mina: An Analysis of the Sources*. Madison: African Studies Program, University of Wisconsin, 1994.

Hair, P. E. H., Adam Jones, and Robin Law, eds., *Barbot on Guinea: The Writings of Jean Barbot on West Africa, 1678-1712*. London: Hakluyt Society, 1992.

Hair, P. E. H., and J. D. Alsop, eds. *English Seamen and Traders in Guinea, 1553-1565: The New Evidence of Their Wills*. Lewiston, N.Y.: Mellen, 1992.

Hair, P. E. H., ed. *To Defend Your Empire and the Faith: Advice on a Global Strategy Offered c. 1590 to Philip, King of Spain and Portugal*. Liverpool: University of Liverpool Press, 1990.

Hair, P. E. H., ed. *Travails in Guinea: Robert Baker's "Brefe Dyscourse."* Liverpool: University of Liverpool Press, 1990.

Hening, William Waller, ed. *The Statutes at Large, Being a Collection of All the Laws of Virginia*. Charlottesville: University Press of Virginia, 1969.

Heyden, Ulrich Van der. *Rote Adler an Afrikas Küste: Die brandenburgisch-preußische Kolonie Großfriedrichsburg in Westafrika*. Berlin: Selignow, 2001.

Hill, Robert A., ed. *Marcus Garvey and the Universal Negro Improvement Association Papers*, 10 vols. Los Angeles: University of California Press, 1983-2006.

Horsmanden Daniel. *The New-York Conspiracy, or a History of the Negro Plot, with the Journal of the Proceedings against the Conspirators at New-York in the Years 1741-2*. New York: Southwick and Pelsue, 1810.

Houdas, Oliver and Maurice Delafosse, eds. and trans. *Tarikh el-Fettach*. Paris: Librairie d'Amérique et d'Orient, Adrien-Maisonneuve, 1964.

Houdas, Oliver, trans. *Tarikh es-Soudan*. Paris: Librairie d'Amérique et d'Orient, Adrien-Maisonneuve, 1981.

J. Rask, *En Kort og Sandfaerdig Rejse-Beskeivelse Til og Fra Guinea*. Trondheim: Trykt hos Jens Christensen Winding, 1754.

J. S. G. *The Detector Detected: or, State of Affairs on the Gold Coast*. London: W. Owen, 1753.

Jones, Adam. *Brandenburg Sources for West African History, 1680-1700*. Wiesbaden: Steiner, 1985.

Jones, Adam. *German Sources for West African History, 1599-1669*. Wiesbaden: Steiner, 1983.

Journal and Correspondence of H. W. Daendels, November 1815 to January 1817. Legon: Institute of African Studies, University of Ghana, 1964.

Justesen, Ole, ed. *Danish Sources for the History of Ghana, 1657-1754*, 2 vols. Copenhagen: Royal Danish Academy of Sciences and Letters, 2005.

Kennedy, Lionel H. and Thomas Parker. *An Official Report on the Trials of Sundry Negroes, Charged with an Attempt to Raise an Insurrection in the State of South-Carolina*. Charleston: James R. Schenck, 1822.

Koelle, Sigismund Wilhelm. *Polyglotta Africana*. London: Church Missionary House, 1854.

La Fleur, James D., ed. and trans. *Pieter Van Den Broecke's Journal of Voyages to Cape Verde, Guinea, and Angola, 1605-1612*. London: Hakluyt Society, 2000.

Levtzion, Nehemia and J. F. P. Hopkins, eds. *Corpus of Early Arabic Sources for West African History*. New York: Cambridge University Press, 1981.

Marcus, Jacob R., and Stanley F. Chyet, eds. *Historical Essay on the Colony of Surinam, 1788*, trans. Simon Cohen. New York: American Jewish Archives and KTAV, 1974.

Marees, Pieter de. *Description and Historical Account of the Gold Kingdom of Guinea*, trans. and ed. Adam Jones and Albert van Dantzig. New York: Oxford University Press, 1987.

Mota, A. Teixeira da and P. E. H. Hair. *East of Mina: Afro-European Relations on the Gold Coast in the 1550s and 1560s, an Essay with Supporting Documents*. Madison: African Studies Program, University of Wisconsin–Madison, 1988.

O'Callaghan Edmund B., and Berthold Fernow, eds. *Documents relative to the Colonial History of the State of New York*. Albany: Weed, Parsons, 1856-1887.

O'Callaghan, Edmund B. *The Documentary History of the State of New York*. Albany: Weed, Parsons, 1850.

Oldendorp, Christian George Andreas. *Historie der caribischen Inseln Sanct Thomas, Sanct Crux, und Sanct Jan, insbesondere der dasigen Neger und der Mission der evangelischen Brüder-Unität Herrnhut, erster Teil*, eds. Gudrun Meier, Stephan Palmié, Peter Stein, and Horst Ulbricht. Berlin: Staatliches Museum für Völkerkunde Dresden, 2000.

Pannet, Pierre J. *Report on the Execrable Conspiracy Carried Out by the Amina Negroes on the Danish Island of St. Jan in America, 1733*, trans. and ed. Aimery P. Caron and Arnold R. Highfield. Christiansted, St. Croix: Antilles Press, 1984.

Pereira, Duarte Pacheco. *Esmeraldo de Situ Orbis*. Lisboa: Academia Portuguesa da História, 1954.

Rivière Peter, ed. *The Guiana Travels of Robert Schomburgk, 1835-1844*. London: Hakluyt Society, 2006.

Roberts, John. *Extracts from an Account of the State of the British Forts, on the Gold Coast of Africa*. London: J. Bew, 1778.

Rømer, L. F. *A Reliable Account of the Coast of Guinea*, trans. and ed. Selena Axelrod Winsnes. New York: Oxford University Press for the British Academy, 2000.

Sandoval, Alonso de. *Un tratado sobre la esclavitud*, ed. Enriqueta Vila Vilar. Madrid: Alianza Editorial, 1987.

Slave Narratives: A Folk History of Slavery in the United States from Interviews with Former Slaves. Washington, D.C.: Library of Congress, 1941.

Stedman, John Gabriel. *Narrative of a Five Years Expedition against the Revolted Negroes of Surinam (1790)*, ed. Richard Price and Sally Price. Baltimore: Johns Hopkins University Press, 1988.

Taylor, Charles E., ed. *Leaflets from the Danish West Indies*. London: Dawson and Sons, 1888.

Tilleman, Erick. *A Short and Simple Account of the Country of Guinea and Its Nature*, trans. and ed. Selena A. Winsnes. Madison: African Studies Program, University of Wisconsin, 1994.

Tyson, George F., and Arnold R. Highfield. *The Kamina Folk: Slavery and Slave Life in the Danish West Indies*. U.S. Virgin Islands: Virgin Islands Humanities Council, 1994.

U.S. Department of Commerce, Bureau of the Census. *Negro Population of the United States, 1790-1915*. Washington, D.C.: Government Printing Office, 1918.

Winsnes, Selena A., ed. *Letters on West Africa and the Slave Trade: Paul Erdman Iserts' Journey to Guinea and the Caribbean Islands on Columbia*. London: Oxford University Press for the British Academy, 1992.

Notes

NOTES TO CHAPTER I

1. Cited in Michael Mullin, *Africa in America: Slave Acculturation and Resistance in the American South and the British Caribbean, 1736–1831* (Urbana: University of Illinois Press, 1992), 14.

2. The data for the biographical sketches of both persons named Coffee and Cudjoe can be found in Gwendolyn Hall's *Afro-Louisiana History and Genealogy* (1719–1820) database at http://www.ibiblio.org/laslave (henceforth, the ALHG database).

3. Calculations for Gold Coast imports to Jamaica are derived from David Eltis, Stephen D. Behrendt, David Richardson, and Herbert S. Klein, *The Transatlantic Slave Trade: A Database on CD-ROM* (New York: Cambridge University Press, 1998). For some recent additions see David Eltis, "The Volume and Structure of the Transatlantic Slave Trade: A Reassessment," *William and Mary Quarterly* 58(1) (2001): 17–46, and the updated, web-based version of the database at http://www.slavevoyages.org.

4. These biographical sketches are from the ALHG database. Gwendolyn Hall notes, in *Slavery and African Ethnicities in the Americas: Restoring the Links* (Chapel Hill: University of North Carolina Press, 2005), 119, 178, that prices for children and the elderly were "surprisingly high" in Louisiana, which might explain why Quaco, the sixty-three-year-old elder, was sold at that age, but Hall does not say why prices were high in Louisiana. Mina men, like Quaco, were more likely than other Africans in Louisiana to be recorded as married and as fathers of children, and most of the Mina women recorded with mates were married to Mina men.

5. Stephen D. Behrendt, David Eltis, and David Richardson, "The Costs of Coercion: African Agency in the Pre-modern Atlantic World," *Economic History Review* 54(3) (2001): 464–467, 472–473.

6. For a discussion of the "Mina" coast and the region east of Mina (Elmina) in the mid-sixteenth century, see A. Teixeira da Mota and P. E. H. Hair, *East of Mina: Afro-European Relations on the Gold Coast in the 1550s and 1560s, an Essay with Supporting Documents* (Madison: African Studies Program, University of Wisconsin–Madison, 1988).

7. Robin Law, "Ethnicities of Enslaved Africans in the Diaspora: On the Meanings of 'Mina' (Again)," *History in Africa* 32 (2005): 251.

8. On the provenance of "Mina de oro" and its variants, see P. E. H. Hair, "Black African Slaves at Valencia, 1482–1516: An Onomastic Inquiry," *History in Africa* 7 (1980): 119–131.

9. Pablo B. Eyzaguirre, "Small Farmers and Estates in Sao Tome, West Africa" (PhD diss.: Yale University, 1986), 35, 102.
10. Ibid., 37.
11. Gwendolyn M. Hall, *Slavery and African Ethnicities in the Americas: Restoring the Links* (Chapel Hill: University of North Carolina Press, 2005), 23, 47.
12. Hall, *Slavery and African Ethnicities*, 112–113.
13. Alonso de Sandoval, *Un tratado sobre la esclavitud*, ed. Enriqueta Vila Vilar (Madrid: Alianza Editorial, 1987), 65. See also Law, "Ethnicities of Enslaved Africans," 264; John Thornton, *Africa and Africans in the Making of the Atlantic World, 1400–1800* (New York: Cambridge University Press, 1998), 184–193.
14. Thomas Phillips, "A Journal of a Voyage made in the *Hannibal* of London," in Awnsham Churchill, *A Collection of Voyages and Travels...* (London: Messrs. Churchill, 1732), vol. 6, 228; P. E. H. Hair, Adam Jones, and Robin Law, eds., *Barbot on Guinea: The Writings of Jean Barbot on West Africa, 1678–1712* (London: Hakluyt Society, 1992), vol. 2, 382.
15. Law, "Ethnicities of Enslaved Africans," 254.
16. See Manuel Moreno Fraginals, "Africa in Cuba: A Quantitative Analysis of the African Populations in the Island of Cuba," *Annals of the New York Academy of Sciences* 292(1) (1977): 187–201. The "Araras," distinct from "Ardas" (Allada), were another broad category.
17. Kent Russel Lohse, "Africans and Their Descendants in Colonial Costa Rica, 1600–1750" (PhD diss., University of Texas at Austin, 2005), 53, 58, 62, 64–65, 84. Lohse listed about 75 of 842 references to "Mina" in Costa Rican notarial documents dated between the 1680s and the 1740s, some of which mentioned Juan Mina, Domingo Mina, and Gertrudis Mina, who baptized her son, Manuel Antonio, in 1748.
18. Ibid., 585, 589; National Archives, Kew, Public Record Office, Treasury 52/26, pp. 196–206.
19. Calculations are derived from the data at http://www.slavevoyages.org. The results of strontium isotope analysis have prompted some researchers to suggest the presence of the Akan via Elmina in the Yucatan and Veracruz regions of Mexico in the late sixteenth and early seventeenth century. See T. Douglas Price, Vera Tresler, and James H. Burton, "Early African Diaspora in Colonial Campeche, Mexico: Strontium Isotopic Evidence," *American Journal of Physical Anthropology* 130 (2006): 485–490.
20. Elizabeth Donnan, *Documents Illustrative of the History of the Slave Trade to America*, 4 vols. (Washington, D.C.: Carnegie Institution of Washington, 1930), vol. 1, 301–302, 391; Hair et al., *Barbot on Guinea*, vol. 2, 789–790.
21. Gonzalo A. Beltrán, "The Rivers of Guinea," *Journal of Negro History* 31(3) (1946): 314–316.
22. Mariza de Carvalho Soares, "From Gbe to Yoruba: Ethnic Change and the Mina Nation in Rio de Janeiro," in *The Yoruba Diaspora in the Atlantic World*, ed. Toyin Falola and Matt D. Childs (Bloomington: Indiana University Press, 2004), 231–232, 235; Thomas Ewbank, *Life in Brazil* (New York: Harper and Brothers, 1856), 111. Ewbank names several African "nations" such as the "Congo, Angola, Minas, Ashantee" (in that order), suggesting contiguous cultural groups.
23. Hall, *Slavery and African Ethnicities*, 123; Law, "Ethnicities of Enslaved Africans," 258. On the *terreiros* of Maranhão, see Mundicarmo Ferretti, *Desceu na*

guma: O caboclo do Tambor de Mina no processo de mudança de um terreiro de São Luis, a Casa Fanti-Ashanti (São Luis do Maranhão: SIOGE, 1993); Manuel Nunes Pereira, *A casa das Minas: Contribuição ao estudo das sobrevivéncias do culto dos Voduns, do panteão daomeano, no Estado do Maranhão, Brasil* (Petrópolis: Vozes, 1979); Sérgio Ferretti, *Querebentam de Zomadonu: Etnografia da Casa das Minas* (São Luis: Universidade Federal do Maranhão, 1986).

24. "Negrice Cristal" expresses the idea of being "clear" about one's black or African consciousness.

25. Liberdade is the name of the neighborhood, and Curuzu is the name of the street where Ilê Aiyê was founded in Salvador, Bahia.

26. Hall, *Slavery and African Ethnicities*, 43.

27. In the ALHG database, I counted 181 Cofi or Kofi (varied spellings), 5 Quaco (Kwaku), 5 Aba (Yaa), 4 Cudjoe (Kwadwo), 1 Quashee (Kwasi), and 1 Ama, as well as 35 and 10 entries under "Gold Coast" and "Fanti," respectively. This totals, excluding "Fanti" and "Gold Coast," about 197 Akan persons by name or about 3 percent of the nine thousand African names contained in the database. Of course, if we included "Mina" and other geographical or ethnic designations, the percentage and presence of Akan speakers would be higher. In addition, Akan "day names" spread along the Mina coast as far as Ouidah, though not solely as the result of a "Mina diaspora," as Law notes, for we must also consider the extent of an Akwamu "empire" that extended to include Ouidah (Whydah) at the beginning of the eighteenth century.

28. Hall, *Slavery and African Ethnicities*, 119.

29. Law, "Ethnicities of Enslaved Africans," 248.

30. See John K. Thornton, *Africa and Africans in the Making of the Atlantic World* (New York: Cambridge University Press, 1998); Douglas B. Chambers, "Ethnicity in the Diaspora: The Slave-trade and the Creation of African 'Nations' in the Americas," *Slavery and Abolition* 22(3) (2001): 26–27; James H. Sweet, "Mistaken Identities? Olaudah Equiano, Domingos Álvares, and the Methodological Challenges of Studying the African Diaspora," *American Historical Review* 114(2) (2009): 300.

31. These calculations are my own. I have used the works of Kwesi Prah and others who have begun reexamining African language classification. See Kwesi K. Prah, ed., *Between Distinction and Extinction: The Harmonisation and Standardisation of African Languages* (Cape Town: CASAS, 2000), and the publications of the Centre for Advanced Studies of African Societies. See also Colin Flight, "Trees and Traps: Strategies for the Classification of African Languages and Their Historical Significance," *History in Africa* 8 (1981): 43–74. For missionary "linguists" in West Africa, see the work of German missionary Sigismund Wilhelm Koelle, *Polyglotta Africana*...(London: Church Missionary House, 1854), and, for the Akan, German missionary Johann Gottlieb Christaller, *A Grammar of the Asante and Fante Language called Tshi based on the Akuapem Dialect with Reference to the other Akan and Fante Dialects* (Basel: Basel Evangelist Missionary Society, 1875), and *A Dictionary of the Asante and Fante Language called Tshi* (Basel: Basel Evangelical Missionary Society, 1933).

32. See David Eltis, "The Volume, Age/Sex Ratios, and African Impact of the Slave Trade: Some Refinements of Paul Lovejoy's Review of the Literature," *Journal of African History* 31 (1990): 489.

33. Byron J. Good, *Medicine, Rationality, and Experience: An Anthropological Perspective* (New York: Cambridge University Press, 1994), 17.

34. T. C. McCaskie, *State and Society in Pre-colonial Asante* (New York: Cambridge University Press, 1995), 142.

35. Ibid., 23, 107, 127, 135.

36. Ibid., 23, 115, 141.

37. David Henige, "John Kabes of Komenda: An Early African Entrepreneur and State Builder," *Journal of African History* 18(1) (1977): 6, 18–19.

38. Richard Price, *Travels with Tooy: History, Memory, and the African American Imagination* (Chicago: University of Chicago Press, 2007), 290.

39. See Brent H. Edwards, "The Uses of Diaspora," *Social Text* 19(1) (2001): 45–73; Colin A. Palmer, "Defining and Studying the Modern African Diaspora," *Journal of African American History* 85(1–2) (2000): 27–32; Joseph E. Harris, ed., *Global Dimensions of the African Diaspora* (Washington, D.C.: Howard University Press, 1993); and Kim Butler, "Defining Diaspora, Refining a Discourse," *Diaspora* 10(2) (2002): 189–219. On "imagined" identities, see Sidney J. Lemelle and Robin D. G. Kelley, *Imagining Home: Class, Culture, and Nationalism in the African Diaspora* (New York: Verso, 1994), and, on the African side of the "Atlantic" equation, V. Y. Mudimbe, *The Invention of Africa* (Bloomington: Indiana University Press, 1988) and the *Idea of Africa* (Bloomington: Indiana University Press, 1994).

40. On the African diaspora contextualized as a "migration," see Tiffany R. Patterson and Robin D. G. Kelley, "Unfinished Migrations: Reflections on the African Diaspora and the Making of the Modern World," *African Studies Review* 43(1) (2000): 11–45.

41. See Linda M. Heywood and John K. Thornton, *Central Africans, Atlantic Creoles, and the Foundation of the Americas, 1585–1660* (New York: Cambridge University Press, 2008).

42. Ira Berlin, "From Creole to African: Atlantic Creoles and the Origins of African-American Society in Mainland North America," *William and Mary Quarterly* 53(2) (1996): 251–88, and *Many Thousands Gone* (Cambridge: Belknap Press of Harvard University Press, 1998).

43. See Sheila S. Walker, ed., *African Roots/American Cultures: Africa in the Creation of the Americas* (New York: Rowman and Littlefield, 2001).

44. On the Yorùbá diaspora, see Toyin Falola and Matt D. Childs, eds., *The Yoruba Diaspora in the Atlantic World* (Bloomington: Indiana University Press, 2004). On the Igbo, see Douglas B. Chambers, *Murder at Montpelier: Igbo Africans in Virginia* (Jackson: University Press of Mississippi, 2005), and a substantive critique by Gloria Chuku on H-Atlantic (http://www.h-net.org/reviews/showrev.php?id=12372), October 2006, which shows many of the pitfalls of assuming that one "ethnicity" contributed this or that to the Americas and discusses a gross misreading of the African side of the diasporic equation. On the Kôngo and Central Africans, see Linda M. Heywood, *Central Africans and Cultural Transformations in the American Diaspora* (New York: Cambridge University Press, 2001); John K. Thornton, *Africa and Africans*; Heywood and Thornton, *Central Africans, Atlantic Creoles*; and Maureen Warner-Lewis, *Central Africa in the Caribbean: Transcending Time, Transcending Cultures* (Kingston: University of the West Indies Press, 2003).

45. The classic study on Maroon societies is Richard Price's *Maroon Societies: Rebel Slave Communities in the Americas* (Baltimore: Johns Hopkins University Press, 1979), wherein the Akan receive limited treatment (29, 261, 263, 335, 351).

NOTES TO CHAPTER 2

1. Roger Blench, "Trees on the March: The Dispersal of Economic Trees in the Prehistory of West-Central Africa" (paper presented at the Society of Africanist Archaeologists conference, Cambridge, 12–15 July, 2001, p. 10).

2. Ivor Wilks, *Forests of Gold: Essays on the Akan and the Kingdom of Asante* (Athens: Ohio University Press, 1993), 94.

3. Ibid., 42, 120. For his most recent restatement of this argument, see Ivor Wilks, "The Forest and the Twis," *Journal des Africanistes* 75(1) (2005): 19–75.

4. Elizabeth Isichei, *A History of African Societies to 1870* (New York: Cambridge University Press, 1997), 241, 515n112.

5. Wilks, *Forests of Gold*, 64, 68.

6. A. Norman Klein, "Slavery and Akan Origins?" *Ethnohistory* 41(4) (1994): 628–629.

7. Ibid., 637. For Wilks's response to Klein's critique and Klein's response to Wilks's commentary, see Ivor Wilks, "Slavery and Akan Origins? A Reply," *Ethnohistory* 41(4) (1994): 657–665; and A. Norman Klein, "Reply to Wilks's Commentary on 'Slavery and Akan Origins?' " *Ethnohistory* 41(4) (1994): 666–667. See also T. C. McCaskie, "Empire State: Asante and the Historians," *Journal of African History* 33 (1992): 471. Arguably, the structure and reliability of the Asante "stool histories" collected and translated by Joseph Agyeman-Duah in the 1960s and used by Wilks are in need of revisiting.

8. Ray A. Kea, *Settlements, Trade, and Polities in the Seventeenth-Century Gold Coast* (Baltimore: The Johns Hopkins University Press, 1982), 44, 92, 198; James C. McCann, *Green Land, Brown Land, Black Land: An Environmental History of Africa, 1800-1990* (Portsmouth, NH: Heinemann, 1999), 120–122.

9. A. Norman Klein, "Toward a New Understanding of Akan Origins," *Africa* 66(2) (1996): 248, 262.

10. Ibid., 264.

11. On West African examples of "classless" societies, see Ann B. Stahl, "Political Economic Mosaics: Archaeology of the Last Two Millennia in Tropical Sub-Saharan Africa," *Annual Review of Anthropology* 33 (2004): 152.

12. John Picton has asked, "Why is it always assumed, however, that it was North Africa that influenced the sub-Saharan region rather than the other way around?" See John Picton, "Tradition, Technology, and Lurex: Some Comments on Textile History and Design in West Africa," in *History, Design, and Craft in West African Strip-woven Cloth* (Washington, D.C.: National Museum of African Art, 1992), 28.

13. Kwaku Effah-Gyamfi, *Bono Manso: An Archaeological Investigation into Early Akan Urbanism* (Calgary: Department of Archaeology, University of Calgary Press, 1985), 12.

14. Blench, "Trees on the March," 1.

15. Ibid., 2–3; G. Chouin, "Sacred Groves in History: Pathways to the Social Shaping of Forest Landscapes in Coastal Ghana," *Institute for Development Studies Bulletin* 33(1) (2002): 39–46.

16. M. Posnansky, "The Search for Asante Origins: Archaeological Evidence," in *Golden Stool: Studies of the Asante Center and Periphery*, ed. Enid Schildkrout, 15 (New York: American Museum of Natural History, 1987).

17. M. R. Talbot, "Lake Bosumtwi, Ghana," *Nyame Akuma* 23 (1983): 11.

18. M. A. Sowunmi, "The Beginnings of Agriculture in West Africa: Botanical Evidence," *Current Anthropology* 26(1) (1985): 127.

19. B. W. Andah, "Identifying Early Farming Traditions of West Africa," in *The Archaeology of Africa: Food, Metals, and Towns*, ed. Thurstan Shaw, Paul Sinclair, Bassey Andah, and Alex Okpoko, 240–254 (New York: Routledge, 1995); Sowunmi, "Beginnings of Agriculture," 128; O. Davies, "The Origins of Agriculture in West Africa," *Current Anthropology* 9(5) (1968): 478, 481.

20. L. E. Newton, "More Kintampo Culture Finds in the Forest Zone of Ghana," *Nyame Akuma* 16 (1980): 8; J. Casey and R. Sawatzky, "Obituary for Boyase Hill: A Kintampo Site in Ashanti Region, Ghana," *Nyame Akuma* 48 (1997): 29; Ann B. Stahl, "Reinvestigation of Kintampo 6 Rock Shelter, Ghana: Implications for the Nature of Culture Change," *African Archaeological Review* 3 (1985): 117–150.

21. F. Korkor, "An Investigation of the Kintampo 'Neolithic' Complex Site at Nkukua Buoho near Kumasi, Ghana," *Nyame Akuma* 55 (2001): 45.

22. M. Cremaschi and S. Di Lernia, "Current Research on the Prehistory of the Tadrart Acacus (Libyan Sahara): Survey and Excavations 1991–1995," *Nyame Akuma* 45 (1996): 57.

23. Andah, "Identifying Early Farming Traditions," 250.

24. Among the Dagomba, a non-Akan setter group in the territory that is now northern and northeastern Ghana, it is said that their founder came from the caves and hills around eastern Mali. See A. Cardinall, *The Natives of the Northern Territories of the Gold Coast* (New York: Negro Universities Press, 1969), 5.

25. George E. Brooks, "Ecological Perspectives on Mande Population Movements, Commercial Networks, and Settlement Patterns from the Atlantic Wet Phase (ca. 5500–2500 B.C.) to the Present," *History in Africa* 16 (1989): 23, 29.

26. A. J. Carpenter, *A West African Nature Study* (New York: Longmans, Green, 1954), 149, 154.

27. J. Anquandah, "The Kintampo Complex: A Case Study of Early Sedentism and Food Production in Sub-Sahelian West Africa," in *The Archaeology of Africa: Food, Metals, and Towns*, ed. Thurstan Shaw, Paul Sinclair, Bassey Andah, and Alex Okpoko, 255, 260 (New York: Routledge, 1995).

28. J. Casey and R. Sawatzky,, "Report of Investigations at the Birimi Site in Northern Ghana," *Nyame Akuma* 48 (1997): 35.

29. Ann B. Stahl, "Early Food Production in West Africa: Rethinking the Role of the Kintampo Culture," *Current Anthropology* 27(5) (1986): 535.

30. E. K. Agorsah, "Before the Flood: The Golden Volta Basin," *Nyame Akuma* 41 (1994): 35; D. Calvocoressi and N. David, "A New Survey of Radiocarbon and Thermoluminescence Dates for West Africa," *Journal of African History* 20(1) (1979): 1–29.

31. Korkor, "Nkukua Buoho," 45; B. C. Vivian, "Recent Excavations at Adansemanso," *Nyame Akuma* 46 (1996): 41–42; P. L. Shinnie and A. Shinnie, *Early Asante* (Calgary: Department of Archeology, University of Calgary, 1995), 12; P. L. Shinnie and B. C. Vivian, "1991 Asante Research Project," *Nyame Akuma* 36 (1991): 5; S. K. McIntosh and R. J. McIntosh, "Current Directions in West African Prehistory," *Annual Review of Anthropology* 12 (1983): 237; S. K. McIntosh and R. J. McIntosh, "Recent Archaeological Research and Dates from West Africa," *Journal of African History* 27 (1986): 441; E. Keteku, "Radiocarbon Dates from Nyanawase," *Nyame*

Akuma 24–25 (1984): 4; J. N. Debrah, "Archaeological Survey of the Krobo Mountain Ancient Settlements," *Nyame Akuma* 21 (1982): 17; Calvocoressi and David, "Radiocarbon and Thermoluminescence Dates," 7; T. Shaw, "Chronology of Excavation at Dawu, Ghana," *Man* 62 (1962): 136.

32. Vivian, "Recent Excavations," 41–42; Shinnie and Shinnie, *Early Asante*, 6–7, 12; Shinnie and Vivian, "1991 Asante Research Project," 6; Talbot, "Lake Bosomtwi," 11; Brooks, "Ecological Perspectives," 29.

33. Vivian, "Recent Excavations," 39; Shinnie and Shinnie, *Early Asante*, 7, 14; Shinnie and Vivian, "1991 Asante Research Project," 5. See also R. S. Rattray, *Ashanti* (Oxford: Clarendon, 1923), 121–133.

34. P. Shinnie, "Early Asante: Is Wilks Right?" in *The Cloth of Many Colored Silks*, ed. J. Hunwick and N. Lawler, 198, 201 (Evanston: Northwestern University Press, 1996). Shinnie's position was cautionary relative to the "accepted" claims of Ivor Wilks on Akan "ethnogensis" since, after all, Shinnie did write this essay as part of a tribute that rightfully honored Wilks.

35. D. W. Phillipson, *African Archaeology* (New York: Cambridge University Press, 2005), 237.

36. K. Effah-Gyamfi, "Bono Manso Archeological Research Project, 1973–1976," *West African Journal of Archeology* 9 (1979): 177; idem, "Some Archeological Reflections on Akan Traditions of Origin," *West African Journal of Archeology* 9 (1979): 192.

37. Calvocoressi and David, "Radiocarbon and Thermoluminescence Dates," 12, 17; Effah-Gyamfi, *Bono Manso*, 16, 204; J. Anquandah, "Urbanization and State Formation in Ghana during the Iron Age," in *The Archaeology of Africa: Food, Metals, and Towns*, ed. Thurstan Shaw, Paul Sinclair, Bassey Andah, and Alex Okpoko, 649 (New York: Routledge, 1995); Phillipson, *African Archaeology*, 237.

38. Stahl, "Early Food Production," 535.

39. Vincent K. Farrar, "Traditional Akan Architecture and Building Construction: A Technological and Historical Study" (PhD diss., University of California–Berkeley, 1988), 192, 195.

40. James L. A. Webb Jr., "Malaria and the Peopling of Early Tropical Africa," *Journal of World History* 16(3) (2005): 278–280, 284. Yams yield high calories and would have contributed to population growth, and iron tools were not necessary for its cultivation.

41. The Duffy gene gives total protection against the *vivax* malarial parasite; this is not the case for *falciparum*.

42. Webb Jr., "Malaria and the Peopling," 281; L. Luca Cavalli-Sforza, Paolo Menozzi, and Alberto Piazza, *The History and Geography of Human Genes* (Princeton: Princeton University Press, 1994), 146.

43. Annual rituals in the context of feast and celebration were performed for such women. A "shrine" called *Abamoo* was created for the tenth-born child and for twins, and the mothers of both types of children acted as custodians of this shrine.

44. Cavalli-Sforza, Menozzi, and Piazza, *Human Genes*, 146.

45. Ibid., 152.

46. Webb Jr., "Malaria and the Peopling," 285.

47. Bassey W. Andah, "Population and Language History of Tropical Africa with Special Reference to West Africa," *West African Journal of Archaeology* 17 (1987): 75–76.

48. Brooks, "Ecological Perspectives," 30–31. Between 700 and 1100 CE, the Akan of Kumase and areas farther south received eighty inches of annual rainfall.

49. Kwame Y. Daaku, *UNESCO Research Project on Oral Traditions: Denkyira, No. 2* (Legon: Institute of African Studies, University of Ghana, 1970), 17. See also C. E. Aidoo, *History of the Denkyiras*, n.p., n.d. (Africana folios, Melville J. Herskovits Library, Northwestern University).

50. Daaku, *Denkyira*, 22.

51. Ibid., 18.

52. Kwame Y. Daaku, *Oral Traditions of Assin-Twifo* (Legon: Institute of African Studies, University of Ghana, 1969). This text is unpaginated, and each set of interviews has its own pagination. Here I am citing the histories of Assin Ekrofuom, p.4, Assin Nyanterkyikrom, p.5, and Assin Andoe, p.1.

53. Ivor Wilks and John Stewart, "The Mande Loan Element in Twi," *Ghana Notes and Queries* 4, (1962); Mary Esther Kropp Dakubu, "The 'Mande Loan Element in Twi' Revisited," *Sprache und Geschichte in Afrika* 16–17 (2001): 274.

54. K. O. Odoom, "A Note on the History of Islam in Brong Ahafo," in *Profile of Brong Kyempim*, ed. Kwame Arhin, 39 (Accra: Afram and the Institute of African Studies of the University of Ghana, 1979).

55. Dakubu, " 'Mande Loan Element in Twi' Revisited," 275.

56. Wilks and Stewart, "Mande Loan Element in Twi," *Ghana Notes and Queries* 4 (1962): 26–28.

57. Maurice Delafosse, *La langue mandingue et ses dialectes (malinké, bambara, dioula)*. Vol. 1, *Grammaire, lexique français-mandingue* (Paris: Geuthner, 1929); vol. 2, *Dictionnaire mandingue-français* (Paris: Geuthner, 1955).

58. Dakuku, " 'Mande Loan Element in Twi' Revisited," 286.

59. Ann B. Stahl, *Making History in Banda: Anthropological Visions of Africa's Past* (New York: Cambridge University Press, 2001), 54–57, 151; Mary Esther Kropp Dakubu, "On the Linguistic Geography of the Area of Ancient Begho," *Transactions of the Linguistic Circle of Accra* 3 (1976): 67.

60. E. Kweku Osam, "The Loss of the Noun Class System in Akan," *Acta Linguistica Hafniensia* 26 (1993): 83.

61. Ibid., 82; Florence Dolphyne, "Dialect Differences and Historical Processes in Akan," *Legon Journal of the Humanities* 2 (1976): 20.

62. Osam, "Loss of the Noun Class," 89; Florence A. Dolphyne, "The Brong Bono Dialect of Akan," in *Profile of Brong Kyempim*, ed. Kwame Arhin, 97, 100–101, 104 (Accra: Afram and the Institute of African Studies of the University of Ghana, 1979).

63. Brooks, "Ecological Perspectives," 30–31.

64. Osam, "Loss of the Noun Class," 90–91. Akan ontology resembles that found in so-called Bantu languages, which have retained a full noun classification system.

65. Here, the prefix o- is in free variation with ɔ-. On noun class erosion in Akan (Twi), the "Koromanti" (Akan-derived) language among Maroons in Jamaica has experienced the same change, wherein noun class prefixes (a-, o-, n-) were lost, even though some words have retained it (e.g., *ananse* [spider], *aprako* [pig], *awisa*, [pepper], and *obroni* [white person, in common parlance]).

66. Osam, "Loss of the Noun Class," 102.

67. Robert T. Soppelsa, "Terracotta Traditions of the Akan of Southeastern Ivory Coast" (PhD diss., Ohio State University, 1982), 424.

68. Thomas Phillips, "A Journal of a Voyage made in the *Hannibal* of London," in Awnsham Churchill, *A Collection of Voyages and Travels*...(London: Messrs. Churchill, 1732), vol. 6, 228.

69. Merrick Posnansky, "Traditional Cloth from the Ewe Heartland," in *History, Design, and Craft in West African Strip-woven Cloth* (Washington, D.C.: National Museum of African Art, 1992), 114. On the Akanization of the Guan, see Kwame A. Labi, "Akanization of the Hill Guan Arts," *Research Review* 18(2) (2002): 1–21. In what is now part of the Akuapem area, the Guan were ruled by the Akwamu through military intervention but fell under Akyem rule through invitation and thereafter adopted Akan political, aesthetic, language, and other institutionalized cultural forms. On the question of language, see E. V. Asihene's *Guan-Anum-Boso-English Dictionary* (Accra: author, n.d.), but its vocabulary is distinctively Akan.

70. Nehemia Levtzion, "Patterns of Islamization in West Africa," in N. Levtzion, ed., *Conversion to Islam* (New York: Holmes and Meier, 1979), 208. For historical treatments of Islam in (West) Africa, see John S. Trimingham, *A History of Islam in West Africa* (New York: Oxford University Press, 1970); Nehemia Levtzion and Randall L. Pouwels, eds., *The History of Islam in Africa* (Athens: Ohio University Press, 2000); and David Robinson, *Muslim Societies in African History* (New York: Cambridge University Press, 2004).

71. Levtzion, "Patterns of Islamization," 209.

72. Nehemia Levtzion and J. F. P. Hopkins, eds., *Corpus of Early Arabic Sources for West African History* (New York: Cambridge University Press, 1981), 360, 356–357.

73. Nehemia Levtzion, "Slavery and Islamization in Africa: A Comparative Study," in *Slaves and Slavery in Muslim Africa: Islam and the Ideology of Enslavement*, vol. 1, ed. J. R. Willis, 182–183 (London: Frank Cass, 1985); idem, "Mamluk Egypt and Takrūr (West Africa)," 193; idem, "Merchants versus Scholars and Clerics in West Africa: Differential and Complementary Roles," in *Rural and Urban Islam in West Africa*, ed. N. Levtzion and H. J. Fisher, 27–28 (Haifa: University of Haifa, 1986); St. Clair Drake, *Black Folks Here and There* (Los Angeles: Center for Afro-American Studies at UCLA, 1990), vol. 2, 151.

74. Ivor Wilks, *Asante in the Nineteenth Century* (New York: Cambridge University Press, 1975), 239–260, 310–319, 344–356, 506–509; Robinson, *Muslim Societies*, 124–137.

75. Ivor Wilks, "The Juula and the Expansion of Islam into the Forest," in *The History of Islam in Africa*, ed. Nehemia Levtzion and Randall L. Pouwels, 94 (Athens: Ohio University Press, 2000); idem, "Wangara, Akan, and Portuguese in the Fifteenth and Sixteenth Centuries, I: The Matter of Bitu," *Journal of African History* 23(3) (1982): 333–349; idem, "A Medieval Trade Route from the Niger to the Gulf of Guinea," *Journal of African History* 3(2) (1962): 338.

76. Oliver Houdas and Maurice Delafosse, eds. and trans., *Tarikh el-Fettach ou Chronique du chercheur pour servir à l'histoire des villes, des armées et des principaux personnages du Tekrour* (Paris: Librairie d'Amérique et d'Orient, Adrien-Maisonneuve, 1964), vol. 2, 65, 68.

77. B. Marie Perinbam, "Perceptions of Bonduku's Contributions to the Western Sudanese Gold Trade: An Assessment of the Evidence," *History in Africa* 13 (1986): 309.

78. Duarte Pacheco Pereira, *Esmeraldo de Situ Orbis* (Lisboa: Academia Portuguesa da História, 1954), 107. Pereira regarded "Toom" as a land of gold, whose "black inhabitants" were described as "monstrous people." He also mentioned "Betu" (i.e., Bitu or Begho) as proximate to the land of "Toom." On Tonawa, see John Leyden's *Historical Account of Discoveries and Travels in Africa* (Edinburgh: Constable, 1817), vol. 2, 289; Robin Hallet, ed., *Records of the African Association, 1788–1831* (New York: Thomas Nelson and Sons, 1964), 96–97; On Tõ, see Delafosse, *La langue mandingue*, vol. 2, 760.

79. Oliver Houdas, trans., *Tarikh es-Soudan* (Paris: Librairie d'Amérique et d'Orient, Adrien-Maisonneuve, 1981), vol. 2, 10–20, 20n7, 25n1.

80. Perinbam, "Bonduku's Contributions," 302; Odoom, "Islam in Brong Ahafo," 39.

81. Wilks "Wangara, Akan, and Portuguese," 346; Odoom, "Islam in Brong Ahafo," 38; Kwame Arhin, "The Brong," in *Profile of Brong Kyempim*, ed. Kwame Arhin, 10 (Accra: Afram and the Institute of African Studies at the University of Ghana, 1979).

82. Anquandah, "Urbanization and State Formation," 650–651; Effah-Gyamfi, "Bono Manso Archeological Research," 173–186.

83. Effah-Gyamfi, *Bono Manso*, 23.

84. Effah-Gyamfi, "Bono Manso Archeological Research," 179.

85. Phillipson, *African Archaeology*, 279–280.

86. J. A. Braimah, H. H. Tomlinson, and O. Amankwatia, *History and Traditions of the Gonja* (Alberta: University of Calgary, 1997), 16; Anquandah, "Urbanization and State Formation," 645.

87. Anquandah, "Urbanization and State Formation," 645.

88. L. B. Crossland, *Pottery from the Begho-B2 Site, Ghana* (Calgary: University of Calgary Press, 1989), 104.

89. Bill Freund, *The African City: A History* (New York: Cambridge University Press, 2007), 13–15; Roderick J. McIntosh and Susan K. McIntosh, "The Inland Niger Delta before the Empire of Mali: Evidence from Jenné-Jeno," *Journal of African History* 22(1) (1981): 1–22.

90. Vivian, "Recent Excavations," 39.

91. Crossland, *Pottery from the Begho*, 9.

92. McLeod, *Asante*, 122–123; Timothy Garrard, *Akan Weights and the Gold Trade* (London: Longman, 1980).

93. Hartmut Mollat, "A New Look at the Akan Gold Weights of West Africa," *Anthropos* 98 (2003): 38–39.

NOTES TO CHAPTER 3

1. For a review of the early sources, see Adam Jones, "Semper Aliquid Veteris: Printed Sources for the History of the Ivory and Gold Coasts, 1500–1750," *Journal of African History* 27 (1986): 215–235.

2. For a sixteenth-century map of Edina (Elmina), see Georg Braun and Frans Hogenberg, "S. Georgii oppidum, Mina nuncupatum…" in *Civitates orbis terrarum*, 1573–1618, British Library, maps C.7.d.1, vol. 1, pl. 54.

3. Arquivo Nacional da Torre do Tombo (ANTT), Corpo Cronológico (CC), parte 2, maço 59, no. 89 (30 July 1515); CC, parte 2, maço 79, no. 25 (2 December 1518); CC, parte 1, maço 72, no. 38 (10 June 1542).

4. ANTT, CC, parte 2, maço 79, no. 25. See also John L. Vogt, "The Early Sao Tome-Principe Slave Trade with Mina, 1500–1540," *International Journal of African Historical Studies* 6(3) (1973): 456, 463.

5. John W. Blake, "O Castello de São Jorge da Mina or Elmina Castle." In *Vice-Almirante A. Teixeira da Mota: In Memoriam*, vol. 1 (Lisbon: Academia de Marinha and Instituto de Investigacão Científica Tropical, 1987), 404. Concerning gold from Mina to Portugal, see João de Barros, *Decadas da Asia* (Lisbon: Na Regia Officina Typografica, 1778), vol. 1, 16–28.

6. For a relatively recent discussion on Caramansa, see P. E. H. Hair, *The Founding of the Castelo de Sao Jorge da Mina: An Analysis of the Sources* (Madison: African Studies Program, University of Wisconsin, 1994), 4, 16, 18, 54–66. In 1471, João de Santarem and Pedro de Escobar started trading in gold at the site that became known as Elmina after having traded for gold at Shama. The merchant with whom de Azambuja spoke was João Bernades, who had a ship trading in "gold with Caramança, lord of that village [Edina]." See G. R. Crone, trans. and ed., *The Voyages of Cadamosto and Other Documents on Western Africa in the Second Half of the Fifteenth Century* (London: Hakluyt Society, 1937), 116.

7. Ivana Elbl, "The Portuguese Trade with West Africa, 1440–1521" (PhD diss., University of Toronto, 1986), 212. For recent studies on Eguafo, see Sam Spiers, "The Eguafo Kingdom: Investigating Complexity in Southern Ghana" (PhD diss., Syracuse University, 2007); Gérard Chouin, *Eguafo: Un Royaume Africain "au coeur François" (1637–1688): Mutations Socio-économiques et Politique Européenne d'un État de la Côte de l'Or (Ghana) au XVIIe siècle* (Paris: Afera éditions, 1998).

8. Ghana National Archives at Cape Coast, Tribal Histories, K. Sekyi, "The Downfall of Tekyiman and the Subsequent Emigration of the Mfantsis"; "The History of the Immigrants from Takyiman," ms., n.d., Manhyia Record Office at Kumase. See also John Kofi Fynn, *Oral Traditions of Fante States*, no. 2, *Eguafo*; no. 3, *Komenda*; no. 4, *Edina (Elmina)* (Legon: Institute of African Studies, University of Ghana, 1974).

9. Ibid., no. 3, *Komenda*, 15–16; Ray A. Kea, *Settlements, Trade, and Polities in the Seventeenth-Century Gold Coast* (Baltimore: Johns Hopkins University Press, 1982), 64.

10. The àbráfoɔ (sg. ɔbrafoɔ; lit., those who forbade) functioned in the capacity of the ɔhene's security force, as enforcer of law rather than executioner (i.e., odumfoɔ) and, in spiritual practice, as an ɔkɔmfoɔ's assistant, who handles many of the animal sacrifices.

11. For a detailed study of Elmina, see Harvey M. Feinberg, *Africans and Europeans in West Africa: Elminas and Dutchmen on the Gold Coast during the Eighteenth Century* (Philadelphia: American Philosophical Society, 1989). Elmina's claim of uniqueness is largely without merit. In fact, the Elmina people also shared key cultural practices and festivals with other forest-based and coastal Akan peoples. Some of those festivals included Bakatue (synonym for the Apoɔ festival in Takyiman and Wankyi), Eguadoɔto (synonym for Awukuadae), and Nyɛye (synonym for Akwasiadae).

12. Duarte Pacheco Pereira, *Esmeraldo de situ orbis* (Lisbon: Imprensa Nacional, 1892), 70. For an English translation by George H. T. Kimble, see Duarte Pacheco Pereira, *Esmeraldo de situ orbis* (London: Hakluyt Society, 1937).

13. Ibid., esp. book 2, chaps. 4–6. See also J. D. Fage, "A Commentary on Duarte Pacheco Pereira's Account of the Lower Guinea Coastlands in His *Esmeraldo de situ orbis* and on Some Other Early Accounts," *History in Africa* 7 (1980): 47–50.

14. John W. Blake, *Europeans in West Africa, 1450–1650* (London: Hakluyt Society, 1941), vol. 1, 47. On the themes of miscegenation, commerce, and Christianity in the Portuguese expansion into Africa, see Francisco Bethencourt and Diogo Ramada Curto, eds., *Portuguese Oceanic Expansion, 1400–1800* (New York: Cambridge University Press, 2007).

15. On the mid-sixteenth-century "Mina" coast and the region to the east of Elmina, see A. Teixeira da Mota and P. E. H. Hair, *East of Mina: Afro-European Relations on the Gold Coast in the 1550s and 1560s: An Essay with Supporting Documents* (Madison: African Studies Program, University of Wisconsin, 1988). See also P. E. H. Hair, ed., *To Defend Your Empire and the Faith: Advice on a Global Strategy Offered c. 1590 to Philip, King of Spain and Portugal* (Liverpool: University of Liverpool Press, 1990), 113.

16. Christopher R. DeCorse, *An Archaeology of Elmina: Africans and Europeans on the Gold Coast, 1400–1900* (Washington, D.C.: Smithsonian Institution Press, 2001), 18.

17. Blake, *Europeans in West Africa*, vol. 1, 31; António Brásio, ed., *Monumenta Missionaria Africana*, vol. 1, *África Ocidental*, 1st series, 15 vols. (Lisbon: Agência Geral do Ultramar, 1952–1988), 10, 20, 49. Henceforth, "MMA."

18. ANTT, CC, parte I, maço 3, doc. 119. Letter of Nuno Vaz de Castello to King Manuel I, 2 October 1502. This letter notes de Castello's arrival and reception at Mina, as well as his visit to Xarife (Xeryfe) of Komenda and perhaps the "king of Efuto [Fetu]."

19. Brásio, *MMA*, vol. 1, 191. On the Portuguese courting African rulers while Duarte Pacheco Pereira was governor of the Elmina fort and town, see ANTT, CC, parte II, maço 85, doc. 200 (20 November 1519), CC, parte II, maço 87, doc. 30 (21 January 1520), CC, parte II, maço 88, doc. 137 (3 April 1520), CC, parte II, maço 89, doc. 80 (7 May 1520), CC, parte II, maço 89, doc. 82 (8 May 1520), CC, parte II, maço 90, doc. 13 (7 June 1520).

20. Elbl, "Portuguese Trade," 226.

21. Da Mota and Hair, *East of Mina*, 93; John Vogt, *Portuguese Rule on the Gold Coast, 1469–1682* (Athens: University of Georgia Press, 1979), 55.

22. Vogt, *Portuguese Rule*, 56. See also Brásio, *MMA*, vol. 8, 185; Ralph M. Wiltgen, *Gold Coast Mission History, 1471–1880* (Techny, Ill.: Divine Word Publications, 1956), 20.

23. Brásio, *MMA*, vol. 1, 426, 444, 502, 519; vol. 2, 351, 513; vol. 4, 87, 136.

24. See R. Addo-Fening, "The 'Akim' or 'Achim' in 17th-century and 18th-century Historical Contexts: Who Were They?" *Research Review* 4(2) (1988): 1–15.

25. Albert van Dantzig, "The Akanists: A West Africa Hansa," in *West African Economic and Social History: Studies in Memory of Marion Johnson*, ed. David Henige and T. C. McCaskie (Madison: African Studies Program, University of Wisconsin Press, 1990), 205.

26. Ibid., 206; Erick Tilleman, *A Short and Simple Account of the Country of Guinea and Its Nature*, trans. and ed. Selena A. Winsnes (Madison: African Studies Program, University of Wisconsin, 1994), 31–32.

27. See Pieter de Marees, *Description and Historical Account of the Gold Kingdom of Guinea*, trans. and ed. Adam Jones and Albert van Dantzig (New York: Oxford University Press, 1987); Johann Wilhelm Müller, *Die afrikanische auf der guineischen Gold-Cust gelegene Landschafft Fetu* (as translated in Adam Jones, *German Sources for West African History, 1599–1669* [Wiesbaden: Steiner, 1983]).

28. Müller, *Die Landschafft Fetu*, 208.

29. See the accounts of Andres Ulsheimer, Samuel Brun, Michael Hemmersam, and Johann Müller in Jones, *German Sources*, 29, 85, 207.

30. Kea, *Settlements, Trade, and Polities*, 322–323.

31. On seventeenth- and eighteenth-century kidnappings ("panyard") and pawning from the perspective of British Cape Coast, see, for example, National Archives (NA), Kew, Public Record Office (PRO), Treasury (T) 70/11, memorandum book kept at Cape Coast Castle 4, 17, 25 February 1703, 19 June 1703, 12 February 1704, 6 and 9 September 1704; T 70/1464, Commenda Fort diary, 15 April 1715, 14 September 1715; T 70/1194, letter from Messrs. Roberts, Husbands, and Boteler to Mr. Clifton at Annamaboe, Cape Coast Castle, 12 February 1749; T 70/1476, J. Roberts to Dutch general, 14 November 1750, p. 323.

32. De Marees, *Historical Account*, 51; Jones, *German Sources*, 172.

33. Müller, *Die Landschafft Fetu*, 218, 257.

34. James D. La Fleur, ed. and trans., *Pieter Van Den Broecke's Journal of Voyages to Cape Verde, Guinea, and Angola, 1605–1612* (London: Hakluyt Society, 2000), 64; E. M. Beekman, *The Crippled Heart: An Introduction to the Life, Times and Works of Willem Godschalck van Focquenbroch* (Leiden: Astraea, 1997), 116.

35. Müller, *Die Landschafft Fetu*, chap. 15, pl. 4, and p. 140; Beekman, *Crippled Heart*, 122. There is still a tree, surrounded by a palisade, standing in the middle of the street leading to the Cape Coast Castle. "Shrines" like the one de Marees described are now round, whitewashed cement structures, sometimes draped with a piece of cloth and topped by a small thatch roof (see de Marees, *Historical Account*, 67n2).

36. De Marees, *Historical Account*, 67. Erick Tilleman, a late seventeenth-century trader stationed at Christiansborg, wrote that "their belief in the Fetissero's magic in everything is found throughout the land." See Tilleman, *Simple Account*, 37.

37. Compare the notion of εkɔm (hunger) and akɔm (spiritual process) to the stomach in Dagara thought: "The emptier [the stomach] is, the easier it will be for you to learn since other things within us are better nurtured when the body is not fed." The Dagara hold that "truth emanates from the belly." See Patrice Malidoma Somé, *Of Water and the Spirit* (New York: Arkana and Penguin, 1994), 205, 305. The term *akɔm*, root of *ɔkɔmfoɔ* and a process of spiritual revelation and remedy, functions much like the Dagara concept of *yielbongura* (the thing that knowledge cannot eat). For an early twentieth-century account of an *ɔkɔmfowa*'s training, see R. S. Rattray, *Religion and Art in Ashanti* (Oxford: Clarendon, 1927), 42–43.

38. De Marees, *Historical Account*, 66.

39. Ibid., 67.

40. Ibid.

41. P. E. H. Hair, Adam Jones, and Robin Law, eds., *Barbot on Guinea: The Writings of Jean Barbot on West Africa, 1678–1712* (London: Hakluyt Society, 1992), vol. 2, 381.

42. Kea, *Settlements, Trade, and Polities*, 121, 315.

43. Willem Bosman, *Naauwkeurige Beschryving van de Guinese Goud-, Tand- en Slave-Kust* (1704), translated as *A New and Accurate Description of the Coast of Guinea* (London: J. Knapton, 1705), 75. See also Müller, *Die Landschafft Fetu*, 170.

44. On 11 April 1922, R. S. Rattray also observed an eight-day Apoɔ festival in Axim; see R. S. Rattray, *Ashanti* (Oxford: Clarendon, 1923), 152.

45. Thomas Thompson, *An Account of Two Missionary Voyages...* (London: Benj. Dod, 1758; rpt. by the Society for Promoting Christian Knowledge, 1937), 70.

46. Samuel Brun, *Des Wundartzt und Burgers zu Basel, Schiffjarten* (as translated in Jones, *German Sources*), 93.

47. Ibid., 91.

48. Ibid., 93.

49. Robert Smith, *Warfare and Diplomacy in Pre-colonial West Africa* (London: Currey, 1989), 136.

50. Stanley B. Alpern, "What Africans Got for Their Slaves: A Master List of European Trade Goods," *History in Africa* 22 (1995): 6.

51. G. Thilmans and N. I. de Moraes, "Villault de Bellefond sur la côte occidentale d'Afrique ..." *Bulletin de l'IFAN* 38 (1976): 281, 290–297.

52. On the Komenda wars, see Bosman, *Accurate Description*, 29–40; Robin Law, "The Komenda Wars, 1694–1700: A Revised Narrative," *History in Africa* 34 (2007): 133–168.

53. Kwame Daaku, *Trade and Politics on the Gold Coast, 1600–1720* (Oxford: Clarendon, 1970), 69, 159.

54. Jones, *German Sources*, 137.

55. Alpern, "What Africans Got for Their Slaves," 5–18.

56. For the extensive Portuguese trade in old cloth and linens bartered on the Gold Coast in exchange for gold, see ANTT, CC, parte 1, maço 4, no. 32; CC, parte 1, maço 8, no. 45.

57. For a cultural history of and Akan desire for *akori* beads, see Edith Suzanne Gott, "Precious Beads and Sacred Gold" (PhD diss., Indiana University, 2002), 21–33.

58. Alpern, "What Africans Got for Their Slaves," 13.

59. P. E. H. Hair, "Material on Africa (Other than the Mediterranean and Red Sea Lands) and on the Atlantic Islands, in the Publications of Samuel Purchas, 1613–1626," *History in Africa* 13 (1986): 126.

60. P. E. H. Hair, "Attitudes to Africans in English Primary Sources on Guinea up to 1650," *History in Africa* 25 (1999): 46, 52, 57.

61. Ibid., 58.

62. See P. E. H. Hair, ed., *Travails in Guinea: Robert Baker's "Brefe Dyscourse"* (Liverpool: University of Liverpool Press, 1990).

63. The first English voyages solely to Guinea occurred in the 1550s and 1560s, of which Richard Eden described the first two and William Towerson the next three. Richard Hakluyt published all of these accounts in 1589.

64. Hair, *Travails in Guinea*, 37, 41. Gold was ubiquitous on the Gold Coast, including the use of "weyghtes [weights] and measures." See P. E. H. Hair and J. D. Alsop, eds., *English Seamen and Traders in Guinea, 1553–1565: The New Evidence of Their Wills* (Lewiston, N.Y.: Mellen, 1992), 18.

65. Hair, *Travails in Guinea*, 42–43.

66. Margaret Makepeace, "English Traders on the Guinea Coast, 1657–1668: An Analysis of the East India Company Archives," *History in Africa* 16 (1989): 237.

67. Ibid., 239.

68. Ibid., 239–241.

69. Tilleman, *Simple Account*, 3–4.

70. Van Dantzig, "Akanists," 211.

71. K. G. Davies, *The Royal African Company* (London: Longmans, 1957), 42–43.

72. Zentrales Staatsarchiv (ZSTA) Merseburg, R.65.7 ff. 174–174v, "Instructions for Captain Joris Bartelsen," 7 and 17 July 1680 (as translated in Adam Jones, *Brandenburg Sources for West African History, 1680–1700* [Wiesbaden: Steiner, 1985]), 17.

73. Ibid.

74. ZSTA Merseburg, R.65.7 ff. 117–118, "Treaty with Three Caboceers of Cape Three Points," 16 May 1681 (as translated in Jones, *Brandenburg Sources*), 17.

75. Jones, *Brandenburg Sources*, 3.

76. Ibid., 7.

77. Albert van Dantzig, *The Dutch and the Guinea Coast, 1674–1742: A Collection of Documents from the General State Archive at the Hague* (Accra: Ghana Academy of Arts and Sciences, 1978), 160, 164, 166, 186, 194–196.

78. Ulrich Van der Heyden, *Rote Adler an Afrikas Küste: Die brandenburgisch-preußische Kolonie Großfriedrichsburg in Westafrika* (Berlin: Selignow, 2001), 83–89.

79. Jones, *Brandenburg Sources*, 10.

80. L. F. Rømer, *Tilforladelig Efterretning om Kysten Guinea* (A Reliable Account of the Coast of Guinea), trans. and ed. Selena Axelrod Winsnes (New York: Oxford University Press for the British Academy, 2000), xvii.

81. For a brief note on the rule of Basua and Ado, see Tilleman, *Simple Account*, 28–30.

82. Kwame Arhin, "The Structure of Greater Ashanti (1700–1824)," *Journal of African History* 8(1) (1967): 68; Ivor Wilks, "The Rise of the Akwamu Empire, 1650–1710," *Transactions of the Historical Society of Ghana* 3(2) (1957): 99–136.

83. See NA: PRO, T 70/1515, Richard Graves to council at Cape Coast, James Fort, Accra, 3 April 1742.

84. Ray A. Kea, "Administration and Trade in the Akwamu Empire, 1681–1730," in *West African Culture Dynamics*, ed. B. K. Swartz and R. A. Dumett (The Hague: Mouton, 1980), 371–392.

85. NA: PRO, T 70/29, Thomas Melvil to the committee of the company of merchants trading with Africa, Cape Coast Castle, 11 and 23 July 1751, pp. 3, 6; 14 March 1752, p. 28.

86. NA: PRO, T 70/30, Thomas Melvil to the committee, Cape Coast Castle, 14 March 1753, p. 10.

87. On Asante's role, see James Sanders, "The Expansion of the Fante and the Emergence of Asante in the Eighteenth Century," *Journal of African History* 20(3) (1979): 349–364.

88. George Metcalf, "A Microcosm of Why Africans Sold Slaves: Akan Consumption Patterns in the 1770s," *Journal of African History* 28 (1987): 391.

89. Ivor Wilks, *Forests of Gold: Essays on the Akan and the Kingdom of Asante* (Athens: Ohio University Press, 1993); idem, "Wangara, Akan, and Portuguese in

the Fifteenth and Sixteenth Centuries: I. The Matter of Bitu," *Journal of African History* 23(3) (1982); idem, "Wangara, Akan, and Portuguese in the Fifteenth and Sixteenth Centuries: II. The Struggle for the Trade," *Journal of African History* 23(4) (1982); Larry Yarak, *Asante and the Dutch, 1744–1873* (Oxford: Clarendon, 1990), 6–7; Thomas J. Lewin, *Asante before the British: The Prempean Years, 1875–1900* (Lawrence: Regents Press of Kansas, 1978), 9; T. C. McCaskie, "Death and the Asantehene: A Historical Meditation," *Journal of African History* 30 (1989): 421.

90. Yarak, *Asante and the Dutch*, 7. ɔbirɛmpɔn (pl. abirɛmpɔn) is a term used at different times and interpreted synonymously as "lord," "sovereign," "hero," or "great man" by European observers on the Gold Coast. See J. Rask, *En Kort og Sandfaerdig Rejse-Beskeivelse Til og Fra Guinea* (Trondheim: Trykt hos Jens Christensen Winding, 1754), 90, 171.

91. Akwasi A. Boaten I, "Kumase: Early Settlement up to the End of the 18th Century," *Research Review* (suppl.) 5 (1993): 1–2, 4; idem, "Asante: The Perception and the Utilization of the Environment before the Twentieth Century," *Research Review* 6(2) (1990): 19–27.

92. Boaten I, "Perception and the Utilization," 19, 21–22; idem, "Kumase: Early Settlement," 10.

93. For an early twentieth-century discussion of ɔbirɛmpɔn and an account of the organization and history of Asanteman divisions, see R. S. Rattray, *Ashanti Law and Constitution* (London: Oxford University Press, 1929), 93–98, 127–269.

94. Lewin, *Asante before the British*, 11; Kwame Arhin, "Greater Ashanti," 69; T. C. McCaskie, "Komfo Anokye of Asante: Meaning, History and Philosophy in an African Society," *Journal of African History* 27 (1986): 331.

95. T. C. McCaskie, "Death and the Asantehene: A Historical Meditation," *Journal of African History* 30 (1989): 417–444.

96. Emmanuel Terray has argued that domestic state slavery in Asante declined and domestic slavery increased after 1820 based upon Wilks's argument that the Asante government vigorously intervened to reorient its economy due to the ending of the slave trade, a point disputed by Joseph LaTorre. See Emmanuel Terray, "Long-distance Exchange and the Formation of the State: The Case of the Abron Kingdom of Gyaman," *Economy and Society* 3(3) (1974): 119; Joseph R. LaTorre, "Wealth Surpasses Everything: An Economic History of Asante, 1750–1874" (PhD diss., University of California–Berkeley, 1978), 444–445.

97. Metcalf, "Akan Consumption Patterns," 380.

98. Kea, *Settlements, Trade, and Polities*, 324.

99. Ibid., 325; Gareth Austin, " 'No Elders Were Present': Commoners and Private Ownership in Asante, 1807–96," *Journal of African History* 37 (1996): 4–5.

100. Smith, *Warfare and Diplomacy*, 21. For Denkyira, see J. K. Kumah, "The Rise and Fall of the Kingdom of Denkyira," *Ghana Notes and Queries* 9 (1966); T. C. McCaskie, "Denkyira in the Making of Asante c. 1660–1720," *Journal of African History* 48(1) (2007): 1–25.

101. Van Dantzig, *Dutch and the Guinea Coast*, 79.

102. Ibid., 189–194.

103. Yarak, *Asante and the Dutch*, 101.

104. On Daendels's efforts, see *Journal and Correspondence of H. W. Daendels, November 1815 to January 1817* (Legon: Institute of African Studies, University of Ghana, 1964); van Dantzig, *Dutch and the Guinea Coast*, 84, 130, 203.

105. See Yarak, *Asante and the Dutch*, 111–112.

106. Ivor Wilks, "A Note on Twifo and Akwamu," *Transactions of the Historical Society of Ghana* 3(3) (1958): 215; idem, "Akwamu Empire," 99.

107. Ole Justesen, ed., *Danish Sources for the History of Ghana, 1657–1754*, 2 vols. (Copenhagen: Royal Danish Academy of Sciences and Letters, 2005), vol. 1, 242–243, 357–365, 406–420.

108. Ole Justesen, "Aspects of Eighteenth-century Ghanaian History as Revealed by Danish Sources," *Ghana Notes and Queries* 12 (1972): 9.

109. See Bosman, *Accurate Description*, 75.

110. Justesen, "Ghanaian History," 9–12.

111. Per O. Hernæs, *Slaves, Danes, and African Coast Society* (Trondheim: University of Trondheim, 1995), 92–94.

112. Ibid., 92.

113. Rømer, *Tilforladelig Efterretning*, 78–187; P. E. Isert, *Reise nach Guinea und den Caribäischen Inseln in Columbie*, translated by Selena A. Winsnes as *Letters on West Africa and the Slave Trade: Paul Erdman Iserts' Journey to Guinea and the Caribbean Islands on Columbia* (London: Oxford University Press for the British Academy, 1992), 31–174.

114. Isert, *Letters on West Africa*, 133–135.

115. Smith, *Warfare and Diplomacy*, 8. See also Robert Smith, "Peace and Palaver: International Relations in Pre-colonial West Africa," *Journal of African History* 14(4) (1973): 599–621; Graham W. Irwin, "Precolonial African Diplomacy: The Example of Asante," *International Journal of African Historical Studies* 8(1) (1975): 81–96.

116. The Fante *asafo* (urban) companies were organized for both war and peacetime communal activities and were associated with the rise of coastal townships in the sixteenth and seventeenth centuries (see Kea, *Settlements, Trade, and Polities*, 132). On the battlefield, these companies were organized into right and left wings, with a center along the forest paths, probably marching in single file.

117. Joseph K. Adjaye, *Diplomacy and Diplomats in Nineteenth-century Asante* (Lanham, Md.: University Press of America, 1984), 234, 243.

118. For an eighteenth-century description of preparations for war on the coast, see Isert's *Letters on West Africa*, 31–58.

119. Van Dantzig, *Dutch and the Guinea Coast*, 17–18.

120. Ibid., 56.

121. Ibid., 74.

122. Export calculations derive from the updated "Trans-Atlantic Slave Trade Database" at http://www.slavevoyages.org.

123. David Henige, "John Kabes of Komenda: An Early African Entrepreneur and State Builder," *Journal of African History* 18(1) (1977): 9.

124. Van Dantzig, *Dutch and the Guinea Coast*, 86–87.

125. Martha J. Ehrlich, "Early Akan Gold from the Wreck of the *Whydah*," *African Arts* 22(4) (1989): 52–57, 87–88. The similarities between these pieces, earlier descriptions, and later Asante and Baule work not only outweigh the differences but also support the idea that "Asante" gold ornaments predate the formation of the Asante confederacy and were based upon earlier models.

126. Bosman, *Accurate Description*, 396–468; Dupuis, *Journal*, 21, 256; John Kofi Fynn, *Asante and Its Neighbors, 1700–1807* (Evanston: Northwestern University Press, 1971), 111.

127. Fynn, *Asante and Its Neighbors*, 121, 124.

128. Smith, *Warfare and Diplomacy*, 80; Wilks, "Wangara, Akan, and Portuguese, II," 464.

129. Müller, *Die Landschafft Fetu*, 193.

130. Nehemia Levtzion, "Early Nineteenth-century Arabic Manuscripts from Kumase," *Transaction of the Historical Society of Ghana* 8 (1965): 99; Robin Law, *The Horse in West African History: The Role of the Horse in the Societies of Pre-colonial West Africa* (New York: Published for the International African Institute by Oxford University Press, 1980), 142–143.

131. Smith, *Warfare and Diplomacy*, 86.

132. D. J. E. Maier, "Military Acquisition of Slaves in Asante," in *West African Economic and Social History: Studies in Memory of Marion Johnson*, ed. David Henige and T. C. McCaskie (Madison: African Studies Program, University of Wisconsin Press, 1990), 119–120, 123, 125.

133. James Langlands, a factor at Anomabu, wrote, "I desire that as soon as possible after my decease that my said executors will invest the whole of my effects into slaves or gold dust." He subsequently remitted his profits to kin in London. See NA: PRO, Probate Records of the Prerogative Court of Canterbury (PROB) 11/916, Will of James Langlands, Factor in the Service of the Committee for the Company of Merchants Trading to Africa at Anomabu, 10 February 1766. On wills and will making see P. E. H. Hair and J. D. Alsop, *English Seamen and Traders in Guinea, 1553–1565: The New Evidence of Their Wills* (Lewiston, N.Y.: Mellen, 1992), 73–103, and see also PROB 11/421 and PROB 11/945.

134. Raymond E. Dumett, "Traditional Slavery in the Akan Region in the Nineteenth Century: Sources, Issues, and Interpretations," in *West African Economic and Social History: Studies in Memory of Marion Johnson*, ed. David Henige and T. C. McCaskie (Madison: African Studies Program, University of Wisconsin Press, 1990), 8. See also Martin A. Klein, "Studying the History of Those Who Would Rather Forget: Oral History and the Experience of Slavery," *History in Africa* 16 (1989): 211.

135. T. C. McCaskie, "Office, Land, and Subjects in the History of the Manwere *Fekuo* of Kumase: An Essay in the Political Economy of the Asante State," *Journal of African History* 21 (1980): 192; Metcalf, "Akan Consumption Patterns," 392.

136. Patrick Manning, *Slavery and African Life: Occidental, Oriental, and African Slave Trades* (New York: Cambridge University Press, 1990), 71–85.

137. On these concepts see Sylviane A. Diouf, ed., *Fighting the Slave Trade: West African Strategies* (Athens: Ohio University Press, 2003).

138. By 1800 the Africanization of the Americas was significant, with some 4.5 million persons of African descent, but after that time, Western Christianity, languages, and schooling spread rapidly in the Americas and in Africa due, ironically, to the partial success of African-descendant missionaries. See Herbert S. Klein, *African Slavery in Latin America and the Caribbean* (New York: Cambridge University Press, 1986), 163–187.

139. Smith, *Warfare and Diplomacy*, 135; David Eltis, *The Rise of African Slavery in the Americas* (New York: Cambridge University Press, 2000), 171; Stephen D. Behrendt, David Eltis, and David Richardson, "The Costs of Coercion: African Agency in the Pre-modern Atlantic World," *Economic History Review* 54(3) (2001): 455, 459, 464.

140. Feinberg, *Africans and Europeans in West Africa*, 63.

141. Jean-Baptiste Durand, *Voyage au Sénégal fait dans les années 1785 et 1786*, 2 vols. (Paris: Dentu, 1807), vol. 1, 291.

142. Joseph E. Inikori, *Africans and the Industrial Revolution in England: A Study in International Trade and Economic Development* (New York: Cambridge University Press, 2002), 148–149, 212, 407–442.

NOTES TO CHAPTER 4

1. Ole Justesen, ed., *Danish Sources for the History of Ghana, 1657–1754*, 2 vols. (Copenhagen: Royal Danish Academy of Sciences and Letters, 2005), vol. 1, 184.

2. Ibid., 213.

3. Ibid., 87.

4. Ibid., 545–548.

5. Ibid., 181, 187.

6. Pierre J. Pannet, *Report on the Execrable Conspiracy Carried Out by the Amina Negroes on the Danish Island of St. Jan in America, 1733*, trans. and ed. Aimery P. Caron and Arnold R. Highfield (Christiansted, St. Croix: Antilles Press, 1984), 17; Christian George Andreas Oldendorp, *A Caribbean Mission*, ed. Johann Jakob Bossard; trans. Arnold R. Highfield and Vladimir Barac (Ann Arbor: Karoma, 1987), 235–236; Waldemar Westergaard, *The Danish West Indies under Company Rule, 1671–1754* (New York: Macmillan, 1917), 166–178; John P. Knox, *A Historical Account of St. Thomas* (New York: Scribner, 1852), 71–77; Ray A. Kea, "'When I Die, I Shall Return to My Own Land': An 'Amina' Slave Rebellion in the Danish West Indies, 1733–1734," in *The Cloth of Many Colored Silks: Papers on History and Society, Ghanaian and Islamic in Honor of Ivor Wilks*, ed. John Hunwicks and Nancy Lawler (Evanston: Northwestern University Press, 1996), 160.

7. The fictional source, which is based on a close reading of the archival evidence, is John L. Anderson's *Night of the Silent Drums* (New York: Scribner, 1975).

8. On Jama and the *Laarurg Galley*, see Justesen, *Danish Sources*, vol. 1, 338, 424, 444, 470.

9. Pannet, *Conspiracy*, 17; Oldendorp, *Caribbean Mission*, 235.

10. Kea, "When I Die," 171–172; Leif Svalesen, *The Slave Ship* Fredensborg (Indianapolis: Indiana University Press, 2000), 199.

11. Kea, "When I Die," 187.

12. Johan Lorentz Carstens, St. Thomas slaveholder who left the island in 1739 and wrote *En Almindelig Beskrivelse om Alle de Danske*, in *The Kamina Folk: Slavery and Slave Life in the Danish West Indies*, ed. George F. Tyson and Arnold R. Highfield (U.S. Virgin Islands: Virgin Islands Humanities Council, 1994), 7. Waldemar Westergaard was also convinced: "The El Mina negroes," the source of the term "Amina," were "liable to grow violently mutinous." See Westergaard, *Danish West Indies*, 44.

13. Neville A. T. Hall, *Slave Society in the Danish West Indies: St. Thomas, St. John, and St. Croix*, ed. B. W. Higman (Kingston: University of the West Indies Press, 1994), 70–71; see also Isidor Paiewonsky, *Eyewitness Accounts of Slavery in the Danish West Indies* (New York: Fordham University Press, 1989).

14. The report of these events is based on the written account of one of the "trial" judges, Engelbret Hesselberg, and was translated by Waldemar Westergaard in "Account of the Negro Rebellion on St. Croix, Danish West Indies, 1759," *Journal of Negro History* 11(1) (1926): 53–56. See also Waldemar Westergaard, "A St. Croix Map of 1766: With a Note on Its Significance in West Indian Plantation Economy," *Journal of Negro History* 23(2) (1938): 225–227 for names and properties of principal white officials involved in the alleged 1759 conspiracy.

15. Westergaard, "Account of the Negro Rebellion," 58–61.

16. According to Hesselberg's account, Prince Qvakoe witnessed an oath wherein two of the key actors "cut themselves in the finger in his presence, mixed the blood with earth and water, and drank it with the assurance [to each other] that they would not confess to the conspiracy no matter what pain they were subjected to." See ibid., 57.

17. Christian George Andreas Oldendorp, *Historie der caribischen Inseln Sanct Thomas, Sanct Crux, und Sanct Jan, insbesondere der dasigen Neger und der Mission der evangelischen Brüder-Unität Herrnhut, erster Teil*, ed. Gudrun Meier, Stephan Palmié, Peter Stein, and Horst Ulbricht (Berlin: Staatliches Museum für Völkerkunde Dresden, 2000), 383–384. I thank John Thornton for a copy of this annotated German edition and Susanna Rudofsky for help with the translation. Johann Jakob Bossard edited Oldendorp's original and lengthy manuscript considerably (to Oldendorp's disapproval), as well as one "full" and one partial English translation, respectively, of Bossard's edited version has been published: Oldendorp's *Caribbean Mission* and Soi-Daniel W. Brown, "From the Tongues of Africa: A Partial Translation of Oldendorp's Interviews," *Plantation Society* 2(1) (1983): 37–61. It should be noted, however, that the Karoma English translation and perhaps Brown's translation (both are based on Bossard's edition) lack many pages found in the German original.

18. Oldendorp asked his informants to say the numbers 1–10, 11, 12, 13, 20, 30, 100, and 1,000 in their indigenous languages. The responses in Akan were relatively the same between the Amina, Akkim, and Akripon, but they departed from Akkran (Gã) and were certainly different from the Papaa (of which, according to Oldendorp, the Arrada [Allada], Affong [Fon], Nagoo [Yorùbá], Apeschi [Kpessi], and Attolli [Tori] all belong). See Oldendorp, *Historie der caribischen*, 458–459, 464, and 460–463, for the following table, which highlights the disparities found in the foregoing comparisons:

Group	God	Sun	Moon	Human	Hand	Foot	Head	Woman
Amina	Jankombum (*Onyankopɔn*)	Erwiaa (*awia*, sun)	Osseram (*osram*, moon)	Ojippa (*onipa*, person)	Ensaa (*nsa*, hand)	Onang (*nan*, leg)	Uettirri (*tiri* or *ti*, head)	Obbaa (*ɔbaa*, woman)
Akkim	Jankombum	Awia	Osseranm	Nippa	Ensaa	Onang	Metih (*me ti*, my head)	Obia
Papaa	Gajiwodu	Wetaga	Su-ede	Emme	Allo	Afo	Ta	Djonnu

19. Ibid., 417.
20. Ibid., 386.
21. Ibid., 387–388.
22. Ibid., 394.
23. Ibid., 383 (emphasis added).
24. Richard Price and Sally Price, eds., *Stedman's Surinam: Life in an Eighteenth-century Slave Society* (Baltimore: John's Hopkins University Press, 1992), 259.
25. Kwasi Konadu, *Indigenous Medicine and Knowledge in African Society* (New York: Routledge, 2007), 33.
26. Oldendorp, *Historie der caribischen*, 677–678.
27. Hall, *Slave Society in the Danish West Indies*, 58, 81.
28. Ibid., 112–113. For a Danish account of obeah or "obi," see Lieutenant Brady's observations in Tyson and Highfield, *Kamina Folks*, 172–174.
29. Oldendorp, *Historie der caribischen*, 482–483.
30. Ibid., 483–484.
31. Westergaard, "St. Croix Map," 219–223; William Chapman, "Slave Villages in the Danish West Indies: Changes of the Late Eighteenth and Early Nineteenth Centuries," *Perspectives in Vernacular Architecture* 4 (1991): 109, 116.
32. Tyson and Highfield, *Kamina Folk*, 121.
33. Caryl Johnson, "A West African Reflection in the Danish West Indies," *Nyame Akuma* 59 (2003): 80–82.
34. Chapman, "Slave Villages," 111.
35. For an eyewitness account of the 1848 "emancipation revolt," see "Stadthauptmand Chamberlain von Scholten's Narrative," in *Leaflets from the Danish West Indies*, ed. Charles E. Taylor (London: Dawson and Sons, 1888), 126–132.
36. Petition for Compensation for the Loss of Slaves by Emancipation in the Danish West Indies, June 1851, St. Thomas and St. John, in *Journal of Negro History* 2(4) (1917): 423.
37. Hall, *Slave Society in the Danish West Indies*, 92, 161. On Coffe Smith, see Tyson and Highfield, *Kamina Folk*, 100–101.
38. Rose Mary Allen, "Di Ki Manera? A Social History of Afro-Curaçaoans, 1863–1917" (PhD diss., University of Utrecht, 2007), 64–65.
39. Albert van Dantzig, *The Dutch and the Guinea Coast, 1674–1742: A Collection of Documents from the General State Archive at the Hague* (Accra: Ghana Academy of Arts and Sciences, 1978), 23, 156.
40. Cornelis Goslinga, *A Short History of the Netherlands Antilles and Surinam* (Boston: Nijhoff, 1979), 108, 134; Christopher R. DeCorse, *An Archaeology of Elmina: Africans and Europeans on the Gold Coast, 1400–1900* (Washington, D.C.: Smithsonian Institution Press, 2001), 27–28. DeCorse takes the position that small numbers of Africans from the Elmina settlement were actually captured and transported to the Americas.
41. Allen, "Social History," 68, 71.
42. Stephen D. Behrendt, David Eltis, and David Richardson, "The Costs of Coercion: African Agency in the Pre-modern Atlantic World," *Economic History Review* 54(3) (2001): 473–474.
43. Van Dantzig, *Dutch and the Guinea Coast*, 84.
44. John Gabriel Stedman, *Narrative of a Five Years Expedition against the Revolted Negroes of Surinam (1790)*, ed. Richard Price and Sally Price (Baltimore: Johns

Hopkins University Press, 1988), 175. See also the abridged version of Stedman's account edited by Price and Price, *Stedman's Surinam*.

45. Van Dantzig, *Dutch and the Guinea Coast*, 121.

46. Price and Price, *Stedman's Surinam*, xii. Richard Price, *Travels with Tooy: History, Memory, and the African American Imagination* (Chicago: University of Chicago Press, 2007), 294.

47. Price, *Travels with Tooy*, 291–294. For Saramaka perspectives on their formative history in Suriname, see Richard Price, *First-time: The Historical Vision of an Afro-American People* (Baltimore: Johns Hopkins University Press, 1983).

48. Stedman, *Narrative*, 175.

49. Price and Price, *Stedman's Surinam*, 260.

50. Behrendt, Eltis, and Richardson, "Costs of Coercion," 467.

51. Wim Hoogbergen, "The History of the Suriname Maroons," in *Resistance and Rebellion in Suriname: Old and New*, ed. Gary Brana-Shute (Williamsburg: College of William and Mary, 1990), 81–82.

52. Robert Schomburgk, an early nineteenth-century surveyor appointed by the British Crown, described Maroon treaty making as follows: "A small quantity of earth was mixed with water in a calabash, and each of the contractors having made an incision in his arm for the purpose of procuring some drops of blood, it was mixed up with the earth, of which the white deputies as well as the Negro Chiefs were obliged to drink in pledge of their faithful obligation to the contract." See Peter Rivière, ed., *The Guiana Travels of Robert Schomburgk, 1835–1844* (London: Hakluyt Society, 2006), vol. 2, 182, 190.

53. Hoogbergen, "Suriname Maroons," 85; *Essai historique sur la Colonie de Surinam* (Paramaribo: s.n., 1788), 91, in Jacob R. Marcus and Stanley F. Chyet, eds., *Historical Essay on the Colony of Surinam, 1788*, trans. Simon Cohen (New York: American Jewish Archives and KTAV, 1974), 67.

54. Marcus and Chyet, *Historical Essay*, 57.

55. Price, *Travels with Tooy*, 298.

56. Hoogbergen, "History of the Suriname Maroons," 66.

57. Price, *Travels with Tooy*, 293, 301.

58. See Ibid., 150. Christian proselytization in the late eighteenth century was also unsuccessful among "freed Negroes and slaves." See Marcus and Chyet, *Historical Essay*, 135.

59. Price, *Travels with Tooy*, 152, 156.

60. Kenneth Bilby, "Swearing by the Past, Swearing to the Future: Sacred Oaths, Alliances, and Treaties among the Guianese and Jamaican Maroons," *Ethnohistory* 44(4) (1997): 674.

61. Melville J. Herskovits and Frances S. Herskovits, *Suriname Folk-Lore* (New York: Columbia University Press, 1936), 62, 65; Bilby, "Swearing by the Past," 683.

62. In early nineteenth-century Jamaica, an old woman of African descent told Matthew Lewis, a British planter, "You no my massa, you my *tata*." Here, *tata* meant "father" in Kikôngo, and there were certainly Kikôngo speakers in nineteenth-century Jamaica. See Matthew Lewis, *Journal of a West India Proprietor*, ed. Judith Terry (New York: Oxford University Press, 1999), 147.

63. Herskovits and Herskovits, *Suriname Folk-Lore*, 44–45, 62, 743–750; Price, *Travels with Tooy*, 290, 298, 313–352. The critiques of Melville Herskovits's

"methodology" for uncovering the African meanings of Saramaka linguistic and cultural materials are duly noted. See Price, *Travels with Tooy*, 302; Richard Price and Sally Price, *The Root of Roots: Or, How Afro-American Anthropology Got Its Start* (Chicago: Prickly Paradigm, 2003).

64. Herskovits and Herskovits, *Suriname Folk-Lore*, 21.
65. Price and Price, *Stedman's Surinam*, 267.
66. Herskovits and Herskovits, *Suriname Folk-Lore*, 97.
67. On the Guan term *dede* or *ɔdede* in Akuapem (Ghana), see Kwame A. Labi, "Akanization of the Hill Guan Arts," *Research Review* 18(2) (2002): 1–21.
68. Price, *Travels with Tooy*, 297, 306.
69. Ibid., 289.
70. Richard Price and Sally Price, *Maroon Arts: Cultural Vitality in the African Diaspora* (Boston: Beacon Press, 1999), 24.
71. J. H. Kwabena Nketia, *Our Drums and Drummers* (Tema: Ghana Publishing, 1968), 10, 16; Stedman, *Narrative*, 539; Jean Hurault, *Africains de Guyane* (The Hague: Mouton, 1970).
72. Price and Price, *Maroon Arts*, 256; Nketia, *Our Drums*, 16. These kinds of drums are also found among the Maroons of Jamaica.
73. Price and Price, *Maroon Arts*, 249. This photo and others show the clear resemblance between "play" and *akɔm* dancing.
74. Marcus and Chyet, *Historical Essay*, 156, 159–160.
75. Price, *First-time*, 155.
76. Marcus and Chyet, *Historical Essay*, 160–162; Price and Price, *Stedman's Surinam*, 300–301, 263.
77. Price, *First-time*, 156–159.
78. Price and Price, *Stedman's Surinam*, 201.
79. Jerome S. Handler and Kenneth M. Bilby, "On the Early Use and Origin of the Term 'Obeah' in Barbados and the Anglophone Caribbean," *Slavery and Abolition* 22(2) (2001): 92.
80. Allen, "Social History," 242. In the non-Catholic spiritual tradition, there exists one *zumbi* (evil spirit) named Kofi but who is described as "a luminous erring spirit."
81. Goslinga, *Short History*, 185–268; Bilby, "Swearing by the Past," 679. Desi Bouterse remains one of the wealthiest and most politically influential men in Suriname, while the vast majority of the country's populace, particularly African descendants, live in acute poverty.
82. Allen, "Social History," 91.
83. Okke ten Hove and Frank Dragtenstein, *Manumissies in Suriname, 1832–1863* (Utrecht: Centrum voor Latijns-Amerikaanse en Caraïbische Studies, University of Utrecht, 1997), 45.
84. Ibid., 52–53.
85. Price and Price, *Stedman's Surinam*, 269.

NOTES TO CHAPTER 5

1. Robin Law, "Ethnicities of Enslaved Africans in the Diaspora: On the Meanings of 'Mina' (Again)," *History in Africa* 32 (2005): 267; E. Kofi Agorsah and

Thomas Butler, "Archaeological Investigations of Historic Kormantse: Cultural Identities," *The African Diaspora Archaeology Network Newsletter*, September 2008, 3.

2. NA: PRO, CO 1/19, no. 5, "A Briefe Narrative of the Trade and Present Condition of the Company of Royall Adventures of English Trading into Africa," 1665; CO 1/17, no. 60, "An Extract of Letters from Cormantin and Other Places in Africa," June to September 1663; CO 1/17, no. 77, "Protest of John Valekenburgh, Director-General of the [Dutch Possessions]... against John Stoaks, Commander-in-Chief of all the English Forces," 3–13 September 1663; CO 1/17 nos. 110–111, "The Company of Royal Adventurers Trading into Africa to [the King]," 1663.

3. See J. S. G, *The Detector Detected: or, State of Affairs on the Gold Coast* (London: W. Owen, 1753); [anonymous], *The Trade to Africa Considered, and Demonstrated to the Improved to the Nations' Benefit* (n.p., 1707?), 1; *An Account of the Royal African Companies Forts and Castles on the Coast of Africa* (n.p., n.d.); John Roberts, *Extracts from an Account of the State of the British Forts, on the Gold Coast of Africa* (London: J. Bew, 1778), 6, 14, 18, 38.

4. Law, "Ethnicities of Enslaved Africans," 261.

5. Calculations derived from David Eltis, Stephen D. Behrendt, David Richardson, and Herbert S. Klein, *The Transatlantic Slave Trade: A Database on CD-ROM* (New York: Cambridge University Press, 1998); David Eltis, "The Volume and Structure of the Transatlantic Slave Trade: A Reassessment," *William and Mary Quarterly* 58(1) (2001): 17–46; and http://www.slavevoyages.org.

6. Committee for Trade and Plantations [Great Britain], *Return from the Commissions for Trade and Plantations, to the Honourable House of Commons...* (London: Committee for Trade and Plantations, 1777), 15; calculations are derived from http://www.slavevoyages.org.

7. Between 1780 and 1792, 124 sampled Gold Coast voyages accounted for a mortality rate of 5.6 percent, compared to much higher rates at less than half of that sample for other West African groups and ports. This is even more remarkable in view of the fact that the decade 1781–1791 saw the highest recorded exportation of people from the Gold Coast (at least 135,000), and planters were willing to pay higher costs, including those incurred as a result of vessel- and plantation-based revolts, for these captives. See Stephen D. Behrendt, "The Annual Volume and Regional Distribution of the British Slave Trade, 1780–1807," *Journal of African History* 38 (1997): 193; Eltis, "Volume and Structure," 17–46.

8. Jerome S. Handler, "Survivors of the Middle Passage: Life Histories of Enslaved Africans in British America," *Slavery and Abolition* 23(1) (2002): 27.

9. For details of these "life stories," see Ibid.

10. Board of Trade [Great Britain], *Journal of the Commissioners for Trade and Plantations, 1704–1782*, 14 vols. (London: His Majesty's Stationery Office, 1925–1938), vol. 14, 134, 141, 144; vol. 5, 259; vol. 9, 6–7, 13.

11. For an account of early English sugar plantations in Barbados during the late 1660s, see NA: PRO, CO 1/22, no. 20.

12. Anonymous, "Great Newes from the Barbadoes or, a True and Faithful Account of the Grand Conspiracy of the Negroes against the English" (London: L. Curtis, 1676), 9.

13. William Hardringe and Nicholas Prideoux to the Royal African Company, 11 February 1692/1693, in Elizabeth Donnan, *Documents Illustrative of the History of the*

Slave Trade to America, 4 vols. (Washington, D.C.: Carnegie Institution of Washington, 1930), vol. 1, 391.

14. For the details of the *James*'s voyage see Donnan, *Documents*, vol. 1, 199–209; NA: PRO, T 70/1211, fol. 100. A century later, the voyage of the sloop *Friends*, which arrived in Barbados from Anomabu en route to Grenada, provides another traumatic story. See Donnan, *Documents*, vol. 3, 74–75.

15. Stephen D. Behrendt, David Eltis, and David Richardson, "The Costs of Coercion: African Agency in the Pre-modern Atlantic World," *Economic History Review* 54(3) (2001): 461.

16. Donnan, *Documents*, vol. 1, 207.

17. David A. Collins, *Practical Rules for the Management and Medical Treatment of Negro Slaves in the Sugar Colonies* (London: J. Barfield, 1803), 39–40; *Journal of the Commissioners*, vol. 9, 13, 20.

18. *Great Newes from the Barbadoes*, 12.

19. Eric J. Sundquist, *Strangers in the Land: Blacks, Jews, post-Holocaust America* (Cambridge, Mass.: Belknap Press of Harvard University Press, 2005), 293.

20. NA: PRO, CO 9/10, Antigua Council Minutes, "Negro's [sic] Conspiracy," fols. 40–91; "A Genuine Narrative of the Intended Conspiracy of the Negroes at Antigua" (Dublin: R. Reilly, 1737), 20–23; David Barry Gaspar, *Bondmen and Rebel: A Study of Master-slave Relations in Antigua with Implications for Colonial British America* (Baltimore: Johns Hopkins University Press, 1985), 30–35. See also the correspondences in NA: PRO, CO 152/22–23.

21. NA: PRO, CO 9/10, fols. 75–76; *Narrative of the Intended Conspiracy*, 8; Gaspar, *Bondmen and Rebel*, 22.

22. John Thornton, "War, the State, and Religious Norms in 'Coromantee' Thought: The Ideology of an African American Nation," in *Possible Pasts: Becoming Colonial in Early America*, ed. Robert Blair St. George (Ithaca: Cornell University Press, 2000), 195.

23. Philip D. Morgan, "Conspiracy Scares," *William and Mary Quarterly* 59(1) (2002): 165.

24. Gaspar, *Bondmen and Rebel*, 9, 249.

25. NA: PRO, CO 9/10, fols. 65–66; *Narrative of the Intended Conspiracy*, 5. On the 1712 New York revolt, see Kenneth Scott, "The Slave Insurrection in New York in 1712," *New York Historical Society Quarterly* 45 (1961): 53; New York Supreme Court of Judicature Minute Book, 6 June 1710–5 June 1714 (engrossed), New York City County Clerk Archives, New York.

26. *Narrative of the Intended Conspiracy*, 4; Willem Bosman, *Naauwkeurige Beschryving van de Guinese Goud-, Tand- en Slave-Kust* (1704), translated as *A New and Accurate Description of the Coast of Guinea* (London: J. Knapton, 1705), 132, 135. Bosman's focus on Axim was explicit: "I shall content myself with describing that [i.e., Axim] only." See also Ray Kea, *Settlements, Trade, and Polities in the Seventeenth-century Gold Coast* (Baltimore: Johns Hopkins University Press, 1981), 101–105; Albert van Dantzig, "English Bosman and Dutch Bosman: A Comparison of the Texts, II," *History in Africa* 3 (1976): 118.

27. NA: PRO, CO 9/10, fol. 91.

28. Bosman, *Accurate Description*, 137.

29. *Narrative of the Intended Conspiracy*, 6, 9.

30. T. E. Bowdich, *Mission from Cape Coast Castle to Ashantee* (London: J. Murray, 1819), 256.

31. *Narrative of the Intended Conspiracy*, 8.

32. T. C. McCaskie, "Time and Calendar in Nineteenth-century Asante: An Exploratory Essay," *History in Africa* 7 (1980): 179–200; idem, *State and Society in Precolonial Asante* (New York: Cambridge University Press, 1995), 145; Ivor Wilks, *Asante in the Nineteenth Century* (New York: Cambridge University Press, 1989), 112.

33. Data for this voyage derive from http://www.slavevoyages.org.

34. *Narrative of the Intended Conspiracy*, 8.

35. Bosman, *Accurate Description*, 33–40; Robin Law, "The Komenda Wars, 1694–1700: A Revised Narrative," *History in Africa* 34 (2007): 149.

36. Bosman, *Accurate Description*, 133–137. Bosman observed that the ɔbirɛmpɔn was usually in the service of an ɔhene, such as Jama of the St. John revolt, who was in the service of Akwamuhene Ansa Kwao.

37. Tomboy, labeled a "creole," could have been Coromantee, and this may clarify a point missed by both David Gaspar and John Thornton, who both argue that an individual named Quashee (Kwasi) was a "creole" because he did not speak Coromantee and was not born on the Gold Coast, though his mother was Coromantee (see NA: PRO, CO 9/10, fol. 66). Yet, when we read this statement and the evidence for Quashee's biography in the context of Akan culture, then by virtue of having an Akan mother, Quashee or any other offspring was born culturally Akan. Quashee himself had made this exact claim.

38. Enslaved witnesses who testified included three individuals named Quamina, Quaco, and Cuffee.

39. NA: PRO, CO 9/10, fol. 91.

40. The "Quashee" stereotype, a version of the "Sambo" character, may have its origin in the Akan (Twi) term *kwasea* (fool), as distinct from the "soul-day name" Kwasi (Sunday-born male). In English and perhaps in other European language pronunciation, *kwasea* would have resembled "Quashea," a probable source for the insult and stereotype "Quashee" rather than the name "Quash" or "Quashie" (Kwasi).

41. On the concept of "dibia" within indigenous Igbo cosmology and spiritual practice, see John Anenechukwu Umeh, *After God Is Dibia: Igbo Cosmology, Divination, and Sacred Science in Nigeria*, 2 vols. (London: Karnak, 1997, 1999).

42. Jerome S. Handler and Kenneth M. Bilby, "On the Early Use and Origin of the Term 'Obeah' in Barbados and the Anglophone Caribbean," *Slavery and Abolition* 22(2) (2001): 89, 93–94. For an insightful discussion of *obeah* and its relation to other African-derived traditions in Jamaica, see Dianne M. Stewart, *Three Eyes for the Journey: African Dimensions of the Jamaican Religious Experience* (New York: Oxford University Press, 2005), 36–58.

43. Artist Romare Bearden had an exhibit in New York City titled "Rituals of the Obeah," celebrating his rural North Carolina past and his (then) current Caribbean residence, as "obeah" is still practiced in those places. See Michael Brenson, "Art: Romare Bearden, 'Ritual of the Obeah,'" *New York Times* (30 November 1984), sec. C, 23.

44. Gaspar, *Bondmen and Rebel*, 90.

45. Kwasi Konadu, *Indigenous Medicine and Knowledge in African Society* (New York: Routledge, 2007), 50–51.

46. Coffy (Kofi) became the national hero of an independent Guyana through its first prime minister and president, Linden Forbes Sampson Burnham.

47. Koninklijk Huisarchief (Dutch Royal House Archives), The Hague, no. G2/54/Ib, letter of Robert Douglas to Earl Bentinck, 25 May 1764, fol. 1. I am grateful archivist L. J. A. Pennings for a copy of this letter.

48. Barbara L. Blair, "Wolfert Simon van Hoogenheim in the Berbice Slave Revolt of 1763–1764," *Bijdragen tot de Taal-, Land- en Volkenkunde* 140(1) (1984): 60–61.

49. Governor W. S. van Hoogenheim's journal of "the revolution of the Negro slaves" began on 28 February, but his fear was no different from that of a colony full of frightened and powerless whites a few days earlier. See the "Journal of W. S. van Hoogenheim, 28 Feb. 1763–31 December 1764," trans. Barbara L. Blair, unpublished manuscript, University of Guyana Library, 1973, 1–11. I am grateful to Hetty London and Gloria Cummings for a copy of this document.

50. Blair, "Slave Revolt," 63–64; James Rodway, *Guiana: British, Dutch, and French* (New York: Scribner, 1912), 96–97.

51. *Journal of van Hoogenheim*, 48–49.

52. Ibid., 47.

53. John Gabriel Stedman, *Narrative of a Five Years Expedition against the Revolted Negroes of Surinam (1790)*, ed. Richard Price and Sally Price (Baltimore: Johns Hopkins University Press, 1988), 76–77; Sundquist, *Strangers in the Land*, 294; Cornelis Goslinga, *A Short History of the Netherlands Antilles and Surinam* (Boston: Martinus Nijhoff, 1979), 117.

54. Robert Douglas to Earl Bentinck, fol. 3.

55. Ibid., fol. 2. Douglas named "Acabre" as "the Chief of the Congo Negroes (Cannibals)," but his fate, as of Douglas's writing, was yet to be decided.

56. *Essequebo and Demerary Gazette* 2(216) (14 February 1807); also 2(61, 63–66) (28 February–4 April 1807).

57. Ibid., 2(65) (28 March 1807).

58. Ibid., 2(53–54, 56–58, 60–61, 89) (3–31 January, 28 February, 12 September 1807).

59. School of Oriental and African Studies (SOAS) Archives, London, CWM/LMS/West Indies and British Guiana/Journals/Box 1, John Smith Papers, John Smith diary, entry for 23 July 1823.

60. Ibid.

61. Ibid., diary entry for 18 August 1823.

62. Brian L. Moore, *Cultural Power, Resistance, and Pluralism: Colonial Guyana, 1838–1900* (Montreal: McGill-Queen's University Press, 1995), 145.

63. Ibid., 138–139.

64. Monica Schuler, "Liberated Central Africans in Nineteenth-century Guyana." Paper presented at the Harriet Tubman Seminar, York University, 24 January 2000, 20, 35n84.

65. Moore, *Cultural Power*, 139.

66. Well after emancipation and increased Christianization of these enslaved peoples, the spiritual practices subsumed under the category of *obeah* endured and had a much wider reach in the Caribbean throughout the nineteenth and twentieth centuries. For example, Pierre, a "free black man" of Grenada, was charged with

practicing *obeah* and was tried and convicted by the supreme court, but he adamantly protested his conviction on the grounds that "no evidence was produced or shewn to the Court or Jury... in the practice of Obeah." See NA: PRO, CO 101/78, no. 5, fol. 19. In 1878 St. Lucia passed an ordinance that made *obeah* punishable by public flogging, though "there have been as yet no cases." See NA: PRO, CO 321/22, no. 12, fol. 160.

67. Schuler, "Liberated Central Africans," 1–3.

68. Ibid., 2.

69. On these matters see Rosanne Adderley, *"New Negroes from Africa": Slave Trade Abolition and Free African Settlements in the Nineteenth-century Caribbean* (Bloomington: Indiana University Press, 2006); Leslie Bethell, "The Mixed Commissions for the Suppression of the Transatlantic Slave Trade in the Nineteenth Century," *Journal of African History* 7(1) (1966): 70–93; Robert Conrad, "Neither Slave nor Free: The Emancipados of Brazil, 1818–1868," *Hispanic American Historical Review* 53(1) (1973): 50–70.

70. Behrendt, "Annual Volume," 199.

71. Goslinga, *Short History*, 157.

72. Calculations derived from Eltis et al., *Transatlantic Slave Trade*; updated at http://www.slavevoyages.org.

73. Richard Cullen Rath, "African Music in Seventeenth-century Jamaica: Cultural Transit and Transition," *William and Mary Quarterly* 50(4) (1993): 707. The "Papa" song was too short, and, thus, it did not form part of Rath's analysis.

74. Ibid., 711.

75. Ibid., 726.

76. Colonel C. L. G. Harris, "The True Traditions of my Ancestors," in *Maroon Heritage: Archaeological, Ethnographic, and Historical Perspectives*, ed. E. Kofi Agorsah (Kingston: Canoe Press, 1994), 36–63. See the text to the compilation of Maroon music by Kenneth Bilby, *Drums of Defiance: Maroon Music from the Earliest Free Black Communities of Jamaica* (Washington, D.C.: Smithsonian/Folkways Recordings, 1992).

77. Kenneth Bilby, *True-born Maroons* (Gainesville: University of Florida Press, 2007), 19.

78. See Jacqueline Cogdell DjeDje, "Remembering Kojo: History, Music, and Gender in the January Sixth Celebration of the Jamaican Accompong Maroons," *Black Music Research Journal* 18(1–2) (1998): 115.

79. Bruce L. Mouser, *A Slaving Voyage to Africa and Jamaica: The Log of the Sandown, 1793–1794* (Bloomington: Indiana University Press, 2002), 115. In 1793 the *Alice* and the *Eagle* each experienced an on-board "slave insurrection" coming from the Gold Coast to Jamaica but landed at the port of Kingston with little loss of its human cargo.

80. *Royal Gazette* (Postscript of the *Royal Gazette*), Kingston, 15(14) (25 October–November 1793), 20, 23–24; see also the *Royal Gazette*, Kingston (4–11 June 1803) for four Coromantee under English names.

81. Thomas Thistlewood's estate included a number of Coromantee: Abba (Yaa), Quashe (Kwasi; b. April 1775), Phibbah (Afia; b. April 1776), Jimmy (a "Coromantee or Shanti [Asante]"), Phoebe, Cudjoe (Kwadwo), and Pompey (an "old Coromantee" described as distempered and with elephantiasis). Jimmy, Cudjoe, and Phoebe were shipmates who disembarked at Lucea (in the western part of Jamaica) and were sold on Monday, 29 April 1765, and branded on the right shoulder with the initials "TT."

See Douglass Hall, *In Miserable Slavery: Thomas Thistlewood in Jamaica, 1750–86* (Kingston: University of the West Indies Press, 1999), 135, 146, 201, 203, 315–316.

82. Bryan Edwards, *History, Civil and Commercial of the British West Indies*, 5 vols. (London: T. Miller, 1819), vol. 2, 80–82, 126–127. This text was first published in 1793.

83. John Thornton, *Africa and Africans in the Making of the Atlantic World, 1400–1800* (New York: Cambridge University Press, 1998), 321; Michael Mullin, *Africa in America: Slave Acculturation and Resistance in the American South and the British Caribbean, 1736–1831* (Urbana: University of Illinois Press, 1992), 30. For his discussion on the Akan, see Thornton, *Africa and Africans*, 320–332. See also Hall, *Miserable Slavery*, 160–161.

84. Bryan Edwards, Jamaican planter and historian, wrote that Gold Coast Africans were known as "Koromantees" in the British Caribbean and claimed that Tacky was a "Chief in Guiney" and had used obeah by an elder "Koromantee" in his rebellion. See Edwards, *History*, vol. 2, 59, 113.

85. Cuafee and Quaco were two of seventeen who were emancipated by an act of the Jamaica Assembly for their loyalty. See NA: PRO, CO 139/21, no. 25, 18 December 1760. Douglass Hall notes that another rebellion in St. Mary led by enslaved Coromantee in 1765 was planned but quelled. In 1767 another Cuafee betrayed a conspiracy or "slave rebellion." See NA: PRO, CO 139/23, no. 113, "Act to free two Negro men slaves and compensate their owner ... ," 21 December 1767.

86. Among other benefits of the treaty, the Maroons of Trelawny Town were granted about fifteen hundred acres of land in 1739 in the parish of St. James. For the text of the treaty, see Mavis C. Campbell, *The Maroons of Jamaica, 1655–1796: A History of Resistance, Collaboration, & Betrayal* (Trenton: Africa World Press, 1990), 126–128.

87. On obeah from the perspective of a Jamaican planter, see Matthew Lewis, *Journal of a West India Proprietor*, ed. Judith Terry (New York: Oxford University Press, 1999), 190–194.

88. On *obeah, myalism, kumina*, and other African-centered spiritual traditions in Jamaica, see Stewart, *Three Eyes for the Journey*, and Lewis, *West India Proprietor*, 84–93, 220, 222–223, 286. On *kumina* and its Bakôngo roots in Jamaica, see Maureen Warner Lewis, *The Nkuyu: Spirit Messengers of the Kumina* (Mona, Kingston: Savacou, 1977); Kenneth Bilby and Fu-Kiau Bunseki, *Kumina: A Kongo-based Tradition in the New World* (Brussels: Centre d'étude et de documentation africaines, 1983); Myrna Dolores Bain, *Kumina: A Field Study of Cultural Resistance in Jamaica* (New York: Author, 1985).

89. On Sharpe's rebellion from December 1831 to the new year of 1832, see NA: PRO, CO 137/184.

90. One example of these crimes and punishments occurred in Hanover, the second smallest parish of Jamaica, between St. James and Westmoreland. See National Library of Jamaica (NLJ), "1832 Calendar of Prisoners for Hanover," MS 769. Some details of other executions in Hanover for previous years can be found in NLJ, "Condemnation of Slaves," MS 729, 14 July 1824.

91. NLJ, "Proclamation [Issued by] Somerset Lowry, Earl of Belmore," MS 1873, 3 February 1832; NA: PRO, CO 137/181, "Notice to Rebellious Slaves," Jamaica, 2 January 1832.

92. NA: PRO, CO 137/192 no. 46, fol. 197, letter addressed to the apprentices, Jamaica, 1834. Governor Sligo also wrote the following in private correspondence: "I can assure you that the feeling between Master and apprentice is decidedly more what it ought to be, than I have yet seen it." See West Yorkshire Archive Service, WYL250/3/West Indies/5, Letters regarding List of Cases Brought before Magistrate of Williamsfield Estate, 1834–1835, Lord Sligo to Lord Harewood, 27 December 1835. I am thankful to Paul Norman at the archive for help with this citation.

93. NA: PRO, CO 137/155, G. Gilbert to Bathurst, 1823. See also CO 137/142, Governor Manchester [William Montagu] to Bathurst, 20 December 1816; CO 137/154, Governor Manchester to Bathurst, 13 October 1823 and 10 November 1823; CO 137/160, Governor Manchester to Bathurst, 31 December 1825; CO 137/167, Governor Keane to Murray, 22 November 1828; CO 137/172, Governor Belmore to Murray, 10 December 1830.

94. Gad Heuman, *"The Killing Time": The Morant Bay Rebellion in Jamaica* (Knoxville: University of Tennessee Press, 1994), 19, 21, 87, 91, 184.

95. See Lewis, *West India Proprietor*, 143–144.

96. Campbell, *Maroons*, 252.

97. Donald R. Hill, "From Coromantese to Cromanti: A Folkloric Account of the Spread of Ghanaian Culture in Carriacou, Grenada," *Humanities Review Journal* 2(1) (2002): 1, 5; Lorna McDaniel, "Musical Thoughts on Unresolved Questions and Recent Findings in Big Drum Research," *Black Music Research Journal* 22(1) (2002): 127.

98. Bonham C. Richardson, "The Overdevelopment of Carriacou," *Geographical Review* 65(3) (1975): 393.

99. McDaniel, "Musical Thoughts," 131, 133–137.

100. Kenneth Bilby, "Swearing by the Past, Swearing to the Future: Sacred Oaths, Alliances, and Treaties among the Guianese and Jamaican Maroons," *Ethnohistory* 44(4) (1997): 656.

101. According to Alexander Lindsay, then governor of Jamaica, the Maroons transported to Halifax (Nova Scotia) were "most impatient to leave the country," and though innocent Maroons were permitted to stay on the island, his justification for the Maroon war of 1795–1796 included the chasing away of the superintendent "placed over them by law," "threatening to kill him," setting fires to houses (including the house of the king of that district), and attacking and killing soldiers. These acts, according to Lindsay, "were my reasons for entering their lands in an hostile manner." See NLJ, "Alex[ander] Lindsay, 6th Earl of [Balcarres]... to his Grace the Duke of Portland in Justification of the Maroon War," MS 613, 1 October 1976. But there was also the fear that those in Jamaica might "establish the tree of liberty on the same basis as their brethren of St. Domingo [Haiti]. See NLJ, "Letter from Capt. Gillespie to Earl Balcarres," MS 1681, 1 October 1796. This letter was written in Spanish town on 24 September 1796. See also Bryan Edwards, *The Proceedings of the Governor and Assembly of Jamaica, in regard to the Maroon Negroes* (London: John Stockdale, 1796), and Kenneth Bilby, "The Treacherous Feast: A Jamaican Maroon Historical Myth," *Bijdragen tot de Taal-, Land- en Volkenkunde* 140(1) (1984): 1–31.

102. NA: PRO, CO 137/356 no. 25, fol. 189, "List of African Immigrants Embarked from the Port of Kingston, Jamaica, for Sierra Leone."

103. Nemata Amelia Blyden, *West Indians in West Africa, 1808–1880: The African Diaspora in Reverse* (Rochester: University of Rochester, 2000), 8–9.

104. Ibid., 30. For a recent yet brief statement on the "Maroon town" of Trelawny, see Claudette M. Gentias, "Maroon or Marooned: A Study of Maroon Town, St. James, Jamaica" (BA thesis, University of the West Indies, 1986).

105. Blyden, *West Indians in West Africa*, 32.

106. NA: PRO, CO 950/167, Memorandum of Evidence from Accompong Maroons to [West India] Royal Commission, 1938. In the 1940s H. A. Rowe was removed from the position of "colonel" after a crisis in leadership. The signatories and apparent political order in Accompong were the colonel, captain, major, and lieutenant, which order reflects changes in the official heads of these Maroons, for the original group leader was the captain, which has changed to colonel and then to chief in recent years.

107. Campbell, *Maroons*, 251.

108. The use of Akan names in early nineteenth-century Jamaica is without question. See NLJ, "List of Cornwall Estate Negroes," MS 1344, 6 August 1817. The same was the case in Barbados, where, in its slave register of 1834, I found 273 Cuffy (Kofi), 162 Cudjoe (Kwadwo), 212 Quash (Kwasi), 34 Quamina (Kwamena), 173 Quaco (Kwaku), 3 Affee (Afia), 1 Amma, and 1 Adjoa. The Barbados slave register for 1834 can be found in NA: PRO, T 71/554–558.

109. NLJ, "The Narrative of the Son of a Slave Woman," in Album of the Society for the Relief of Negro Slaves [presented to Lord Dudley], MS 193, 1825.

NOTES TO CHAPTER 6

1. Michael A. Gomez, *Exchanging Our Country Marks: The Transformation of African Identities in the Colonial and Antebellum South* (Chapel Hill: University of North Carolina Press, 1988), 88, 107.

2. *Slave Narratives: A Folk History of Slavery in the United States from Interviews with Former Slaves* (Washington, D.C.: Library of Congress, 1941), vol. 14, 252, pt. 1; vol. 11, 3, pt. 3; vol. 2, 39, 222, 254, pts. 2, 3, 6. The nature of these narratives raises important issues, and they have been duly noted. See Gomez, *Exchanging our Country Marks*, 297–298.

3. *Slave Narratives*, vol. 1, 263.

4. John Thornton, "Central African Names and African-American Naming Patterns," *William and Mary Quarterly* 50(4) (1993): 727–728. Newbell Pucket found the male Akan names Cuffee (and its variants), Cudjo, Quaco/Quacko, Quamina, Quash (the most prevalent were Cuffee and Cudjo) and the female Akan names Abah/Abba, Affee, Ama, and Bena(h) present in largely southern and a few northern states throughout the eighteenth and nineteenth centuries. See Newbell Niles Puckett, *Black Names in America*, ed. Murray Heller (Boston: Hall, 1975), 20–23, 30–32, 72, 77, 84, 90–95, 111, 171–172, 188, and 227.

5. *Slave Narratives*, vol. 14, 107, pt. 2.

6. *South Carolina Gazette* (29 October 1763; 22 January–29 January 1754).

7. The Gulf states of Texas, Louisiana, Mississippi, Alabama, and Florida received slightly more than one thousand (recorded) Gold Coast Africans over the course of the slave trade to North America.

8. Zora Neale Hurston, "Cudjo's Own Story of the Last African Slaver," *Journal of Negro History* 12(4) (1927): 648–663; idem, *Dust Tracks on a Road* (New York: Harper Perennial, 1991), 144–148.

9. Allen D. Candler, *The Colonial Records of the State of Georgia* (Atlanta: Franklin, 1904), 50, 55–62, 216, 555.

10. Mitsuhiro Wada, "Running from Bondage: An Analysis of the Newspaper Advertisements of Runaway Slaves in Colonial Maryland and Georgia," *Journal of the School of Letters* (Japan) 2, (2006): 11–21.

11. Elizabeth Donnan, *Documents Illustrative of the History of the Slave Trade to America*, 4 vols. (Washington, D.C.: Carnegie Institution of Washington, 1930), vol. 4, 612–625. See NA: PRO, CO 700/Georgia, 12, 1755, Map of the Inhabited Part of Georgia.

12. *Georgia Gazette* (Savannah) (2 August and 25 October 1764, 4 July and 15 August 1765).

13. Donnan, *Documents*, vol. 4, 633.

14. *Gazette of the State of Georgia* (Savannah) (11 May 1786).

15. *Georgia Gazette* (Savannah) (30 March 1768).

16. Ibid. (15 June and 7 September 1774; 22 March 1775).

17. Ibid. (27 July 1774).

18. Ibid. (6 June 1765).

19. *Royal Georgia Gazette* (Savannah) (25 January 1781).

20. *Gazette of the State of Georgia* (Savannah) (29 December 1785).

21. *Georgia State Gazette or Independent Register* (Augusta) (23 December 1786).

22. William Francis Allen, *Slave Songs of the United States* (New York: Simpson, 1867), 48.

23. *Freedman's Bank Records on CD-ROM* (Salt Lake City: Intellectual Reserve and the Christ of Jesus Christ and Latter-Day Saints, 2000). The Freedman's Bank records include approximately 480,000 names of African descendants who established accounts between 1865 and 1874.

24. Ibid.

25. Ibid.

26. Ibid.

27. See the Department of Commerce, Bureau of the Census, *Fourteenth Census of the United States 1920 Population* (Washington, D.C.: Government Printing Office, 1921), Georgia, Glynn Co., 8 June 1920, sheet no. 3B.

28. See Wada, "Running from Bondage," 11–21.

29. *Maryland Gazette* (Annapolis) (7 June 1749).

30. Ibid. (9 June 1747).

31. *Maryland Journal and Baltimore Advertiser* (Baltimore) (29 July 1783).

32. Lorena S. Walsh, "The Chesapeake Slave Trade: Regional Patterns, African Origins, and Some Implications," *William and Mary Quarterly* 58(1) (2001): 167.

33. Donnan, *Documents*, vol. 4, 17–18, 21, 172–181; see also Board of Trade (Great Britain), *Journal of the Commissioners for Trade and Plantations, 1704–1782*, 14 vols. (London: His Majesty's Stationery Office, 1925–1938), vol. 2, 55.

34. Gomez, *Exchanging our Country Marks*, 113.

35. Ibid., 242.

36. See T. H. Breen and Stephen Innes, *"Myne Owne Ground": Race and Freedom on Virginia's Eastern Shore, 1640–1676* (New York: Oxford University Press, 1980).

37. For one of the earliest references to Africans ("Negroes") in early Virginia, see NA: PRO, CO 1/3, no. 2, List of Names of the Living in Virginia, 16 February 1624. On indentured servants, see Russell R. Menard, "From Servants to Slaves: The Transformation of the Chesapeake Labor System," *Southern Studies* 16(3) (1977): 355–390; David Galenson, "White Servitude and the Growth of Black Slavery in Colonial America," *Journal of Economic History* 41(1) (1981): 39–47.

38. "Colonial William Byrd on Slavery and Indentured Servants, 1736, 1739," *American Historical Review* 1 (1895): 88–89.

39. William Waller Hening, ed., *The Statutes at Large, Being a Collection of All the Laws of Virginia* (Charlottesville: University Press of Virginia, 1969), vol. 2, 170.

40. Ibid., 260.

41. Donnan, *Documents*, vol. 4, 172–181.

42. Hening, *Statutes at Large*, vol. 7, 388–389; vol. 8, 336–337.

43. On the numbers of Gold Coast captives and the difficulty calculations present, see Stephanie E. Smallwood, *Saltwater Slavery: A Middle Passage from Africa to American Diaspora* (Cambridge, Mass.: Harvard University Press, 2007), 3, 20, 177. On the Royal African Company (RAC) and Virginia, see Kenneth Gordon Davies, *The Royal African Company* (London: Longmans, 1957), 214–232, and, on overall African imports under the RAC, see Susan Westbury, "Slaves of Colonial Virginia: Where They Came From," *William and Mary Quarterly* 42(2) (1985): 236.

44. Walsh, "Chesapeake Slave Trade," 166; Donnan, *Documents*, vol. 4, 183–185.

45. Donnan, *Documents*, vol. 4, 188–234.

46. *Virginia Gazette* (Williamsburg) (8 June 1739).

47. Ibid. (9 July and 10 August 1772, 21 May and 3 June 1773).

48. Donnan, *Documents*, vol. 3, 195.

49. Walsh, "Chesapeake Slave Trade," 150.

50. On social organization and principles of succession in Senegambia, see Boubacar Barry, *Senegambia and the Atlantic Slave Trade* (New York: Cambridge University Press, 1998), 16, 27, 83. Most of the literature on the Angola region suggests a "double-descent" system, and the largely patrilineal Igbo—though some are matrilineal—or the matrilineal Akan from the Gold Coast have been well noted.

51. Kevin Roberts, *African-Virginian Extended Kin: The Prevalence of West African Family Forms among Slaves in Virginia, 1740–1870* (Master's thesis, Virginia Polytechnic Institute and State University, 1999), 58. On Pharsalia and the planters and enslaved Africans who created it, see Lynn A. Nelson, *Pharsalia: An Environmental Biography of a Southern Plantation, 1780–1880* (Athens: University of Georgia Press, 2007).

52. *Virginia Gazette* (Williamsburg) (3–10 December 1736).

53. Ibid. (4 October 1770). For an account of English language use or value on the mid-eighteenth-century Gold Coast, see Peter Wood, *Black Majority: Negroes in Colonial South Carolina from 1670 through the Stono Rebellion* (New York: Knopf, 1974), 173.

54. *Slave Narratives*, vol. 11, 372, pt. 1.

55. *Virginia Gazette* (Williamsburg) (24 September 1772).

56. Ibid. (7 March 1766; 15 January 1767).

57. Ibid. (8 November 1776); *Virginia Gazette and Weekly Advertiser* (5 November 1785).

58. *North Carolina Gazette* (5 May 1775).

59. Rachel Malcolm-Woods curated an exhibit at the Ridderhof Martin Gallery, University of Mary Washington, titled "Taking History in Material Culture: Igbo and Akan Signs in Early Virginia," 25 January–2 March 2007. The exhibit documented the skilled Akan artisans who used fabric, stone carving, and other media to create graphic signs to communicate and preserve culture among peoples who constructed log cabins and other types of housing contiguous with family graveyards and ancestral shrines. On the African Burial Ground in New York City, see Cheryl J. LaRoche and Michael L. Blakey, "Seizing Intellectual Power: The Dialogue at the New York African Burial Ground," *Historical Archaeology* 31(3) (1997): 95. Akan persons executed in the 1712 New York revolt were buried in the "Negro Burial Ground," and it is more probable they used the Sankofa or other symbols to convey a message of going home.

60. In 1856 Robert Taylor Scott wrote his wife about an anticipated "slave revolt" in Prince William and Fauquier country, Virginia. See Robert Taylor Scott to Fanny Scott, 31 December 1856, Keith Family Papers, 1830–1979, Virginia Historical Society.

61. U.S. Department of Commerce, Bureau of the Census, *Negro Population of the United States, 1790–1915* (Washington, D.C.: Government Printing Office, 1918), 57.

62. Walter B. Edgar, *South Carolina: A History* (Columbia: University of South Carolina Press, 1998), 140, 267; Alexander S. Salley, "The Introduction of Rice Culture into South Carolina," *Bulletin of the Historical Commission of South Carolina* 6 (1919), 1–23. On rice cultivation and slavery, see Daniel Littlefield, *Rice and Slaves: Ethnicity and the Slave Trade in Colonial South Carolina* (Baton Rouge: Louisiana State University, 1981), 80, 98, 114; Judith A. Carney, *Black Rice: The African Origins of Rice Cultivation in the Americas* (Cambridge, Mass.: Harvard University Press, 2001), 81, 165.

63. *South Carolina Gazette* (15 July 1732). This newspaper was established in 1732.

64. Ibid. (23 February 1734, 27 February 1757, 27 April 1765, 2 July 1772, 31 May 1773, 14 June 1773, 20 June 1774, 13 June 1785, 22 March and 21 July 1786, 20 September 1786, 15 December 1804, 24 April and 22 June 1805, 7 April and 1 May 1806, 15 May 1806, 25 March and 9 May 1807).

65. Wood, *Black Majority*, 59–60, 201, 335.

66. Donnan, *Documents*, vol. 4, 274.

67. Margaret Washington Creel, *"A Peculiar People": Slave Religion and Community-Culture among the Gullahs* (New York: New York University Press, 1988), 4, 10, 114, 158, 326.

68. William S. Pollitzer, *The Gullah People and Their African Heritage* (Athens: University of Georgia Press, 1999), 114–115. The classic text on the Gullah language is Lorenzo D. Turner, *Africanisms in the Gullah Dialect* (Chicago: University of Chicago Press, 1949).

69. Pollitzer, *Gullah People*, 119.

70. *Slave Narratives*, vol. 14, 65, pt. 3.
71. *South Carolina Gazette* (19–26 August 1732).
72. List of slaves, ca. 1779, Butler Family Papers; Butler Island Plantation Hospital Book, 1838–1842; various slave lists (1775–1815), Butler Family Papers, Historical Society of Pennsylvania.
73. *South Carolina Gazette* (1 April 1745; 26 May 1746; 12 January 1747).
74. Ibid. (22 September 1746).
75. Ibid. (14 September–21 September 1747).
76. *South Carolina and American General Gazette* (11 February 1772).
77. *Gazette of the State of Georgia* (Savannah) (11 May 1786).
78. *South Carolina Gazette* (27 September 1773).
79. *South Carolina and American General Gazette* (21 February 1781).
80. *South Carolina Gazette* (25 May–1 June 1748).
81. *Freedman's Bank Records on CD-ROM*.
82. Patrick S. Brady, "The Slave Trade and Sectionalism in South Carolina, 1787–1808," *Journal of Southern History* 38(4) (1972): 618.
83. Ibid.
84. Ibid., 618, 620.
85. *Freedman's Bank Records on CD-ROM*.
86. Ibid.
87. *The History of Prince Lee Boo, to which is added, The life of Paul Cuffee, a Man of Colour...* (Dublin: C. Crookes, 1820), 149–170. See also Paul Cuffee, *A Brief Account of the Settlement and Present Situation of the Colony of Sierra Leone, in Africa* (New York: Samuel Wood, 1812).
88. Donnan, *Documents*, vol. 3, 24–25.
89. Ibid., 27, 29, 68.
90. The updated "Trans-Atlantic Slave Trade Database" (http://www.slavevoyages.org) lists only one voyage under Captain Robert Ball from the Gold Coast to Massachusetts in 1748 and cites Donnan, *Documents*, vol. 3, 66, but Donnan does not include any such voyage, and there was no vessel under Captain Robert Ball listed for 1748 (see Donnan, *Documents*, vol. 3, 65–67). For a recent biography on Paul Cuffee, see Lamont D. Thomas, *Rise to Be a People: A Biography of Paul Cuffee* (Urbana: University of Illinois Press, 1986).
91. Committee for Trade and Plantations (Great Britain), *Return from the Commissioners for Trade and Plantations, to the Honourable House of Commons...* (London: Committee for Trade and Plantations, 1777), 5.
92. On Quaco Walker, see William Cushing Judicial Notebook, 1783, ms., Massachusetts Historical Society, 89–99; John D. Cushing, "The Cushing Court and the Abolition of Slavery in Massachusetts: More Notes on the 'Quock Walker Case,'" *American Journal of Legal History* 5(2) (1961): 120–133; Robert M. Spector, "The Quock Walker Cases (1781–83): Slavery, Its Abolition, and Negro Citizenship in Early Massachusetts," *Journal of Negro History* 53(1) (1968): 12, 24, 32. For Cuffee and Quoma, see "Warrant for the Arrest of Ann Grafton, Cuffee (a slave), and Quoma (a slave)," 12 July 1748, Miscellaneous Bound Manuscripts, Massachusetts Historical Society, 1–2.
93. Cushing Judicial Notebook, 90.
94. Spector, "Quock Walker," 32.
95. Calculations derive from http://www.slavevoyages.org.

96. Donnan, *Documents*, vol. 3, 223.

97. Ibid., 144, 165–188, 174–185, 204, 210, 295.

98. Ibid., 81, 268–269, 388–393.

99. Calculations derive from http://www.slavevoyages.org.

100. Donnan, *Documents*, vol. 3, 422–423, 426–434.

101. Thelma Foote, *Black and White Manhattan: The History of Racial Formation in Colonial New York City* (New York: Oxford University Press, 2005), 37, 65, 67–69; James G. Lydon, "New York and the Slave Trade, 1700–1774," *William and Mary Quarterly* 35(2) (1978): 382–383.

102. Edmund B. O'Callaghan, *The Documentary History of the State of New York* (Albany: Weed, Parsons, 1850), vol. 1, 482.

103. Donnan, *Documents*, vol. 3, 462–510.

104. Ibid., 510–512.

105. O'Callaghan, *Documentary History*, vol. 1, 446, 469.

106. Edmund B. O'Callaghan and Berthold Fernow, eds., *Documents relative to the Colonial History of the State of New York* (Albany: Weed, Parsons, 1856–1887), vol. 1, 364–365; Charles T. Gehring, trans. and ed., *Correspondence, 1647–1653, New Netherlands Documents Series* (Syracuse: Syracuse University Press, 2000), vol. 12, 134–135.

107. Calculations derived from David Eltis, Stephen D. Behrendt, David Richardson, and Herbert S. Klein, *The Transatlantic Slave Trade: A Database on CD-ROM* (Cambridge: Cambridge University Press, 1998); updated at http://www.slavevoyages.org.

108. John Sharpe's letter dated 23 June 1712 to the secretary of the Society for the Propagation of the Gospel in Foreign Parts appeared in Roswell Randall Hoes, "The Negro Plot of 1712," *New York Genealogical and Biographical Record* 21 (1890): 162.

109. One account of the revolt that follows the general course of events is by Governor Robert Hunter, who was royal governor of New York and New Jersey between 1710 and 1719. For Hunter's account, see O'Callaghan and Fernow, *Documents*, vol. 5, 341–342. See also Court of General and Quarter Sessions of the Peace, 1691–1731, and New York Supreme Court of Judicature Minute Book, 6 June 1710–5 June 1714 (engrossed), New York City County Clerk Archives, New York.

110. O'Callaghan and Fernow, *Documents*, vol. 5, 342; Court of General and Quarter Sessions of the Peace, 1691–1731, 221, 227r; Kenneth Scott, "The Slave Insurrection in New York in 1712," *New York Historical Society Quarterly* 45 (1961): 63; Foote, *Black and White Manhattan*, 130–138.

111. Court of General and Quarter Sessions of the Peace, 1691–1731, 213, 215–219, 221, 227.

112. Hoes, "Negro Plot," 163; Court of General and Quarter Sessions of the Peace, 1691–1731, New York City County Clerk Archives, New York, 212.

113. Hoes, "Negro Plot," 162.

114. Foote, *Black and White Manhattan*, 133, and esp. 134–139, for a perspective on the Akan role and objective in the 1712 revolt. See also Graham Russell Hodges, *Roots and Branch: African Americans in New York and East Jersey, 1613–1863* (Chapel Hill: University of North Carolina Press, 1999), 65.

115. Hoes, "Negro Plot," 162–163.

116. Scott, "Slave Insurrection," 71–76.

117. O'Callaghan and Fernow, *Documents*, vol. 5, 356–357, 460–461, 525; *Minutes of the Common Council of the City of New York* (1713), vol. 3, 27–31.

118. William J. Allinson, *Memoir of Quamino Buccau: A Pious Methodist* (Philadelphia: Henry Longstreth, 1851), 5.

119. *New York Gazette* (18 May 1730).

120. *New York Weekly Post-Boy* (18 August 1746).

121. *Pennsylvania Gazette* (Philadelphia) (29 October 1747).

122. *Pennsylvania Journal and the Weekly Advertiser* (Philadelphia) (20 August 1761).

123. *New Jersey Gazette* (Burlington) (31 December 1777).

124. *Pennsylvania Gazette* (Philadelphia) (31 March 1773).

125. Ibid. (24 May 1775; 11 October 1775; 17 July 1776).

126. *Royal Gazette* (New York) (5 January 1782).

127. *Pennsylvania Gazette* (Philadelphia) (18 January 1770); Charles R. Foy, "Seeking Freedom in the Atlantic World, 1713–1783," *Early American Studies* 4(1) (2006): 59.

128. *Pennsylvania Gazette* (Philadelphia) (30 August 1775).

129. *Royal Gazette* (New York) (5 November 1783).

130. Daniel Horsmanden, *The New-York Conspiracy, or a History of the Negro Plot, with the Journal of the Proceedings against the Conspirators at New-York in the Years 1741-2* (New York: Southwick and Pelsue, 1810), 97–98.

131. Ibid., 100.

132. Lionel H. Kennedy and Thomas Parker, *An Official Report on the Trials of Sundry Negroes, Charged with an Attempt to Raise an Insurrection in the State of South-Carolina* (Charleston: James R. Schenck, 1822), 186.

133. Ibid., 187,

134. Philip D. Morgan, "Conspiracy Scares," *William and Mary Quarterly* 59(1) (2002): 164.

135. Horsmanden, *New-York Conspiracy*, 41–42.

136. Ibid., 44, 100, 213–214.

137. Leopold S. Launitz-Schurer Jr., "Slave Resistance in Colonial New York: An Interpretation of Daniel Horsmanden's New York Conspiracy," *Phylon* 41(2) (1980): 151.

138. Horsmanden, *New-York Conspiracy*, 212, 265–266.

NOTES TO CHAPTER 7

1. Harold Connolly, "Blacks in Brooklyn from 1900 to 1960" (PhD diss., New York University, 1973); Robert J. Swan, "Did Brooklyn (N.Y.) Blacks Have Unusual Control over Their Schools? Period I: 1815–1845," *Afro-Americans in New York Life and History* 7(2) (1983): 25.

2. Robert A. Hill, ed., *Marcus Garvey and the Universal Negro Improvement Association Papers* (Los Angeles: University of California Press, 1983), vol. 1, 536–537, 540.

3. "African 'Paradise' Lure for Negroes," *New York Times* (11 February 1914), 5; "British Warning for 'Chief Sam,' " *New York Times* (26 February 1914), 7; "Chief Sam Stirs British," *New York Times* (27 February 1914), 4; " 'Chief' Sam's Ship

Gone," *New York Times* (8 March 1914), 8; "Negroes for Gold Coast," *New York Times* (24 March 1914), 21; "Chief Sam Party Missing," *New York Times* (12 June 1915), 5.

4. J. Ayo Langley, "Chief Sam's African Movement and Race Consciousness in West Africa," *Phylon* 32(2) (1971): 165; Hill, *Marcus Garvey*, vol. 1, 538.

5. "New West African Scheme," *New York Times* (22 March 1914), C5; "200 Going 'Back to Africa,' " *New York Times* (29 March 1914), C5.

6. "War Maroons Chief Sam's Colony," *New York Times* (16 December 1915), 10; "Abandoned *Liberia* Here," *New York Times* (4 December 1916), 15.

7. Hill, *Marcus Garvey*, vol. 1, 546.

8. Louis R. Harlan and Raymond W. Smock, eds., *The Booker T. Washington Papers* (Champaign: University of Illinois Press, 1982), vol. 12, 437–438; Langley, "Chief Sam's African Movement," 167–169, 173–175. All the persistent charges by British, North American, and Gold Coast authorities and their agencies were without merit and ultimately dropped, though pursed vehemently in terms of Chief Sam's legal and political entanglements.

9. Hill, *Marcus Garvey*, vol. 1, 543.

10. "King of Gold Coast Here on *Aquitania*," *New York Times* (26 September 1925), 8; Alexander B. Holmes IV, "Economic and Political Organizations in the Gold Coast, 1920–1945" (PhD diss., University of Chicago, 1972), 114, 118.

11. Ibid.; "African Chief Arrives to Study Negroes Here," *New York Times* (11 October 1925), XX15.

12. On Nana Amoah's participation in the Pan-African Congresses, see David L. Lewis, ed., *W.E.B. Du Bois: A Reader* (New York: Holt, 1995), 671; idem, *W.E.B. Du Bois: The Fight for Equality and the American Century, 1919–1963* (New York: Holt, 2001), 112, 209. The Schomburg Library has a copy of Nana Amoah's 1927 lecture; see the Arthur A. Schomburg Papers, Sc micro R-2798, box 15, f. 2. r. 11, New York Public Library, Schomburg Center for Research in Black Culture and Life.

13. "African Chief Arrives to Study Negroes Here."

14. "Gold Coast King Asks Pride in Negro Race," *New York Times* (17 October 1925), 4. James Emman Kwegyir Aggrey was a relative of Nana Amoah III. An unscrupulous individual named Tete Ansa in Harlem joined Amoah, though Ansa's fraudulence was eventually exposed after Amoah created some distance between himself and Ansa. Evidently Ansa continued his efforts in Harlem among diasporic Africans, but a number of the latter maintained a healthy skepticism about Ansa's commercial project since the memories of Chief Sam's and Marcus Garvey's recent movements were still fresh in their minds. A century before Nana Amoah lectured in Harlem, A. W. Hanson, "a native of the Gold Coast of Africa," lectured on similar topics related to the history, language, and culture of the Gold Coast in 1839. We can be assured that Hanson came from the westward coastal areas in the 1830s, and he and Amoah would have ideologically shared much. See *Daily Courant* (Hartford, Conn.), 10 July 1839, 2.

15. In their three-volume work, *An Index of British Treaties* (London: Her Majesty's Stationery Office, 1970), compilers Clive Parry and Charity Hopkins list no such treaty of 1897.

16. Holmes, *Economic and Political Organizations*, 116.

17. Ibid., 129.

18. Roger Gocking, "Creole Society and the Revival of Traditional Culture in Cape Coast during the Colonial Period," *International Journal of African Historical Studies* 17(4) (1984): 602.

19. Ibid., 604, 613, 615–616.

20. Michael A. Gomez, *Exchanging our Country Marks: The Transformation of African Identities in the Colonial and Antebellum South* (Chapel Hill: University of North Carolina Press, 1988), 290–292.

21. Nana Yao Opare Dinizulu, *The Akan Priests in America* (Queens: Aims of Modzawe, 1974), 8.

22. Ibid., 7

23. For an excellent documentary film on contemporary Akan and Yorùbá spiritual practices in New York, see Alfred Santana's film *Voices of the Gods* (Brooklyn: Al Santana Productions, 1985).

24. In the early 1980s, the Ooni of Ile-Ife, the sacred home of the Yorùbá, formally recognized Oseijeman as Oba (ruler) of Oyotunji village through a coronation ceremony (hence, Oba Ofuntola Oseijeman Adelabu Adefunmi).

25. Nana Kwabena Brown, interview by author, Washington, D.C., 5 December 2001.

26. Dinizulu, *Akan Priests*, 6.

27. Ibid., 5. His statements are well supported by the historical and anthropological record.

28. See "A Look at the Akan Religion in America," *Black News* 3(1) (1977): 18. See also Laurent Fourchard, René Otayek, and André Mary, eds., *Entreprises religieuses transnationales en Afrique de l'Ouest* (Paris: Éditions Karthala, 2005), and Stefania Capone, *Les Yoruba du Nouveau Monde: Religion, ethnicité, et nationalisme noir aux États-Unis* (Paris: Éditions Karthala, 2005), 111. According to Nana Kwabena Brown, "even though the place was called Bosum Dzemawodzi, most of the [deities] worshipped there were Yorùbá for the next two years until he [Nana Dinizulu] went to Ghana." Brown, interview.

29. One source suggests that Nana Oparebea's travels to North America and her establishment of shrines and a branch of the Ghana Psychic and Traditional Healing Association in the country was in part due to her desire to "secure Black American financial support to help her build a traditional hospital so she can better do her work in Ghana." See Doris V. Bright, "The Quest to Legitimize the Akan Religion in America (Phase One), A Cross-cultural Analysis of Traditional Religion: The Akonedi Shrine, Larteh, Ghana, and the Bosum Dzemawodzi, Long Island City, New York" (PhD diss., Union Institute and University, 1977), 11.

30. Ibid., 14; Kofi Asare Opoku, "Training the Priestess at the Akonnedi Shrine," *Research Review* 6(2) (1970): 34.

31. Opoku, "Training the Priestess," 44.

32. This information comes from the funeral program for Nana Akua Oparebea, who passed away in 1995. Her funeral was held in Larteh on 10 January 1996. A copy of the funeral program is in the author's possession.

33. Brown, interview.

34. Ibid.

35. Zaro's House of Africa was established in 1968 and was named after Nana Kwabena Brown's maternal great-great-grandfather, Zaro Isaac, who was a well-known healer.

36. Dinizulu, *Akan Priests*, 9. Ajaibo is of further interest since he was part of Nana Dinizulu's first group of trainees under Bosum Dzemawodzi in New York and at the Akonnedi shrine in Larteh. While in Larteh in 1972, he was "possessed" not by an Akan ɔbosom but by a Yorùbá òrìsà named Shango (Sango). According to Doris Bright, a witness to this phenomenon and a doctoral student who studied Dinizulu's efforts in New York and Larteh, this was "Shango's first appearance at Awukugua," home of one of the most famous ɔkɔmfoɔ in Akan and Asante history, ɔkɔmfoɔ Anokye (i.e., Kwame Frempɔn Anɔkye Kotowbere). This occasion was critical for the "legitimization" of Nana Oparebea's and Nana Dinizulu's efforts to establish Akan spirituality in its Larteh form in North America. See Bright, "Quest to Legitimize the Akan Religion," 20, 25–27, 208.

37. Brown, interview.
38. Ibid.
39. Ibid.
40. Ibid.
41. For a list of other Akan-based houses in and around the District of Columbia, see African Traditional Spiritual Coalition, "A Sacred Healing Circle" (Washington, D.C.: Author, 2000).
42. On Akua Kyerewaa, see Bright, "Quest to Legitimize the Akan Religion," 175, 205.
43. See Angela Terrell, "Psychic Powers, Healing Herbs," *Washington Post* (6 July 1973), B3.
44. For a discussion of *akɔm*, see Kwasi Konadu, *Indigenous Medicine and Knowledge in African Society* (New York: Routledge, 2007), 45, 54, 64–65.
45. Nana Kwabena Brown, "A Brief Survey of African Traditional Religion with Notes on Its Afro-American Perspectives," unpublished manuscript, 1981, 6.
46. Brown, interview.
47. Ibid.
48. Ibid.
49. Ibid.
50. Ibid.
51. Ibid.
52. Brown, "Brief Survey," 7.
53. Lee A. Daniels, "Child Becomes Woman in Traditional Akan Rite," *New York Times* (15 July 1991), B2.
54. Ibid.
55. Howard W. French, "King of Ashanti in U.S. Stresses Cultural Pride," *New York Times* (29 May 1989), 25–27.
56. Bright, "Quest to Legitimize the Akan Religion," 182, 192. For rare interviews with Nana Dinizulu in the 1970s, see 192–204, 239–240.
57. Cynthia A. Roby, "Two Women Seated as Ghanaian Priestesses," *Broward Times* (Broward, Fla.) (9 November 2007).
58. Kwadwo Konadu-Agyemang, Baffour K. Takyi, and John Arthur, eds., *The New African Diaspora in North America: Trends, Community Building, and Adaptation* (Lanham, Md.: Lexington, 2006), 116–117.
59. See Sandra Riley, *Homeward Bound: A History of the Bahama Islands to 1850* (Miami: Island Research, 2000).

60. NA: PRO 30/55/100, Guy Carleton Papers no. 10427 (Book of Negroes), 53–53. The Book of Negroes has been reproduced as a searchable database at http://www.gov.ns.ca/nsarm.

61. Ibid., 117–118.

62. Ibid. 98–99, 123–124, 131–132.

63. Ibid., 31–32, 119–120; Nova Scotia Archives and Records Management (NSARM), MG9, Shelburne Transcripts, 1782–1807, Muster Book of Free Black Settlement of Birchtown, September 1784. I am grateful to the staff of the Black Loyalist Heritage Society in Shelburne (Nova Scotia) for the reference to the latter archival source and for putting me in contact with the NSARM.

64. Thomas Y. Owusu, "The Role of Ghanaian Immigrant Associations in Toronto, Canada," *International Migration Review* 34(4) (2000): 1155–1160.

65. Ibid., 1173–1174.

66. Kwabena O. Akurang-Parry, "Passionate Voices of Those Left Behind: Conversations with Ghanaian Professionals on the Brain Drain and Its Net Gains," *African Issues* 30(1) (2002): 57–58.

67. Hein de Haas, "The Myth of Invasion: Irregular Migration from West Africa to the Maghreb and the European Union," International Migration Institute research report, Oxford University, October 2007, iv (emphasis in the original).

68. Edward M. Bruner, "Tourism in Ghana: The Representation of Slavery and the Return of the Black Diaspora," *American Anthropologist* 98(2) (1996): 291.

69. Ibid., 293–294.

70. For the Joshua Project, see the very meticulous data collected on and marshaled toward the "unreached peoples" of the globe at http://www.joshuaproject.net. Another organization of a related nature is the Church of Jesus Christ of Latter-Day Saints (Mormons), which has amassed approximately two billion names that are now stored in a secured vault in Salt Lake City; the church has sought to "baptize the dead" from among those names. Moreover, it continues to baptize African ancestors as a prerequisite of "salvation." The issue is that not only does this process add to the Mormon membership but also that those ancestors are being claimed without consent. Although Jewish and Catholic communities have protested this practice for their adherents, no one has yet argued the African and African diasporic case.

71. Bruner, "Tourism in Ghana," 300–301.

72. Lydia Polgreen, "Ghana's Uneasy Embrace of Slavery's Diaspora," *New York Times* (27 December 2005), sec. 4, p. 1.

73. Pamela Woodford, "Filming Slavery: A Conversation with Haile Gerima," *Transition* 64 (1994): 90–104.

74. Ibid., 101, 103.

75. Obiagele Lake, "Toward a Pan-African Identity: Diaspora African Repatriates in Ghana," *Anthropological Quarterly* 68(1) (1995): 22.

76. Ibid., 33.

77. Ibid.

78. J. D. Y. Peel, "Historicity and Pluralism in Some Recent Studies of Yorùbá Religion," *Africa* 64(1) (1994): 163.

Index

Abaan, Kwabena (ɔhene), 71
Abankɛseɛse (Dɛnkyira capital), 42
abosom (spiritual agencies), 18
   Asanteman and, 78
   communication with, 66
   defined, 40, 238–239
   in diasporic Africans' spiritual practice, 215, 216–217
   Fante polities, 75–76, 216
   Gã-Adangme term for, 213
   in homes, 59
   in Maroon groups, 114–115, 117, 118, 119
   physical abodes of, 42, 65
   resistance to outside religions, 54, 61–62
   in rituals/festivals, 67, 135
   Tanɔ river, 41, 61, 114–115, 118, 221, xi
   water-derived, 20, 41, 42–43, 163, 216
   See also Akan Creator (Onyankopɔn); spiritual culture, Akan
Aboure people, 47
abrafoɔ (brassos/braffoes), 60, 61, 76, 136, 237, 251*n*10
Abramsz, Heerman (Dutch director-general), 86
Abrem "nation," 56–57, 69, 70
Accompong (Maroon settlement in Jamaica), 150
   spiritual culture, 151, 152–153
   treaty of, 157, 160–161, 271*n*106
   Westernization, 159
Accra
   Asante relations, 87
   British relationship, 82, 123
   conflicts involving, 70
   Danish relationship, 82
   Dutch relationship, 69, 82, 83
   expatriates from Americas in, 231
   as Gã terminus, 74, 138
   landscape, 84
   map, 56–57
   Portuguese relationship, 58
Acomane. *See* Komenda
Act of Emancipation (Britain, 1834), 146
Ada settlement, 56–57, 83
Adade Kofi ɔbosom, 216, 220
adaduanan. *See* calendrical cycle
Adansemanso (archaeological site), 34, 35, 52
Adebɔ, Nana Ayɛkra, 42, 43
Adefunmi, Oba Ofuntola Oseijeman Adelabu (contemporary Yorùbá spiritualist), 210, 213, 279*n*24
adinkra symbols, 180, 238
Ado (Akwamuhene), 74–75
Adom settlement, Dutch involvment with, 69
Adoom (Asante "prince"), 79
Afram, Nana Afum (Assin leader), 42
African American Association of Ghana, 230
African Blood Brotherhood (ABB), 204–205
African Burial Grounds (New York City), 180, 200, 274*n*59
African Cultural and Religious Society (ACRS), 220
African diaspora. *See* diasporic Africans
African School no. 2 (Brooklyn), 204
African studies, 90, 231–232
African Town, Alabama, 166
African Union Company, 206
African Union Society (Brooklyn), 204

283

Agona "nation," 56–57, 70
  See also Dɛnkyira
agriculture in Americas
  in arid regions, 107
  crops raised, 167, 172, 177, 182, 189
  Maroon communities, 112–113
  reliance on enslaved labor, 96, 108–109
  tobacco, 105, 167, 170, 172, 177
  See also sugar and sugar production
agriculture in West Africa
  distribution of surplus, 65
  domestic animals, 36
  domestic enslavement, 78, 80, 81
  efficiency of, 64
  forest fallow system, 29
  important crops, 30, 31, 32, 64, 73
  proto-Akan society, 30, 31, 32, 40, 53
  seasonality of, 58
  spiritual culture and, 33, 40, 53
Agyeman-Duah, Joseph, 245n7
Ahanta "nation," 56–57, 74, 82
Akan Creator (Onyankopɔn)
  human links to, 20, 163
  in Maroon groups, 113–114, 152
  matrilineality and, 232
  myriad manifestations of, 53
  offspring of, 40, 59, 114, 117, 118, xi
  prayers to, 68, 102
  terms for, 46, 102, 238
  See also abosom (spiritual agencies)
Akan culture in Americas
  composite nature of, 5–6, 22, 150, 151, 159, 177, 235
  disproportionate influence of, 6, 142, 149–150, 155, 163–164, 174
  transmission of, 20, 150, 153, 164, 177, 225–226
  See also Akan/African spiritual movement in North America; biographical sketches of slaves; Maroon groups; names and naming patterns, Akan; obeah
Akan culture in West Africa, 3
  animal symbolism, 122
  composite nature of, 22, 232–233, 235
  conflation with Asante culture, 77–78
  death (*See* death)
  defined, 17
  diasporic African engagement with, 202–203, 220–221, 227–232, 233
  early evidence of, 34
  elite ambivalence toward, 211–212, 229–230
  formation of, 6, 23, 24, 27–29, 247n34
  Mande commercial contact, 45, 51
  social rank, 135
  See also leadership/political structure; matrilineal system; names and naming patterns, Akan; oral histories; proto-Akan society; scarification, Akan; spiritual culture, Akan
Akan language, 237–240
  in British colonies, 136, 146, 154–155
  in Danish colonies, 101
  in Dutch colonies, 110
  as Gold Coast lingua franca, 8, 44
  in Gullah language, 185
  linguistic differentiation and, 39, 46
  linguistic family of, 45
  loss of, 233
  Mande cultural diffusion myth, 43–45
  in Maroon settlements, 150, 151, 159
  Mina term and, 9–10, 12, 101, 123
  in New York, 195
  noun prefixal system, 43, 45–46, 248nn64–65
  number words, 260n17
  proto-Akan, 45–46
  spiritual lexicon, 114–115, 117–118
  translation of, 68
Akan people. *See* biographical sketches of slaves; Coromantee term; Ghana; Gold Coast captives; Mina term; names and naming patterns, Akan
Akan polities
  conflicts and alliances, 74–76, 82–83, 85
  major disagreements, 64–65
  organization of, 62–64
  social order in, 138
  See also names of polities and "nations"

Index

The Akan Priests in America (Dinizulu), 212–213
Akan-Abrem battle (1920), 69
Akan/African spiritual movement in North America, 212–222
  composite nature of, 213, 216–217, 221–222
  training, 215–216, 218–219, 220, 224
  See also back-to-Africa movements
Akan-European commercial encounters, 58–76
  Akani merchants, 63–64, 76
  British relations, 71–73, 88–89, 91–92, 208–209
  Christianization, 62, 66–68
  Danish relations, 82–83
  depopulation, 76
  diplomacy, 85, 88
  Dutch relations, 68–70, 71, 81–82, 83, 86, 88–89
  European colonial armies, 82
  European involvement in local politics, 59–60
  firearms trade, 88–89
  French relations, 69–70
  German relations, 73–74
  goods traded, 70–71, 72, 74
  international enslavement enterprise, 89–92
  intra-Akan conflicts and alliances, 65, 69, 74–76, 86
  mutual exploitation of rivalries, 83–84
  Portuguese relations, 61–62, 88
  as window into Akan culture, 55
  See also European competition on Gold Coast; international enslavement enterprise
Akani merchants, 63–64, 76
Akanization process, 6, 29–30, 54
  Akan culture importation to Americas, 149–150
  empire (*See under* Akwamu; Akyem "nation"; Asanteman)
  enslavement within West Africa, 239
  evidence of in Americas, 155
  in spiritual culture, 216–217
Akara (1763 Berbice revolt leader), 144
Akasini (regent of Assinie), 66–67
Akatakyi. *See* Komenda

Akim Trading Company Limited, 205–206, 208
Akong settlement (Queen Anne's Point), 56–57
Akonnedi Abena shrine, 215–216, 219–220, 280n36
akɔm, 221, 223, 238, 253n37
akɔmfoɔ
  in African culture movement, 215, 218–220, 221, 224
  assistant to, 237, 251n10
  defined, 239
  European observations, 84, 102–103
  Komfo ritual, 146
  in Maroon groups, 115, 117, 119, 151
  scarification of, 103
  training of, 65–66, 146, 216, 221
  See also spiritual culture, Akan
Akuapem polity, 48, 87, 239–240, 249n69
Akwamu (archaeological site), 34
Akwamu "nation"
  Akyem relationship, 82
  Asanteman and, 75, 78
  collapse of, 98
  conflicts involving, 70
  Danish relationship with, 82, 95
  empire, 9, 48, 74–75, 243n27, 249n69
  map, 56–57
Akwida (Akoda) settlement, 56–57, 73–74
Akwonno (Aquando, Akwamuhene), 75, 82
Akyem "nation"
  Akwamu relationship, 75, 82
  Asante-Aowin war (1715), 87
  Asanteman and, 75, 78, 82–83
  Chief Sam's movement, 205
  Danish relationship, 82, 95
  empire, 48, 249n69
  Fante relationship, 83
  Gã people and, 74
  map, 56–57
  organization of, 63–64
ALHG (Afro-Louisiana History and Genealogy) database, 243n27
Allen, Rose Mary, 118
Aluku Maroons (French Guiana), 112

Amanahia settlement, 87
Amankwaa, Kwaa (Edina leader), 59
Amankwakurom (Eguafo town), 59
Amerindians, 120, 142
Amina term. *See* Mina term
Amo, Anton W. (African-descended missionary), 67
Amoah, Nana III, 208–209, 210, 278*n*14
Amowi rock shelter (archaeological site), 35
Ananse stories, 110, 117, 142, 159, 161
ancestry as basis for cultural identity, 215, 232
Angola
　double descent system, 273*n*50
　enslaved captives imported from, 176, 185
　Kôngo-Angola region, 22, 108, 122, 185, 195
　Loango-Angola region, 109, 110
　Maroon culture and, 150–151
　slaves imported from, 195
Animah (Akkonedi Abena ɔkɔmfoɔ), 216
Anokye (Asante ɔkɔmfoɔ), 75, 138, 280*n*36
Anomabu settlement
　British relationship, 123
　as embarkation point for enslaved captives, 124–126, 127, 132, 153–154, 169, 192
　as embarkation point for non-Akan captives, 130
　as Fante polity, 60
　as homeland of enslaved captives, 127, 131, 154, 161
　map, 56–57
Anomansa (Anomee) village, 59
Ansa, Amma (Akonnedi Abena ɔkɔmfoɔ), 216
Ansa, Tete (pan-African businessman), 278*n*14
Antamá (Saramaka Maroon leader), 113
antelope as symbol of wisdom, 122
anthropology, 16, 17, 18
anti-draft riots of 1863 (New York City), 204

Antigua, 133–140
　1736 conspiracy trial, 134, 139
　Akan names in, 133, 138, 140
　Akan people in, 126–127, 217
　Akan rituals in, 134–137, 139–140
　Gold Coast voyages to, 124
　intra-African alliances in, 138–139
　obeah in, 140, 141
　transshipment from, 195
Aowin polity, 83, 87
Apínti drum, 110, 116, 117, 118
apprenticeship system, 156–157, 270*n*92
Aquashiba (1733 St. John rebellion), 99
archaeology. *See* names of West African sites; proto-Akan society
architectural traditions, Akan
　archaeological evidence, 33, 36–37, 39, 52
　in Danish colonies, 105–106
　in Maroon groups, 116, 118
　in Virginia, 180
Arguim (West African island), 58
Aruba (Curaçao Islands), 107
asafo (paramilitary groups), 60, 61, 211, 257*n*116
asamando (ancestral dwelling place), 19–20, 99, 143, 163
Asameni (freed slave on Gold Coast), 93
Asamoah, Nana Opoku (Asantefoɔhene), 223, 225
Asante people
　as distinct from Asanteman, 77
　as enslaved captives shipped to Americas, 124, 127, 154
　goldwork, 257*n*125
　interest in Elmina fort, 228
　in North America, 190, 223
Asante-Aowin war (1715), 87
Asanteman (Asante nation), 77–78
　anthropological perspectives, 18–19
　architectural traditions, 36–37
　diplomacy, 85, 87–88, 89
　as distinct from Asante people, 77
　domestic enslavement, 78, 80–81, 88, 89, 256*n*96
　empire building, 11–12, 25, 45, 47, 74, 75, 78, 80–81
　European relationships, 81–82, 95

Index

map, 56–57
national symbol, 117
odwira festival, 78, 136–137
political-organizational model, 75
ruling clan, 79
stool histories, 77, 245n7
town/village organization, 80
trade dominance, 64, 76, 78, 80–81
warfare, 75, 78, 80, 82–83, 86–88, 89, 216
Asanteman Association, 223, 225
Asantemanso (archaeological site), 34, 35
Asebu polity, 7, 56–57, 68, 69
Ashnati Goldfields Corporation, 209
Ashy (Barbados slave), 126
Assin Akenkasu settlement, 42
Assin polity, 42–43, 83, 101
Assinie settlement, 41, 66–67, 73
assongou (terracotta tradition), 47
Asuo Gyebi shrine, 220
Atta (1763 Berbice revolt leader), 143, 144
Attandansu settlement, 42
Atwetwebooso rock shelter (archaeological site), 35
Austin, Iyalode Ida, 217, 218
autobiographical accounts.
  See biographical sketches
Axim town
  Asanteman and, 87
  Christianization, 61, 211
  Dutch involvement with, 68–69, 69, 108
  as embarkation point for enslaved Africans, 7
  festivals, 67
  German involvement with, 73
  map, 56–57
  Portuguese involvement with, 58, 61
  social order of, 135, 138

ba (terracotta tradition), 47
back-to-Africa movements, 204, 206, 207–208, 209–210, 278n14
  See also Akan/African spiritual movement in North America; pan-Africanism
Bacon's rebellion (1676), 175

Bahamas, African-descendants immigration to, 225
Baker, Robert, 71–72
Bakr, Abu (Jamaican slave), 126
"Baptist" rebellion of 1831 (Jamaica), 155–156
Barbados
  Akan people in, 126, 127, 131, 217
  conspiracy to revolt in (1675), 130–131, 132–133
  Gold Coast voyages to, 73, 124, 127
  transshipment from, 172, 176, 182, 191, 195
Barbot, Jean (European slaver), 10, 63, 67
Basua (Akwamuhene), 74
Baule people, 9
Bearden, Romare, 266n43
Begho (Bew, archaeological site), 50–52
  age of, 34–36
  Mande diffusion myth, 44, 50–51, 250n78
  marginalization of Islam in, 54
Bénin, Bight of. *See* Slave Coast (Bight of Bénin)
Benyo Lagoon, 59
Berber people, 48–49
Berbice, 142–144, 267n49
Berlin, Ira, 21–22
Bew. *See* Begho (Bew, archaeological site)
Biafra, Bight of, 94, 176, 177, 185, 233
Bible, the, 66
Bibly, Kenneth, 113–114, 151
biographical sketches of slaves
  Akan culture in, 162–163
  Akan naming patterns in, 170–171, 189–190, 190–191, 225
  legal cases, 191–192
  marriage and family, 161, 189–190
  paths to enslavement, 103–105, 121, 124, 126–127, 154, 166
  as windows into African experience, 4
  See also runaway advertisements
Birchtown settlement, Nova Scotia, 225
Bitu-Bitugu. *See* Begho (Bew, archaeological site)
Blyden, Edward Wilmot, 207
Boakye, Nana Kofi Asinor (African spiritualist in North America), 218, 219

Boaten, Akwasi, 77
Bogle, Paul (Morant Bay rebellion leader), 157, 160
Bolton, Quash (Georgia slave), 171
Bonaire (Curaçao Islands), 107
Bonduku-Gyaman location, 50
Boni Maroons (French Guiana), 112
Bonny, Bight of. *See* Biafra, Bight of
Bono people
    architectural traditions, 36–37, 52
    language, 45–46
    Mande diffusion myth, 44–46, 51
    proto-Akan culture, 52
    terms for, 50
Bono-Manso (archaeological site)
    age of, 34–36
    early Akan trade, 51, 52–53
    marginalization of Islam in, 51–52, 54
    settlement organization, 52, 80
Bonsu, Mensa (Asantehene), 19
"Book of Negroes" (1783), 224–225
Bornu, enslaved captives from, 127
Borribori (Bɔrebɔre). *See* Akan Creator (Onyankopɔn)
Bosman, Willem (Dutch merchant), 67, 135, 136, 138, 266n36
Bosome polity, 75
Bosomfoɔ (Assin *abosom*), 42–43
Bosompra cave (archaeological site), 32, 34, 35
Bosomtwe, Lake, 31–32, 34
Boston (Djuka Maroon chief), 111
Boston Gazette (newspaper), 191
Bosuaba (ancient settlement), 44
Bosum Dzemawodzi (African spiritual organization)
    Ajaibo Waldron and, 280n36
    claims to Akan spiritual practice, 213, 215, 217
    Ghanaian-born *akɔmfoɔ*, 220
    Nana Kwabena Brown and, 213, 218, 219
Bouterse, Desi (Suriname military dictator), 120, 263n81
Bowdich, Thomas, 136
Boyase Hill (archaeological site), 31–32, 34, 35
Braffo, Ambro (Fante leader), 122

braffoes/brassos (*abrafoɔ*), 60, 61, 76, 136, 237, 251n10
Brandenburg African Company, 73–74
branding of slaves, 108–109, 268n81
Brazil, 8, 10–12, 11–12, 124, 130
Briggs, Cyril V. (African Blood Brotherhood), 205
Bright, Doris, 280n36
Britain, 91–92, 226
    See also British colonies in Americas; British presence in Gold Coast
British colonies in Americas, 122–161
    Akan language in, 136, 146, 154–155
    Akan names in, 133, 138, 140, 164
    Akan people in, 126–127, 131, 142, 148–149, 217, 268n81
    Akan rituals in, 134–137, 139–140
    apprenticeship system, 156–157, 270n92
    conspiracies in, 130–131, 132–133, 134, 139
    Coromantee term in, 6, 123–124
    Danish relations, 106
    Demerara, 144–146
    Dutch relations, 109, 130, 141
    emancipation, 141, 145, 146, 147–148, 156–157
    French relations, 159
    Gold Coast captives shipped to, 4, 73, 124, 124–127, 127, 141, 153–154, 169
    insurrections in, 140–142, 144–146, 155–156
    intra-African alliances in, 138
    Maroon groups in (*See* Maroon groups)
    obeah in, 140, 141
    transshipment from, 169, 172, 176, 179, 182, 191, 195
    white anxiety in, 156, 267n49, 270n101
    See also Antigua; Barbados; Guyana; Jamaica; names of North American colonies/states
British presence in Gold Coast
    abolition of international enslavement enterprise, 81–82, 144, 147

Asante relations, 85, 87–88, 89, 216
back-to-Africa movements, 206, 207, 209
commercial monopoly, 208–209, 209
early voyages, 254n63
European competition, 71–73, 123
Gold Coast elites and, 211–212
growth of British economy and, 91–92
Komenda relations, 70, 123
Kormantin, 71, 72, 122–123
Broeke, Pieter van dan, 65
Brong-Ahafo region in Ghana, 44
Brooklyn, New York, 204
Brooks, George, 39, 45
Brown, Alice. *See* Dinizulu, Afua Owusua (Alice Brown)
Brown, Nana Kwabena, 26, 202, 213, 217–222, 279n35
Brown, William. *See* Brown, Nana Kwabena
brua. *See* obeah
Brun, Samuel, 69
Burkina Faso, 47
Burnham, Linden Forbes Sampson (Guyana prime minister), 267n46
Burton, Mary (witness in 1741 New York conspiracy), 200, 201
Byrd, William II, 175

cacao. *See* cocoa trade
calendrical cycle *(adaduanan)*, 40, 137
California, Akan spiritual practice in, 215
Campbell, Mavis, 160
Canada, 215, 224–226, 270n101
Cape Coast
 diasporic Africans in, 207
 Dutch presence in, 69
 European observations of spiritual culture, 65, 67–68, 75
 Gold Coast intelligentsia, 209–210
 sacred trees and, 65, 253n35
 terms for, 60
Cape Coast Castle
 Asante relations, 85, 87
 British involvement with, 71, 72, 123
 diasporic African tourists and, 227–228, 230–231

 as embarkation point for enslaved captives, 93, 97–98, 124, 125–126, 127, 131
 map, 56–57
 slave vessel insurrection near, 183
Cape Three Points, 56–57, 73
Capuchins, 66
Caramansa (Kwamena Ansa), 58, 60, 61, 71
Carriacou, 157–158
Carribean, map of, 128–129
Carsville, New York, 204
Castelo de São Jorge da Mina, 7, 58–59
caves. *See* rock shelters
ceramic traditions, 47, 52
Charles Town (Maroon settlement in Jamaica), 152
Charleston, South Carolina, 183, 185–186
Chesapeake Bay, Virginia, 172, 176
Chickasaw Indians, 187
Chief Sam. *See* Sam, Alfred Charles (Chief Sam)
Christianization
 African-descended missionaries, 67, 258n138
 Akan-European commercial encounters and, 62, 66–68
 among Gold Coast elites, 191, 209–212, 230
 in British controlled Gold Coast, 214
 of Chinese indentured workers, 148
 of ex-slaves, 121, 146
 in Ghana, 203, 227, 229–230, 233
 insurrections and, 155–156
 Maroon groups, 159
 obeah's decline, 103
 as perceived path to freedom in Americas, 176
 proximate African-European contact, 61, 67
 racial identities and, 174
Christianization, resistance to, 23
 Akan spiritual culture and, 13, 54, 55, 61–62, 62, 66–67, 232–233
 contradictions in slave society, 159, 180–181
 European/white observations of, 84, 102, 196

Christianization (*continued*)
  in Maroon groups, 23, 113, 115–116, 262n58
  obeah and, 146–147, 267n66
Christiansborg, Fort
  African attempt to capture, 93
  Asante relations, 85
  Danish control of, 95
  as embarkation point for enslaved Africans, 97–98, 99, 104
  European observations from, 84, 253n36
  map, 56–57
Church of Jesus Christ of Latter-Day Saints, 281n70
Claes, King (King of Adampe), 99
Claessen, Jan (John Cloice), 72–73
cocoa trade, 142, 206, 208
coffee, 142, 206
Coffy (Guyana national hero), 142–143, 144, 267n46
Cojo, Kormantin (Djuka captain), 111
Coker, Daniel, 207
commerce on Gold Coast
  Asante, 64, 76, 78, 80–81
  British monopoly, 208–209
  firearms, 76, 88–89
  goods and commodities, 70–71, 72, 74, 78, 192
  ivory trade, 72, 74, 86, 192
  proto-Akan society, 36, 39, 44
  rivalries, 85
  trade routes, 49, 75, 87
  trans-Saharan, 49
  See also Akan-European commercial encounters; European competition on Gold Coast; gold trade in West Africa; international enslavement enterprise
Conny, Jan (John Konny), 74
conspiracies
  Akan leadership in, 123, 201
  in Antigua (1736), 133–140
  in Barbados (1675), 130–131, 132–133
  dubious evidence for, 200–201
  Gabriel's (1800), 188
  New York (1741), 196–197, 199, 200–201
  oaths/rituals, 101, 131, 135–136, 195–196, 260n16
  obeah and, 136, 137
  punishments, 101, 132, 139, 199, 201
  rewards to informers, 139
  in South Carolina (1822), 138, 190, 199–200
  in St. Croix (1759), 100–101, 135, 139
  in Virginia, 175, 274n60
  See also insurrections
Coromantee term, 5, 6, 10
  Akan names, 14
  British use of, 6, 123–124
  evidence for Akan people, 131
  in Jamaica, 148
  Kormantin as source of, 60–61, 117, 122–123, 206
  non-Akan people included in, 130
  North American use of, 196
  origin of, 122–123
Costa Rica, 9–10, 242n17
cotton, 82, 105, 142, 167
country marks. *See* scarification, Akan
Court (Coromantee slave in 1736 Antigua conspiracy), 134, 135, 136–137, 137–139
crime in Akan settlements, 84
Crisis (publication), 207
Crommelin, Wigbold (Governor of Suriname), 111
Crossland, L. B., 52
Cuba, Mina term in, 9–10
Cudjo (St. Croix conspiracy of 1759), 100–101
Cudjoe (Jamaican Maroon leader), 157, 158, 159
Cuffee (1736 Antigua conspiracy informer), 139
Cuffee, Paul (African-descended entrepreneur), 15, 190–191, 207
Cugoano, Ottobah Kobina, 91, 127
culture, 15–17, 25
  language and, 46
  spirituality and, 17–18, 19–20
Cummings, Cuffy (Birchtown settler), 225
Curaçao, 107–108, 119–121
currency systems, 52–53, 71, 104

Index

Dabokrom (Ahanta village), 82
Dagomba polity, 6, 49, 87, 88, 246n24
Dahomey, 75, 91, 146
    See also Slave Coast (Bight of Bénin)
Dakubu, Mary, 44
Damballa Hwedo, Order of (diasporic African religious institution), 213
Danish colonies in Americas, 95–107
    Akan captives imported to, 95–96
    Akan culture, 101–105, 105–106
    Akan people in, 106–107
    conspiracies in, 100–101
    emancipation, 96, 106
    enslaved populations in, 96, 100, 105
    Gold Coast voyages to, 105, 124
    insurrections in, 98–100
    Mina term in, 6
    "slave code" of 1733, 96
Danish presence in Gold Coast, 82–83
    Asante relations, 85, 87–88
    Christianization attempts, 66
    Danish West India and Guinea Company, 95, 96
    decline of, 70
    slave escapes and revolts, 93
Dapper, Olfert, 136
Dasina (spiritual healer in Suriname), 119
Davis, William (St. Croix conspiracy of 1759), 100–101
Dawu-Akwapem (archaeological site), 34
de Azambuja, Diogo, 58, 60, 71, 251n6
de Haas, Hein, 226
death
    African Burial Grounds (New York City), 180, 200, 274n59
    asamando (ancestral dwelling place), 19–20, 99, 143, 163
    burial practices and sites, 65, 102, 152–153, 274n59
    stories of, 116
    See also suicide
Delafosse, Maurice, 44
Demerara, 1823 insurrection in, 144–146
Dεnkyira
    Asanteman and, 64, 78, 81, 83, 86
    diplomacy, 85

    map, 56–57
    origins of, 42
Denmark Vesey conspiracy (1822, Charleston), 138, 190, 199–200
diaspora, 20–21
diasporic Africans
    acceptance of white social order, 212
    Akan spiritual culture and, 215, 216–217
    dialogue between modern Akan & African descendants, 223–224, 229–230
    engagement with Akan culture, 202–203, 207, 220–221, 227–232, 233
    in Ghana, 205, 209, 213, 215, 219–220, 228–230
    modern Ghanaian, 222–226
    slave castles and, 23, 24, 203, 226–228
    study of, 21–24
    See also Akan/African spiritual movement in North America; back-to-Africa movements
Dinizulu, Afua Owusua (Alice Brown), 213, 232
Dinizulu, Nana Yao Opare, 26, 202
    Ajaibo and, 280n36
    claims of Akan spiritual practice in North America, 210, 212–213, 215, 217
    death of, 222
    Kwabena Brown and, 218, 219
diplomacy, 69–70, 85, 87–88, 89, 111
disease, 29, 66, 97
    See also malaria
Djabaku, Tetteh (Ada leader), 83
Djuka Maroons (Suriname), 111–112, 119
Dokyi, Kwame (Akyem omanhene), 205
domestic animals in West Africa, 36
drums and drumming
    African cultural movement in North America, 212
    drum language, 152, 162
    drum songs, 158–159, xi–xii
    drum texts, 27, 41, 55, 110, 122, 162
    in Maroon groups, 116, 117, 118–119

drums (*continued*)
  modern diasporic Ghanaians, 223
  styles of, 116, 118, 151, 152
  See also musical traditions
Du Bois, W. E. B., 207
Dutch and British war of 1665–1668, 123
Dutch colonies in Americas, 107–121
  Akan language in, 110
  Berbice, 142–144, 267n49
  British relations, 109, 130, 141
  Coromantee term in, 6
  Curaçao, 107–108, 119–121
  emancipation, 110, 119–120, 121
  enslaved populations, 107–108, 109
  Gold Coast voyages to, 107, 109, 124
  insurrections on, 142–144
  Maroon conflicts, 111–112, 120
  New Amsterdam, 109, 193
  See also Saramaka society (Maroon group in Suriname); Suriname
Dutch East Indies army, 82
Dutch Guianas. *See* Dutch colonies in Americas; Suriname
Dutch presence in Gold Coast, 68–70
  Asante relations, 76, 81–82, 85, 87–88
  vs. Dutch colonies in Americas, 108
  Elmina fort/settlement and, 7, 68–69, 228
  European competition, 71, 81, 83, 123
  firearms, 88, 89
  gold mining, 82
  international enslavement enterprise, 81–82
  involvement in local conflicts, 86
  Mina term, 8
Dutch West India Company, 60, 81
Dyula traders. *See* Juula (Dyula) traders

East India Company (British), 72, 73
Edwards, Augustus. *See* Dinizulu, Nana Yao Opare
Edwards, Bryan, 269n84
Effah-Gyamfi, Kwaku, 30
Eguafo polity, 58–59, 60, 138
Ejo (Akkonedi Abena ɔkɔmfoɔ), 216
elephants as symbol of wealth, 122, 136–137

Elmina fort/castle
  Asante relations, 85
  Castelo de São Jorge da Mina, 7, 58–59
  diasporic African tourists and, 227–228, 230
  trade routes, 87
Elmina (Edina) settlement
  Akan culture in, 251n11
  Dutch relations, 68–69
  map, 56–57
  origins and sociopolitical structure, 59–60
  Portuguese relations, 58–60, 61, 62, 88, 251n6
emancipation
  apprenticeship system, 147, 156–157, 270n92
  in British colonies, 141, 145, 146, 156–157
  continued exploitation of ex-slaves, 5, 119–120, 147–148, 203
  continued protest/rebellion, 96, 106, 141, 146, 157
  in Danish colonies, 96, 106
  in Dutch colonies, 110, 119–120, 121
  in Guyana, 141
  in Jamaica, 156–157
  Jim Crowism, 204
  in Massachusetts, 191–192
  in New York, 203
  sharecropping/tenant farming, 106, 166, 170
  in Suriname, 110, 119–120, 121
  in United States, 166, 170, 181
  See also freedom; manumission
England. *See* entries beginning with British
England, Akan people in, 127
enslaved African populations
  Akan proportions, 100, 147, 148–149
  in British colonies, 131, 141, 142
  in Danish colonies, 96, 100, 105
  in Dutch colonies, 107–108, 109
  in Georgia, 168
  in Maryland, 173
  in Massachusetts, 191
  mortality, 96, 182–183

Index 293

in New York, 193–195
in South Carolina, 164, 181, 184
in Virginia, 175, 178, 180–181
See also Gold Coast captives
enslavement within Europe, 91
enslavement within West Africa
Akanization, 239
in Asanteman, 78–80, 80–81, 88, 89, 256n96
Dutch participation in, 82, 108
forest clearance, 28–29, 76–77
Portuguese participation in, 58
trans-Saharan trade, 49
enstoolment/destoolment
in modern diaspora, 223, 224
of Nana Amoah, 208
political unrest and, 59
role in slave conspiracies, 134, 135–136, 137
See also stools
Eotile people, 29, 47
Esi Ketewa shrine, 220
Essai de manuel pratique de la langue mandé ou mandinque (Delafosse), 44
ethnicity, 14, 150, 174, 244n44
Etsi people, 59
European competition on Gold Coast, 123
Akan manipulation of, 25, 69–70, 72–73, 83–84
Akani traders and, 64
increased cost of captives, 78
increased exportation of captives, 81, 88, 149
national trading companies, 89–90
trade agreements with Akan people, 68, 69–70, 71, 83–84
See also Akan-European commercial encounters; gold trade in West Africa; international enslavement enterprise
Ewbank, Thomas, 242n19
Ewe language, 8, 48, 101

Faduma, Orishatuke (African nationalist), 207, 208
falciparum malaria, 37–39, 247n41
family. *See* marriage and family

Fante people
coastal migrations of, 59
diasporic African tourists and, 227–228
as enslaved captives shipped to Americas, 124, 126, 127, 154, 192
language of, 45–46
name forms, 188
Fante polities
abosom of, 75–76, 216
Akyem relationship, 83
alliances of, 83
Asante-Aowin war (1715), 87–88
Asanteman and, 76, 78
coastal townships, 60–61, 257n116
diplomacy, 85
enstoolment, 208
European relations, 69, 75–76, 95, 122
Mankessim as capital, 75–76
map, 56–57
fertility, 29, 37
Fetu "nation"
conflicts involving, 70, 131
European relations, 58–59, 72–73, 95
map, 56–57
resistance to Christianization, 61, 66
spiritual culture, 65, 67
firearms
availability of on Gold Coast, 62, 65, 69, 70, 76, 88–89, 101
in conspiracies and insurrections, 98–99, 134, 142, 183, 195
intra-Akan conflicts, 75, 82–83
restricted African access to in North America, 175, 196
Florida, 224, 271n7
Focquenbroch, Willem van, 65
Foote, Thelma, 196
forest clearance, 28–29, 31–32, 40, 53, 76–77
Forest of Gold (Wilks), 27–29
forests and warfare, 84–85
Fourteenth Amendment (U. S. constitution, 1868), 181
Franginals, Moreno (Cuban historian), 9
Frederiksborg castle, 70, 95
free African populations, 99, 105, 180–181, 196

Freedman's Bank, 171, 190, 272n23
freedom
  Christianization and, 176
  evidence in naming patterns, 190
  letters of, 93
  levels of, 96–97, 174, 181
  self-purchases, 180–181
  suing for, 191–192
  See also emancipation; insurrections; manumission; Maroon groups; runaways
Freeman, Thomas B. (Wesleyan Methodist missionary), 19
Freetown, Sierra Leone, 159–160
French colonies in Americas
  aid to Danish colonies, 98, 99
  British relations, 159
  Gold Coast voyages to, 124
  Maroon groups, 112, 114–115, 117–118
  Mina term in, 6
French Guiana, 112, 114–115, 117–118
French presence in Gold Coast, 6, 69–70

Gã people, 9, 10, 74, 82, 95, 98
Gã-Adangme language
  Akanization, 6, 48
  in diasporic African spiritual practice, 213
  marginality of, 8
  Mina term, 9, 10, 12, 123
  multilingualism and, 101
  names, 138
  number words, 260n18
Gabriel's conspiracy (1800), 188
Gardelin, Philip (governor, Danish colonies), 96
Garrard, Timothy, 52–53
Garvey, Marcus, 204–205, 208
Gaspar, David, 134–135, 266n37
Gbe languages, 146
  Ewe language, 8, 48, 101
  Mina term and, 8, 9, 10, 12, 101
Georgia, 166–171, 174, 189
Georgia Gazette, 169
Gerima, Haile (filmmaker), 230–231
German presence in Gold Coast, 73–74, 88
Ghana, 233–235
  Christianization in, 203, 227, 229–230, 233
  culture loss in, 233
  diasporic Africans in, 205, 209, 213, 215, 219, 219–220, 228–230
  dual citizenship, 223, 226, 229
  modern diaspora from, 222–226
  slave castles in, 23, 24, 226–228
  tourism, 227–232
Ghana Psychic and Traditional Healing Association, 215, 279n29
Ghana-Caribbean Association, 230
Ghanas (Dinizulu organization), 212
gods. *See abosom* (spiritual agencies); Akan Creator (Onyankopɔn); spiritual culture, Akan
Gold Coast, 7–8, 56–57, 94
Gold Coast captives
  to British colonies, 4, 73, 124–127, 141, 153–154, 169
  to Costa Rica, 242n17
  to Danish colonies, 105, 124
  demand for, 10, 131, 140, 148, 185, 264n7
  to Dutch colonies, 107, 109, 124
  to Florida, 271n7
  increased exportation of, 81, 88, 149
  to New York, 193, 195
  non-Akan people exported, 130
  reputation among other African slaves, 110
  sales/selling value of, 131–132, 177, 191, 241n4
  seasoning process of newly imported slaves, 108–109, 111
  to South Carolina, 164, 182–183
  total exported, 3
  See also enslaved African populations; slave vessels
Gold Coast colony, 75
Gold Coast intelligentsia, 208, 209–210, 210–212
gold mining, 58, 64, 82
gold ornaments, 257n125
gold trade in West Africa, 65
  domestic enslavement, 76–77
  European involvement, 58, 68–69, 72, 192, 251n6
  gold as currency, 71

Index

gold weights, 52–53, 72
  importance of, 63, 74
  vs. international enslavement enterprise, 64, 78, 81
  Islam and, 49
  warfare and, 86
Gomes, Fernão, 58
Gomez, Michael, 162, 163, 172–174, 212
Gousari (1763 Berbice revolt leader), 144
Gramsci, Antonio, 18–19
Grant, Affie (Georgia slave), 171
Greenburg, Joseph, 14
Grenada, 100, 127
Gronniosaw, James Albert Ukawsaw (freed slave), 127
Groote, Arent (Dutch merchant), 122
Gross Friedrichsburg, 56–57, 73, 74
Guan language, 48, 115, 117, 216, 249n69
Guinea Company (British), 72
Gullah community, 164, 185
gunpowder, 88–89
Guyana
  Akan people in, 142
  Gold Coast captives shipped to, 124, 141
  insurrections in, 142–146
  Maroon groups in, 144
  national hero of, 267n46
  post-emancipation racial hierarchy, 147–148
Gyaanewa, Nana Kɔkɔɔ (Assin leader), 42
Gyamma (King June, Akwamu commander), 99
Gyebi, Nana Asuo, 216

Hair, Paul, 71
Haiti (Saint Domingue), 123–124
  African-descendants' immigration to, 204
  Haitian revolution (1791), 100, 188
  Mina term in, 10
  spiritual practice, 213
Hall, Gwendolyn, 8–9, 11, 12, 241n4
Handler, Jerome, 124
Hani. *See* Begho (Bew, archaeological site)
Hanson, A. W., 278n14
Harlem, New York
  African spiritual practice in, 213, 222–223
  back-to-Africa movements, 204, 208, 278n14
  street-orator tradition, 205
Harleston, Quash (1822 Denmark Vesey conspiracy), 199–200
Harrison, Hubert, 205
Hawkins, John, 71
healing, Akan indigenous
  African culture movement and, 213
  culture resistance and, 62, 146
  European praise for, 84, 103, 119, 120
  as evidence of Akan descent, 123, 163
  Ghana Psychic and Traditional Healing Association, 215–216, 279n29
  loss of knowledge, 233
  in Maroon groups, 113, 117, 144, 151
  See also obeah
hegemony. *See* Akanization process; racism and racial identities
hemoglobin, malaria and, 38, 39
Hennequa, Jan, 72–73
Herskovits, Melville J. and Frances S., 113–114, 114–115
Herskovits-Frazier debate, 21
Hesselberg, Engelbret (judge, St. Croix conspiracy of 1759), 100–101, 260n16
Heywood, Linda, 21–22
Hoogenheim, Wolfert S. van (Berbice governor), 142, 143, 267n49
Horsmanden, David (judge in 1741 New York conspiracy), 199, 200, 201
Hughson, John (1741 New York conspiracy), 199, 201
Hunter, Robert (royal governor of New York), 276n109
hunters, Akan, 40–42, 43, 53, 59, 77
Hurston, Zora Neale, 166

ideational culture, 16
  architectural traditions and, 106
  lexicon for, 114–115, 117–118
  politics as, 131

ideational culture (*continued*)
  vs. spiritual and material culture, 17, 235
immigration, 159–160, 204, 205, 209, 225–226
  See also back-to-Africa movements
indentured workers, 147–148, 175
indigo, 167
Inikori, Joseph, 91–92
inselbergs, 32, 35
insurrections
  Akan leadership of, 98–99, 111, 123, 148–149
  in Antigua (1736), 100–101
  in Berbice (1763), 142–144
  costs of international enslavement enterprise, 105
  in Demerara (1823), 144–146
  on Gold Coast, 93
  in Grenada (1795), 100
  Haitian revolution (1791), 100, 188
  in Jamaica (1760, 1831), 155–156, 269n84
  as means to understand culture, 25
  in New York (1712), 134, 193–196, 199, 274n59, 276n109
  punishments for, 99, 100, 143–144, 146, 195, 199–200
  rewards for informants, 107, 155, 269n85
  in St. Croix (1878), 106
  in St. Vincent (1795), 100
  See also conspiracies; insurrections on slave vessels
insurrections on slave vessels, 90
  British vessels, 133, 139, 149, 169, 183, 198, 268n79
  Danish vessels, 97–98, 105
  Dutch vessels, 111
  See also slave vessels
international enslavement enterprise, 21, 94
  abolition of, 81–82, 144, 147, 188
  costs of, 90, 96, 105
  vs. domestic enslavement, 89, 189
  vs. gold trade, 64, 78, 81
  human costs of, 89–92
  See also Akan-European commercial encounters; Gold Coast captives;

names of European *n*ations and colonies; transshipment
Isert, P. E., 84
Islamization, 48–53
  Akan resistance to, 13, 23, 28, 50
  marginalization of, 48, 50, 54
Ivory Coast (Côte d'Ivoire)
  Akan populations in, 9, 29, 47, 49
  Akan town-marker in, 44, 47
  Asanteman and, 80
  European trade links with other regions, 7–8
ivory trade, 72, 74, 86, 192

Jamaica, 148–161
  Akan language in, 154–155
  Akan people in, 126, 131, 148–149, 268n81
  apprenticeship system in, 156–157, 270n92
  British relocation from Suriname, 109
  deportation of Maroons from, 270n101
  Gold Coast captives imported to, 4, 124, 153–154, 169
  insurrections in, 155–156, 269n84
  John Crow stories, 118
  Kikôngo language in, 262n62
  Maroon groups, 110, 111, 119, 150–153, 158–161, 228, 248n65
  transshipment from, 169, 179, 191, 195
Jenné-Jeno (ancient commercial town), 50–51, 52
Jim Crowism, 204
Johnson, Affie (Georgia slave), 171
Johnson, Elijah, 207
Joseph, John (Asante prisoner of war), 4, 127
Joseph Project (Ghanaian tourism effort), 228–229
Joshua Project (Christian missionary organization), 228–229, 281n70
Jukwa settlement, 42
Juula (Dyula) traders, 48, 49, 50, 51, 54

Kabes, John (Gold Coast merchant), 19, 87, 138
Kea, Ray, 65, 99

Kikôngo language, 262n62
Kintampo archaeological sites, 31–32, 33, 34–37, 44
Klein, A. Norman, 28–29
Kofi-maka (Kwinti Maroon leader), 112
Komenda town
  Asanteman and, 87
  European relationships, 62, 69, 69–70, 70, 86, 123
  Komenda wars (ca. 1694–1700), 70, 109, 138
  map, 56–57
  sociopolitical structure, 59–60
Kôngo-Angola region, 22, 108, 122, 185, 195
Konkom sacred forest, 42
Konny, John (Jan Conny), 74
Kormantin settlement
  British relationship, 71, 72, 122–123
  Coromantee term and, 60–61, 117, 122–123, 206
  map, 56–57
Kormantin-Kodjogron (Aluku Maroon settlement), 112
Krobo (archaeological site), 34
Kromanti music (Maroon music), 151, 152–153
Kuma, Takyi (Eguafo leader), 138
Kumah, Nana Baah (Asante hunter), 77
Kumase town
  agriculture, 78, 80
  Asante capital, 75, 87
  Christianization in, 214
  diasporic Africans in, 231
  marginalization of Islam in, 54
  proto-Akan society, 77
kumina spiritual tradition, 155
Kwa languages, 38, 45, 195
  See also Akan language; Gã-Adangme language
Kwaman. *See* Kumase
Kwame, Osei (Asantehene), 88
Kwao, Ansa (Akwamuhene), 82, 99, 266n36
Kwinti Maroons (Suriname), 112

La langue mandingue et ses dialectes (Delafosse), 44
lack of support for slave revolts, 101

lagoon culture, 47
Lake, Obiagele, 231
Lamptey, Jake Obetsebi (Ministry of Tourism and Diaspora Relations), 228
Langlands, James, 258n133
language, 14, 17, 43, 46
  See also Akan language; multilingualism; proto-Akan society, indigenous development of; names of languages
Larteh-Kubease, Ghana, 215, 216, 219–220, 280n36
LaTorre, Joseph, 256n96
Law, Robin, 11, 12, 243n27
laws upholding slavocracy
  in British colonies, 146–147, 157
  in Danish colonies, 96
  in New York, 196, 197
  obeah and, 103, 141, 147, 267n66
  in South Carolina, 183
  in Virginia, 174–176, 181
leadership/political structure
  abrafoɔ (brassos/braffoes), 60, 61, 76, 136, 237, 251n10
  ahemfoɔ/nhemmaa, 60, 239
  asafo (paramilitary groups), 60, 61, 211, 257n116
  confederations, 143
  hunters and, 40–42, 43, 53, 59, 77
  town/polity organization, 50, 51, 61, 62–64, 75, 80
  See also akɔmfoɔ; enstoolment/destoolment; matrilineal system; stools
Levtzion, Nehemia, 48
Lewis, Cudjo (slave interviewed), 166
Liberia (Chief Sam's ship), 205, 206
Lindsay, Alexander (governor of Jamaica), 270n101
linen, 65, 67
linguistic differentiation, 39, 46
literacy, 179–180, 183
Little Popo (Aného), 8, 95
Loango-Angola region, 109, 110
loanwords, 44
Lohse, Kent Russel, 242n17
London Missionary Society, 145, 146
Louisiana, 4, 127, 241n4, 271n7

Louisiana Slave Database, 12
Loyer, Godefroy, 66–67

maize, 64, 73
malaria, 37–39
　adaptation to, 53, 247n41
　in Americas, 182–183
　back-to-Africa movement, 206
Malcolm X, 205, 217
Malcolm-Woods, Rachel, 274n59
Mali, 49, 50
Malinké people, 48
Mande commerce with proto-Akan people, 39
Mande cultural diffusion myth, 29–30, 43–46, 47, 50–53, 54, 250n78
Mande language, 185, 195
manilas (copper bracelets), 70–71
Mankessim town, 59, 60, 75–76
manumission
　discouragement of, 196
　in Dutch colonies, 120–121
　for information on conspiracies/rebellions, 107, 139, 155, 269n85
　in Virginia, 180–181
　See also emancipation; freedom
Maravilha, César, 11
Marees, Pieter de, 64, 65, 253n35
Maroon Arts (Price), 116
Maroon Creator (Nana Kediama Kediampon), 113, 114, 117
Maroon groups, 107–121, 148–161
　aid to plantocracy by, 155, 156, 157, 159, 160, 269n86
　Akan cultural elements, 114–116, 117–118, 119, 153
　Akan people and, 5, 22, 95, 123, 148
　British conflicts, 144, 158, 159, 160, 270n101
　Christianization and, 23, 113, 115–116, 159, 262n58
　composite culture formation, 109–110, 112–114, 151
　cultural transmission, 20, 153
　Dutch conflicts, 111–112, 120
　geographic conditions and, 110–111, 133, 175
　lack of participation in slave revolts, 99
　language, 114–115, 117–118, 228, 248n65
　music, 150–153, 159
　oath making, 111–112, 135, 159, 262n52
　political order within, 271n106
　relationship to European social order, 5, 107, 120
　in Sierra Leone, 159–160
　treaties as symbols, 157, 160–161
　white anxiety, 96–97, 270n101
　See also Accompong (Maroon settlement in Jamaica); Saramaka society (Maroon group in Suriname)
marriage and family
　Akan name transmission, 15, 170–171, 179, 189–190, 190–191
　among Mina slaves, 102, 241n4
　customs of, 104
　extended kinship groupings, 177, 179, 185
　nuclear family in elite Gold Coast, 211
　running away and, 170, 179, 187
　transshipment and, 161
Maryland, 164, 167–169, 172–174
Massachusetts, 126–127, 191–192, 275n90
material culture
　as historical evidence, 34
　vs. ideational and spiritual culture, 17, 235
　lexicon for, 114–115, 117–118
　in Maroon groups, 116, 118
　preservation of, 274n59
　stools, 54, 118, 131
　in Virginia slave society, 180
　See also architectural traditions, Akan
matrilineal system, 18, 266n37
　architectural traditions and, 39, 180
　in coastal towns, 61
　cultural transmission and, 177
　European incursion in local politics, 66–67
　as evidence of Akan culture, 15, 47, 77, 102, 273n50
　historical/ancestral basis, 42, 43, 117, 232

hunters and, 41, 43, 53
malaria and, 38
in Maroon groups, 112, 114, 117
matriclan structure, 27–28, 29, 112, 237
See also mothers and motherhood
McCaskie, Thomas, 18–19
medicine, indigenous. *See* healing, Akan indigenous
Melvil, Thomas, 75–76
Mende language, 185
Messenger (publication), 205
millet, 64, 107
millie (Turkish corn or wheat), 64
Mina, Antonio Cofi (Louisiana slave), 12, 14
Mina, Joseph (Louisiana slave), 12, 14
Mina term, 5, 6–13, 122
  Akan language and, 9–10, 12, 101, 123
  Akan names, 14
  broadness of, 7–8, 10–12
  Gbe language and, 8, 9, 10, 12, 101
Ministry of Tourism and Diaspora Relations (Ghana), 228–229
miscegenation, 61, 120–121, 167–169, 172
missionaries. *See* Christianization
mma (terracotta tradition), 47
mobility in West Africa, 46, 232–233
Mollat, Hartmut, 53
Monrad, H. C., 84
Moore, Brian, 146
Moore, Richard B., 205
Moore Town (Maroon settlement), 150
Morant Bay rebellion (1865), 157, 160
Morgan, Philip, 134–135
Mori settlement, 69
mosquitoes, 37
mothers and motherhood
  childbirth, 84, 114
  esteem for, 37, 247n43
  pressures to reproduce, 189
  as source of enslaved status, 175–176
Müller, Johann Wilhelm, 64, 65, 66, 67, 68
multilingualism
  in Africa, 13, 14, 101
  in Akan slaves, 84
  Mina term and, 9

running away and, 167, 179–180, 197–198
musical traditions, 150–153, 159, 166, 170
See also drums and drumming
muskets, 80, 88 *See also* firearms
mutual-aid organizations, 11, 123

Namasa settlement, 44, 51
names and naming patterns, Akan
  after emancipation, 121
  among enslaved Africans in Louisiana, 4
  archived in Carribean songs, 159
  as archives of Akan culture, 142, 161
  in census records, 189
  in conspiracy/insurrection records, 99, 133, 138, 139–140, 199–200
  day names, 101, 164–165, 243n27
  in evacuation records, 225
  as evidence of Akan descent, 12, 14–15, 138
  family transmission of, 15, 170–171, 179, 189, 190–191
  in Freedman's Bank records, 190
  frequency of occurrence in Americas, 188
  of gold weights, 53
  in Gullah language, 185
  Maroon groups, 112–113
  in plantation records, 186–189, 268n81, 271n4, 271n108
  renaming of slaves, 109
  in runaway advertisements, 144, 154, 165, 169–170, 179–180, 197–198
  self-ownership and, 190
  in slave vessel records, 10
  towns and settlements, 30, 44, 46–47, 77, 113
Nana Adade Shrine (South Florida), 224
Nananom Mpow (sacred grove), 75–76
Nanny (Maroon leader), 157, 159
"The Narrative of the Son of a Slave Woman" (unknown author), 161
Nassau, Fort, 69, 142
nation concept, 14, 18–19
National Congress of Ghanaian Canadians, 226
Negrice Cristal (Brazilian song), 11

Negro Act of 1740 (South Carolina), 183
The Netherlands. *See* entries beginning with Dutch
new African diaspora. *See under* Ghana
The New African Diaspora in North America (Konadu-Agyemang, Takyi, and Arthur), 224
New Amsterdam, 109, 193
New Jersey, 193
New York and New York City, 193–201
  abolishment of slavery in, 203
  African spiritual movement in, 212, 215
  African-descended communities in, 204
  Akan and Akan descendants in, 210, 223
  enslaved African population in, 193–195
  New Amsterdam, 109, 193
  1712 revolt, 134, 193–196, 199, 274n59, 276n109
  1741 conspiracy, 196–197, 199, 200–201
  transshipment to, 192, 193, 195
  See also Dinizulu, Nana Yao Opare
New York Times (newspaper), 205, 208, 209
Niger-Congo linguistic family, 45
Ningo (Fredensborg), 56–57, 83
Nkrumah, Kwame (Ghanaian prime minister), 215–216
Nkukua Buoho (archaeological site), 31–32, 34, 35
North America. *See* names of states and countries
northern factor, 29–30, 36, 245n12
  See also Mande cultural diffusion myth
noun prefixal system, 43, 45–46, 248nn64–65
Nova Scotia, Canada, 224–225, 270n101
Nseserekeseso ancestral site, 35
Nsokɔ (Nsawkaw). *See* Begho (Bew, archaeological site)
Ntsiful (Wassahene), 87–88
Nyendael, David van, 81

oaths
  Akan spiritual culture, 61, 111, 131, 135–136, 159, 195–196
  Asanteman and, 78
  in conspiracies, 101, 131, 135–136, 195–196, 260n16
  in Maroon groups, 111–112, 135, 159, 262n52
obeah
  Akan origin of, 139–140, 146–147
  Christianization and, 103
  Christianization resistance, 146–147, 267n66
  conspiracies and, 136, 137
  endurance of in Caribbean, 266n43, 267n66
  insurrections and, 142, 146, 155, 156, 269n84
  in Maroon settlements, 151
  positive connotations of, 119
  punishments for practicing, 103, 141, 147, 267n66
  See also healing, Akan indigenous; spiritual culture, Akan
oburoni concept, 58, 228–230, 237
O'Callaghan, E. B., 193
odekuro (Asante village head), 80
odum tree, 30, 113–114
odwira festival, 78, 135, 136–137
Ofaa, Nana (Assin leader), 42
Ofori (Offorie, Akyemhene), 82
ogyedua tree, 55
ɔhene. *See* hunters, Akan; leadership/political structure
oil palm *(Elaeis guineensis)*, 30, 31, 32–33, 40, 53
Oklahoma, 204, 206
Oldendorp, Christian (Moravian clergyman), 100, 101–105, 169, 260nn17–18
Onipa Abusia (Akan religious organization in U.S.), 223
Opare, Nana Aba Nsia (African spiritualist in North America), 218, 219
Opare, Nana Yao Odum (African spiritualist in North America), 218, 219
Oparebea, Nana Akua, 213, 215–216, 219–220, 279n29

oral histories, 28
  Akan origins and, 32, 34, 36, 45, 46, 51, 52
  Akan spiritual culture and, 61, 114
  Asante stool histories, 77, 245n7
  Mande diffusion myth, 44
Osam, Kweku, 46
Osu. *See* Accra
Oteng, Otelia (diasporic Ghanaian), 222–223
Ouidah settlement
  Akan names, 243n27
  Akan people in, 8
  Akwamu hegemony in, 9, 74, 75
  captives procured from, 10, 95, 97, 126, 140
Owens, Ama (Alabama slave/servant), 171
Oyotunji village, South Carolina, 210, 213, 279n24

pan-Africanism, 205, 207, 208, 217, 231
  See also Akan/African spiritual movement in North America; back-to-Africa movements
Panama, Mina term in, 9–10
Panin, Kwaku Dua (Asantehene), 19
patrilineal principle, 61, 211, 273n50
A Peculiar People (Washington), 185
Peel, John D., 234–235
Pennsylvania, Gold Coast captives in, 193
Pereira, Pacheco, 50, 60, 61, 250n78
Pernambuco, Brazil, 130
Pharsalia plantation (Virginia), 179
Philadelphia, Akan spiritual practice in, 215
Philips, Thomas (British slaver), 8–9
Picot, Thomas R. (Wesleyan Methodist missionary), 19
Picton, John, 245n12
plantain, 64, 118
plantations. *See* agriculture in Americas; conspiracies; insurrections; sugar and sugar production; white anxiety
Pointe Coupee conspiracy (1795), 4, 12
Pokesu settlement, 73

political structures. *See* leadership/political structure
Pollitzer, William, 185
Popo (Hula), 93
Portuguese colonies in Americas, 6, 7, 124, 164
Portuguese presence in Gold Coast
  Christianization and, 54, 61–62
  decline of, 68–69, 73
  dominance of, 24–25, 58–60
  early voyages, 251n6
  intrusion into local politics, 58–60, 61, 62, 71
  Mina term, 7, 8
  use of armed Africans for protection, 88
Prempeh, Nana Agyeman I (Asante resistor to British), 228
Price, Richard, 20, 109–110, 113–114, 116, 118
Price, Sally, 116
Propheet, Hans (cartographer), 7
proto-Akan society, indigenous development of, 29–48, 54, 77
  agriculture, 30, 31, 32, 40, 53
  archeological evidence, 30–37, 51–53
  architectural evidence, 33, 36–37, 39, 52
  biomedical evidence, 37–39
  hunters in, 40–41, 42–43, 53
  linguistic evidence, 36, 43–48, 54
  oral historical evidence, 32, 34, 36, 44, 45, 51, 52
  regional commerce, 36, 39, 44
  See also Mande cultural diffusion myth
Protten, Christian (African descended missionary), 67
Pucket, Newbell, 271n4
Purchas, Samuel, 71

Quabena (Gold Coast slave), 93–94
Quacco (Stedman's slave), 121
Quamina (1736 Antigua conspiracy informer), 139
Quamina, Deacon (1823 Demerara revolt leader), 145
Quaque, Philip (African-descended missionary), 67–68
Quassy (spiritual healer in Suriname), 119

Quawcoo (Antigua obeah practitioner), 136, 137, 138, 139, 140
Queen Anne's Point, 56–57
Queens, New York, 213
Quereampum (Tweadeampɔn). *See* Akan Creator (Onyankopɔn)
Qvakoe (Kwaku, St. Croix conspiracy of 1759), 100–101, 260n16
Qvau (Quaco, St. Croix conspiracy of 1759), 100–101

racism and racial identities
　class and, 212
　composite culture and, 177
　in Ghana, 228–230
　hereditary enslavement, 91, 162, 175–176
　in historical accounts of Africa, 92, 231–232
　modern diaspora and, 224
　postemancipation social order, 119–120, 147–148, 203
　white defining of, 107, 119–120, 174, 175, 200–201
　See also back-to-Africa movements; pan-Africanism; white anxiety
rainfall in West Africa, 32–33, 248n48
Randolph, A. Philip *(Messenger)*, 205
Rask, Johannes, 84
Rath, Richard, 150
Raule, Benjamin, 73
rebellions. *See* insurrections
Reconstruction, 166, 204
Relation du Voyage du Royaume d'Issyny (Loyer), 66–67
religion, 16, 17–18
　See also abosom (spiritual agencies); Akan Creator (Onyankopɔn); Akan/African spiritual movement in North America; Christianization; Islamization; obeah; spiritual culture, Akan
revolts. *See* insurrections
Rhode Island, Gold Coast captives imported to, 192
rivers and streams, spiritual significance of, 41, 42, 146, 216
　See also under abosom (spiritual agencies); Tanɔ; river; Volta river

Robin (1736 Antigua conspiracy informer), 139
rock shelters, 32, 35
Rodney, Walter, 92
Rømer, L. F., 84
Rowe, H. A. (Accompong Maroon leader), 160, 271n106
Royal, Fort, 123
Royal Adventurers, 73, 123
Royal African Company (Britain), 123, 131–132, 137–138, 176
Royal Library in Copenhagen, 88
Royall, Belinda (Massachusetts slave), 126–127
rubber, 78, 205–206, 207
rum, 105, 192
runaway advertisements, 165–166
　Akan names, 144, 154, 165, 169–170, 179–180, 197–198
　as evidence of Akan culture, 172
　as window into African lives, 187–188
runaways
　biographical sketches, 162–163
　difficulties facing newly arrived Africans, 179
　in Gold Coast, 93
　laws concerning, 175
　profiles of, 165–166, 167, 187–188, 197
　returning to Africa, 3

sacred days, Akan, 66, 78
St. Croix, 95–96, 98
　Christianization in, 103
　importance as sugar-producing colony, 105, 106
　slave conspiracy of 1759, 100–101, 135, 139
Saint Domingue/Dominique (Haiti), 10, 123–124
　See also Haiti (Saint Domingue)
St. John, 95, 96–100, 266n36
St. Thomas, 74, 95–96
St. Vincent slave rebellion (1795), 100
Sakyi, Nana Kwaku (diasporic ɔkɔmfoɔ), 221
Saltpond settlement (Chief Sam), 206, 208

Index

Saltwater Slavery (Smallwood), 23
Sam, Alfred Charles (Chief Sam), 204, 205–208, 278*n*8
Sandoval, Alonso de, 8
Sankofa (Gerima), 230–231
Sankofa symbol, 180, 274*n*59
São Antonio de Axem (Axim), 58
São Jorge de Mina fort (Elmina), 58, 62
São Sebastião (Shama), 58
São Tomé, 7–8
Saramaka society (Maroon group in Suriname)
   Akan cultural elements, 111–118
   composite culture, 109–110
   language, 114–115, 117–118
   spiritual culture, 20, 113, 114–116
   treaty of, 111–112
Sasatia (Dɛnkyira *abosom*), 42
Sasaxy (Fetu leader), 62
Sasraku, Ansa (Akwamuhene), 74
scarification, Akan, 102–103, 169
   in runaway advertisements, 180, 187
Schomburgk, Robert (British surveyor), 262*n*52
Schuler, Monica, 146
Scott's Hall (Maroon settlement in Jamaica), 150, 152, 155
Secondi (Antigua conspirator 1736), 136, 139
Sefwi settlement, 83
Semprendre, Kofi (Djuka captain), 111
Senegambia
   captive exports, 109, 169, 176, 177, 185, 193–194
   map, 94
   resistance traditions, 5
sensan tree, 55
Sereer people, resistance to enslavement of, 5
Sessarakoo, William Unsah, 127
Shama settlement
   Dutch relationship, 69, 108
   map, 56–57
   Portuguese relationship, 58, 61, 251*n*6
sharecropping and tenant farming, 106, 166, 170, 208
Sharpe, John (observer of 1712 New York uprising), 196, 199
Sharpe, Sam (1831 "Baptist" rebellion), 155–156
sheep, 36, 104
shield ceremony, 134–135
Shinnie, Peter, 34, 247*n*34
ships. *See* slave vessels
sickle cell anemia, 37–38
Sierra Leone
   African-descendants immigration to, 225
   back-to-Africa movements, 208, 210
   captive exports, 109, 169
   in composite culture, 151
   map, 94
   Maroons in, 159–160
Sierra Leone Company, 159
Singleton, Benjamin "Pap," 204
skin lightening, 233, 234
slave castles
   depictions of, 230–231
   diasporic African experience of, 23, 24, 203, 226–228
   whitening of, 227, 230
Slave Coast (Bight of Bénin)
   Akan names and people in, 47, 75, 95, 101
   captive exports, 109
   Christianization, 233
   Dahomey, 75, 91, 146
   European trade links with other regions, 7–8
   Gbe language, 8, 146
   in Gullah names, 185
   map, 94
   Maroon culture formation, 110
   Mina term, 9, 10
slave vessels, 164
   African experience on, 131–132
   British, 125–126, 131–132, 137–138, 139, 177
   condemned, 10
   Danish, 93, 95, 97–98, 99
   to Massachusetts, 275*n*90
   mortality, 97, 125–126, 132, 137–138, 183, 192, 264*n*7
   numbers of Gold Coast voyages, 124
   See also Gold Coast captives; insurrections on slave vessels; transshipment

slavery. *See* agriculture in Americas; conspiracies; enslaved African populations; enslavement within West Africa; insurrections; international enslavement enterprise
Slavery and African Ethnicities in the Americas (Hall), 8–9, 241n4
slaves. *See* enslavement within West Africa; Gold Coast captives; international enslavement enterprise
Sligo, Marquess (governor of Jamaica 1834–1836), 156, 270n92
Sloane, Hans, 150
Smallwood, Stephanie, 23
Smith, A. E. (Akim Trading Company Limited), 205
Smith, John (British missionary to Guyana), 145–146
Smith, Venture (North American freed slave), 127
Snees, Jantie (Cape Coast merchant), 67
Society for the Propagation of the Gospel in Foreign Parts, 196
Songhay Empire, 49
Soninke people, 48
Soppelsa, Robert, 47
South Carolina, 164, 181–190
  Akan names, 186–189
  Akan people in, 127
  contemporary Yorùbá spiritual practice, 210
  enslaved African populations in, 164, 184, 189
  free African populations in, 181
  Gold Coast captives imported to, 164, 182–183, 183
  Gullah language, 185
  Lowcountry, 185, 186
  runaway advertisements, 187–188
  white anxiety, 183, 188–189
South East Africa, 94
South Potomac, Virginia, 176
South Sea Company (British), 9–10
Spanish colonies in Americas, 6, 9–10, 164
spiritual culture, Akan
  agriculture and, 33, 40, 53
  in Akan language, 114–115, 117–118
  Akanization and, 216–217
  akɔm, 221, 223, 238, 253n37
  asamando (ancestral dwelling place), 19–20, 99, 143, 163
  Asanteman and, 77–78, 136–137
  Christianization resistance and, 13, 54, 55, 61–62, 66–67, 232–233
  defined, 16–18
  European observations of, 65, 67–68, 75
  festivals, 67, 78, 135, 136–137, 251n11
  as fetishism, 17, 62
  insurrections and, 195, 196
  modern Ghana and, 233–235
  oaths, 61, 111, 131, 135–136, 159, 195–196
  obeah and, 139–140, 146–147
  as proxy for cultural identity, 233, 234–235
  rituals, 134–137, 139–140, 146–147, 222–223
  sacred days, 78, 137
  sacred groves, 75–76
  See also abosom (spiritual agencies); Akan Creator (Onyankopɔn); Akan/African spiritual movement in North America; *akɔmfoɔ*; death; healing, Akan indigenous; Maroon groups; oral histories; trees
spiritualists. *See akɔmfoɔ*
Stahl, Ann, 33, 36
Stedman, John, 102–103, 108–109, 110, 111, 114, 119, 121
stereotypes of Akan people in Americas, 4–5, 99, 100, 108, 123, 133, 162, 266n40
Stewart, John, 43–44
Stono rebellion of 1739, 183
stools
  as material culture, 54, 118, 131
  stool histories, 77, 245n7
  succession, 61, 211
  as symbols of political authority, 42, 60, 78–80, 131
  See also enstoolment/destoolment
stories
  Ananse stories, 110, 117, 142, 159, 161
  John Crow/King Buzzard, 118

Index   305

See also biographical sketches of slaves; oral histories
Sudan, 50
sugar and sugar production
  in Africa, 7, 108
  in Akan diets, 64
  in British colonies, 73, 130, 142, 148, 167
  as commodity, 105, 132, 192
  conspiracies/insurrections and, 99–100, 131, 156
  skills in, 133, 161
  in St. Croix, 96, 105, 106
suicide
  on board slave vessels, 97, 132
  conspiracies, 132–133
  failed insurrections, 99, 143, 195
  See also death
Suriname
  Akan language, 114–115, 117–118
  Akan material culture, 116, 118
  Akan spiritual culture, 20
  economic disparity in, 263n81
  emancipation, 110, 119–120, 121
  Gold Coast captives imported to, 107, 109
  manumission, 120–121
  slave seasoning process in, 108–109
  See also Saramaka society (Maroon group in Suriname)
Svane, Frederick P. (African-descended missionary), 67

Ta Kora. *See* Tanɔ; river
Tacky's revolt (Jamaica, 1760), 155, 269n84
Takoradi settlement, 56–57, 74
Takrama settlement, 74
Takyiman settlement, 59, 67, 76, 221
talismans, 85, 102
Tambu (Maroon music), 151
Tanɔ river
  as boundary of Mina coast, 7
  as source of *abosom*, 41, 61, 114–115, 118, 221, xi
Ta'rikh al-Fattash, 50
Ta'rikh al-Sudan, 50

Tata Odun (Maroon god), 113–114
taxes, 65, 78, 183
Temple of Nyame (Nana Kwabena Brown), 220, 221
temporal culture, 16
  See also material culture
tenant farming, 170
terracotta traditions, 47
Terray, Emmanuel, 256n96
textiles, 48, 70, 72, 116
Thompson, Thomas (English missionary), 67–68
Thompson, Thomas P. (Sierra Leone governor), 160
Thornton, John, 21–22, 134–135, 154–155, 266n37
Tigare ɔbosom, 216, 220
Tilleman, Erick (Dutch trader), 93, 253n36
tobacco, 105, 167, 170, 172, 177
Togo, Akan town names in, 47
Toronto, Canada, 215, 224, 225
towns and settlements, Akan
  naming patterns for, 30, 44, 46–47, 77, 113
  organization of, 50, 51, 61, 80
  urbanization, 65, 257n116
  See also leadership/political structure; names of towns or settlements
trade. *See* Akan-European commercial encounters; commerce on Gold Coast; gold trade in West Africa; international enslavement enterprise
Trans-Atlantic Slave Trade Database, 124
transshipment
  after emancipation, 147
  from Barbados, 172, 176, 182, 191, 195
  in biographical sketches, 126–127, 161
  from Curaçao, 107
  frequency of, 3, 164
  to Georgia, 169
  from Jamaica, 169, 179, 191, 195
  to Maryland, 172
  to Massachusetts, 191
  to New York, 192, 193, 195
  to Virginia, 172, 176, 179

trees
  in Akan town names, 30
  sacred, 65, 77, 113–114, 116, 118, 253n35
  sacred groves, 75–76
  symbolism of, 55
Trelawny Town Maroon group (Jamaica), 160, 269n86
trypanosomiasis, 36
Turner, Henry McNeil (bishop), 206, 207
Tutu, Osei (Asantehene), 75, 81, 138
Tutu, Osei II (Asantehene), 222
Twi language. *See* Akan language
Twifoɔ polity, 56–57, 83, 86, 87

United States, emancipation in, 166, 170, 181
  See also names of states
uprisings. *See* insurrections
Utrecht, Treaty of (1713), 9–10

Vai language, 185
van Scholten, Peter (Danish Governor General), 106
van Sevenhuysen, J., 86
Veracruz region, Akan people in, 242n19
Vesey, Denmark (1822 Charleston conspiracy), 138, 190, 199–200
vessels. *See* slave vessels
Virginia, 174–181
  Akan people in, 127, 217
  conspiracies (1856), 175, 274n60
  enslaved populations in, 175, 178, 180–181
  Gold Coast shipments to, 164, 176–177
  laws upholding slavocracy, 174–176, 181
  slave imports to, 177–179
  transshipments to, 172, 176, 179
vivax malaria, 37, 247n41
Vivian, Brian, 52
Volta river
  as boundary of Gold Coast, 7, 15, 17, 31, 95, 140
  map, 35, 56–57

Wagadu (Soninke polity), 48, 49
Wagadugu polity, 35, 85

Waldron, Ajaibo (Bosum Dzemawodzi), 218, 280n36
Walker, Quaco, 191–192
Walsh, Lorena, 172
Wangara trading communities, 49
Ware, Opoku (Asantehene), 83, 154
warfare, 84–92
  Akan-Abrem battle (1920), 69
  Akani merchant conflicts, 64
  Akyem-Akwamu conflict, 82
  Asanteman and, 75, 78, 80, 82–83, 86–88, 89
  availability of enslaved captives and, 89, 98, 109, 126, 149
  against British incursion, 216
  Dutch and British war of 1665–1668, 123
  European involvement in Akan, 69, 71
  forest, 84–85
  Komenda wars (ca. 1694–1700), 70, 109, 138
  Maroon groups and (*See under* Maroon groups)
  protocols of, 85
  suicide and, 143
  See also insurrections
Washington, Booker T., 204
Washington, D. C., Akan spiritual practice in, 215, 218–219
Washington, Margaret, 185
Wassa polity, 56–57, 83, 87–88
Weber, Max, 18
Weeksville, New York, 204
Weiga (Wergan, Fante ɔbosom), 75–76
Wells, Quabner (20th century Akan descendant), 171
Wesleyan Methodist Church, Axim, 211
West Africa
  diaspora studies and, 21–22
  maps, 35, 56–57, 94
  See also names of polities and nations
West Central Africa, 21–22, 94
  See also names of polities and nations
Westernization. *See* Christianization
white anxiety
  in British colonies, 156, 267n49, 270n101
  in Danish colonies, 96–97, 99–100

levels of African freedom and, 96–97, 181
Maroons and, 96–97, 270n101
in New York, 196–197, 200–201
in South Carolina, 183, 188–189, 189
in Virginia, 175, 181
See also racism and racial identities
white populations
in Danish colonies, 105
in Georgia, 167, 168, 189
in Maryland, 173
in New York, 193, 194
in South Carolina, 184
in Virginia, 178, 180
Wieme (ɔbosom's abode), 42
Wilhelm, Friedrich I, 73
Wilhelm, Friedrich III, 74
Wilks, Ivor
on Asanteman, 18, 256n96
late Akan culture formation, 27–29, 49–50, 76–77, 247n34
Mande cultural diffusion, 43–44
Windward Coast, 94, 172

Winneba settlement, 123, 125–126, 132
Wolf, Adjuba Sara (manumitted slave), 121
Wolof people, resistance to enslavement of, 5
women, 15, 42, 43, 144, 216
See also matrilineal system; mothers and motherhood

Xeryfe (Komenda leader), 62

Yaa Asantewaa war (1900), 216
yams, 30, 31, 40, 64, 73
Yarak, Larry, 76–77
Yorùbá culture
language, 10
scarification, 102
spiritual practice, 210, 213, 217, 234–235
Yucatan region, 242n19

Zaro's House of Africa (African-oriented store), 218, 279n35

www.ingramcontent.com/pod-product-compliance
Lightning Source LLC
Chambersburg PA
CBHW052052110526
44591CB00013B/2184